In praise of *The Orvis Fly-Fishing Guide*

Of the many primers meant for beginning and intermediate fly-fishers, Tom Rosenbauer's is the best I know —a comprehensive guide for all species and all waters from the trout stream to the bonefish flats, from the bass pond to the salmon river, from selecting tackle to caring for it, repairing it, and deftly deploying it in almost every conceivable situation. *The Orvis Fly-Fishing Guide* is the right entry point for new fly fishers, and a trusted path for experienced fly fishers looking to expand their horizons.

—James R. Babb, Editor
Gray's Sporting Journal

There is a bunch of fly-fishing guides out there, but none of them benefits from the depth and breadth of knowledge that Tom Rosenbauer brings to this revision of his classic book. Tom's not just a fine angler, but a great teacher, as well, and the central argument of this book is that fly fishing is not as difficult as many people believe. Tom's concise writing and Bob White's clear illustrations make it even easier. Whether you are a beginner looking to catch your first fish on a fly or an intermediate angler looking to become an expert, this book is an invaluable resource.

—Phil Monahan, Editor
American Angler

Tom Rosenbauer's wholly revised *Orvis Fly Fishing Guide* is the most comprehensive, and best, introduction to fly fishing that I have seen. All aspects of our sport are explained with clear, common-sense explanations. It makes understandable what often seems arcane and frustrating for most beginning and intermediate anglers.

—John Randolph, Editor
Fly Fisherman

The ultimate reference book for fly fishers of all stripes. Tom Rosenbauer's clear and contemporary answers to fly fishing's knottiest problems give all anglers a refreshingly open path to success on the water.

—John Merwin, Fishing Editor
Field & Stream

This is simply the best, most comprehensive, most understandable book for newcomers to our sport that I've ever seen. It also belongs in the reference library of experienced fly fishers who need a quick education about a fish species or a technique they haven't used before.

—Howell Raines
Pulitzer Prize–winning journalist and author of
The One that Got Away and *Fly Fishing Through the Midlife Crisis.*

A splendid guide including everything an angler needs.

—Jim Harrison
Author of *Plain Song* (poems), *The Raw and the Cooked* (essays),
and *Legends of the Fall* (fiction), and contributing editor to *Field & Stream*

Books by Tom Rosenbauer

The Orvis Fly-Tying Manual, 2nd Edition
The Orvis Fly-Tying Guide
The Orvis Guide to Reading Trout Streams
The Orvis Streamside Guide to Leaders, Knots, and Tippets
The Orvis Streamside Guide to Approach and Presentation
The Orvis Streamside Guide to Trout Foods and Their Imitations
Prospecting for Trout
Casting Illusions
Fly Fishing in America

THE
ORVIS

Fly-Fishing Guide

Completely Revised and Updated, with Over 400
New Color Photos and Illustrations

Tom Rosenbauer

PHOTOGRAPHS BY TOM ROSENBAUER
& THE ORVIS COMPANY

ILLUSTRATIONS BY BOB WHITE

The Lyons Press

GUILFORD, CONNECTICUT
An imprint of The Globe Pequot Press

The Lyons Press is an imprint of The Globe Pequot Press.

10 9 8 7 6 5 4 3 2 1

Printed in the United States

Designed by Sheryl P. Kober

ISBN-13: 978-1-59228-818-2
ISBN-10: 1-59228-818-9

The Library of Congress has previously catalogued an earlier edition as follows:

Rosenbauer, Tom.
Orvis fly-fishing guide/Tom Rosenbauer
p. cm.
ISBN 0-941130-91-6
ISBN 0-941130-92-4 (pbk.)
1. Fly fishing.   I. Title
SH456.R66 1984
799.1'2   83-25898

Contents

Acknowledgments

I'd like to thank the following people for showing me new techniques to use and new species to fish for; for their help with photography and Photoshop, and their editorial gems; and for some wonderful places to research this book.

For the first edition (1984): Spider Andreson, Bob Bachman, Mark Bressler, the late Vern Bressler, Bill Bryson, Silvio Calabi, Carl Coleman, Greg Comar, the late Leigh Condit, Alan Crossley, John Dembeck, Cooper Gilkes, the late Pat Gill, Bob Gotshall, John Harder, Chuck Knauf, Dave Linde, Nick Lyons, Ron and Maggie MacMillan, Del Mazza, John Merwin, Cook Neilson, Dave Perkins, Leigh Perkins, Perk Perkins, Neil Ringler, Rick Rishell, Paul Schullery, Tom Shubat, the late Tony Skilton, the late Howard Steere, Jim Sulham, Walter Ungermann, Herb Van Dyke, Wayne Walts, the late Richard Wolters, and Ron Zawoyski.

For the second edition (2007): John Arlotta, Jim Babb, Dave Barber, Jeremy Benn, Rich Benson, Tony Biski, Scott Bowen, Joe Bressler, Paul Bruun, David Carmona, Jay Cassell, Marty Cecil, Monroe Coleman, Pat Crow, Nick Curcione, Marshall Cutchin, Joe Demalderis, Rick Eck, Brett Ference, Charles Gaines, Mike Gawtry, Andy Goode, Rick Grasset, Todd Green, Kevin Gregory, Jim Harrison, Steve Hemkens, Steve Huff, Patrick Keller, Art Lee, Jim Lepage, Jim Logan, John Maron, Pat McCord, Jay McCullough, Jim McFadyean, Galen Mercer, Truel Meyers, Tom Montgomery, Pat Neuner, Margot Page, John Rano, Eric Rickstad, Paul Roos, Dave Ruddock, Rick Ruoff, George Ryan, John Stalcup, Lou Tabory, Glister Wallace, Jeff Walther, Bob White, and Victoria Woodruff.

Thanks to all my friends and coworkers at The Orvis Company. It's a wonderful opportunity to be able to work with people who share the same passions.

And finally, to my wife, Robin, and children, Brett and Brooke, thanks for being so patient with my late nights sequestered in my study.

Introduction

I wrote the original *Orvis Fly-Fishing Guide* in 1983, and this much revised and updated edition in 2006, to be the book I would have wanted to read when I first tried fly fishing in the late 1960s and very much needed a good guidebook. In the nearly forty years that I've been involved in the fly-fishing business, I've always listened carefully to novices, both in my years as a fly-fishing instructor and afterward. And I've studied how-to books on photography, cross-country skiing, kayaking, and even books on macroeconomics or foreign policy, for ideas on how to present a complex process to the uninitiated. When I find someone who can explain in an elegant way a topic unfamiliar to me, I'll go back and study his or her approach again and again. So if you're new to fly fishing, I've been thinking of you. I want this book to be your reliable reference for at least your first few years, and, hopefully, longer.

I wrote *The Orvis Fly-Fishing Guide* to fill the real and specific needs of anglers. This book presents a starting point for the soon-to-be fly fisher and serves the rea-sonably proficient fly fisher as a reference. (Even quite capable anglers may need a refresher course on some specialized aspect of fly fishing, such as saltwater knots, the how-to care for waders, or how to fish a dry fly in tricky currents.) I have tried to offer a balanced view of all the various elements and kinds of fly fishing—including tackle selection, casting, flies, presentation, tactics, and a host of other subjects, for all the major gamefish in both fresh and salt water.

Fly fishing has a long and colorful history, and contains significant technical issues. No single book can explain it all, and that is partly why many serious anglers have large libraries. This book will provide a sensible jumping-off point for a sport that is simple in purpose, yet often amazingly—and quite wonderfully—complex in execution. Hopefully, *The Orvis Fly-Fishing Guide* will be a valuable introduction to fly fishing, an endeavor that will give you immense pleasure, the chance to meet some wonderful people along the way, and more than a glimpse of some of the world's most beautiful places.

Tom Rosenbauer
Pawlet, Vermont
April 2006

{ THE GORGE }

Chapter One

What Is Fly Fishing?

FLY CASTING MAKES IT POSSIBLE to deliver a relatively weightless lure or imitation of a living creature on target, using line weight to develop momentum. That's a fairly dry way of saying that, using a fly rod, you can catch fish with an artificial lure that can't be presented by any other method. It means that you can successfully fool a trout that feeds upon tiny insects measuring less than an eighth of an inch long—or lure a 150-pound tarpon into striking a 6-inch feathered lure. Artificial flies are used to catch sunfish, bass, trout, pike, bluefish, shark, bonefish, sailfish, salmon, walleye, and even catfish. The possibilities are endless. Any fish that eats insects, minnows, or crustaceans can be hooked with an artificial fly. *Landing* a 500-pound bluefin tuna on a fly rod is another story, but I'm quite sure you could *hook* one, as they often feed on 6-inch sand eels. Even shad, which are plankton feeders, can be angered into striking an artificial fly when they ascend freshwater rivers on their spawning run from the sea.

Fly fishing is most commonly associated with trout and salmon in streams; in fact, in most Atlantic salmon rivers in North America, fly-fishing gear is the only kind allowed by law. But the same tackle used for a 9-foot, 6-weight trout rod can provide endless hours of fascination in a Midwestern farm pond, fishing for bluegills. The heart-stopping leap of a smallmouth bass hooked on a fly-rod bug can be experienced on the Potomac River in Washington, D.C. A fly fisher who lives in Florida, hundreds of miles from the nearest trout stream, can use the same fly-rod outfit to catch largemouth bass one day, baby tarpon and snook in brackish canals the next, bone-

Fly fishing can be as physical and exhilarating as catching a tarpon in salt water.

fish on shallow saltwater flats the next, and bluefish and Spanish mackerel in the open ocean for a grand finale.

Fly fishing is an ancient pursuit, perhaps practiced first by the Roman poet Martial (A.D. 40–104), who reportedly used a feathered hook to capture a saltwater fish similar to a weakfish. History also documents Aelian, another Roman, as observing Macedonian anglers catching trout on artificial flies a hundred years later.

This streamer fly and a spinning lure both imitate baitfish, but the streamer fly weighs a tenth of what the spinning lure weighs.

Contrary to popular stereotypes, fly fishing is much more than stream fishing for trout.

Throughout the Middle Ages and into the Renaissance, references are made to the imitation of artificial flies when fishing for trout. The early fly fishers surely did not think of themselves as sportsmen; they were deceiving trout for more pragmatic reasons. Mayflies and other delicate creatures do not stay on a hook very well, nor do they retain their lifelike qualities after being impaled. The early fly fishers were merely utilizing a bait that would last for dozens of fish without falling off the hook.

Fly-fishing tackle has changed considerably. Early anglers had no fly lines as we know them today. They fished with long rods—sometimes over 20 feet long—and long leaders. Using a technique called *dapping*, which suspends the fly over the fish, they would tease him into striking. Any distance required was obtained from the long rods they used. Reels were nonexistent, and the line was tied to the end of the rod.

Today's "flies" may imitate anything fish would think of eating, from their own eggs to frogs, insects, mice,

leeches, crabs, moths, minnows, and even snails. Rods from space-age fibers and reels constructed of the latest lightweight metallic alloys cast floating fly lines made by an ingenious process in which tiny glass bubbles (called *microballoons*) are homogenized into a plastic line coating. Fur and feathers are being replaced to a large degree by synthetics, although many fly tiers prefer the traditional materials. But the principle is still the same: A relatively weightless lure is delivered to the fish via a long, flexible rod and a weighted line. And fly fishers are still searching for the perfect imitation, the fly that will catch a fish on every cast. Let's hope that we never reach the end of that rainbow.

Almost everyone today has used or seen a spinning outfit, and to understand just what fly casting is, a comparison of it and spin casting may be helpful. Let's take a look at two anglers, both casting from a boat for bass, both using a minnow imitation.

A typical spin fisher's lure weighs about a quarter of an ounce. One common type of spinning lure is carved from balsa wood or cast from plastic and is shaped like a minnow. It has a silvery painted finish, and a cup-shaped lip in the front makes it wiggle like a minnow when retrieved through the water. His tackle consists of a 6½-foot spin rod and an ultralight spinning reel that contains 200 yards of level 6-pound-test monofilament line. The lure is tied directly onto his line. Holding the rod at about the 10:00 position in front of him, he uses his wrist to bring the tip of the rod back to 12:30, beyond his

Because flies weigh almost nothing, these insect imitations need a weighted line to deliver them to a fish.

Flies can even imitate worms. The worm imitated by these San Juan worm flies are aquatic worms, but they look a lot like the common garden variety toted around in bait cans.

shoulder; then a snap of the wrist quickly brings it back to 10:00, in front of him at eye level. At the same time, he straightens his index finger, which has been crooked around the line. The flex of the rod snaps the lure off into space, pulling the line smoothly off the reel. Air resistance and gravity slow the lure's trajectory about 60 feet away, and it hits the water with a gentle splat. The angler retrieves his line and fishes the lure by turning a crank on the side of the reel; a mechanical bail gathers the line back onto the spool, moving the lure through the water with a minnow-like swimming motion. When the lure reaches the boat, he reels in more line until the lure is hanging a few inches below the tip of the rod. He is ready to make another cast.

Now let's take a look at the fly fisher. His objective is the same, but both his lure and the tackle that presents it are quite different. The lure consists of a hook dressed with tinsel and feathers. The tinsel is wound around the straight part of the hook, forming a shiny "body" that reflects light in imitation of a minnow's silvery scales. The "wing" of the fly consists of two chicken feathers. The feathers, which have black centers with white edges, are an impressionistic view of a minnow's black medial stripe. This fly is called a *streamer fly*, and it would take maybe a couple dozen of them to equal the weight of the spin fisher's balsa-wood version.

As the fly has virtually no weight, it lacks the momentum necessary to peel line off the front of the spinning reel. Even if you take a fly in your hand and heave it as far as you can, it won't get 10 feet away. You can always dap the fly off the end of your spinning rod, literally dipping it to the surface of the water as our primitive ancestors did with their embryonic fishing tackle, but there are more efficient ways to present a fly.

Instead of a long, level piece of nylon, the fly fisher relies upon a weighted line to deliver his fly. The line may float or sink once it hits the water, but it has enough weight mass to deliver the fly over 100 feet away (although the average cast is much less, more like 30 feet). The thick fly line is separated from the fly by a leader of tapered nylon monofilament, basically the same stuff the spin fisher's entire line is made of. The leader provides a flexible, relatively invisible connection between the fly line and the fly. It makes the fly appear lifelike and unattached on the water, and its air resistance allows the fly to settle gently to the water's surface.

Let's observe a fly fisher in action. After tying the fly to his leader, he pulls 10 feet of fly line out beyond the tip of his fly rod. Then he pulls 30 feet of fly line off the reel and holds it, coiled, in his left hand. With a quick back-and-forth flicking motion, using his right forearm and wrist, he moves the tip of the fly rod from straight out in

3

This crab imitation is made from mostly synthetic materials.

front of him to just past the vertical. As the fly line moves through the air it describes a tight, elongated arc, called a *casting loop*. The arc flattens, parallel to the water, both behind and in front of him. He does this three or four times, without letting the fly or line hit the water, releasing some of the coiled fly line in his left hand every time he finishes a forward stroke. When he finishes the fourth *false cast*, as they are called, his fly, leader, and line settle gently to the water, 40 feet away.

The streamer, a type of wet fly, sinks slowly beneath the surface, pulling the leader along. The fly fisher begins to retrieve line, moving the fly through the water. Instead of using his reel to retrieve line, as the spin fisher does, he hooks the fly line over the index finger of the hand that is holding the rod and pulls the fly line with his other hand. Each pull of the line makes the fly dart through the water like a minnow. And each length of line is carefully coiled in his left hand, ready to be worked out on the next cast. When the fly is about 10 feet from the boat, our fly fisher will begin another cast, repeating the process.

At first glance, it appears that the fly fisher has to go through a lot of effort for a single cast. All the spin fisher has to do to deliver the lure is flick the tip of his rod once, while the fly fisher has to move his rod a few times before his fly reaches an effective fishing distance. But fly fishing has its advantages. For one, if the fly fisher suddenly sees a feeding fish, he can pick up that entire 40-foot length of line, change the direction of his cast in midair, and lay it down right in front of the fish. The spin fisher must reel in all his line before he can even think about making a cast to another spot. And there are other advantages.

How hard is it to learn? Like many things, it depends on how well you observe and listen, and how much hand-eye coordination you possess. Most people think it's about as difficult as golf or tennis to learn, and like those

Fly casting places that weightless fly in a precise spot, as well as ensuring the casting loop is formed properly.

Fly fishing is also a lazy day catching sunfish on little poppers.

So to feel comfortable with a fly rod probably takes a few years. Fly fishing became almost a craze in the late 1990s when the movie *A River Runs Through It* hit the screens, but the people who flocked to fly fishing soon discovered it required a big commitment in time and effort, and gave up. Fly fishing has one of the highest dropout rates of any sport, so if you stick with it, you can be proud of yourself.

Fly fishing is thought by the uninitiated to be expensive, but it does not have to be. There is great satisfaction in owning fine tackle, and better equipment *can* give you an edge in performance. But you can buy an entire outfit for under $100 that can catch any trout that swims, and many of the smaller saltwater species. (Hard-running saltwater fish do often require more expensive tackle, but it's a pittance after acquiring the boat or hiring the guide to get to them.)

sports, you'll never be completely satisfied with your skills. I've been fly-fishing for forty years, and there are some days I feel completely helpless on the water. To understand this, imagine relying on your own mechanical dexterity for the fly-casting aspect, then throw in the uncertainties of wind, water conditions, and an animal that some days just won't eat anything.

How old must a child be before he or she can learn? I can teach any five-year-old to cast a fly rod in half an hour, but that child then needs to have the patience to tie on a fly, observe the water, and then maybe go without a strike for hours. Can your child handle that? I've seen many kids turned off to fly fishing because their father or mother took them on a trout stream for their first outing, adding

You can fly fish from a boat in the ocean.

You can also walk or wade the edges of a stream or lake.

the complexities of current and a fish that has the moody feeding habits of a toddler. If you want to introduce a young child to fly fishing, take her to a small pond filled with sunfish, where she can see the fish, catch them on almost every cast, and learn how to play and land them. If you want to take a five-year-old trout fishing, get a push-button spincast reel rod, a can of worms, and a bobber.

Although fly fishing is probably the most enjoyable way to fish for trout, it is not always the most efficient method. In early spring, when the water is cold, the trout are not inclined to move for a drifting fly. A worm put right in front of their noses is much more appealing. One early-spring afternoon, I was walking the bank of my favorite river, searching for surface-feeding trout. An angler using worms was carefully and methodically working one of the runs, and I envied his ability to place his worm right on the bottom. Bait is effective just sitting there, but a fly must move or drift with the current in order to entice trout.

I sat on the bank, keeping my eyes peeled for those characteristic rings on the surface of the water that indicate trout feeding on emerging insects. At this time of year I could expect to see grayish-colored mayflies emerging at about 2:00 P.M. The trout often feed on these insects to the exclusion of other types of food.

Sure enough, at about 1:45 I saw the sailboat wings of the mayflies glittering in the weak spring sunlight as they rode the currents, drying their wings. A dozen adult mayflies were soon airborne, flying slowly but steadily upstream. Then two dozen; then three. By 2:00, the surface of the water was covered with struggling mayfly adults, and the trout finally took notice, as mayfly after mayfly disappeared into the concentric rings of surface-feeding trout. It was the kind of opportunity that fly fishers yearn for but seldom see.

I waded out into the pool with a light-gray dry fly, an imitation of the floating mayfly, tied to my leader. The normally elusive brown and brook trout of this river must have forgotten the lessons they had learned the previous season. It seemed that every time I put my fly over a fish, it was taken. I was elated—so elated that I forgot about the worm fisherman sitting on the bank behind me until he started exclaiming: "Ooh! Oh my God! Oh!" Every time I hooked a fish, his awe became more apparent. Finally he gave in.

"What kind of bait are you using?"

"Dry flies," I said.

"Live ones?"

"No, artificials made out of fur and feathers."

"I've been fishing worms all morning, couldn't get a strike," he complained. "Usually worms work out pretty good."

"Guess they just want flies today," I replied. "It isn't always this easy."

He pelted me with more questions, while I played and released fish almost continuously. Finally the worm fisherman thanked me for my patience with his questions and began walking to his car, dejection showing in the slump of his shoulders. He turned to me once more.

"Is it hard to learn?"

Don't let anyone tell you the right or the wrong way to fish with a fly. You'll hear some prima donnas say that nymph fishing with a strike indicator is not really fly fishing, or that trolling a streamer fly is not fly fishing, or that fishing for steelhead with an egg imitation is not fly fishing. Who cares? As long as the gear you are using is legal (some fly-fishing-only areas prohibit weighted flies or have other gear restrictions) and you're having fun, how you play the game should matter to no one but you. If you want to keep a few fish for dinner, don't feel guilty. If you are strictly a catch-and-release fly fisher, don't preach. Habitat protection and access to water is the key to the future of fishing, not stockpiling fish for a few years. It is vir-tually impossible to completely eradicate a fish population by sportfishing, but if the habitat is ruined, then the fish may never come back.

Make sure that while you enjoy your fun, you don't ruin it for others. Littering is an obvious example of boor-ish behavior, but even worse is forgetting to close a cattle gate or pushing down a fence. Less obvious to neophytes is the ability to gauge how much distance to give another angler. In lakes or on the ocean, don't run your boat through a school of feeding fish, and always leave plenty of room for other boats. On trout streams, give other anglers as wide a berth as possible: Even if there is only one person in a pool, don't fish that pool if there is another empty one close by. Or if all the pools are full of anglers, find a riffle or a side channel somewhere. On even the most crowded trout streams in the country, you'll always be able to find a place to fish where you won't be bothering others. You will find one of the great pleasures of the sport is solitude.

{ MAPS }

Chapter Two

Fly Rods and Line Sizes

A FLY ROD IS A TOOL FOR CASTING and repositioning line and playing fish. But because it seems to have a personality of its own, you might think of a fly rod as an extension of your own anatomy—a long, skinny finger.

The phrase *casting a fly* is not really an accurate description of what you do when you wave a fly rod back and forth. A fly rod casts a weighted fly line; the leader and fly go along for the ride. Casting energy is transferred from your forearm and wrist through the rod to the line, which provides the energy to drive the leader and fly up

to 90, or even 100 feet away. (But you'll be happy to know most fish are caught with less than a 40-foot cast.) Thus, it's difficult to discuss fly rods without talking about fly lines. In fact, when we name a fly rod, we generally describe it by length and line size: 8½-foot for 6-weight line, or 9-foot for 9-weight line. The material the rod is constructed from and the weight of the rod are also important parameters, though less important than length and line size.

Too often, fly fishers will ask: "I have a 3⅞-ounce bamboo rod. What kind of fishing can I do with it?"

A fly rod's main purpose is to cast the line.

Describing your fly rod by weight alone is like describing someone by saying he weighs 190 pounds. Giving a rod's length, line size, and material, however, is like describing his personality, his purpose in life, his faults, and his strong points, as well as all his physical dimensions.

A fly rod can also reposition the line on the water.

And of course a fly rod acts as a flexible lever to play and land a fish without breaking the leader.

FLY-ROD TERMINOLOGY

Before we discuss fly-rod line sizes, lengths, and materials, let's identify the parts of a fly rod. Although one-piece fly rods do exist, they are not terribly practical, because it's hard to fit an 8-foot rod inside the trunk of your car. The most common fly rods are two-piece, although three- and four-piece versions are also available and are quite practical. Two-piece rods used to be the most common, but today, four-piece rods—because they are easier to pack and to get on an airline or into a car trunk—have surpassed two-piece rods. Today's technology makes it possible to construct a seven-piece fly rod that will be a supremely practical tool, with no sacrifice in casting qualities or "feel."

In a two-piece fly rod, the thicker, lower section (the piece that includes the handle) is called the *butt*, while the skinny top section is called the *tip*. On four-piece rods, the section the reel attaches to is still called the butt, the next section up is the butt-middle, followed by the tip-middle, and finally, the tip. Don't even ask me what all the sections on a seven-piece rod are called. If you have to talk to a rod repair person, just describe the section as "the fifth one up from the butt" or something equally imaginative.

Starting at the extreme bottom of the fly rod, the metal cap is called the *end plug*. On some large saltwater and salmon rods, this plug can be removed and replaced with a detachable *butt extension* or *fighting butt*, although most rods for this purpose come with a fixed fighting butt that extends from 1 to 2 inches below the reel seat. This attachment is used when the fly fisher expects to be playing large fish for a long time. Bracing it against your stomach or belt can take a lot of the strain off your arms—a most pleasant weariness that generally accompanies big-game fishing.

The end plug is attached to the *reel seat*, which is available in an almost endless variety of materials. Although the reel seat's sole purpose is to hold the fly reel securely to the rod, fly-rod manufacturers and amateur rod builders often spend an inordinate amount of time discussing the relative merits of designs and materials. The reel seat usually consists of a metal frame (which actually holds the reel) and a filler. The frame is usually a strong, lightweight aluminum alloy. The filler, for practical and cosmetic reasons, may be made from cork, walnut, maple, zebra wood, synthetic composites, or other exotic plastic-impregnated wood laminates. Premium hardware is often made from jewelry-grade nickel-silver (heavier and more expensive, but exquisite in appearance). In most saltwater

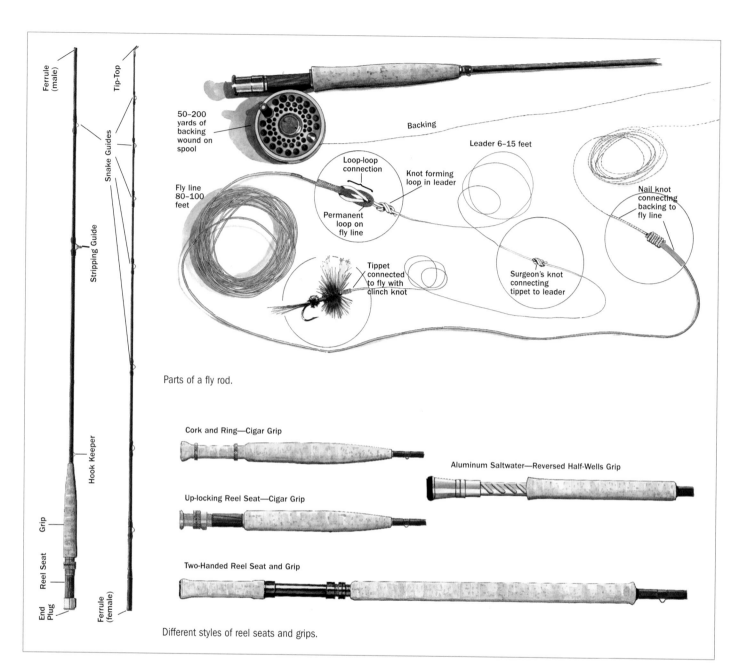

Parts of a fly rod.

Different styles of reel seats and grips.

rods, the entire reel seat is made from anodized aluminum, which is necessary to hold heavy saltwater reels and to resist the corrosive action of salt water.

A sample of the reel seats offered by modern fly-rod manufacturers includes:

Ring type. Designed for small reels and light fly rods, the ring type consists of two thin metal bands that are forced over the feet of the fly reel. Although they are more secure than they appear, avoid reels that weigh over 3 ounces with this type of reel seat.

Screw-locking. This type consists of a fixed metal hood at the bottom of the seat, combined with a hood at the top, which can be screwed down over the reel-seat foot. This is probably the most popular type of reel seat.

Reversed screw-locking. Exactly the same as the screw-locking, except that the fixed hood is at the other end of the seat, and is often buried inside the cork grip. The screw band screws *up* toward the grip—in fact, this type is often called *up-locking*, as opposed to the *down-locking* reel seat above. This is the most common type of reel seat used today.

Most other reel seats are simply variations on the above three types, incorporating such features as fixed fighting butts, or, in the case of the two-handed salmon or Spey rod, a second long grip located below the reel seat. As long as your reel seat is of the correct size to accommodate your reel, you should select a type for aesthetic reasons.

The grip functions as the handle of your fly rod. On all quality fly rods it is constructed from cork that was filed on a lathe and sanded smooth. Grip style, which varies in diameter size and in shape, is a matter of personal taste. Grips commonly used, in order of increasing diameter, include superfine, cigar, half wells, and full wells. People with small hands generally prefer the smaller-diameter grips; those with big hands feel more comfortable with something like a full-wells grip.

Working your way up along the rod, you'll find a small metal ring or hook called the *hook keeper*. When you are not fishing, your fly is hooked here to keep it from catching in streamside brush (or your clothing). Not all rods feature a hook keeper, as in saltwater rods it tends to get in the way when shooting long lengths of line. If your rod does not have a hook keeper, simply wrap the leader around the base of the reel seat and bring the fly back up to one of the guides, where it can be hung to keep it out of mischief.

Next you'll encounter the first guide, called the *stripping guide*. The purpose of fly-rod guides is threefold: to hold the line to the rod during casting; to funnel the line along the length of the rod when shooting line (releasing extra line to obtain additional distance); and to distribute properly along the entire length of the rod, the stress of playing the fish. The stripping guide, being the first part of the rod the line encounters after leaving the reel, receives a lot of wear and tear. To reduce friction, the stripping guide is made from an abrasion-resistant material, usually hard chrome or ceramic. Some saltwater rods feature two stripping guides. The rest of the guides, of which there should be at least as many as the rod is long in feet, are simple bent pieces of wire called *snake guides*. Guides are distributed along a rod according to a specific formula that is unique to each length of rod and are attached to the rod with nylon thread, which is epoxied or varnished two or three times for durability and protection from the elements. The last guide, which sits at the extreme top of the tip section, is called the *tip-top*.

Some fly rods feature ceramic stripping guides or single-foot ceramic guides along the entire length of the rod, instead of snake guides. But these are so heavy and air-resistant that they change the action of the rod. The idea is to lessen the friction between guides, enabling the caster to shoot more line.

Ferrules are the joints that connect the sections of multiple-piece rods. They are designed to hold the pieces of a rod together throughout a day of fishing, yet pull apart easily when you want to put your rod away. Ferrules on bamboo rods are made of nickel-silver metal, while those on graphite, fiberglass rods, and boron/graphite are *self-ferrules*, which involve a tapered sleeve of the rod material itself, glued to the tip section, which fits snugly over the butt section.

LINE SIZES

To understand why line size is so important, you must realize that fly fishing is immensely versatile. If everyone fished with flies that were ¼ to ¾ of an inch long, in streams 15 to 30 feet wide, in a place where winds were always moderate to light, we'd need only one line size. But flies range in size from ⅛ of an inch to over 6 inches in length, and the corresponding differences in air resistance of these different-sized flies require lines of different weights. Generally, the heavier the fly line, the larger the fly you'll be able to cast, the fewer problems you'll have with wind, and the farther you can cast. The lighter your line, the more delicate and accurate your presentation will be with smaller flies.

A well-made fly rod is designed for a particular line size. The shape of the loop on your line cast is very important, and it is necessary to keep the fly line moving through the air in a special fashion. To cast properly, a fly rod must exhibit a happy medium between flexibility and stiffness. A pretty and efficient cast comes from a well-designed fly rod, good casting form, and the weight of the fly line pulling on the rod. A heavy fly line will exert more pull on a fly rod during casting; thus, a rod designed for throwing large flies into the wind will be stiffer than a rod designed to present tiny dry flies with a light fly line.

In order to cast a line, a fly rod must flex in a special fashion. This flex cannot come from the weight of either the fly or the leader; it must come from the weight of the line. "Fly-rod balance" is the key. If a line is too light for your rod, the rod will not flex enough, making you work extra hard in order to cast. If the line is too heavy, it will overload the rod and cause sloppy presentation. A severely overloaded rod can even break on a long cast.

Eventually, every fly fisher asks: "Can I get one fly rod that will do everything for me?" That depends upon what is meant by "everything." If you will be fishing for, say, trout—and nothing else—the answer could be yes. However, if you want to fish for many different kinds of fish on rivers, lakes, ponds, and oceans, you will probably need a number of fly rods.

The all-purpose fly rod can be likened to an all-purpose golf club. It's possible to play eighteen holes of golf with a putter, but it's certainly not efficient (and not much fun).

Table 1 shows the range of line weights used by fly fishers, the fly sizes paired to them, and the kinds of species that can be pursued with those flies. The number designation of each weight corresponds to the weight in grains (437.5 grains = 1 ounce) of the first 30 feet of line.

This system was adopted by the American Fishing Tackle Manufacturers Association in 1961 and is used throughout the world by all fly-line manufacturers. This weight may range from 100 grains for a 3-weight line to 380 grains for a 12-weight.

Why do we use weight at all? Why not diameter? Actually, before 1961 fly lines were classed by diameter, with letters of the alphabet referring to particular diameters. All lines were made of silk, so diameters were consistent with weight. With the advent of modern floating, sinking, and intermediate-weight lines, with their varying densities, this system had to be scrapped and was replaced with the modern system based on weight.

Table 1: Matching Line Sizes to Fish Species and Flies

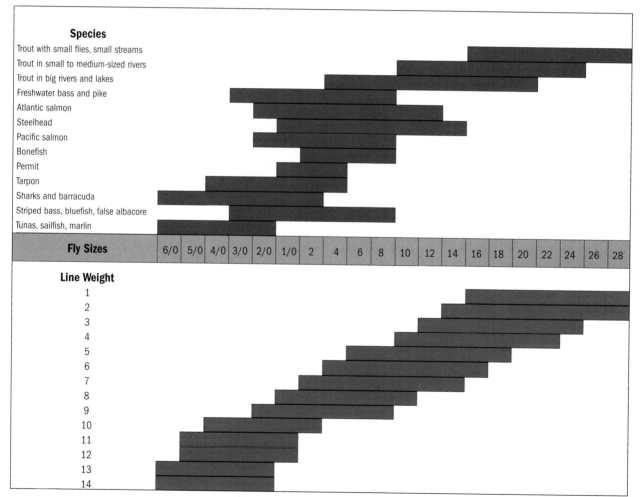

The chart above shows how to choose the correct line size according to the species you are going to pursue. For instance, if you'll be fishing for trout in large rivers or lakes, you'll see that you might be fishing fly sizes in anything from a size 4 through a size 20. Looking down, you'll see that line sizes could be anything from a 1-weight to a 9-weight. Unless you will only be fishing big size-4 streamers all the time, you can rule out line sizes 8 and 9, and unless you'll only be fishing tiny flies, you can forget about the 1, 2, and 3 weights. That still leaves you with the possible line sizes 4, 5, 6, and 7. If most of your flies will be on the smaller size, stick with the smaller line size 4. If most of your flies will be larger, or you you'll encounter a lot of wind, go with the heavier 6 or 7 weight. And, of course, if you want to cover all your bases, choose the 5—which is the most popular trout line size by a large margin.

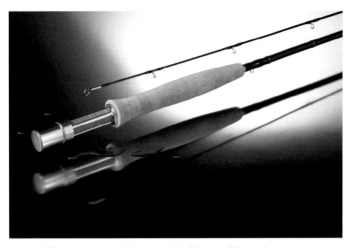

This two-piece graphite trout rod is light, sensitive, and very strong.

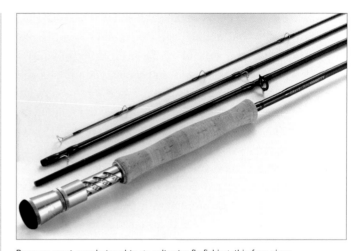

Because most people travel to go saltwater fly fishing, this four-piece graphite saltwater rod fits easily in a duffle bag or can be carried onto an airplane.

Some fly rods, especially modern graphite and boron/graphite rods, will cast two or three line sizes with minor adjustments in casting technique. Whether a particular rod can do this depends on its design, and you will have to try different lines on a rod to find this out. As a rule of thumb, you can get away with one line size heavier if your casts will be consistently under 30 feet, and one line size lighter if they will be consistently longer than 40 feet.

Again referring to Table 1, you can see that, for any type of fishing or fly-size range, you have a choice of two, or perhaps even three, line sizes. This leeway allows you to choose your line size to fit prevailing weather and water conditions. For example, in stream trout fishing we generally use fly sizes 12 through 18. These would call for a 4-, 5-, or 6-weight line. If casts are frequently long and the wind is a constant factor, or if you plan to fish weighted flies or with weight on your leader, the 6-weight would be the best choice. If your streams lie in protected valleys and winds are light, or if the fish are skittish, the 4-weight might be a better choice. For a little bit of both, go with the 5-weight.

Rods that call for 12- to 14-weight lines are unlike any other kind of rod, because they are designed as much for playing large fish as they are for casting. Usually called "big-game" rods, they allow the fly fisher to muscle large tarpon, trevally, sailfish, or sharks. You might be able to hook and play a 150-pound tarpon with a lighter 7-weight fly rod without breaking it, but a lighter model will bend to such a degree that you'll never be able to put enough pressure on a huge fish to land it.

All fly rods made by reputable manufacturers are marked with the recommended line size. This recommendation is usually either engraved on the butt plate or inscribed on the butt section of the rod, just above the cork grip.

With modern graphite fly-rod construction, even a seven-piece rod can be built with no sacrifice in casting quality—and it literally fits into a briefcase.

This Spey rod, for two-handed casting, has a grip in front of and behind the reel seat.

ROD MATERIALS

In selecting a fly rod, the variables involved are material, length, price, and action (or flex index). The material that the rod is made of will to some degree determine the personality of the rod, or the casting tempo or "action" it exhibits. The material will definitely determine both the appearance and the price of your rod. While I will talk about bamboo and fiberglass fly rods, 95 percent of the quality fly rods built today are made of some kind of graphite composite.

Bamboo

A bamboo fly rod, or "split bamboo" or "split cane" rod, is known even to non-fly fishers as the hallmark of the affluent anglers. Fly rods handcrafted from bamboo, with a heritage dating back well over a hundred years, are sometimes thought to be fragile and easily broken. This belief has about as much basis in truth as does the proverbial story of the young boy with a bent pin outfishing the experienced sport. The finished bamboo fly rod is a solid, six-sided shaft. The glowing brown-and-amber bamboo is polished and varnished to produce a fishing rod that is unmatched in appearance. Most of the steps in making a bamboo rod are hand operations performed by craftspeople, and other than electric saws and milling machines, they use hand tools. It takes a month or more to produce each quality bamboo fly rod.

Briefly, raw bamboo is graded and sorted, strips are cut from the bamboo poles, and the strips are tapered on a milling machine to tolerances of a few thousandths of an inch. Six strips are glued together to form the solid rod; next, the outside of the rod is lightly sanded; and only then can the reel seat, grip, guides, and ferrules be mounted to the rod. A bamboo fly rod carries a pride of ownership that only the fly fisher and perhaps a custom woodworker can appreciate.

Before the advent of fly rods made from synthetic materials, starting with fiberglass in the mid-1940s and continuing with graphite and boron in the 1970s and '80s, bamboo was the only material of any significance, at

A section of raw bamboo, cut in half, next to a finished, solid, six-sided blank.

Bamboo fly rods are the epitome of a rodmaker's craft, and with their heavier, solid construction they feel much different than the light, hollow tubes used to make graphite rods.

least in the twentieth century. Manufacturers experimented with other types of wood and with tubular steel, but these produced inferior fly rods. Thus, bamboo was used for all types of fly rods, from the biggest, heaviest saltwater and salmon rods to the most delicate trout rods.

Bamboo rods are heavier for a particular class of rod than any of the synthetics, and in the 8- to 12-weight sizes, they have been edged out of the market by the lighter and more powerful synthetics. Who wants to cast all day with a 9-ounce bamboo fly rod when a 4-ounce graphite rod can do the job as well, or better?

The strong, elastic fibers of the bamboo plant lend their personality to the bamboo rod, giving it a special casting sensation that is unique. These fly rods are neither better nor worse than those made from synthetic materials, but they *are* different. Bamboo fly rods feel more flexible when casting, lending themselves to a relaxed casting style. This is because bamboo fibers stretch more than, say, graphite, to deliver the same amount of power. Some fly fishers, myself included, feel that bamboo is superior for delivering tiny, delicate flies to sophisticated trout in clear water.

A beginner should not shy away from a bamboo fly rod, but merely respect its limitations—namely, weight and price. For fly fishing in salt water, or wherever large flies must be cast long distances, bamboo is surely not as efficient as graphite or boron/graphite. This is not to say that bamboo is more fragile. A good bamboo rod can withstand the shock of being whacked against a tree limb

or steady thrumming against a boat gunwale much better than synthetic rods, with their hollow construction. For trout fishing, pan fishing, or fishing with the smaller bass flies, at normal casting ranges (up to 60 feet), bamboo is as good as any synthetic fly rod, and many aficionados feel it is better.

Fiberglass

Fiberglass was the first successful synthetic material used to make fly rods, and it is still with us today. Since the 1950s, fiberglass has been improved with new resin systems and fibers that are more consistent in their properties. Fiberglass fly rods are round and hollow, because they are formed by wrapping fiberglass around a stainless-steel form, or *mandrel*, under pressure. The mandrel is removed, leaving the hollow fly rod.

Fiberglass is lighter than bamboo, but it must bend more to deliver the same power; thus, when stressed on a long, powerful cast, a fiberglass rod will lose its power, or reach its elastic limit, under less stress than will a bamboo, graphite, or boron/graphite rod. However, this limit can be reached only within the abilities of a tournament caster and is something that we ordinary mortals don't have to worry about. But fiberglass is also less sensitive to casting subtleties and less forgiving of casting mistakes.

Fiberglass rods used to have a big edge on all other types of modern fly rods in that a good one costs about half the price of a graphite or boron/graphite rod and about a quarter of the price of a bamboo rod. Fiberglass is an inexpensive raw material, and the fabrication techniques require much less labor. But the inexpensive nature of fiberglass has led to many poor-quality, mass-produced rods that are little more than spin rods with fly-rod guides. You can still find fiberglass fly rods in big-box stores, but I'd avoid them, because you can get a decent graphite rod today for under a hundred dollars—and it will be much more fun to use. There is at least one custom maker of fiberglass fly rods today, and these are beautiful rods, very slow and delicate. But they cost as much as medium-priced graphite rods, and I'm afraid their appeal is limited to those who have nostalgic memories of their old fiberglass rods.

Buy your fiberglass fly rod from a reputable *fly-rod* salesman, not a sporting-goods clerk who feels more comfortable selling tennis rackets or bicycles.

Fiberglass rods are made for all types of fly fishing, from trout to tarpon. They are also very rugged; thus, they lend themselves well to youngsters, who tend to be impatient with things like fly rods.

Graphite

Graphite is a polyester carbon fiber that has been subjected to intense heat and pressure. (In fact, if you live in the UK, what we Americans call graphite rods are usually referred to as "carbon-fibre" rods.) It was developed by the aerospace industry as a light, strong, flexible, heat-resistant alternative to metals. As used in fly rods, graphite consists of thousands of tiny, hair-like filaments held together by some type of resin system, along with a layer of strengthening fibers called *scrim*. A flat layer of graphite fibers, cut to a taper, is rolled around a tapered mandrel along with a layer of scrim, and perhaps a small amount of boron fibers for strength, and subjected to heat and pressure, after which the mandrel is removed. The resulting hollow fly-rod *blank* (the rod tube itself before the guides, grip, or reel seat are attached) is extremely light, has tensile strength greater than steel, and, most important to us, makes a very fine fly rod.

Making a graphite fly rod is a complex process. If you read much of the advertising literature, you'd think they were made from a solid tube of graphite. But each rod is a combination of graphite fibers, the resin system that holds them together, the scrim that provides strength to the walls of the hollow tube, and finally, the taper cre-

Steps in the construction of a graphite rod. At far left is a flat graphite flag that is wrapped around a steel mandrel and then wrapped with heat-shrink tape. Next is a hollow blank after the tape is removed, showing the ridges formed on the outside of the blank. Next is a blank that has been sanded, and finally a finished blank, painted with a maroon color and then coated with a hard, clear finish.

ated when the fibers are cut to a precise shape and then wrapped over a mandrel that also has a precise taper. Just as with other high-technology products, most of us mortals are never going to understand (or care) exactly what materials are in a rod, as long as it feels good in the hand, performs well in casting and playing fish, and is strong enough to play a fish without breaking.

You'll hear the expression *modulus (degree) of elasticity* trumpeted, especially "high-modulus." This term refers to a material's resistance to bending. To a certain degree, a high modulus is desirable, because the higher the modulus, the stiffer the fibers, allowing you to produce a lighter, thinner rod. The problem is that as you increase in modulus, you also increase in brittleness, which can be offset by higher-quality resin systems made of thermoplastic. But without knowing the taper of a rod, its wall thickness, the resin system used to hold the fibers together, and the type and amount of scrim used, knowing the modulus of elasticity of the graphite fibers used is meaningless.

One of graphite's special virtues is a comparatively high modulus of elasticity. This means that graphite has a high resistance to bending—or, quite simply, it's stiffer. Being stiffer without breaking is desirable up to a point, as it enables a rod to flex less to deliver the same length of line; this means that it will hold a longer length of line in the air, will have a quicker response rate between back and forward casts, and can be made thinner, cutting down on air resistance. All of these factors produce a higher line speed. More line speed produces more line momentum, so your fly line travels farther than if you expended the same effort with a bamboo or fiberglass fly rod.

In order to direct the fly line to the proper spot, your fly rod should bend when you direct it to and stay still when you want it to. The high modulus of elasticity also means that graphite rods have a quick recovery rate. When you finish your forward cast and the rod is pointing to where you want the line to go, the less your rod wiggles, the more efficient and accurate your casting will be. Graphite fly rods are the most efficient casting rods known today.

Obviously, graphite's qualities lend themselves well to rods for big flies and heavy line sizes. How about delicate fishing and light line sizes? Because graphite is stiffer than bamboo or fiberglass, long (over 8-foot) rods for light fly lines (3-, 4-, and 5-weights) can be practical fishing tools, rods that would not be possible with either bamboo or fiberglass.

Graphite is also more forgiving of casting mistakes than any other material, and our years of experience in the Orvis Fly Fishing Schools have substantiated this belief. The hardest problem a beginning caster encounters is producing a high, flat backcast. Mistakes in timing that would be disastrous with a bamboo rod can produce a passable presentation with a graphite rod.

That a graphite fly rod is lighter than a bamboo or fiberglass rod is not terribly significant when you are comparing trout-size models, as the difference in weight is a fraction of an ounce. When you compare the longer, thicker-walled saltwater, salmon, or bass rods, however, the weight differential is extremely significant. The fact that a 9-foot bamboo salmon rod weighs almost 7 ounces and a fiberglass rod almost 6, while a graphite rod weighs only 3, doesn't sound significant—but when you are wielding this rod through hundreds of casts a day, using only the muscles of your wrist and forearm, you appreciate the difference.

You do generally get what you pay for, because the better materials are more labor-intensive to work with, and the cost of the raw material itself is higher. And fly-rod makers put their best reel seats, cork, and guides on their better rods. So as you go up the scale in price, you get a lighter, stronger, and more responsive rod—and usually a better-looking one, if that matters to you.

ACTION

Fly fishers often say, "That rod has good action," or "The action of this rod is poor." Great—all that tells us is that these anglers like the way one rod feels in their hands, with their own particular casting style, and they don't like the other. *Action* merely describes the way a fly rod flexes under stress.

In the golden age of bamboo rods, action was supposed to dictate what kind of flies could be used with a particular rod. "Fast action" was stiffer, and this type of rod flexed almost entirely in the top 25 percent of the rod. Flicking excess water from a dry fly was its purpose. "Slow-action" rods flexed all the way into the grip during casting and were designed *not* to flick the water off a wet fly. "Fast action" became synonymous with dry-fly action, and "slow action" was equal to wet-fly action. "Medium action," obviously, was somewhere in between. The "slow" and "fast" came from the fact that it takes a lot more time to develop the

power needed for a cast when the rod bends all the way into its lower sections than it does for a rod to flex just at the tip.

The fact that modern graphite, boron, and synthetic fiber rods behave so differently from bamboo rods has made comparisons of actions obsolete. For rods of comparable length and line size, fiberglass is usually the slowest, bamboo is next, and graphite faster, with boron or boron/graphite the fastest. This comparison is based only on the stiffness of the materials involved. Theoretically, by thickening the walls on a fiberglass rod you could make it faster than graphite, but it would be extremely thick and heavy.

There is still no system of measuring action that crosses all makers of rods, but in the late 1990s Orvis devised a system called the Flex Index that at least allows you to compare one Orvis rod to another—even if they have different retail prices. The Flex Index is a numbering system from 1 to 12, where a rod with the theoretical flex index of 1 is about as soft as a noodle, and a rod with a flex index of 12 approaches the characteristics of a broom handle. The Index is divided into three broad groups: Full-Flex Action, Mid-Flex Action, and Tip-Flex Action. All will cast a fly line beautifully, and the choice of flex index is partially a matter of your casting style and temperament, and partly a matter of the fishing conditions you find yourself in the most.

The Orvis Flex Index

Full-Flex Action: 2–5
- Well suited for close-range, delicate casting
- Protects light tippets best because of full-flex shock absorption
- Responds well to a gentle casting stroke
- Offers superior "feel" on close-range casts
- A favorite traditional action of anglers for many years

Mid-Flex Action: 6–9
- Excellent performance over a wide range of conditions
- Suits a wide range of casting styles
- Great combination of butt strength for fighting fish and medium flex for casting ease
- An excellent measure of tippet protection
- For the angler who needs one rod for a variety of conditions

Tip-Flex Action: 10–12

- Light tip for a "light-in-the-hand" feel
- Helps the caster maximize line speed
- Suits casters with quicker, shorter casting strokes
- Strong butt section (in upper line weights) for fish-fighting "backbone"

The numbering system does take some subjectivity out of the equation, because if you find a rod that you like—let's say an 8½-foot, 5-weight mid-flex trout rod—you can get the same kind of casting sensation in a bonefish rod by buying a 9-foot, 8-weight rod that has the closest flex index to the one you like. This is not going to do you much good when you buy your first rod. Don't worry about the numbering system; just decide whether you think you'd be best suited with one of the three broad groups and pick a rod with that general flex index. You may even find that you like different flex indexes for different kinds of fishing: I like a full-flex action for small-stream trout fishing, mid-flex for stripers and steelhead, and tip-flex when making long casts with dry flies.

Most modern fly rods are built to a *progressive taper* or *progressive action*, which means that as the rod is loaded with more line, it flexes lower and lower. Variations in action occur between manufacturers and between different models made by the same manufacturer. There are really no set rules for building fly-rod action.

LENGTH

Standard lengths for trout and bass fly rods run from 7½ to 9 feet. These particular lengths in line sizes 4, 5, 6, 7, and 8 (the most common line sizes used today) achieve a balance between lightness, manageability, and casting efficiency. As rod length becomes shorter, casting efficiency decreases, because the mechanical advantage obtained (the whole reason for using a fly rod) decreases as the arc through which the tip of the rod moves decreases. A fly rod less than 6 feet long is a novelty and not particularly pleasant to cast. To a lesser degree, fly rods longer than these lengths also decrease in efficiency, mainly because of added weight and air resistance. With graphite, though, it is possible to make a practical fly rod for a 6-weight line as long as 10½ feet. Saltwater fly rods are almost universally 9 feet long, with a few a half-foot longer or shorter. Single-handed rods for steelhead and salmon fishing are typically between 9 and 10 feet long, with the 10-footers getting the edge today because the longer rod helps control the fly line on bigger rivers.

Two-handed rods are made as long as 15 feet, but these are most commonly used for salmon and steelhead, although dedicated two-handed fly fishers use them in trout streams and in the surf off the northeast coast. These long, powerful rods are capable of picking up 80 feet of line and redirecting it to another spot in the river in a single cast.

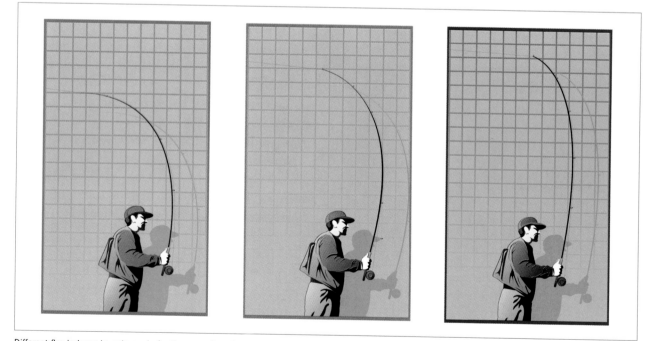

Different flex indexes in rods made for the same line size: Full-flex (green), mid-flex (red), and tip-flex (blue).

Short fly rods have their advocates, and a 6½-foot fly rod is more manageable than an 8-footer in brushy country; it is lighter by almost a full ounce, and it has faster action than a longer rod for a corresponding line size. The shorter rod is faster because it is stiffer, as the same amount of line weight has to be held in the air by less material. Short fly rods make it easier to drive in a fly under overhanging brush, because of their faster line speed and greater maneuverability. Short fly rods are also deadly efficient tools for fighting large fish. It is much easier to lead a fish into the net at close quarters with a short fly rod.

The practicality of longer fly rods is due to graphite fiber. For example, a 9-foot fly rod for a 4-weight line in bamboo or fiberglass would be heavy and as limp as cooked spaghetti, yet such graphite rods are commonplace today. Long (over 8½ feet) fly rods for line sizes 9 to 12 have always been made, because a 7-foot rod for a 10-weight line would have to be so stiff that it would hardly bend at all. But graphite's light weight has almost entirely edged bamboo out of the area of heavy lines/long rods. Long fiberglass rods are also used, but almost entirely in the heavy line sizes.

Thus, a fly fisher with an eye toward big gamefish in the open ocean or salmon on a raging Norwegian river almost *has* to choose a longer rod. What about the trout-and-bass fly fisher? Should they consider a rod over 8½ feet long, even if their casts are never over 40 feet?

The question of fly-rod length can become quite personal, and if a fly fisher likes the idea of an ultralight, short

fly rod, or a long rod, more power to him (or her). Long fly rods have their advantages under certain circumstances, and it's important to recognize the helping hand that a long fly rod can provide. Remembering that a fly rod is merely an extension of your hand and arm, it's obvious that a rod over 8½ feet long will be a great help when the fishing situation calls for repositioning the fly line and/or fly on the water once the cast has been made. For example, imagine that you are standing in an area of fast water in the middle of a trout stream, and trout are rising in the slower water against the far bank. With a short rod, as soon as the fly line hits the water, the fast current at your feet will immediately begin to pull on it, whisking the fly out of the slower water. A long rod will extend your reach, enabling you to hold the fly line above the fast water. By repositioning line on the water, you can also control the speed at which a wet fly drifts through the current.

Anglers who wade in the edges of small lakes and ponds prefer long fly rods for a number of reasons. One advantage of a long rod is that it will keep a fly line out of the vegetation along the shoreline, enabling you to control your fly or bug with greater precision. Whether you fish in lakes or in streams, a long rod, with its greater vertical reach, will keep your backcast out of low trees and shrubs. When you're casting from a sitting position in a boat, a long fly rod will also keep your fly line from slapping the water behind you.

Long fly rods also offer certain casting advantages. They are a great help when the situation calls for a long cast, holding more line in the air, helping you to overcome gravity on your backcast. By enabling you to pick up more line off the water, a long fly rod can also place your fly back on the water with a single cast. A 6-foot fly rod just cannot develop enough momentum to pick up 60 feet of line with a single casting stroke.

Fly rods longer than 7½ feet also offer smoother, longer roll casts. (This is getting ahead of ourselves a bit; a *roll cast* is essentially a cast that has no backcast. The roll cast is a lifesaver when you find yourself backed up against a wall of streamside brush and trees.)

ROD WEIGHT

Rod weight—at least, the physical weight of a fly rod—is a relatively unimportant consideration. In any given line size, an ounce is the difference between a really light one

Tight quarters like this small mountain stream call for a short fly rod, between 6 and 7½ feet.

Long casts, lots of wind, and a high bank behind the angler means his rod should be at least 9 feet long.

plain feel livelier in your hand. Unfortunately, levered weight is not something fly-rod manufacturers use in their specifications, so if it's really important to you, pick up various rods in a fly shop and see which one feels lightest in the hand. Because fly reels weigh much more than rods, you can make a rod feel lighter in the hand just by putting a somewhat heavier reel on it.

FLY-ROD SELECTION

I'll stick my neck out and recommend that your first fly rod be between 8½ and 9 feet long, and be made from graphite. This seems to be the most efficient length for easy fly casting, and graphite is more forgiving of casting mistakes than any other material. If you fish small streams, lean toward an 8½-footer; if you fish big rivers, lakes, or salt water, a 9-foot rod will be easier for long casts or when the wind is blowing.

Because these lengths are the most popular among fly rodders, they come in the complete range of line sizes. If all your fly fishing will be done for trout in clear water, or for panfish, pick a rod that calls for a 4- to 5-weight line. For all-around trout fishing, choose a 5-weight rod, by far the most common line size used by trout anglers. For both trout and bass, get a 6-weight outfit. For just bass, salmon, and smaller, inshore saltwater species, get an 8-weight. Only if you are fly-fishing for the larger saltwater species or salmon or steelhead should you go as heavy as a 9-weight outfit, in order to throw bigger flies, play bigger fish, and fight heavy winds. These rods are heavier and more tiring than trout or bass rods of the same length.

Take time before you choose. Ask a knowledgeable friend or a trusted fly-fishing dealer. Good fly-fishing schools can provide solid advice. Always try the rod with a matching line before you buy. And buy from a reputable shop, catalog, or website that will exchange the rod for a different model if you decide you don't like it.

and a heavyweight. Fly rods can be as light as a single ounce for a tiny small-stream rod to as much as 11 ounces for a large two-handed salmon rod. But most trout rods run between 2 and 3½ ounces, and most saltwater or salmon rods run between 4 and 6 ounces. But it's really the reel-seat hardware that determines most of the weight, not the material used to construct the rod blank. A 4-ounce saltwater rod might tire you less than a 6-ounce rod over eight hours of fishing, but your casting style, how far you cast, and how many big fish (hopefully) you have to play will affect your casting arm far more.

What you feel when you pick up a rod that feels really light as compared to others is *levered* (or *swing*) *weight*. It's the difference in weight between the tip and butt section, and how the rod balances when you hold it by the cork grip. Rods with a lower levered weight have more of the mass concentrated near the handle of the rod and can actually reduce fatigue somewhat. And they just

{ One Last Look—Brook Trout }

Chapter Three

Lines and Reels

FLY-LINE OPTIONS

You are now the proud owner of a new fly-rod outfit, including rod, reel, and a weight-forward floating line of the proper size for your rod. Is this line the only one you'll need? Can you fish wet flies with a floating line? What's the difference between a double taper and a weight-forward taper?

Modern fly lines come in an array of tapers and densities. A battery of different fly lines, mounted on extra spools that fit your fly reel, can help you increase the distance of your casts and keep your fly just under the surface, 20 feet below the surface, or anywhere in between.

Take a look at the line packages in a fly shop. You'll see them marked with a code that might read "DT5F" or "WF6S" or "ST8F/S." You already know the meaning of the number—it's the line size. The first two letters designate the taper, or how the line varies in thickness throughout its length. The last letter or letters tell you the line type—whether the line floats, sinks quickly, sinks slowly, or only partly sinks.

Taper

Standard fly lines are between 80 and 90 feet in length. The weight distribution along this length is tapered, except in *level* (L) lines, which are practically worthless in terms of their casting and presentation qualities. Many of us made the mistake of trying to learn how to fly-fish with a level line. After all, a tapered line costs two to three times as much. Why spend all that money on something you may give up after a season?

Giving up after a season is exactly what you may do if you start with a level line. Tapered lines are designed to take advantage of a gradual decrease in weight that transmits energy smoothly to the leader and fly, resulting in that feather-light delivery we associate with no other method of fishing. An accomplished caster can appreciate the niceties of increased accuracy and delicacy, but even a first-time fly caster can see how much easier it is to cast with a tapered line.

All fly lines start thin at the end to which the leader is attached, to minimize the disturbance when your cast touches the water. The line gradually thickens into what is called the *belly*, which is at least 30 feet long. This is the portion of your line that you hold in the air when casting. *Weight-forward* (WF) lines taper down quickly after 30 feet of head to a thin running line that takes up the rest of the length. *Double-taper* (DT) lines form a mirror image if you cut them in half; the belly does not thin and extends through to a taper on the opposite end (imagine an elongated hour-glass shape). *Shooting-taper* (ST) or *shooting-head* lines replace the running line with fine-diameter floating-level fly line or monofilament. The actual fly-line part of a shooting head is only 28 to 40 feet long. A loop is spliced into the back end of the line and into the running line, making a quick change from a floating to a sinking line without your having to replace the reel spool.

Weight-forward lines are best for the beginning caster, because they cast and shoot easier than a double taper. They were originally designed for distance casting, because concentrating the weight up front enables the caster to shoot longer lengths of line with less effort.

Table 2: Fly-Line Letter Designations

Letter Designation	Refers to	Means
WF	Taper	Weight Forward
DT	Taper	Double Taper
ST	Taper	Shooting Head
L	Taper	Level
F	Sink Rate	Floating
S	Sink Rate	Full Sinking
F/S	Sink Rate	Sink Tip
I	Sink Rate	Intermediate

Example: **WF5F**

Taper is weight forward   Line size is a 5   Line is a floating line

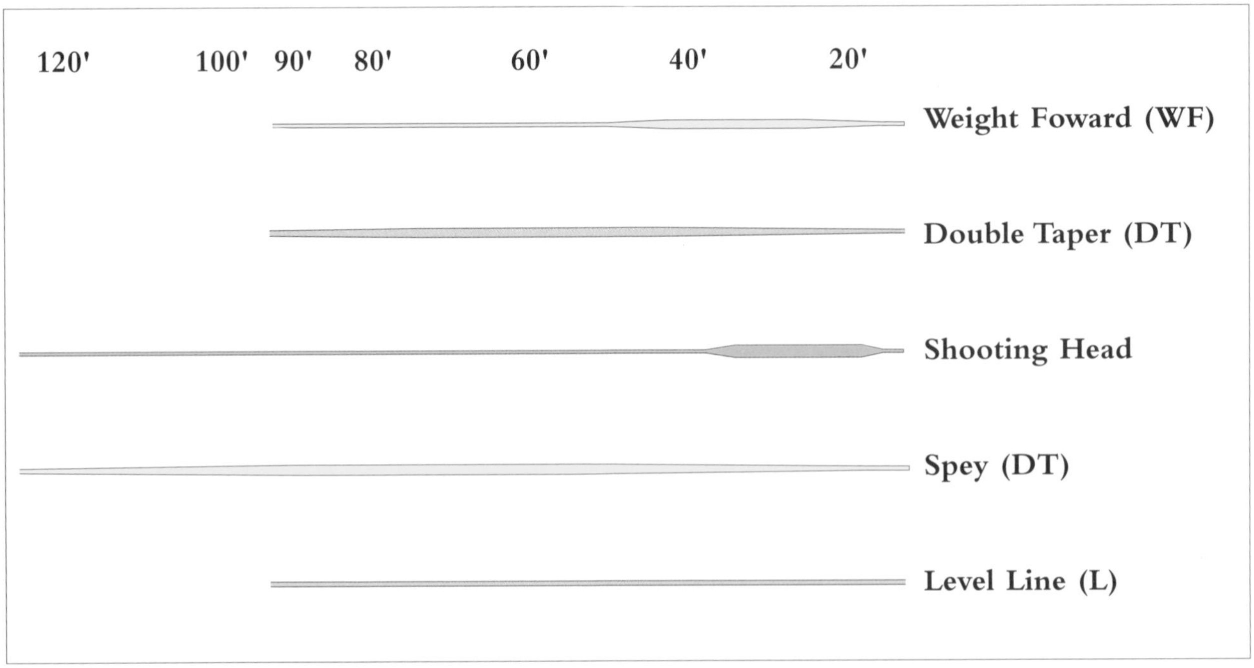

120'   100' 90'   80'   60'   40'   20'

Weight Foward (WF)

Double Taper (DT)

Shooting Head

Spey (DT)

Level Line (L)

The basic fly-line tapers and their relative dimensions.

Modern weight-forward lines have a gentle front taper and are every bit as delicate as the traditional double-taper line. Each line follows the standard weight-forward formula, but exactly how the line tapers in diameter is carefully chosen to maximize the efficiency for the conditions you'd encounter with each species. The taper on a weight-forward trout line is designed to maximize both delicacy and distance with smaller flies, and the taper on saltwater-specific lines is steeper and more aggressive, to throw bigger flies and make long casts into the wind.

Besides the standard weight forward, you may also see lines listed as *bass-bug* or *saltwater tapers*. These are lines with a steep front taper, designed especially for casting large flies into the wind. These lines are not versatile, because they lack delicacy, so many bass and saltwater fly fishers stick with standard weight-forward lines.

Double-taper lines offer the advantage of economy, because if one end of the line becomes damaged or worn out, it can be reversed. The myth that double-taper lines are more delicate than weight-forwards does not hold true today because of the gentle tapers incorporated into modern weight-forward lines. Double-tapers will roll-cast long lines well, because the heavier middle portion helps to develop the roll, rather than the hinging effect that occurs when you try to roll-cast a weight-forward line with more than 30 feet of line on the water. The purported ability of double-taper lines to false-cast long lengths of line is dubious at best; a 50-foot false cast can be controlled only by a most skillful fly caster. Using a weight-forward line's shooting properties is a much more efficient way to get distance. For small-stream work, though, the double taper is a most efficient and economical fly line, with its roll-casting advantages and reversibility.

The original shooting tapers (also called shooting heads) were originally designed for tournament casting; they were never intended to be used in practical fishing situations. Replacing the running line of a weight-forward line with a running line greatly reduced in diameter reduced both friction between rod guides and air resistance. A group of ingenious West Coast steelhead anglers discovered that by using shooting-taper lines, not only could they reach the far bank of unwadable rivers, but they could also cheat strong winds and get their flies deeper in fast-moving rivers. The same qualities that lessen air resistance also help fast-sinking shooting heads cut through heavy river currents.

Shooting-taper lines are now used in all types of fly fishing where extra-long casts and strong winds are the rule. They are limited in their application, though, because they lack delicacy. Many fly fishers also find it difficult to handle shooting tapers, because those coils of thin running line tangle much more easily than the thicker fly line. Anglers who employ shooting heads may strip coils of line in a stripping basket that straps onto their waist when wading, or use an improvised plastic garbage can when fishing from a boat. These devices let them shoot great lengths of line with less chance of tangling.

Line Type

Most fly fishers use a *floating* line (F) as their basic line. Floating fly lines incorporate tiny glass microballoons in the coating that forms the taper of the line. Although they need to be cleaned periodically, they need no grease or line dressing to float them, as did the old silk lines. The better floating fly lines actually have a hydrophobic coating that repels water and helps them float and shoot through the guides better. These coatings are always closely guarded secrets, with each manufacturer using a different formula.

Also important to note is the difference between cold-water and warm-water fly lines. *Cold-water fly lines*, those used for trout and salmon (and saltwater fish in northern latitudes) are designed to stay supple in water as cold as 40 degrees. They also utilize a core (the thin center of the line over which the tapered coating is applied) of nylon braid. *Warm-water fly lines*, for water temperatures over 70 degrees, feel stiffer because they are made with a braided monofilament and have a harder coating. These lines won't get sticky on the hot deck of a boat or in 80-degree water, so they retain their shooting abilities better.

Floating lines are the workhorses of fly fishing; they are not limited to use only with floating flies. Wet flies sink of their own accord, because they are tied on heavy wire hooks; they can also be weighted with lead wire wrapped around the shank of the hook before the fly is tied. Leaders can be weighted with tiny split shot or lead strips. Thus, floating fly lines can be used to fish wet flies several feet below the surface; in small streams and shallow ponds, a floating line is all you'll need. Sinking lines do not offer the same versatility, as they cannot be used with floating flies.

Floating lines are the easiest of all lines to cast and handle, for a number of reasons: they pick up off the water easily, they're easiest to manipulate on the water, and they're the most air-resistant of all lines. Greater air resistance means that it will be much less of a chore to keep the line high on your backcast. Sinking lines, with their greater density (less air resistance), need an experienced sense of timing to cast; otherwise, your backcast will fall below the rod tip, with a resulting loss of power. Needless to say, your first attempts at fly casting and fly fishing should be made with a floating line.

We'd all like to fish with floating lines 100 percent of the time; they're pleasant to use. Sooner or later, though, you'll need some sort of sinking line. Sitting in a boat with only a floating line, knowing that the smallmouth bass are on a shoal 10 feet below you, makes you feel helpless; likewise, being on a deep, rushing steelhead river when you just can't get your fly down to the fish. *Sinking* lines sink throughout their length. They come in various types, such as sinking, fast-sinking, and extra-fast-sinking. You might also see them rated in classes from II through V, with V being the densest and fastest-sinking. For instance, a Class II line sinks at about 2 inches per second, and a Class V at about 6 inches per second. The sink rate is usually listed on the package. It can vary from 1½ inches per second to almost 10 inches per second. The deeper or faster the water you want to fish, the greater the sink rate you should choose. For real bottom-scratching, sinking shooting heads sink quicker than standard sinking lines, because the thin running line presents less resistance to the water.

You can tell this is a sink-tip line because of the two different colors. The dark brown tip portion sinks, and the remaining yellow line floats.

Full-sinking lines are inconvenient in some respects. The fact that they sink means you have to retrieve most of your line before you can make another cast. (Picture trying to pick up 50 feet of sunken line and throwing it back over your shoulder with a single casting stroke.) For the same reason, *line mending*, or repositioning the line when it is on the water, is almost impossible with sinking lines. But sinking lines offer an important advantage—when you retrieve them through the water, the fly swims at an angle to the bottom. When fish are hugging the bottom and not chasing insects or baitfish up to the surface, you'll keep your fly in their strike zone longer. I've learned the hard way over the years that if you chase trout in lakes or striped bass

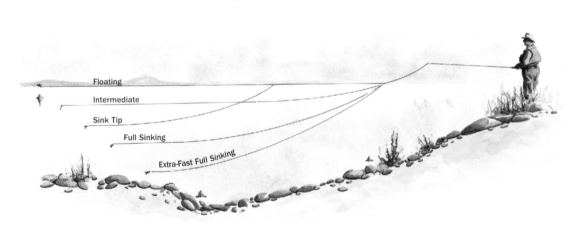

The various types of fly lines and their relative sink rates.

over deep water, you'll miss a lot of the action if you don't have a full-sinking line.

Sinking-tip (F/S) lines are a practical compromise. They offer a 4- to 20-foot tip of sinking line, with the remainder of the line standard floating line. Although they don't reach the depths that full-sinking lines do, sinking-tip lines get deep enough to be practical on small to medium rivers, and all but the deepest parts of shallower ponds and lakes. The floating portion lets you mend line easily in currents, and picking up line for another cast is less of a struggle. For trout fishing in moving water, a sinking-tip line should be the line you carry, in addition to a floater.

Another alternative to full-sinking lines are *intermediate-weight* lines. Just slightly denser than water, intermediate-weight lines sink very slowly and are quite useful in shallow, weedy lakes where even a sink-tip line would drag your fly into the weeds on every cast. Intermediate-weight lines are also very thin and can be cast into the wind more easily than corresponding floating lines of the same weight. Because they ride just under the surface, intermediate-weight lines can be fished on a choppy lake surface without being affected by wave action. The casting characteristics of these lines are so pleasant that many fly fishers prefer them to floating lines, and Atlantic salmon and steelhead anglers prefer them for fishing wet flies just under the surface. In fact, in a pinch, an intermediate line will float when periodically greased with line dressing.

Fly-Line Color

Fly-line color is a minor consideration but one that is worth a few thoughts. It is generally agreed that sinking lines should be dark, as subdued colors are less noticeable to the fish and blend with the background colors of a stream or lake. A fish is surrounded by drifting debris all his life, and unless a subsurface object makes a threatening move, it's usually ignored.

The color of a floating line is probably immaterial from the fish's vantage point. I subscribe to the theory that all floating fly lines are equally visible against a backlit sky, but I've seen some theories that run contrary to this. There is an argument that light-colored lines are more visible to the fish when they are in the air. I have seen instances where shy trout or bonefish in shallow water would spook when a bright line is cast over their heads, but this can usually be corrected by trying to cast off to one side of them. The perfect fly line would be

You can get a single reel with an assortment of extra spools so you can change line types quickly.

completely transparent. Both floating and intermediate lines can be made out of a clear coating over a monofilament core, but even leaders, which are close to being transparent, cast shadows on the bottom.

There are good reasons for using floating lines that are bright, even garish, in color. Fluorescent lines in shades of yellow, orange, and red are more visible to you than other colors in early-morning and late-evening light. Under these conditions you'll seldom be able to see your fly, but if you can see the end of your fly line, you'll at least have a clue. Keeping an eye on your fly line when it's in the air also helps correct casting problems. Most casting difficulties originate when the line is behind you, and bright colors show up vividly against streamside foliage. Incidentally, this quality makes them photograph extremely well in color, and in black-and-white when a yellow filter is used.

Backing

Backing is a thin, inexpensive, supple Dacron line that is knotted or spliced to the "back" end of your fly line. Because fly lines are only 80 to 110 feet long, and many game-fish can run for 100 yards before slowing, backing lets you keep control of a frisky fish when you run out of fly line. A tarpon angler, for instance, will make sure that his fly reel holds not only a 12-weight fly line but also at least 200 yards of backing. Small-stream trout fishers also use backing (usually only 50 yards or so), not so much for insurance as to fill up the narrow diameter of a small single-action reel.

A spool loaded with 150 yards of 30-pound Dacron.

The same spool loaded with 250 yards of 35-pound gel-spun backing. Note that despite the greater break strength and 100 more yards of baking on the spool, the gel-spun takes up less space.

Fly line that is tied directly to a reel spool tends to retain tight coils when stripped from the reel, coils that might interfere with casting and shooting line.

Braided Dacron materials are the best for backing; regular monofilament line retains coils that may foul on rod guides. Freshwater fly fishers generally use 20-pound-test Dacron braided nylon or Dacron for backing. For saltwater, salmon, and steelhead, 30-pound braided nylon or 35-pound gel-spun polyester are best. Gel-spun backing is extremely fine in diameter for its strength, and you can get 60 percent more of it on a reel for the same strength as braided nylon. It's preferred by fly fishers who go after long-running fish because the ability to put 200 (or even 400) yards of backing on a reel, plus a fly line, is important to them. But gel-spun is more than twice as expensive as braided nylon, so you don't need to go that route for most trout fishing.

Each fly-line weight fills up a different amount of displacement on a reel spool, because as line sizes get heavier, their diameter increases. To get minimum line coil and maximum retrieve rate, a fly line and backing combination should fill a spool to within ½ to ¼ inch of the rim. So when buying a reel and line combination, you have to buy the correct length of backing. This could be a tricky process, but luckily, good fly shops spool lines and backing on reels all day long and they use motorized line-winding machines with counters. They know exactly how much backing to wind on a spool before knotting and winding on the fly line. If you plan on winding line and backing on a reel yourself, you'll find each reel's capacity listed in catalogs, on websites, or in the owner's manual that comes with the reel. You should know that stated capacities are for floating lines, which are the biggest in diameter. You can get about 20 percent more backing on a reel when spooling it with a sinking line—not for its strength, but because the larger diameter has much less chance of binding on the underlying layers when reeled under the heavy pressure of a big fish.

FLY REELS

A fly reel's purpose is to store line, provide smooth, uninterrupted tension (drag) when a fish makes a long run, and counterbalance the weight of your fly rod when casting. In general, as the size and tenacity of the fish you catch increase, so does the importance of your reel.

Fly reels are simple devices, and even the most complicated has fewer moving parts than a spinning reel. Fly reels consist of a foot that secures the reel to the rod, a handle, an outside frame, a spool that turns around a pillar or spindle attached to the frame, and some sort of drag system that puts tension on the revolving spool. Somewhere on the outside of the reel you'll find two levers or knobs: one is the *spool release*, which enables you to change spools; the other is the *drag adjustment*, which regulates the tension on the spool.

Drag Systems

Fly-reel drag systems have two purposes: they prevent spool overrun (with its resulting line tangles) when you strip line from your reel during casting, and they tire running fish by exerting tension against line running in the opposite direction. Fly fishers who catch fish that weigh less than a pound, such as small trout or bluegill, may never use the drag of their reel when fighting a fish, choosing instead to strip the fish in by hand. Their reels are simply line-storage devices. In the tight, brushy confines of small streams, fly reels keep excess line away from clutching branches and abrasive streamside gravel

On the other hand, a bonefish, tarpon, salmon, or even a large trout can strip a hundred yards of line from

A simple spring-and-pawl reel. The triangular pawl in the frame at the left is under tension from the leaf spring above it. The teeth on the gears of the spool engage the tooth of the pawl to give light drag and form that distinctive fly-reel sound.

You can tell this reel has an offset disc drag system because the drag components (located under the brass plate) are offset from the center arbor of the spool.

a reel in seconds; in this case, the reel can become the most important part of your tackle. The tension put on a running fish must be smooth, because a drag that stutters can cause an uneven buildup of pressure on your leader. The mechanical, adjustable tension that a drag system provides is smoother and more consistent than anything you could ever achieve by pinching the outgoing line between your fingers.

Mechanical drag systems may be either *ratchet-and-pawl*, a system which clicks audibly when the spool is revolving; *caliper drags*, in which calipers like those found in bicycle brakes rub against a plate attached to the reel spool; *disc drags*, a silent system where pressure is applied to plates that then apply pressure to the spool; or a combination of the latter two systems. Many reels also feature a spool rim that is exposed on the outside of the reel, allowing the angler to exert additional drag by placing his palm up against the bottom of the reel.

Ratchet-and-pawl drag systems are the simplest and most common. A ratchet on the inside of the spool engages a pawl or a pair of pawls mounted on the reel frame. A leaf spring is connected to a knob on the outside of the spool, and variable tension can be applied to the drag pawl by turning the drag adjustment knob. The pawls are shaped so that the tension on the spool is always light when you're reeling in line. The tension on the spool when the line is running out can be made lesser or greater, depending upon the strength of your leader and how much pressure you dare put on the fish. This drag system is used on the lightest trout reels. Its advantage is its simplicity and light weight. Its disadvantage is that strong drag cannot be applied to the spool.

Caliper drags are used on some inexpensive reels. Because disc drags are smoother and more efficient, caliper drags aren't used much today, and really offer no advantage to a well-designed disc drag.

Disc-drag systems incorporate cork or Teflon plastic pads (or discs) that exert pressure directly on the reel spool. These reels apply pressure in varying amounts—anything from almost no pressure (just the friction of the spool on the spindle and pawls that may be used to add noise to an outgoing drag), to strong pressure that can only be budged by a sprinting tuna. The tension on the drag surface is controlled by springs, washers, or a combination of the two. One type utilizes a disc that rests on the rim of the spool, with tension provided by a leaf

spring. Another type, similar to drum brakes on a car, features a pad on the inside of the spool face. Tension on this type is provided by a coil spring inside the spool pillar, adjusted by a nut on the outside of the pillar.

Disc drags are most often used when fish will be heavy or strong and where leaders will be correspondingly heavy. Disc drags can exert a great amount of smooth pressure against a reel spool without seizing up. There are as many disc-drag systems as there are models of fly reels, and every reel designer has his theories on what is best. Less expensive disc-drag reels utilize an offset drag system, where a gear that is offset from the center of the reel receives the pressure from the drag. This gear then engages a gear on the spool. Offset drags are fine for trout reels or those used for smaller salmon, steelhead, and saltwater species. But because the drag is one step removed from the spool, when the pressure is on they tend to give a slightly erratic pressure.

The best drags are known as *center-line drags*, because the drag system is in the center of the reel, surrounding the spool. Engineers say this is the best type of drag system, because the drag pressure is applied right to the spool close to its axis of rotation. The drag surfaces can be cork against the polished aluminum of the inside of the spool, or a sandwich of materials that might include cork and exotic plastics like Teflon, Brofolon, or Rulon. You typically get what you pay for—the more expensive reels have drag systems that can handle a 100-pound bluefin tuna running at 20 mph for hours without literally burning up and smoking. The finest reels also incorporate a heat-sink design to dissipate the heat buildup by a spool rotating as high as 6,000 rpms.

Reel Materials

Very cheap reels are made from stamped metal. Avoid them. Next in quality are reels made from cast aluminum. Although these reels are not as strong as reels machined from a solid piece of aluminum, they can still be as strong as you'll ever need for most fishing, and they are light in weight and inexpensive. All of the best reels are made from aircraft-grade aluminum bar stock and machined to very precise tolerances. They are very strong for their weight and just look gorgeous; the holes in the spool and frame are sharp and clean, and they are typically highly polished and anodized against corrosion. A black-colored reel is theoretically the best color, as it won't flash in the sun and frighten spooky fish. But shiny silver and gold reels are just as popular. Who says fly fishing always has to be so practical?

The drag components of this center-line-drag reel are all located around the center arbor.

Traditional Retrieve Systems

Fly reels offer three types of retrieve systems: single-action, multiplying, and automatic. Because the reel is not used to retrieve line after every cast, this aspect of the reel is not as important to the fly fisher as it is to the spin or bait caster.

The *single-action* reel, by far the most popular variety, gets the vote of most fly fishers because it is light and simple to maintain and has only a few moving parts to wear out or break down. One complete turn of the handle completes one turn of the spool.

Multiplying fly reels add a multiplying gear, which retrieves line faster than a 1:1 ratio. In other words, one turn of the handle produces anywhere from one and a half to two turns of the reel spool. The faster line retrieve comes in handy if you're fishing for such fish as Atlantic salmon, which sometimes run toward the angler at terrific speeds. Another time you might want to get excess line out of harm's way and onto the reel is when fishing from a boat with gear strewn all over. When a fish makes its initial run, you want those loose coils of line packed neatly into your reel, not wound around canoe paddles, cameras, or tackle boxes. I don't know of any such reels that are still made today, but you might find one at a yard sale. They are heavy, clunky, and the drag systems were never as smooth as they should have been.

The *automatic* fly reel, another dinosaur, incorporates a large coiled spring that surrounds the inside of the reel spool. The spring becomes progressively tighter as each length of line is pulled from the reel. By pressing a release lever, the angler can retrieve great lengths of line in just a few seconds. I must confess a prejudice against automatic fly reels that dates back to my first attempt at field maintenance. Upon prying the spool apart, I found myself surrounded by a twitching mass of steel springs that were impossible to squeeze back into their original position. Automatic reels are also substantially heavier than single-action reels of the same capacity, and their drag systems tend to be quite heavy-handed, making them unsuitable for use with light leaders. Extra spools are also difficult to obtain and tricky to exchange, making changing from a floating to a sinking line time-consuming (or impossible). Their weight and drag systems are even worse than those on multiplying reels, and I don't think one has been manufactured for thirty years. Still, they're fun to play with, and you might find one in your grandmother's attic.

Large-Arbor Fly Reels

Large-arbor reels have a wider-diameter inner spool than traditional reels. The idea is to increase the length of line you can retrieve with a single turn of the reel handle. It's

You'll notice that although the large-arbor reel on the left retrieves line faster, it's also bigger in diameter. Both reels hold the same size line and backing.

an elegant alternative to clumsy multiplying reels. Large-arbor reels can retrieve line twice as fast as a reel with conventional narrow spools. This is handy when moving from one spot to another, when you want to get your line onto the spool instead of dragging it along the bank. But you really see a large-arbor's advantage when fishing for fast-running fish like bonefish, which can often turn and run right at you after peeling 100 yards of line from your reel. If you don't gather that line, it can wrap around a mangrove stem or a propeller blade, and you'll lose your prized trophy in a heartbeat.

Are there any disadvantages to a large-arbor reel? Of course; by design, they have to be bigger overall, and some anglers feel they look oversized on a small trout reel. Some of them even look strange on a big saltwater rod. So, the *mid-arbor* reel was designed, with an inner spool diameter about halfway between a skinny traditional spindle and a big large-arbor spool. You get a reel that looks more traditional with a slight increase in retrieve speed.

Anti-Reverse Reels

Anti-reverse reels are often merely upscale versions of single-action trout reels. They may incorporate disc drags or ratchet-and-pawl drags; regardless of the drag system used, however, they must be capable of applying heavy pressure without seizing up. A 150-pound tarpon can put an incredible amount of strain and heat buildup on a fly reel. The reel frame itself must also be substantial, so anti-reverse reels are quite heavy—between 6 and 10 ounces, as opposed to 3 to 6 ounces for freshwater fly reels.

These reels may be either direct-drive or anti-reverse. In most fly reels, called *direct-drive* reels, the reel handle turns as the line is running out, which sometimes makes a mess of careless knuckles. Anti-reverse reels have a locking mechanism that prevents the handle from turning, yet allows the spool to rotate under drag tension when the line is running out. By necessity these reels are heavier, more expensive, and contain more moving parts to wear out or seize up from corrosion buildup. I'd only spring for one if you're really forgetful and think you might reach for the reel handle at the wrong moment.

All other considerations aside, an anti-reverse fly reel must be constructed from corrosion-resistant materials, usually anodized aluminum for the frame (to save on weight) and stainless or chromed or cadmium-plated steel for internal parts. Salt water is extremely corrosive and can cause electrolysis between unlike metals.

Choosing a Fly Reel

The most important consideration when purchasing a fly reel is its capacity. All good fly reels are rated for capacity; you can find this information on the box, in the instruction sheets, on a website, or in catalog copy if you're buying through the mail. Typical capacity information will read something like this: "To WF8F with 150 yds. backing." Because lighter line sizes are smaller in diameter, you know that a WF7F line is also okay on this reel, with at least 150 yards of backing (probably 175 yards). Sinking lines are finer in diameter than floaters, so you can probably fit a WF9S line on the same reel with the same amount of backing. Double-taper lines fill up a spool more than weight-forwards, so our same reel with a DT8F line will most likely hold only 100 yards of backing.

Except for the smallest and simplest single-action reels, fly reels are available in right- and left-hand retrieve versions. The difference is merely in which direction the drag tension is applied. In single-action reels with ratchet-and-pawl systems, switching from right- to left-hand retrieve is accomplished by merely removing a pawl from its post and flipping it over. Some single-action reels offer a double-pawl system, which means one pawl can be engaged for right-hand retrieve while the other merely acts as a spare and does not engage the ratchet. The second pawl may also be flipped to achieve a stronger drag.

Some reels have metal line guards at the bottom, which are usually attached by one or two screws. When you switch from right- to left-hand retrieve, also switch the line guard by loosening the screws and reversing the direction the line guard is facing.

Disc drags are usually a bit more difficult to switch over. Some require a completely different set of parts and cannot be changed over without returning the reel to the manufacturer. Before ordering a fly reel with one of the more complicated drag systems, you should decide whether you want to crank right- or left-handed.

If you're right-handed and spin- or bait-cast as well as fly-fish, you'll probably want to crank left-handed, as nothing is more frustrating than to reach for the handle of your reel in the excitement of playing a fish and find it on the opposite side of the reel. Many right-handers, however, are oriented so strongly in that direction that they find it uncomfortable to reel with their left hand. This necessitates switching the rod from right to left hand when reeling in line or playing a fish, but it becomes almost second nature and really presents no problem at all.

Regardless of whether you are right- or left-handed, decide which way is more comfortable for you and purchase or convert your fly reels accordingly.

Some fly fishers say that the reel should balance the weight of the rod beyond the grip; when the reel is mounted on the rod, the whole arrangement should balance perfectly when the middle of the grip is placed on the index finger. Others contend that the fly reel should be as light as possible. A third faction feel comfortable with a reel that is heavier than custom dictates, especially if they pursue long-running fish and need extra capacity for added backing. Rest assured that if you own a fly rod that calls for a 6-weight line, a single-action reel that will hold a WF6F line plus 150 yards of backing will be perfectly comfortable. At both extremes of fly-fishing tackle, you may have to be a little careful in choosing a fly reel—those little cork-and-ring reel seats used on tiny 2-weight rods may only fit over the thin feet of the lighter fly reels, and the substantial feet on the heaviest saltwater reels may require a full-metal saltwater reel seat.

Noise or Not? Right Hand or Left?

Two of the biggest debates on fly-reel design amount to a whole lot of racket and not much substance. First is the issue of whether a fly reel should make a clicking noise or should be completely silent. Many anglers, myself included, like to hear the satisfying click of a finely machined reel when we reel in line, and also like an even noisier click when a fish takes line. When a truly speedy fish takes line, the pitch becomes higher with the speed until it sounds almost like a scream—thus the term "screaming reels" you might have read about. I also appreciate a noisy drag when night-fishing, so I can tell how fast a striped bass is taking line on a night with no moon. Because disc drags are silent by nature, you will usually see some sort of pawl system on these reels. Usually it contributes little to the pressure applied to a running fish, and

you can even disengage the pawls to create a silent reel with no ill effects. Some anglers just don't like the noise, and I'll leave it up to you to decide which type you prefer. Just don't let anybody tell you which is right or wrong.

The second issue, one that often confuses people just starting out in fly fishing, is whether you should reel with your right or left hand. This is not as simple as it seems. "Of course, because I'm right-handed and cast with my right hand, I have to reel with my left," some people say. Many right-handed anglers also reel with their right hand. So they cast with their right hand and strip line with their left, but when it comes time to play a fish, they put the rod in their left hand and reel with their right. Why?

Some of it is due to tradition, as this is the way it was done fifty years ago. Supposedly the idea came from Atlantic salmon fishing, where you would have cast a heavy 10-ounce bamboo rod for hours at a time. When you finally hooked a fish, it was nice to give that casting arm a break when trying to muscle a big fish. But most people these days take up fly fishing after doing some spin fishing, where right-handers always cast with their right and reel with their left. I am right-handed and cast and reel with my right, so I have to switch hands when playing a fish. It's just the way I was taught. But I have to admit that after casting and playing fish all day long on a particularly good day, I have sometimes been thankful I learned that way, as it is sure nice to give your right arm a break.

Set up your reels any way you wish, and it won't be wrong. Just remember that it makes a difference which way you wind line on a reel, and also that you might have to switch the drag over from one direction to another because the "line out" direction of a spool rotation is the one that receives the drag pressure, and the "line in" direction offers much less resistance. Most modern fly reels are shipped in left-hand retrieve, but it's a simple matter to switch the drag over in just a few minutes. All reels come with simple instructions on how to do this.

{ MIDWINTER DAYDREAMS }

Chapter Four

Leaders and Knots

 ## HOW LEADERS ARE MADE

The leader is not only as important as the rod, reel, and line, but at times more important than the correct fly pattern. The leader is a device for deception as well as presentation. It deceives by being transparent, and even more by its flexibility. With the proper leader, your fly should appear unattached. It should move freely with every shift of the current or sink unhindered.

Leaders are made from solid nylon, PVDF (polyvinylidene fluoride, also known as fluorocarbon), or polyethylene. Solid leaders are called monofilament leaders because they are made from a single solid filament. Leaders can also be made from tiny braided filaments. They are often classified either as *braided leaders*, which have a hollow core and utilize very tiny strands, or *furled leaders*, made from slightly bigger strands with no hollow space in the middle.

Before nylon was first used for leaders, in the late 1940s, leaders were made from drawn silkworm gut. Level pieces of gut were joined with knots to form tapered leaders, which cast and straightened very well. However, gut is brittle unless soaked in water for a few hours, and it mildews and rots if not carefully dried and put away. Gut cannot be drawn with any kind of quality control in diameters less than .009-inch. Today we use nylon in diameters as fine as .003-inch, and a nylon leader is two or three times as strong as a gut leader of the same diameter.

Gut did have one advantage over nylon: it was straight. Because leaders are so long, they must be stored coiled, and nylon retains a "memory" that must be removed. You can easily remove almost all the kinks and curls from nylon leaders by carefully stretching sections between your hands or drawing them through a piece of gum rubber or leather. The heat generated by this process, along with the slow, steady pull, realigns the molecules in the nylon and eliminates most of the memory.

Leaders designed to present flies properly follow tapers developed by theory and by trial and error, just as fly rods and fly lines are tapered. In fact, the whole system is one continuous taper, from the butt section of the rod to the hair-thin end of the leader. All three work together to transmit and dampen the tremendous speed and energy developed in your casting arm, to place the line, leader, and fly on the water so gently they barely ripple the surface. Leader tapers are critical to your success. I've seen people try fly rods with a poorly designed leader on the end and swear that the rod was no good.

Leaders made from solid nylon or PVDF monofilament are tapered either by machine, in which case they are called knotless leaders, or by joining sections of "level" (untapered) material together. One special kind of knotless nylon leader is constructed with special air chambers inside so it floats better than standard solid leaders (nylon is slightly heavier than water and sinks slowly).

Twenty years ago, the best leaders were the knotted variety because they could be made in compound tapers, where the diameter does not decrease at a constant rate. Don't ask me why; the physics are too much for me. But leaders with compound tapers just cast much better. However, the process used to make knotless leaders has been greatly improved, to the point where compound tapers are now easy to create without knots. It's hard to find a commercially made knotted leader today.

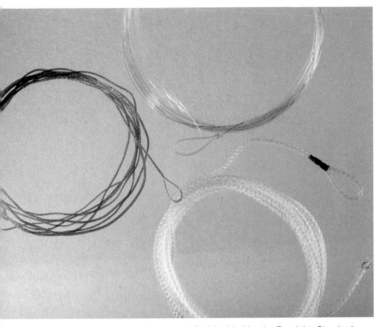

Different types of leaders. Left: A braided leader. Top right: Standard nylon knotless tapered leader. Bottom right: Furled leader. The nylon leader already has a tippet as an integral part, but the braided loop on the thin end of the braided leader and the metal ring on the end of the furled leader need to have a separate tippet attached with a loop-to-loop connection.

Making knotless leaders is an amazing process, where hot nylon or PVDF is extruded through nozzles that change in diameter as the material comes out, into a bath of either water or oil. The leaders are then run down a long line of machines with rollers that heat, cool, and stretch the leaders until the taper is perfect.

Braided leaders are made on machines that start with a given number of filaments and then gradually reduce the number of filaments as you approach the tippet, thus creating the taper. The cut-off ends of the filaments are tucked into the tightly woven braid so they don't unravel. Furled leaders are made by twisting strands of ordinary fishing line (or even thread) around a jig, and the taper is created by the way they are twisted. Unlike braided leaders, they can be made at home with a simple jig. You can find the plans to make them with a basic Internet search. Both braided leaders and furled leaders are always finished with a monofilament tippet, either nylon or PVDF. The tippet can be knotted to the fine end of the braid, looped over a loop that is at the end of the braid, or some-

times knotted to a tiny metal ring that is tied to the end of a furled leader.

A knotless leader is a single, continuous piece of nylon that gradually decreases in diameter. The diameter of a knotless leader must decrease at a constant rate, due to the manufacturing process that extrudes the leader.

Knotted leaders do not decrease in diameter at a constant rate. The most common formula for a compound-tapered leader consists of about 60 percent heavy material called the *butt section*, a 20-percent section of a number of pieces that step down the taper quickly, and a final 20 percent of a level piece on the end called a *tippet*. The heavy butt section connects to the fly line and assures a smooth transmission of casting energy; the step-down sections continue this process into the tippet. The level tippet is very air-resistant and makes sure the fly lands softly. Of course, in a knotless leader you don't see these as separate sections, but you can figure out about where one ends and the other begins by looking at the way the material tapers.

HOW TO CHOOSE A LEADER

Leader Type

There is a confusing array of leaders on the market today. As long as you pick a good-quality leader, it really does not make that much difference whether you buy a knotless tapered leader, a knotted leader, or a furled or braided leader. (Because the fishing qualities of braided leaders and furled leaders are very similar—despite what some people might tell you—I'll treat them together, and from here on will just call them *braided leaders*.) Besides, you'll spend ten bucks for the most expensive leader, and most run around four bucks each. Try different types and experiment until you find what works best for you.

Ninety-five percent of fly fishers today use standard knotless tapered leaders, for everything from trout fishing in Maine to redfishing on the Texas Gulf Coast. They're inexpensive, they don't have a lot of knots to catch on weeds or coral, and they cast beautifully. You could spend the rest of your life fishing just knotless tapered leaders and be happy as a clam.

Knotted leaders don't offer any advantages besides the fact that you can make your own and save a few pennies, and perhaps because you can experiment with different leader tapers if so inclined. But all those knots create potential weak spots; they catch on weeds and streamside brush, and in salt water, they can catch on pieces of coral or oyster shells, resulting in an instant parting of the ways. Still, many of us fished with them for decades and were quite happy with them until the knotless leader tapers got better.

Braided leaders do offer some advantages in delicacy. Because they are so air-resistant, they land softer than a monofilament leader. But perhaps that advantage is neutralized because they are more opaque and thus more visible to fish. They are also suppler than solid leaders, which theoretically makes your presentation better because they are closer in suppleness to fly lines, thus ensuring tighter, more accurate casting loops. They are also amazing at straightening a very long tippet—up to 5 or 6 feet, which is not easy with solid leaders. So, if you fish a lot of small trout flies in clear water over spooky trout, you might play around with these.

Braided leaders do hold more water than solid leaders, and some anglers object to the spray they throw when casting, claiming it frightens trout. There are two ways to avoid this: either make a quick cast off to the side to flick off the water, or treat the braid with paste silicone fly floatant. One variety of braided leader is even sold already pretreated with a waterproof coating.

Should My Leader Float or Sink?

The answer to this one is not as easy as you think. And to be honest, there is no right answer. When you are fishing wet flies like nymphs or streamers with a sinking line, it's true that you want your leader to sink. Why else would you be using a sinking fly line? But when fishing floating flies, not everyone wants a leader that floats as high as a dry fly. If you cast a floating leader and look at the bottom of a shallow pool, you'll see that the shadow of the leader casts a large blob on the bottom. It must be quite glaring to trout or other skittish fish, and thus some anglers go to great lengths to get at least the last few feet of their leader to sink, rubbing mud, clay, glycerin wetting agent, and other magic potions onto the leader. However, if you had an entire 9-foot leader that sunk, it would pull a tiny dry fly underwater after a short drift, and that's not so great if the fish are rising to floating insects.

Also, when fishing a weighted nymph with a *strike indicator* (a small piece of yarn, cork, or foam that lets you see when a fish takes your fly unseen below the surface—in other words, a tiny bobber), if your leader pulls the strike indicator underwater, you're defeating the purpose of using one. Luckily, braids can be left untreated to sink slowly or treated to float high. PVDF has a specific gravity of 1.76 (water is 1.00), so it sinks faster than nylon, which at 1.1 has almost neutral buoyancy. Nylon gets interesting, because if you rub on a little silicone fly paste (or even oil from your nose), it will float like a cork; yet if you rub it with toothpaste or clean it with alcohol, or use a commercial leader sinking agent, it will sink slowly.

So if you are fishing dry flies in smooth water where a shadow is visible, you can clean the last few feet of a nylon leader to keep that ugly shadow away from your fly. Or if you want a strike indicator to float higher in choppy water, you can grease the butt end of your leader. I'll often use a tippet of PVDF tied to a hollow-chambered nylon leader, which sinks my tippet near the fly but keeps the rest of the leader floating, both to keep a strike indicator floating high and to keep the entire leader from pulling a dry fly under. Of course, you can also get the same effect by using just a plain nylon leader, cleaning the last several feet to make them sink, and greasing the rest of the leader to keep it floating.

HATE KNOTS?—
USE LOOPS

You can avoid tying knots in leaders by using loops. For instance, you can attach a permanent loop to the end of your fly line and then make a loop-to-loop connection to attach a leader. Leaders are almost always sold with loops on the butt end. The loop at the end of a fly line can be any of the following:

- Just a 6-inch piece of monofilament nail knotted to the end of the line. You can do this yourself or ask a kindly fly shop employee to do it for you.
- A fused loop, where the core of the line itself is permanently welded to itself at the factory.
- Braided loops can also be purchased or made at home with a crochet hook. The hollow end opposite the loop is inserted over the end of the fly line, a piece of stretchy tubing is usually passed over the connection, and then the whole arrangement gets a tiny drop of superglue to hold it in place. Again,

this can be put on by a knowledgeable fly shop employee, or you can try it yourself.

- The strongest (but bulkiest) way to put a loop on the end of a fly line is to double over the last 2 inches of the line and then tie three tiny nail knots using 10-pound nylon over the line. These are usually only used on bigger saltwater lines where strength is valued over delicacy. And if you want one, I'd really recommend you ask an expert to do it for you until you get really comfortable with nail knots. (See below on how to tie a nail knot.)

Loop-Loop Connection

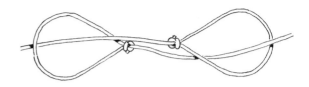

Pass the end of the leader through the loop on the end of the fly line.

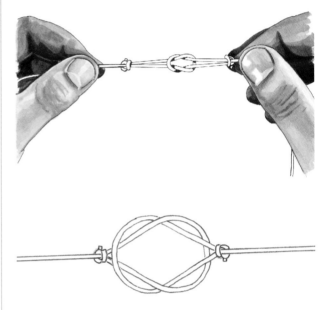

Pass the line loop up through the loop on the end of your leader.

Pull the loops in opposite directions until they slide together to form what looks like a square knot.

Placing a Braided Loop on a Line

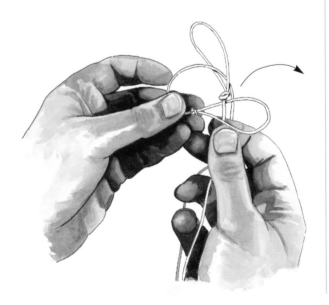

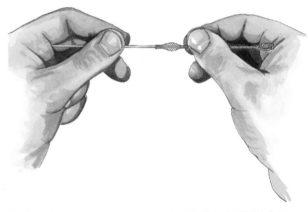

Gently work the fly line up inside the open end of the braid. It helps to pinch it against the line and "inchworm" it forward. The fly line should go all the way into the braid, until it hits the point where the loop is glued.

Pull a 6-inch piece of tippet material into the braided loop. Even up the ends.

Thread the elastic tube onto the piece of tippet material. Hold onto the end of the tippet and use it to guide the tube onto the braided loop.

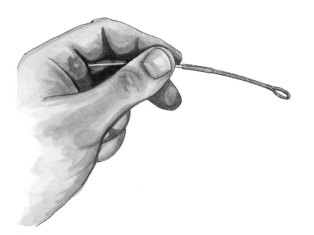

Carefully work the tube down over the braid until it covers the raw open end of the braid opposite the loop. Add a tiny drop of superglue or similar at both ends of the tube and allow to dry before using.

You can also continue the loop process at the other end of the leader, to attach a tippet. Knotless leaders already come with a tippet as an integral part of the leader, but after a while, that section gets too short and the end

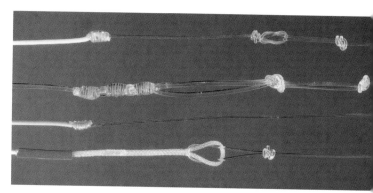

Various ways of connecting a leader to a fly line. In all cases the fly line is on the left and the leader is the piece continuing to the right. Top: A short piece of butt material nail knotted to the fly line, with a perfection loop at the other end. Second from top: A fly line (in this case a clear monofilament fly line) that has been doubled over itself to form a loop. Three nail knots are tied over the loop to secure it. This is the strongest but bulkiest arrangement. Third from top: A leader that has been nail knotted directly to the fly line. This is the smoothest connection but if you need to change leaders you'll have to tie knots instead of just a simple loop-to-loop connection. Bottom: A braided loop glued to the fly line. This type of connection can be used with both braided and standard nylon leaders.

of the leader is too heavy. So instead of throwing the whole leader away, you tie on a piece of tippet material with a knot and keep on fishing. But instead of tying a knot every time you need to attach a new tippet, what if you tied a tiny loop at the fine end of the leader, right where your new tippet would go? You can then tie up a bunch of tippets with loops on them at home, where the light is good and the bugs aren't bothering you, and simply make a loop-to-loop connection every time you need a new tippet.

You can also buy premade tippets with Bimini loops already tied for you. The Bimini twist is the strongest loop you can tie in monofilament, but it is very tricky to tie in fine diameters, which is why people are willing to pay to have someone else tie the knot for them. And braided leaders, which are typically sold with loops at both ends, are often sold in a set with looped monofilament tippets in the package.

Nail or Tube Knot

The nail knot can be used to permanently attach a 6-inch section of heavy monofilament to your fly line, with a perfection loop on the other end. This makes it easy to change leaders, with a loop-to-loop connection. You can also attach the butt section of your leader directly to the fly line with this knot.

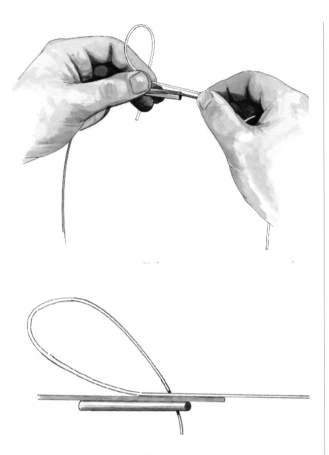

About an inch from the end of the fly line, pinch the monofilament against the line and begin winding the tag end back over itself, over the fly line, and over the tube. The wraps must progress toward the end of the fly line. The hardest part is to take that first wind because it needs to double over itself in a direction it does not want to travel. Each turn should be tight against the preceding one, with absolutely no gap between winds. The fifth turn will still be some distance from the end of the line but that's OK; the knot tends to slip off the end of the line if you get too close. You can cut a full 2 inches off the end of a fly line without hurting its performance in the slightest.

It helps to have a tube to tie this knot, and makes it much easier to do than with just a nail. It also helps to make sure the end of your fly line and the monofilament are as straight as you can get them. Stretch both in your hands. Place the tube parallel to the fly line, making sure that the open end of the tube (if one end is closed) points toward the end of the fly line. Lay the piece of monofilament alongside both the line and the tube. The long part of the leader (the part that will not be trimmed) should be coming off the end of the line and about 10 inches of tag end should run up along the fly line.

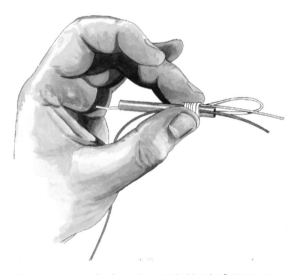

Now slide the thumb and forefinger that are pinching the first wrap up over the wraps—and keep pinching them.

Pass the tag end through the tube so that it passes under the turns you just made. You don't have to pass the whole thing under as long as the end of the tag end is now beyond the first wrap you made. You should still be pinching the five wraps.

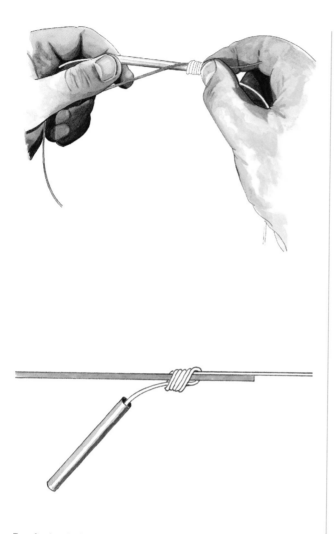

Once you are satisfied with your coils, pull tightly on both ends of the monofilament. It helps to wrap the butt of the leader around your hand and hold the tag end with a pair of pliers. Finally, pull on the fly line and the standing part of the leader with nearly as much force as you can with your hands. This snugs the knot completely and tests the knot before you put it into action. Trim the tag end of the leader and the end of the fly line as close to the knot as you can.

Tests have shown that the butt section of leaders used with 3- and 4-weight lines should be about .019 inch; with 5- through 9-weights, .021 inch; and for the real heavy 10-, 11-, and 12-weight lines, .023 inch. The permanent loop that you attach to your fly line should be of the same diameter material as the butt section of your leaders.

Transfer the pinching to the other hand without letting go of the coils. Pull the tube out in a direction opposite the end of the fly line. It should be withdrawn quickly, and you should still be pinching those five wraps tightly. Don't look at the wraps and don't stop pinching. Have faith.

Loop Knots

Loops can be tied in the butt section of your leader or in a tippet with one of two knots, either the perfection knot or the surgeon's loop. They have equal strength; the perfection knot is a little neater and the surgeon's loop is easier to tie.

Double Surgeon's Loop

Still without taking your fingers off the wraps, pull gently on the tag end until it tightens against the wraps. Switch pinching hands again and pull on the standing end. You may want to repeat this a few times until the turns are snug but not tight up against the fly line. Now you can stop pinching and check your coils. If they are not smooth and even, you can try working them back into position at this point with your fingernail. You can even position the knot to move it closer to the end of the fly line now if you wish. If things look too bad, slip the mono off the end of the line and start over.

Make a loop and overlap the tag end with the standing part of the leader for about 5 inches. Pinch the material close to the top of the loop and near the bottom of the overlap.

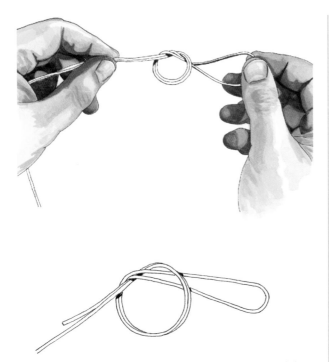

Tie a loose overhand knot in the doubled section and pass the single loop through the double loop you have just formed. Don't tighten.

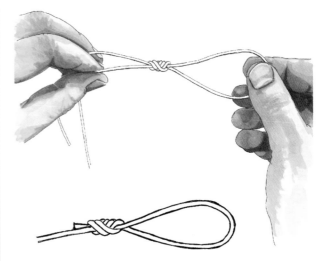

Moisten the knot. Tighten it by pulling the loop away from both the tag end and the standing part of the line. Unlike the perfection l

Perfection Loop

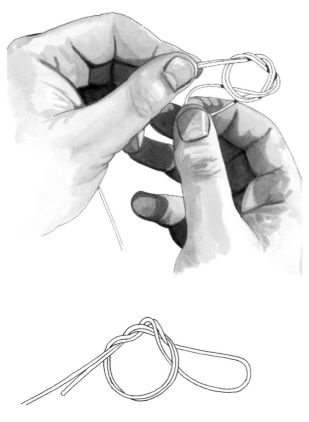

Make another turn of the single loop through the doubled loop. In other words, make a double overhand knot in the doubled section.

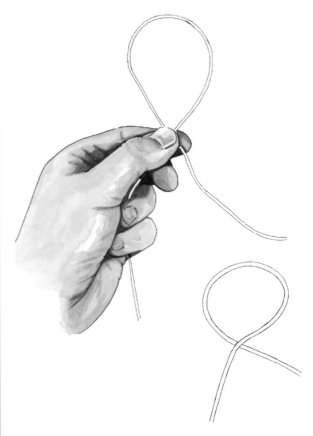

Form a single loop by bringing the tag end behind the standing part of the leader. The tag end should be pointing toward the right, at a right angle to the standing part of the line.

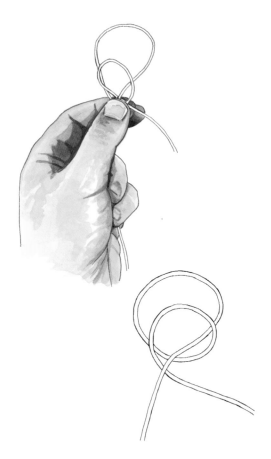

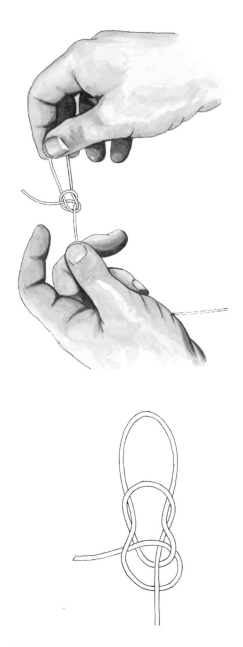

Form a second, smaller loop in front of the first one by rolling the tag end around the front of the first loop, then behind it. The second loop should be pushed flat against the first with your thumb, and the tag end should again end up on the right side, pointing at a right angle away from the standing part.

Take the tag end and fold it to the opposite side, passing it between the two loops. It should end up on the left, pointing at a right angle to the standing part of the line. Push it to the bottom of the point where the two loops overlap. Pinch it in place here with your thumb.

Reach behind the first loop and pull the second smaller loop through the first loop. Make sure the tag end stays put, on the left at a right angle to the standing part. Tighten by pulling the second loop straight in line with the standing part of the leader. Do not hold the tag end or put any pressure on it.

Notice that ordinary square knots were not used. Nylon monofilament is slippery stuff, and knots that hold in rope will slip right out when tied with nylon. You also may have observed that there is never more than .002-inch difference in diameter between connecting leader sections. The greater the difference in adjacent strands, the weaker the connecting knots, especially if you use the barrel knot.

ers that are available commercially. It's a smooth, neat knot, but it requires some practice to tie properly. It's a good idea to practice this knot and all other fly-fishing knots with heavy string or rope before you try your hand with thin, slippery leader material.

The barrel knot will not slip if properly tied. If, when you inspect your finished knot, both tag ends stick out the same side, the knot is not properly tied and may break. When tied correctly, the tag ends should emerge from the knot at a 180-degree angle to each other.

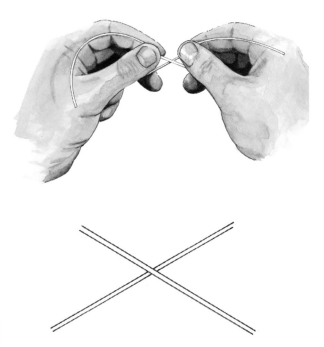

Begin the barrel knot by crossing the two sections of leader material over each other. If you're new to this knot, leave about 2 inches of overlap on each tag end.

Tighten the knot fully and inspect it. The tag end should still be pointing at a right angle to the standing part of the leader, and the loop itself should be in line with the standing part. If not, cut the knot and try again. Trim the tag end when you are satisfied the knot is tied properly.

KNOTS FOR JOINING PIECES OF LEADER MATERIAL

Barrel Knot

The *barrel knot* (also known as the *blood knot*) is the traditional knot you'll see used most often in knotted lead-

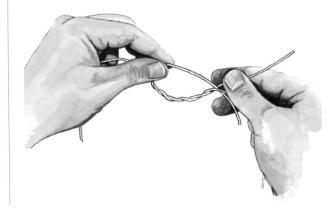

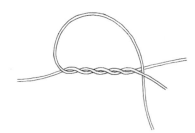

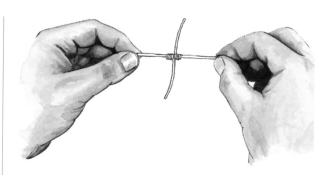

Pinch the place where the two ends overlap with the thumb and forefinger of one hand to keep a loop open. With the other hand, wind a tag end around the standing part of the leader three to five times—three times in diameters heavier than 3X, four times in 4X and 5X, and five times in 6X or 7X. Pass the tag end of the piece you have just been winding back inside the loop you've been holding open (where the sections originally crossed).

Moisten the knot and pull the standing ends away from each other. Make sure the tag ends don't slip out. Some people hold the tag ends in their teeth while tightening.

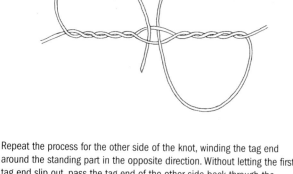

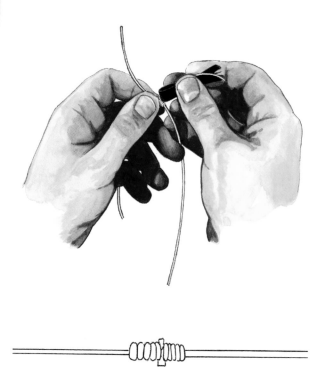

Repeat the process for the other side of the knot, winding the tag end around the standing part in the opposite direction. Without letting the first tag end slip out, pass the tag end of the other side back through the same place as the first, but it should come from the opposite direction. This is the trickiest part. If you have problems, leave a longer overlap and work hard to keep that section where the pieces overlap large.

Trim both tag ends as close to the knot as possible without cutting into the knot. Tag ends that are too long won't make the knot any stronger, and they will catch on the rest of your leader when casting.

Triple Surgeon's Knot

The triple surgeon's knot is slightly stronger than the barrel knot and is easier to tie. It is not quite as neat in the larger diameters; most anglers use it for tippets and for the finer sections of tapered leaders. If you have to join pieces of leader material that differ more than .003 inch in diameter, the surgeon's knot is stronger than the barrel knot.

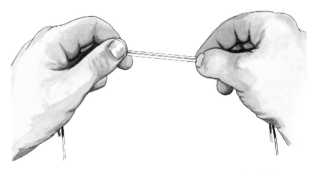

Overlap the tag ends of the two strands you are joining by 4 to 6 inches.

Make an overhand knot by passing both the tippet (or the thinner piece) and the tag end laying alongside it through the loop.

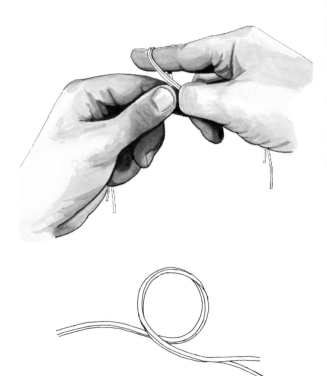

Form a loop in the overlapped strand.

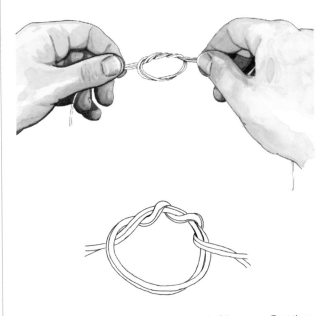

Make two more turns around the loop for a total of three turns. Treat them as a single piece; if you wet them with saliva they'll stay together easier.

Pinch the junction of the loop with the thumb and forefinger of one hand.

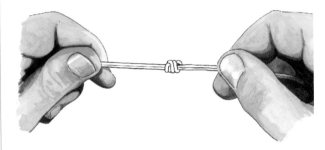

Tighten this knot by holding both short and long ends on each side and pulling quickly and tightly. Make sure they all tighten together—if they do not, this knot will fail.

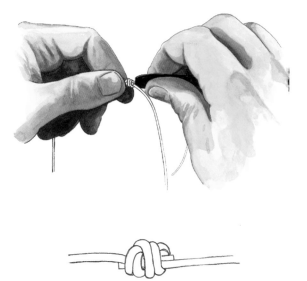

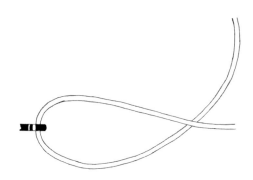

Give yourself plenty of tippet for this one. Pass the tippet through the eye of the fly from the top and form a loop by bringing the tag end over the standing part of the tippet on the *far* side.

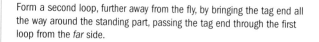

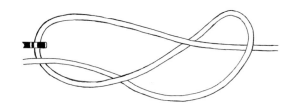

Trim the tags ends as close to the knot as possible. Like the barrel knot, tag ends that stick out could cause tangles in your leader.

Form a second loop, further away from the fly, by bringing the tag end all the way around the standing part, passing the tag end through the first loop from the *far* side.

Knots for Tying the Fly to the Tippet

The two best knots for tying freshwater flies to the tippet are the clinch and the Orvis knot. The clinch is easiest to tie, it is stronger, and you generally don't use up as much leader material when you tie on a new fly. The clinch knot can sometimes cock the fly off to one side. Both are easy to tie—the clinch is a more traditional knot and is known to most serious fly fishers, whether they fly or spin fish. The Orvis knot is a newer knot that is slightly stronger and is especially good with bigger streamer flies, nymphs, and saltwater flies.

The Orvis Knot

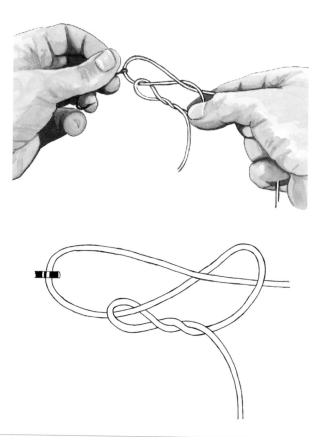

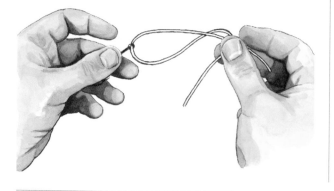

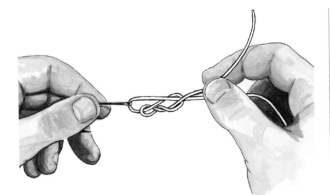

Fold the tag end over and take two turns around the loop just formed (the second loop).

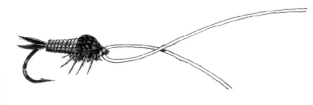

Begin the clinch knot by passing the tippet through the eye of the hook. It doesn't matter whether you come from above or below the hook eye. Make sure you keep a loop in front of the eye open because you'll have to pass the tag end through it.

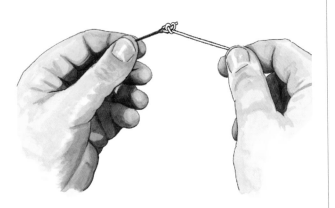

Lubricate the knot. Tighten the second loop against the standing part by pulling on the fly and the tag end. Then let go of the tag end and pull on the fly and the standing part until the knot snugs neatly against the eye. Trim the tag end as close to the fly as possible.

Twist the tag end of the tippet around the standing part five times. Any fewer turns and it's a weaker knot, and any more do not do you any good.

Clinch Knot

Pass the tag end of the tippet through the loop you've held open in front of the hook.

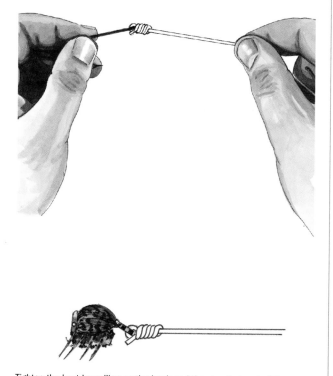

Tighten the knot by pulling on the hook and the standing part of the leader. Don't pull on the tag end, but it helps to hold it in place so that it does not slip back through the loop. Like all knots, the final tightening should be with a quick, firm pull, and the knot should be wetted with water or saliva to lubricate it before you tighten. Trim the tag end as close to the knot as you can without cutting into the knot itself.

Another reason for preferring the clinch knot is that you can remove the knot simply by grasping the knot just ahead of the hook eye with your fingernail and pulling away from the fly. The coils will come undone. The double turle knot must be clipped off when you replace flies.

The improved clinch knot, in which the tag end is passed back through the large loop, is needed only when the diameter of the hook eye is much greater than the diameter of your tippet.

TIPPETS

The tippet is the most important tool for deception in a fly fisher's bag of tricks. At least when trout fishing, a .001-inch difference in the diameter of your tippet can make a marked difference in your success. Diameter increases the relative flexibility or stiffness of your final connection to the fly, and thus the fly's credibility as an unattached morsel of food.

Leaders are described by their length and tippet size. Though tippets may be identified by their diameter in inches, in the finer sizes a more common system is to assign "X" numbers to specific diameters. The system, which is universal regardless of the manufacturer of the leader material, is as follows:

Table 3: Tippet Size Matched to Fly Size			
TIPPET SIZE	**DIAMETER** (INCHES)	**BALANCES WITH FLY SIZES**	**APPROXIMATE BREAKING STRENGTH** (POUND-TEST)*
0X	.011	2, 1/0	16
1X	.010	4-6-8	14
2X	.009	6-8-10	12
3X	.008	10-12-14	9
4X	.007	12-14-16	6.5
5X	.006	14-16-18	5
6X	.005	16-18-20-22	3.5
7X	.004	18-20-22-24	2.5
8X	.003	22-24-26-28	1.75

* Exact breaking strength varies with material and manufacturer, and strengths improve with new technology. The strengths listed here are current for Orvis tippet material in 2006.

The diameter of your leader tippet must exhibit a happy medium between stiffness for proper presentation and flexibility for deception. Flies vary greatly in terms of size and air resistance, so you must be adaptable in your choice of leaders.

For example, if I'm going to fish for trout with a size-14 dry fly, I'll usually choose a leader with a 4X tippet. From experience I know that a 2X tippet is too stiff and will make the fly behave unnaturally as it drifts in the currents. If I use a 6X tippet, I find that the last half of the leader won't straighten, because the 6X material is too fine to overcome the air resistance of a size-14 fly. If I can't straighten my leader, the fly won't go where it's supposed to—and if the tippet falls in a big heap around the fly, it's tough to fool the fish.

If you look at the tippet size/fly size table, you'll see that I could use a 3X or 5X tippet. If the water is very clear or if conflicting currents are pulling on the leader and making the fly drift unnaturally, I'll use 5X. If the water is dirty or fast and the fish are easier to fool, I might use 3X instead, with its greater breaking strength.

There are two easy formulas that will help you remember tippet sizes, diameters, and what size fly to choose. The diameter in thousandths of an inch is always 11 minus the X size, so a 6X tippet is 11-6, or .005". And to get the approximate tippet size for a fly, divide the fly size by 3. By this formula, a size-12 fly takes a 4X tippet, and a size-14 fly is a 5X tippet. Just don't forget that in clear water, you might want to go to one size tippet smaller, and in dirty water, you might go to one size heavier.

TIPPET MATERIALS

Tippets can be made of either nylon or PVDF. Nylon has more stretch and is about half the price of PVDF. PVDF is more abrasion-resistant, has a greater specific gravity (so it sinks faster), and is less visible in water because its refractive index is very close to water. Nylon is fine in faster, more riffled water where the fish don't get a good look at your tippet and is also just fine when you're moving a fly quickly through the water, so fish don't get a good look at your presentation. Because it's cheaper, nylon is also perfect for fish like freshwater bass, pike, and panfish, which don't seem to be leader-shy. But for trout in slow, clear water and for most saltwater species, where abrasion resistance is critical, PVDF seems to hold the edge.

PVDF also has one dirty little secret that frustrates some fly fishers: it is more difficult to knot. You can be pretty casual about tying knots in nylon, but when using PVDF tippets, always tie your knots very carefully and make sure you wet the knot with water or saliva before drawing it tight (actually, a good practice with nylon as well). So if you are just starting out, use nylon for all your fishing until you get more comfortable with knots, then go to PVDF tippets for really fussy fish.

You can knot PVDF to nylon without any problems. Just make sure your knots are carefully tied and secure. Most anglers feel that when tying nylon to PVDF, a triple surgeon's knot is better than a barrel knot.

Note that in both PVDF and nylon, tippets of the same diameter will vary in strength depending on the brand. A piece of tippet material marked 4X on the spool should always be .007" in diameter, no matter what brand and whether it is made from PVDF or nylon. But 4X from one manufacturer might break at 3 pounds, where 4X from another could be as strong as 7 pounds. If you went by pound-test, you might end up choosing the wrong tippet size because the ability of a tippet to straighten with a given fly size (yet still land with delicacy on the water) is related to diameter, not break strength.

When fishing for bass, salmon, steelhead, and the saltwater species, you'll want a heavier tippet, because the flies will be larger, casts will be longer, and you are not concerned with a delicate presentation. The tippet sizes used are larger, too large for the X system. The following designations are used:

Table 4: Heavy Tippet Designations			
	DIAMETER (INCHES)	APPROXIMATE POUND-TEST	FLY SIZES
Ex. Light	.011	16	8, 10, 12
Light	.013	18	4, 6, 8
Medium	.015	20	1/0, 2, 4
Heavy	.017	25	3/0, 2/0, 1/0
Ex. Heavy	.019	30	5/0, 4/0, 3/0

Thus, a 9-foot leader with a tippet of .007 inch will be called a "9-foot 4X leader." With the heavy saltwater, bass-bug, or salmon leaders, the tippets are often larger than 0X. We would call a 9-foot leader with a .015-inch tippet a "9-foot .015 leader," or a "9-foot medium salmon leader," or even a "9-foot 11-pound leader." The 11 pounds refers to the minimum breaking strength or pound-test of that .015-inch section.

Leader Length

Leaders also come in varying lengths, from as short as 3 feet to as long as 15 feet. Very short (3- to 6-foot) leaders are used with sinking or sink-tip lines. The specific gravity of nylon is so close to that of water that leaders tend to float, especially if contaminated with line dressing or grease from your hands. Even PVDF leaders don't sink as quickly as sinking fly lines. So a long leader with a sinking line tends to buoy the fly toward the surface, defeating the purpose of using a sinking line. Sinking lines are seldom used under clear, shallow-water conditions where the fish are spooky, so having the heavy line in close proximity to the fly is not a problem.

The slap of a fly line seldom scares voracious fish like largemouth bass, northern pike, or bluefish, and short leaders, from 3 to 7½ feet, are used for these species. When fishing for bluefish with big poppers, in fact, I've used a level piece of 60-pound monofilament. Bluefish aren't afraid of much, and I could conceivably tie the popper right to the fly line. The only problem is that the teeth of a bluefish can cut through fly line in a single chop, whereas nylon is more resistant to abrasion by sharp teeth.

Certain fish are what is called *leader-shy*, but *line-shy* is actually a more appropriate term. Trout in freshwater as well as saltwater, bonefish, permit, and sometimes striped bass fall into this category. If a heavy fly line lands too near them, they may cease feeding or actually bolt for cover. Whenever this kind of nervous fish is found in calm, clear water, it's best to use a leader longer than 7½ feet.

Because a leader is thinner and more air-resistant than fly line, a longer leader gives you added delicacy. Nine- or 10-foot leaders are considered standard for trout and bonefish under most conditions. At times, when the water is very shallow and clear, or on a calm lake surface, you may find that even a 10-foot leader will frighten the fish. Longer leaders, 12- to 15-footers, may be used under these demanding conditions.

Unless it is windy, a properly made 12-foot leader will straighten as well as a 7½-footer, as long as the casts you make are over 20 feet. In small, narrow trout streams, though, the short casts you make seldom develop enough line speed to straighten a 9-foot leader. Luckily, trout in small streams usually aren't very leader-shy, and you can get away with a 7½-foot leader.

Your leader can be modified during a day's fishing; in fact, you should be prepared to change your tippet quite frequently. Suppose you start fishing with a 9-foot 4X leader. The tippet on this leader, as it comes to you in the package, will be about 2 feet long. Every time you change flies, you'll have to tie a new one on with a clinch, double turle, or Orvis knot, losing a small piece of tippet in the process. As the tippet shortens with each fly change, the delicacy of your presentation decreases, especially when it gets down to 15 or 16 inches. You need that 2 feet of air-resistant tippet to slow down your fly at the end of the cast. Because your knotless tapered leader gets heavier as you use up the level tippet, it just won't present the fly with the same delicacy it did with a fresh leader. If you're properly prepared, you'll have spools of tippet material in your fishing vest; merely pull off a piece that's just over 2 feet long (you'll lose some tying it to your leader). Then just attach it to the rest of the leader, and you're ready to go. Of course, the taper won't be exactly the same as that fresh leader, but it will be close. I usually start a day of fishing with one leader and use it all day (or even weeks) without changing it. I simply tie on new tippets when needed. When I get to about my fourth tippet change and it looks like I'm tying the tippet to a piece that's too different in diameter than the tippet, I'll just add 6 inches of the next size up and tie my new tippets to that.

For example, let's say I started the day with a 9-foot 5X leader. I've had a bad day—losing flies on the bottom, breaking them off in trees, and parting company with a couple of large trout. I've already had to tie on four new tippets. But on the fifth one, I see that the piece of leader I'm tying my tippet to looks much bigger in diameter than my 5X tippet. It looks more like 2X. From painful experience, I know that if I tie 5X to 2X with a barrel knot, my leader won't straighten gently and my knots won't hold. So I tie on an 8-inch section of either 3X or 4X (either one will be acceptable, as they are both within .002 inches of both 2X and 5X).

How can I tell that my leader was down to 2X? After forty years, I can just tell by eyeballing it. How can you tell? You can carry a micrometer or leader gauge (they work like a feeler gauge for spark plugs) and check the diameter, or you can pull out spools of tippet material of a known size and compare them side by side until you find a match.

It's easy to change tippet sizes. Suppose you need to fish a smaller fly, say a size 22, with that 9-foot 5X leader. The 5X tippet is too heavy for a size-20 fly. If the leader is fresh and you have not tied a new tippet on, just fold back the tippet over the rest of the leader until you find the place where the diameter starts to increase. From that point, leave about 6 inches of tippet and tie on a 2-foot piece of 6X. Or, if you had already tied on a new tippet, just cut the 5X tippet back to 6 inches and, again, tie on a 2-foot piece of 6X.

Yes, you now have a 9½-foot 6X leader, and the taper varies slightly from a store-bought one. However, as long as that 60-20-20 butt-mid-tippet formula remains relatively intact, you can add or subtract a few midsections without affecting the leader's casting dynamics. Don't forget not to jump more than .002 inch between diameters. In the same light, you can change that 9-foot 5X leader to a heavier (but shorter) 3X leader just by cutting it back about 3 feet and adding 2 feet of 3X tippet. Clip off the remaining 4X tippet and tie on a new one.

Windy conditions and certain casting problems can put what are called *wind knots* in your tippet. Wind knots are simple overhand knots. They should be removed immediately, as they can weaken the breaking strength of your tippet by as much as 50 percent. Check your leader frequently while fishing; if you see a knot where it isn't supposed to be, remove the tippet and tie on a fresh one. It's almost impossible to untie these tiny overhand knots, and even if you can pick them apart, I still wouldn't trust that tippet. Once the damage to the tippet is done, it is irreparable.

BIG GAME LEADERS

When fishing for bass, salmon, and the saltwater species, you'll want a heavier tippet, because the flies will be larger, casts will be longer, and you are not concerned with a delicate presentation. The tippet sizes used are larger, too large for the X system. So in these fisheries, even though diameter can vary with the brand of leader material and whether it is made from PVDF or nylon, people still speak in "pound-test."

For steelhead, salmon, bass, and most saltwater species like striped bass, redfish, bonefish, and permit, you'll just need a standard knotless or knotted leader. For nearly all of these species under normal conditions, a 9-foot 12-pound leader is most often used. However, where fish get spooky and are frightened by your presentation or turn away from the fly, the first thing to do is lengthen your leader.

If you can't find a 12-pound leader longer than 9 feet, you can always add an extra 3 to 6 inches of monofilament in the same diameter as the butt section of your leader (this is usually listed on the package or on the manufacturer's website). For instance, suppose I'm using a 9-foot 12-pound leader on striped bass and they keep bolting when I cast to them. I look on the leader package and see that the butt section of this leader measures .023 inches. I remove the leader from the fly line, pull out a spool of .023" material (you should always carry extra spools of at least the tippet sizes and the butt size you'll be using), and measure off about 7 inches. Tie a perfection loop in the end of this material, and then cut the loop off the leader you just removed. Join the two pieces with a barrel knot. Then, attach the new, 15-foot leader to your fly line and you're ready to go.

You can also go to a lighter tippet, but most saltwater species are not "tippet-shy" and don't seem to respond to a lighter tippet the way trout will. On the other end of the scale, if you keep breaking off fish and they don't seem to be spooky, just cut a few feet off the end of your knotless leader. You'll increase the pound-test because you are cutting back to a thicker section.

If you want to get really simple with saltwater leaders, you can make a basic 9-foot 12-pound leader yourself. Put a loop on the end of a 6-foot piece of 25-pound-test, attach about 18 inches of 16-pound-test with a surgeon's knot, and then add an 18-inch tippet of 12-pound. Or, if you want to get really simple, some fish, like king salmon fresh from the ocean, striped bass in the surf, bluefish, or largemouth bass in heavy weeds are not leader-shy at all. Just tie on about 7 feet of straight 20-pound-test and have at it. You won't get much delicacy in your presentation, but in these circumstances you don't need it.

For tying your fly to these heavier leaders, I don't recommend you use a standard clinch knot. It doesn't seem to hold well to the heavier wire diameters used in the bigger fly hooks. One knot I've used with great success is a Trilene knot, a simple variation on the clinch knot where you go through the eye twice before finishing the same as a standard clinch. The Orvis knot also works well in materials under 16-pound-test. A third knot for big game leaders is the non-slip mono loop. Because it forms a free-swinging loop next to the fly, some anglers believe it gives their flies better action. I have never lost a fish to a bad non-slip mono loop, so I just trust it.

Non-Slip Mono Loop

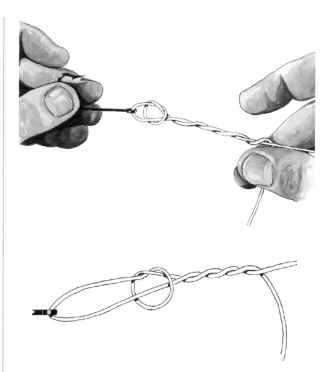

Start this knot by making an overhand knot in the leader before doing anything with the fly. In this case, you should allow about 10 inches of tag end. Don't tighten the loop. Pass the tag end of the leader through the eye of the hook.

Wrap the tag end around the standing part of the leader, just as you would in tying a clinch knot. Make six turns for material under 8-pound test, five turns for material from 8 to 12-pound, and four turns for material up to 40-pound. (For heavier material use an improved Homer Rhode loop.)

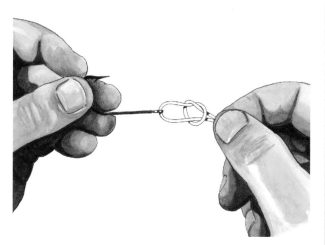

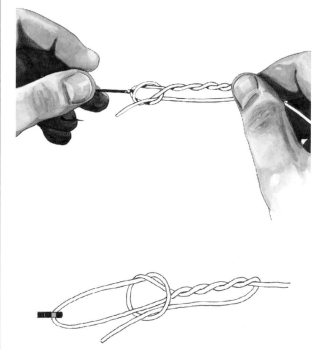

Bring the tag end back through the overhand knot, making sure that it enters the loop formed by the overhand knot on the same side as it exited when you tied the overhand. The distance between the fly and the overhand knot determines the size of your loop, so work the knot up or down the standing part of the leader until you get the size loop you want.

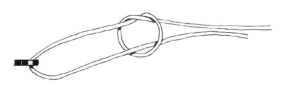

Pass the tag end back through the original overhand knot for a final time. Again, it must enter the loop on the same side you have been using.

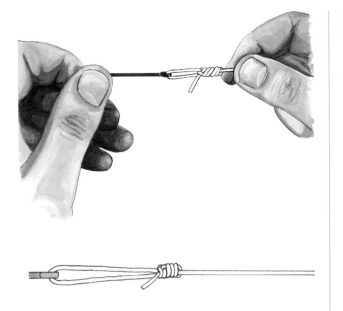

Tighten the knot by first pulling on the tag end until the turns tighten against the overhand. Next pull tightly on the fly and the standing part of the leader to finish the knot. Trim the tag end.

SALTWATER SHOCK AND WIRE LEADERS

There are times when you have to deviate from a standard knotless leader, almost always because you're fishing for guys with sharp teeth, gill plates, or rough skin. Northern pike, sea trout, bluefish, barracuda, sharks, and even the little Spanish mackerel have needle-sharp teeth that can cut through 20-pound monofilament. Sharks are double trouble because their sandpaper skin can wear through a leader if their teeth don't get it first. Tarpon and snook have very sharp gill plates that can wear through a leader in short order. So you need to add either a wire tippet or a monofilament shock tippet to the end of your leader.

There are as many types of shock-leader formulas and knot suggestions for shock leaders as there are fishing guides in the Florida Keys. In fact, if you're going to fish anywhere with an experienced saltwater guide, don't even bother bringing your own leaders. Their business depends on strong leaders and good knots, and most will immediately cut off any leader you have and throw it in the trash bucket, replacing it with one of their own.

However, you may be going to a remote destination without experienced guides, or you may be just fishing by yourself. The next best thing is to buy some premade shock leaders or leaders with wire tippets already attached. However, at some point you'll need to replace a section, or you'll get sick of replacing $10 leaders every time you need a new one.

Monofilament shock tippets can be anything from 20-pound for small sea trout to 80-pound for large tarpon. Saltwater shock leaders are usually constructed like this: 2 feet of 25- to 40-pound monofilament, 18 inches of tippet (called the *class tippet* because records are classified by the pound-test-class the fish has been caught with), and 12 inches of heavy 40- to 100-pound monofilament. The tippet is there to make things more sporting. To qualify for International Game Fish Association (IGFA) records, it must be at least 15 inches long; the shock tippet must be no more than 12 inches long.

The butt section of a saltwater leader can be connected to the class tippet by tying surgeon's loops in both pieces. Connect them with the same loop-to-loop connection you use to attach your leader to a permanent fly-line loop. The shock tippet is then attached to the tippet with an Albright knot, or, better yet, a Huffnagle knot (see the paragraphs about these knots at the end of this section). By permanently attaching a butt section to your fly line and tying a surgeon's loop on the other end, you can tie up extra tippet–shock tippet sections in advance. If you wish to change tippets, it's an easy matter to make a simple loop-to-loop connection.

Albright Knot

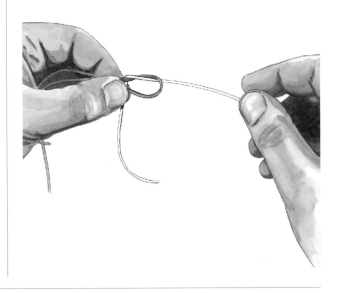

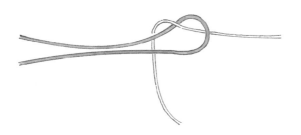

Bend a loop in the tag end of the heavier leader material or wire and allow at least 4 inches of overlap. Pass the lighter material through this loop and pinch it against the heavier material about 2 inches from the end. You should leave yourself at least 3 inches of material to work with beyond this point.

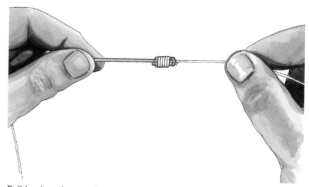

Pull hard on the standing part of the light and heavy ends to make sure the knot will not slip. You can't be too careful with this one. Trim the tag ends of the heavy and light materials.

Huffnagle Knot

Make a double overhand knot in the shock tippet about 2 inches from the end of the tippet.

With smooth, closely spaced turns, wind the smaller material over the doubled section of bigger material, working toward the loop. Take at least five turns, and up to twelve turns where the smaller material is much finer than the heavier material. Pass the smaller material through the loop on the same side of the loop that it entered.

Slowly pull on the standing parts of the lighter material and heavier material (this is one knot that should never be tightened quickly) and work the coils toward the end of the loop, being careful they don't slip off the end. When the coils are near the end, pull gently on the tag end of the smaller material to snug the coils, then pull gently on the standing part of the lighter material. Keep alternating between pulling on these ends until the knot is tightened neatly against the loop. Now use a pair of pliers or forceps to take one last tight pull on the tag end.

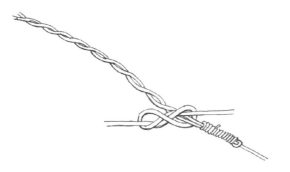

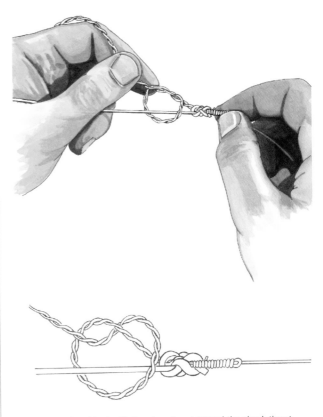

Pass the loop at the end of a class tippet (which already has a Bimini twist in it—either you've bought one, or had one tied for you) through the loop in the shock tippet. Stop when you get to the end of the Bimini twist as shown.

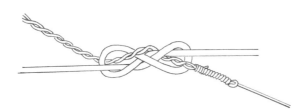

The doubled part of the class tippet should then be passed through the second loop of the figure-8 and should exit the loop on the same side as the end of the shock tippet.

Make an overhand knot with the class tippet around the shock tippet. Tighten. Make another overhand knot and tighten.

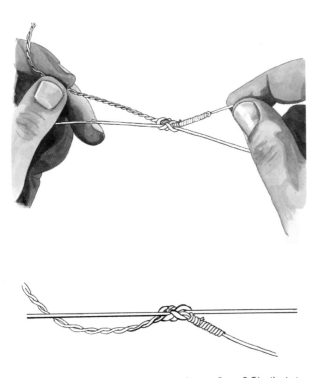

Tighten the knot in the shock tippet until it forms a figure-8. Trim the tag end of the shock tippet knot.

Make a third overhand knot, but this time take five turns around the shock tippet, working back toward the figure-8.

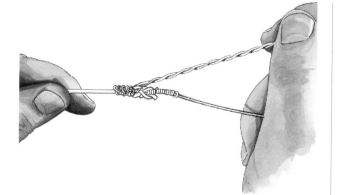

Tighten this by pulling on the tag end, stroking the coils back toward the standing part of the shock tippet to keep the coils from wrapping over themselves, and repeating until the coils are snug against the rest of the knot.

Tighten completely by pulling the tag end toward the class tippet, by pulling on the tag end of the class tippet, and the standing part of the shock tippet. Trim the tag end.

A Word about Albright and Huffnagle Knots

The Albright knot is a good knot for attaching backing to fly line. It can also be used any place where you need to join sections of monofilament that vary greatly in diameter. Both of these knots are used to tie together materials of greatly different diameters. The Albright knot is often used to tie backing to fly lines and to tie a shock tippet to a leader. Although this knot looks easy to tie, it is difficult to tie *properly* because it must be tightened perfectly to form a secure connection. The only place I recommend you use this knot is to tie a piece of wire to the rest of your leader. For tying backing to fly lines for trout, I just use a seven-turn nail knot of the backing over the fly line, and then I hit the knot with a small drop of superglue. For tying backing to lines used in salt water, a more secure connection is to double the fly line over and secure this loop with three small nail knots, then make a loop in the backing using a Bimini twist and attach the two with a loop-to-loop connection.

The Huffnagle is a far better knot for attaching a shock tippet to a saltwater leader. Although it is a little tricky, it's actually easier to tie *properly*. I've lost a few fly lines and quite a few fish over the years to my own poorly tied Albright knots, but have never lost a fish to a bad Huffnagle.

Now here's where it gets confusing. Anglers who are very concerned with records want to make sure they have the strongest knots possible in the weakest link, the class tippet. For extra insurance, they double both ends of the tippet with a knot called a Bimini twist. The Bimini twist is about the most complicated knot you'll ever encounter and beyond the scope of this book. I recommend that you buy these pre-made, or if you're really stubborn you can find directions for tying them in *The Orvis Pocket Guide to Leaders, Knots, and Tippets*. They then tie a loop in the end of the doubled section that attaches to the butt, and tie the other doubled end to the shock tippet with either an Albright or a Huffnagle knot. The reason this is so secure is that no knot is truly 100 percent effective—in other words, when you make a loop in a 16-pound tippet,

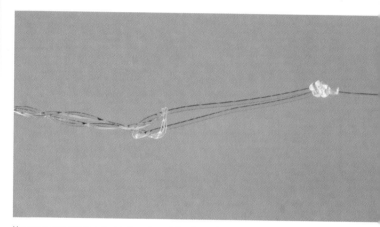

Here you can see the doubled portion of the tippet, in which a Bimini twist has been tied, looped to the butt section of the leader on the right.

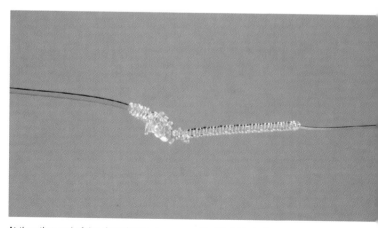

At the other end of the class tippet, you can see the Bimini twist knot itself, tied to the shock tippet coming from the left. Although the Bimini twist is bulky, it preserves 100 percent of the tippet strength.

the effective breaking strength of the arrangement is somewhere around 15 pounds. Because the Bimini twist doubles the line and is close to 100 percent effective, when you tie a loop in the end of this section it will test somewhere just shy of 32 pounds. So you lose no breaking strength to knots, and you can be sure that if your tippet tests at 16 pounds, so will the whole leader.

Many tarpon guides (and clients) are uninterested in the record books and just want a simple leader that is easy to tie in a rocking boat, will hold fish subjected to strong pressure (the quicker you can get a fish to the boat, the better its chances of survival when released), and one with a shock tippet longer than the official 12 inches so they can easily grab the heavier shock tippet when the fish is near the boat. They also feel that the standard tarpon leader, with its assortment of bulky knots, will spook fish in places with heavy fishing pressure.

A simple tarpon leader used by guides is as follows: A butt section of 4 feet of 50-pound nylon, a tippet of 3 feet of 25-pound nylon, and a shock tippet of 5 feet of 60-pound PVDF (for its greater abrasion resistance). The butt section has a loop to attach to the fly line and is attached to the tippet with an improved barrel knot, which is tied like a standard three-turn barrel knot, but the smaller-diameter 25-pound section is doubled over before the knot is tied. The shock tippet can be attached with this same knot, but the improved barrel knot is difficult to tie with such a big diameter, and many guides use a Huffnagle knot instead.

Improved Blood Knot

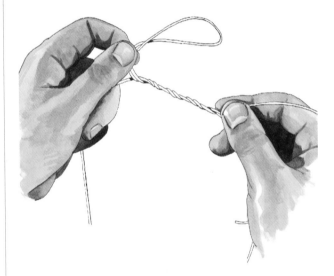

Practice the regular blood knot before you try this one. Double about 4 inches of the thinner strand, then cross this doubled section over the heavier strand, about 4 inches from the end of the heavier strand.

Try to keep a loop pinched open where these strands crossed. Wind the doubled strand four times over the heavier strand, working away from the point where they first crossed.

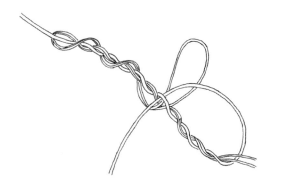

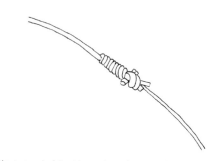

Poke the loop end of the doubled strand through the place where they first crossed. Then take three turns with the heavier strand around the standing part of the doubled strand and pass it back through the same point, from the opposite direction.

Trim the tag end of the bigger piece, the end of the loop of the doubled section, and the extra loose end of the doubled section.

Shock leaders are so thick that you can't use standard fly-to-leader knots to attach the fly. The most popular knot used to tie a fly to a shock tippet is an improved Homer Rhode loop. This loop knot is not particularly strong, but it's one of the few you can use with 80-pound monofilament. And when your class tippet is at 20 pounds, who cares if your fly-to-shock tippet connection only tests at 40?

Improved Homer Rhode Loop Knot

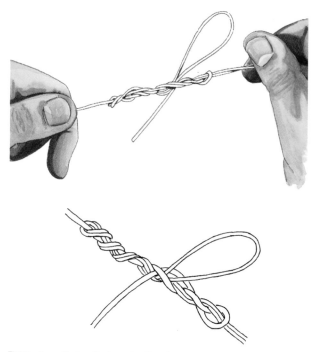

Tighten by pulling on the two standing pieces.

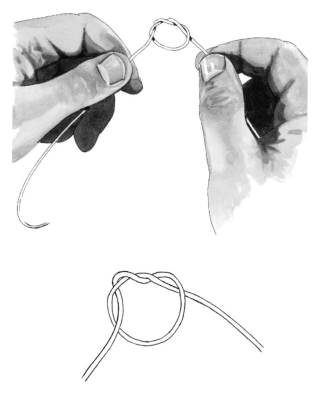

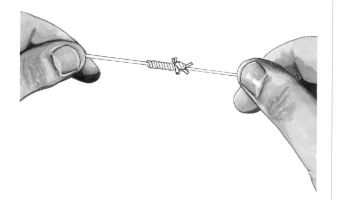

Tie a double overhand knot in the end of a heavy piece of shock tippet, leaving yourself at least 4 inches of tag end to work with.

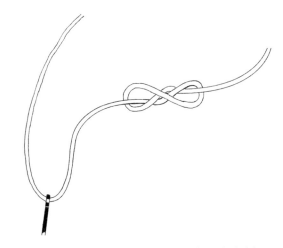

Pull on the shock tippet knot until it forms a figure-8 but don't tighten completely.

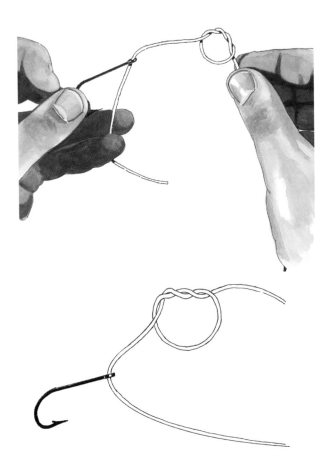

Pass the tag end of the shock tippet through the eye of the hook.

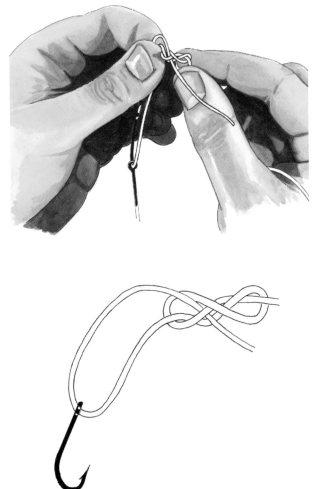

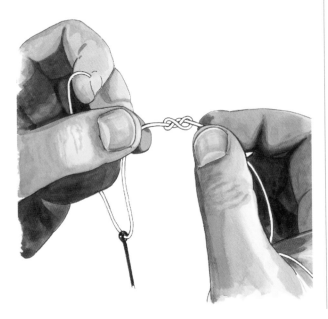

Pass the tag end of the shock tippet through the loop of the figure-8 closest to the fly, on the same side the piece that leads to the fly exits.

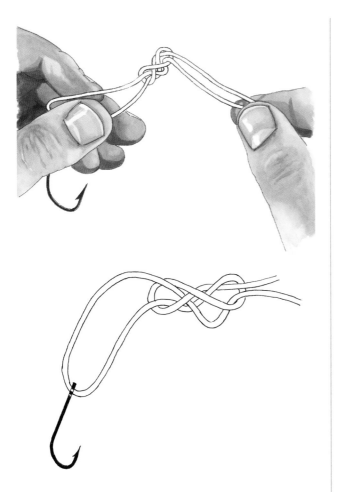

Now pass the tag end of the shock tippet through the second loop, exiting on the same side as the standing part of the shock tippet.

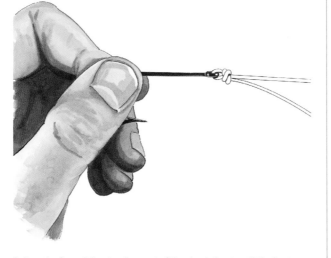

Pull on the fly and the standing part of the shock tippet until the knot snugs down against the eye of the hook.

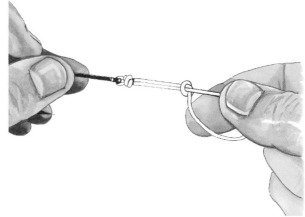

Tie an overhand knot with the tag end of the tippet around the standing part. The distance between this knot and the first knot will determine the size of your loop.

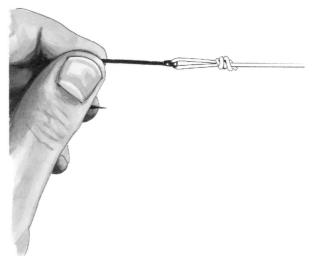

Pull on the fly and the standing part of the shock tippet. The two knots will snap together, forming a loop in front of the fly. Trim the tag end.

Wire Tippets

Wire shock tippets are sometimes used for species with very sharp teeth, like bluefish or barracuda. The wire can be multistrand plastic-coated wire or fine solid wire, which need special knots or a crimping tool, or some of the newer wires that can be tied to leader material and the fly with standard knots. The wire should be attached to the rest of your leader with an Albright knot. Because wire is stiff and will affect the action of your fly, use no more than 6 inches.

Flies can be attached to plastic-coated braided wire with a loop. Attach the fly to the wire by threading the fly on the leader and then tying a surgeon's or perfection loop in the end, so that the fly is inside the loop and able to swing free. A three-turn clinch knot can also be used, but will not allow the fly to move in the water as well. Flies should be attached to single-strand wire with a hay-wire twist.

You can also buy premade wire tippets that have a loop made in one end, so that you can tie one on the end of a regular monofilament leader. The fly end of the leader has a premade haywire twist in it, covered with a plastic sleeve. All you have to do is slip up the sleeve, untwist the wire, thread on the fly, and then twist the loop back together and slip the sleeve back up (it's easier to do than it sounds).

Haywire Twist

If you make your own wire leaders out of stiff, single-strand wire, you'll need to attach the fly with a Haywire twist.

Pass the wire through the eye of the hook and bend it back toward the standing part of the wire.

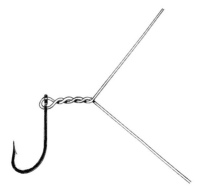

Twist the tag end of the wire five times around the standing part of the wire, working away from the fly.

Turn the tag end of the wire 90 degrees to the standing part and make three barrel coils around the standing part.

Put a 90 degree bend in the tag end of the wire. Twist this little handle back and forth until the tag end breaks right next to the standing part. (If you try to cut the end of the wire, it leaves a razor-sharp edge that can cut your fingers.)

PUTTING BACKING AND FLY LINE ON YOUR REEL

Attach the backing to the back end of your fly line. You should have a spool of backing of the length specified for your reel model with the particular line size you're using. Tie one end of the backing to the reel spool with an arbor knot and wind it on with fairly tight turns, level-winding it from side to side so it goes on evenly.

When all but a few feet are on the reel, tie the backing to the fly line with a smooth, secure knot. A nail knot with seven or eight turns instead of the usual five is fine.

Now wind on your fly line, using the same technique to distribute the line across the spool. The fly line should be wound firmly, but not too tight, because when you're fishing you seldom take the time to wind it tight. The line should come no closer to the rim of the spool than about a quarter-inch, or you'll have trouble changing spools and the line will bind up against the frame of the reel.

Arbor Knot

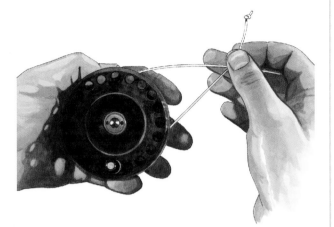

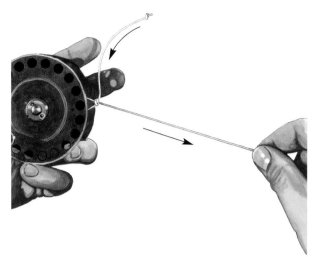

Tie an overhand knot in the end of the backing. Loop the backing around the arbor of the spool.

Pull the knot snug against the arbor and tighten the knotted tag end to the second knot against the arbor.

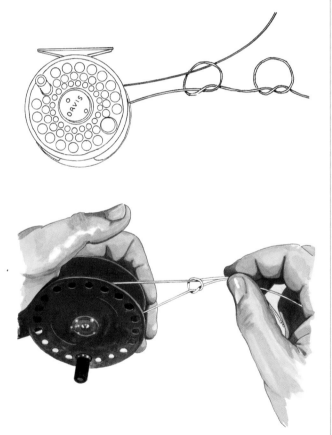

Tie a second overhand knot with the tag end of the backing around the standing part.

A supposedly clever trick is to wind the fly line onto the reel first, attach the backing and wind it on, then take the whole thing off and wind it back on in reverse order. The idea is to see exactly how much backing you need, cutting it at the proper point. The problem is you then end up with about 100 yards of backing and 30 yards of fly line in a big heap that you have to untangle and wind back on the reel. I prefer to trust the reel manufacturer's specifications and wind everything on in the proper order. If I find the spool is filled too much, I'll just strip off the fly line, cut off some of the backing, and tie a new nail knot to the fly line.

Take care that the knot you use to attach the backing is as smooth as possible and all tag ends are trimmed closely. You may not need your backing very often, but if that trophy of a lifetime runs away with your fly line, you don't want your backing connection to catch on one of the guides on your fly rod.

Most fly fishers pay less attention to their leaders and knots than they should. A change in leader length or tippet size will sometimes be more important than a change in fly patterns.

{ Top of the Canyon }

Chapter Five

Fly Casting

THE BASICS OF FLY CASTING ARE easy. You can learn to cast well enough to catch fish with just a few hours of practice. It's easier to learn to spin-cast than to fly-cast, but fly casting is less mechanical and requires more manipulation by the fly fisher. This greater control and sensitivity is fly fishing's greatest appeal.

As with any skill that requires hand-eye coordination, like tennis or golf, there will be times when almost no expertise is required; other times you'll have to call upon every minute you've ever spent practicing the art. I have to warn you that you'll probably never be totally satisfied with your casting. While it's easy to learn the basics, polishing your casting to the point where you can place a fly exactly where you want it to go ten times in a row will take years of practice. Luckily, fish aren't nearly as critical as we are of ourselves.

The first step toward learning to fly-cast is to relax and think about what you're doing. Don't relate fly casting to spin casting. Don't think about throwing a fly as you would cast a spinning lure. Never lose sight of the fact that you cast a *weighted line* that propels the fly and leader.

I'd be foolish if I told you that you can learn fly fishing as well with this (or any) book as you can with a

You can practice your casting anywhere you have room. These gentlemen are practicing in a city park in Salzburg, Austria.

A fly-fishing school is probably the best way to learn fly casting, unless you have a patient friend who is also a good instructor.

might consider a DVD on fly casting that features a highly regarded fly-fishing instructor, either as a way to learn outright, or as a way to brush up on your technique after you attend a school.

There's nothing wrong with learning to fly-cast from a book—it just takes longer. If you do expect to learn from this book, proceed slowly and patiently. Watch other fly casters in action. Practice as often as you can, even if it's in a back alley or on your lawn. Some amazing athletes can pick up fly casting after a few practice sessions, but for most of us mortals, the more we practice, the better we'll get—and the more fun we'll have on the water. Above all, don't try to fish while you're practicing—at least for a couple of sessions.

GETTING READY

Find a quiet, unobstructed place to practice. The ideal place would be a pond that contains no fish, but a lawn will do, at least for the basic forward cast. Find a place away from prying eyes. I know that my laboriously slow progress in fly casting was partly the result of neighbors snickering over a young boy with a book lying open on the lawn next to him, flailing away with a long, skinny fishing pole.

For practice you'll need a properly balanced rod, reel, and line combination, plus a leader. Leave the flies at home. Flies weigh almost nothing, so they add nothing to the cast. Besides, they're distracting, and until you've practiced a bit, they tend to embed themselves in pants, shirts, and ears. But don't forget to attach a leader to your line. I'd start with a 7½-footer, and any size tippet will do. A fly line without an air-resistant leader at the end to slow it down has a nasty tendency to bounce.

Take the rod out of its case and seat the ferrules by pushing them together until they're hand-tight. You can prevent damage to your rod by holding the rod close to the ferrules when you do this. Line up the guides by eye, or by using the little dots painted on the ferrules. When taking a rod apart, it's best to hold the rod out in front of you with one hand above and the other below the ferrule. Shrug one shoulder back, and twist the sections away from each other with your wrists, making sure that you get a straight pull. Bending the rod while unseating a ferrule is the easiest way to damage a rod and is a common reason for careless rod breakage. Fiberglass, graphite, and boron

When you put your rod together or take it apart, keeps your hands close to the ferrules to prevent damage.

Doubling the fly line over and passing it through the guides is much easier than trying to thread the thin leader through them—and if you let go of the line, it stays in place.

teacher standing at your side. I learned how to cast a fly rod from books, borrowed from the library (and usually returned late), because I didn't know anyone who used a fly rod, and I was a kid before the time of videos and DVDs. And I can tell you it took me three years to learn what you can learn during a weekend fly-fishing school, or a week spent watching a good casting DVD. If your budget and time allow, your best bet is to go to a fly-fishing school. Organized fly-fishing schools are reasonably priced, and the instructors are experienced in picking out exactly what you're doing wrong. Second best is a patient fly-fishing friend, preferably not a relative or spouse. However, a great caster is not always an adequate teacher; I've watched famous casters on sports shows (who are often more interested in showing off than teaching) confuse beginners to the point of frustration. You

rods should be twisted slightly, but metal ferrules on bamboo rods should never be twisted, so when you put a bamboo rod together or take it apart, just pull the ferrules straight away from each other when you unseat them.

Attach the reel securely to the rod, making sure that the handle is on the correct side and that the line guard, if there is one, is facing forward. Pull off about 10 feet of fly line from the reel. While resting the butt of the rod against the ground (a great idea is to lay your hat on the ground so the reel doesn't get dirty), string up the rod by doubling the fly line just near its junction with the leader. Doubling the fly line is easier than trying to pull the fine leader through the guides, as you invariably lose your grip on the leader just as you reach the last guide—and if the line slips out of your fingers near the last guide, it catches before it slips down the length of the rod.

Set the rod down again and pull out about 25 feet of line beyond the tip of the rod. Ready to cast? I bet you're holding that rod like you have a rattlesnake by the neck. A death grip on a fly rod doesn't help at all—it fatigues you quicker, and it will make your motions too jerky. Most fly rods are light and don't need much strength. Think of a bird in your hand rather than a reptile. Check behind you for obstructions. Now, get the line out in front of you any way you can. Thrash around a little bit; get the feel of the rod and forget about technique for a moment. You're ready to start when that 25 feet of line is straight out in front of you, the rod and line are both at a 90-degree angle to your body, the rod is pointing straight out in front of you at waist level, and your feet are planted comfortably with toes pointing straight out in front of you. You may also wish to angle your body slightly to one side (to the right side if you're right-handed), enough so that when the line goes back over your shoulder, you can watch it by just turning your head and not your entire body. At this stage, being able to see the line behind and in front of you is critical. By watching the line and rod in both directions, it will be easier to improve your timing and develop correct muscle memory.

HOLDING THE ROD

How are you gripping the rod? There are two basic grips: the *thumb-on-top* and the *index-finger-on-top*. If you don't have one or the other on top of the grip, you won't

be able to point the rod precisely and, as a result, may sacrifice some accuracy. Most people find using the thumb more comfortable and less tiring, but use whichever style feels more natural to you. You can cast a fly rod with your index finger on top of the grip, with the V between your thumb and forefinger on top, or with your thumb on top. Most people use their thumb, and that's the way I recommend you start. Think of your thumb as the rudder that controls your cast—the line will go wherever you point your thumb, assuming the rest of your casting form is decent.

Holding the rod with your thumb on top is the most popular way to hold a fly rod.

Sometimes, especially with very light rods, the index finger on top gives you more control.

There is a third, little-used grip called the *free-hand* or *V grip*. This grip puts the V between your thumb and forefinger on top of the rod grip. It is supposed to be

The V grip, with the V between your thumb on forefinger at the top of the grip, is another perfectly fine way to hold a fly rod.

The perfect starting position for fly casting—arm at your side at waist level, wrist bent down just slightly.

more comfortable and efficient on long casts, but I've never seen anyone other than tournament casters use it consistently. You might want to switch to the V grip occasionally, to relieve cramping in your casting hand.

If you're right-handed, you should cast a fly rod with your right hand; left-handers should cast with their left hands. If you are totally ambidextrous, I would recommend that you learn to cast with one hand and stick with it. Trying to learn to cast with both hands usually results in a mediocre ambidextrous caster, rather than an accomplished one-handed caster.

Your other hand, which I'll refer to as the line hand, actually does more work when you're fishing. The line

hand controls your line and, as a result, is always doing something. The casting hand operates only when you're casting or mending line or playing fish.

When you first begin practicing, you should think about your casting hand and not about the other. Grasp the line between the reel and the stripping guide with your line hand and, as you cast, allow the line hand to follow the rod as it comes up into the backcast. As you finish the backcast and are ready to begin the forward cast, your line hand should be level with your chest. Keep this hand in front of you and at about waist level, gripping the line so that it does not slide through your fingers. We'll worry about the line hand later.

THE BASIC OVERHEAD CAST

Make sure the rod is pointing out in front of you, below waist level, with the tip of the rod pointing at the water. Your wrist should be bent downward slightly. Using your forearm as a lever, lift the tip of the rod straight up to the point just past the vertical. If you were looking at yourself from the side, the rod should start at the 9:00 position and stop at the 1:00 position. Start to move the line off the water by lifting the tip of the rod. As soon as the end of the line (where it joins the leader) leaves the water, accelerate the tip of the rod to a quick stop when your thumb is level with your ear. The easiest way to pull off this speed-up-and-stop motion—referred to as the "power stroke"—is to do most of it with your forearm, straightening your wrist with a snap at the moment just before the stop. Turn your head and see where the fly line goes. With proper technique, the line should form a loop as you're moving the rod and then straighten beyond the tip of the rod, forming a line that is parallel to the ground.

Most problems on the backcast come from using too much wrist and not enough forearm, and from "breaking" the wrist so that it rotates beyond a position where it is straight in line with your arm. To get a sense of this, put down your rod and point your forearm straight out in front of you, with your elbow at a comfortable position along the side of your body. Bend your wrist down slightly toward the ground. Now snap your wrist up until it is straight in line with your forearm. This is where your wrist should end on the backcast. Notice that if you break your wrist by bending it up until your thumb points up, the motion is tiring. So not only does breaking the wrist destroy a good backcast, but it also fatigues your wrist.

When you finish the backcast, the line should be bending your rod as it straightens behind you. The line will shortly fall to the ground, because you haven't yet learned the forward cast, but during actual casting the fly line should never drop below the tip of the rod on the backcast. The rod must flex in order to transmit casting energy properly to the line, and if you bring your rod back too far by breaking your wrist, the rod will not flex enough.

You should be able to feel the rod bending as you cast. Some fly casters liken a fly rod to a spring: the energy that is built up by the fly line bending the rod is released, slinging the line out in front of you. Nonsense, others say; the

fly rod must bend because it allows the tip to travel in a straight line, obtaining a greater mechanical advantage between your casting hand and the energy it imparts to the fly line.

As you practice the overhead cast, which is by far the most important cast, keep in mind that while the line travels back and forth while you cast, fly casting is really an up-and-down motion of your forearm and rod, working together as a single unit. This motion keeps the fly line pulling at an almost perpendicular angle to the rod, which puts the fly rod to its best mechanical advantage.

With 30 or 40 feet of line on the water in front of you, lifting all of that line out of the water, into the air, and back behind you is a lot to ask of a simple movement of your forearm. This is where the mechanical advantage of the fly rod becomes apparent. Don't shortchange yourself

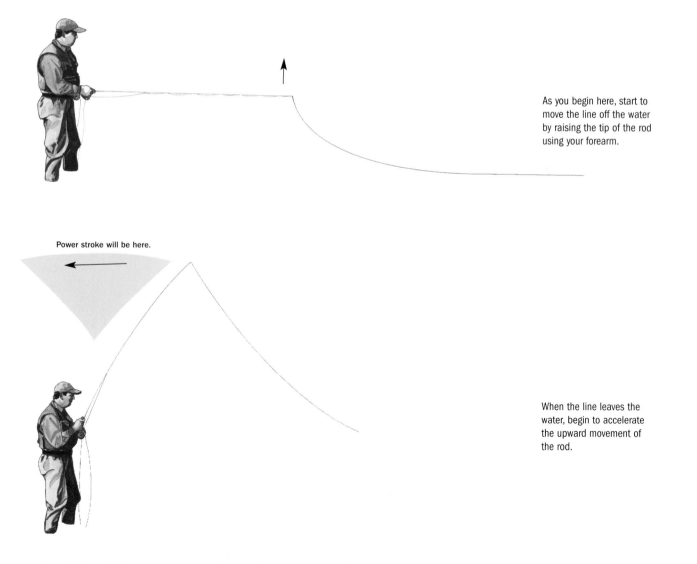

As you begin here, start to move the line off the water by raising the tip of the rod using your forearm.

Power stroke will be here.

When the line leaves the water, begin to accelerate the upward movement of the rod.

At the end of the acceleration, apply a little wrist snap. Notice that the caster is watching his back cast, and that his wrist is not tilting his thumb back over his shoulder.

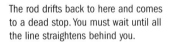

The rod drifts back to here and comes to a dead stop. You must wait until all the line straightens behind you.

Dead stop here

Power stroke here

On the forward cast, begin to accelerate the rod here.

Casting loop diameter

Your acceleration on the forward cast ends here.

Release line now if shooting for extra distance.

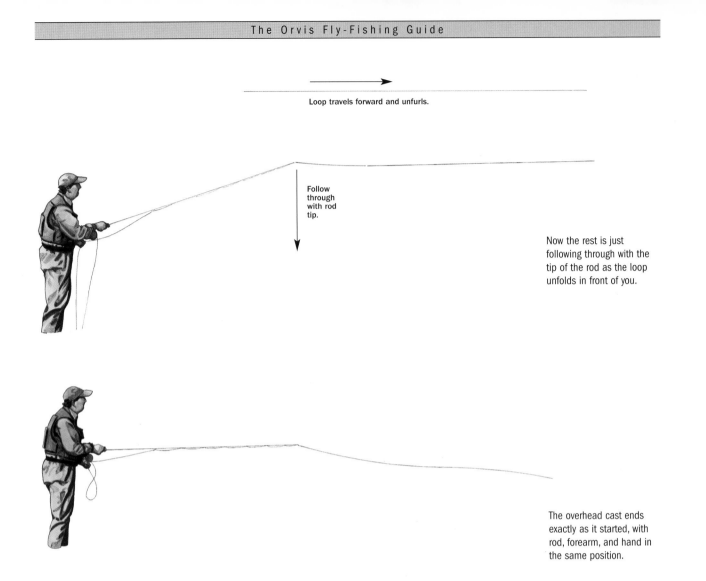

Loop travels forward and unfurls.

Follow through with rod tip.

Now the rest is just following through with the tip of the rod as the loop unfolds in front of you.

The overhead cast ends exactly as it started, with rod, forearm, and hand in the same position.

by starting a cast with the fly rod held too high. You can't move much fly line by starting a cast at 10:30 (with your rod tip in the air) and stopping at 1:00 (by your ear).

Too much slack line on the water presents a similar problem on a backcast. Your fly rod will work properly only when the fly line is bending it throughout the execution of a overhead cast. Otherwise, you might as well be casting with a broomstick. If you start a backcast with slack line on the water, the rod won't bend enough, until all the slack is lifted off the water, which doesn't give you much room to lift the rest of the line into the air.

To get the most out of your fly rod on a overhead cast, always either lower the rod tip and eliminate any slack by stripping in some line before starting the cast or make a roll cast to straighten the line. I realize I haven't taught you how to strip line or how to make a roll cast yet—you might want to read ahead if you need to do either.

Get the line back out in front of you and make another backcast. This time, though, turn your head and

With a nice, flat, high backcast like this, it's very difficult to make a bad forward cast.

watch for the instant that the line is perfectly straight behind the tip of the rod. With a hammering motion that uses both forearm and wrist, quickly bring the rod tip back to its starting position in front of you. This is an-

This is the place your arm and wrist should stop at the completion of the backcast.

This is called "breaking the wrist," and it's sure to result in a sloppy cast. The wrist is bent back way too far.

limp "spaghetti rods" popular in those days. With today's progressive-taper rods, casting with the elbow tucked tightly into your side is not only impractical, it's plain uncomfortable.

On the forward cast, your elbow should start by hanging comfortably at your side, at about waist level. During the backcast it should come up to the level of your shoulder, returning to that relaxed position at your side on the forward cast. Your elbow movement should always be more of an up-and-down motion than a back-and-forth one.

Your first cast probably did not look like poetry in motion. Relax, and don't let it bother you. Most likely you tried to use your wrist too much. Try to take your mind off the grip of the rod. Thinking about where you're holding the rod as you also think about the position of the tip, because the tip directs the line, makes you use your wrist as the pivot point of the cast. Instead, make your forearm pivot around your elbow. If the wrist is not locked into position at the end of the backcast, it may dip the rod tip too far back, throwing the line below the point where it is effectively pulling on the rod.

If you have trouble with your wrist breaking on the backcast, try this: Before starting the cast, while the rod is pointing straight out in front of you, notice the angle between the rod and your forearm. Make a couple of back-casts, never taking your eyes off your wrist. Forget about

Notice the flex in this rod at the start of a nice backcast.

other speed-up-and-stop motion, just like the backcast, except its mirror image. You get the wrist snap at the end by bending your wrist down from its straight position. Don't try to throw the line; merely direct it out in front of you with the tip of the rod.

Back in the days of long, limber bamboo fly rods, students were taught to cast with a book under their elbow, using a flick of the wrist to move the rod. Any greater effort on their part would have overpowered the

the line for a moment. On the backcast, that angle between your forearm and wrist should remain constant. Now look at your backcast. Is it flat and parallel to the ground?

If your rod tip is coming to a dead stop at 1:00 (by your ear) every time, and the backcast drops too low, you may not be putting enough emphasis into the backcast. If you try to throw the fly line up in the air over your head rather than over your shoulder, it may be easier to keep the backcast where it belongs.

The backcast should be a gradually increasing acceleration, starting low at 9:00, and ending at a dead stop at 1:00, when your thumb reaches your ear. Watch the fly line on the water. As you begin to raise your rod tip, the fly line will begin moving toward you; then it will suddenly leave the water. At this point, increase your acceleration to a maximum. As mentioned earlier, this is called the *power stroke*. It's a difficult concept to visualize until you've done it correctly once or twice. Some instructors like to call it a speed-up-and-stop motion.

Once the backcast is mastered, you have accomplished more than half the task. It's easy to make a good forward cast once you have a good backcast, but nearly impossible to make one with a poor backcast. (Putting together a good backcast with a good forward cast composes what I've been calling the "overhead" cast—two parts making the whole that is the basic cast in fly fishing.)

The timing of the forward cast is important. If you begin to come forward before the backcast has straightened, you'll probably hear a sharp crack—and the line will fall in a big puddle in front of you. You cannot develop enough power on the forward cast until the line is straight behind the tip of the rod, pulling on the rod. If you wait too long, gravity will take over, causing the fly line to fall below the tip of the rod. Again, you're not getting maximum power out of your fly rod.

You should always begin the forward cast at the instant just before the fly line straightens behind you. It's perfectly all right to turn your head and look; even the best casters turn and check their backcasts occasionally. After some practice this timing will be almost intuitive, and you won't have to look. Different lengths of line require different timing. With a short cast the pause is very short, but with a long cast it takes longer to straighten all that line behind you.

The forward cast is almost like pounding a nail into a wall that is about 1 foot in front of you. When pounding nails, most of the power comes from the forearm, with the wrist adding that final crispness to the stroke. Just as you wouldn't throw your arm forward too far when pounding that nail, try not to throw your arm forward on the cast. Your upper arm can move a little on the forward cast, but you shouldn't end up with it any farther forward than your shoulder. The forearm should end up exactly where it started—at below waist level pointing straight out over the water. If you're wading in deep water, over your waist, the forearm will end up

Too much power too soon will give you a tailing loop, where the loop closes on itself. With this problem, the fly often catches on the leader or the rod.

higher than waist level, but it should end up parallel to the water.

Problems sometimes occur on the forward cast because power is not directed properly. There is a power stroke on the forward cast, and it should be applied between the 1:00 position and as soon as you see your thumb (if you are looking straight ahead), and just like the backcast, it comes from a quick snap of the wrist. Too much power too late will make the line splash on the water instead of straightening just above the water and settling gently to the surface. Too much power too soon will give you what's called a *tailing loop*, where the casting loop catches on itself as it unrolls. If it happens while you're fishing, you'll often catch the fly on the tip of your rod or on the line.

Misdirecting the forward cast can also cause the line to splash or puddle. Don't forget that the tip of the rod directs the line. Keep your eyes on it. If you aim the tip of the rod *on* the water, you will *put* the line on the water. You're actually trying to straighten the line 2 to 3 feet above the water, letting the air resistance of the line and leader take over at the end to produce a delicate delivery. There are two ways of looking at this, and you should use whichever idea works best for you: either aim 2 feet high, or else make sure that the tip of the rod never ends up pointing below the horizontal when you complete the forward cast.

Now we're ready for some fine points. You may have hit your shoulder or the back of your head with the leader as the rod came forward. Make sure that, for now, the tip of your rod moves through a vertical plane as you cast. In other words, as you lift the rod on the forward cast, you slice upward through a vertical plane; make sure that you slice back through this same plane on the forward cast. Now this plane does not have to be exactly straight up and down; in fact, it is more comfortable to cast at a slight angle off to your side, maybe 20 degrees from the vertical. Just make sure that your rod follows that same angle on both the forward and backcasts.

Another fine point to note, during the power stroke on both the forward and backcasts, is that the tip of your rod follows the same horizontal line above your head. The Orvis instructors like to call this "painting the ceiling of a *house*" as opposed to "painting the ceiling of an *igloo*." When you apply that quick power to the fly line, you get the most efficient power by applying it in a straight line. By dipping the tip of the rod up or down (painting the igloo), you don't keep constant tension on the tip of the rod, so the energy you could potentially build up—the energy that drives the fly line—is mostly lost.

You may also have hit the rod itself with the leader or line. If you had a fly on the leader, it would probably be hooking on the leader or line as you came forward—the dreaded tailing loop—which usually happens because you are pushing and pulling, rather than raising and lowering your forearm. If you push forward, the rod tip, leader, and line all move forward in the same plane and something has to tangle. Dropping your arm on the forward cast gets that rod tip out of the way as the line, leader, and fly pass over your head.

SHOOTING LINE

It's time to lengthen your cast. This technique, called *shooting line*, is done by pulling some line off the reel, holding it with your line hand, and releasing it on the forward cast. The momentum of the line traveling forward on the forward cast will pull this line through the guides.

Make a 30-foot cast and leave this line on the water. Strip about 10 feet of line from your reel. Hold this line tightly so that the slack is below your line hand (between your line hand and the reel, not between your line hand and the stripping guide). The line between this hand and your stripping guide should be tight. The slack line can be coiled in this hand, but for now just let it hang to the ground. Start a backcast, making sure that the line is held tightly between your thumb and forefinger. Don't release any line while the line is behind you. As your rod comes forward, at about 10:30 (right when you begin to see the fly line), release the line you're holding. It should slip through the guides and add another 10 feet to the cast.

It will take some practice to determine exactly when you should release the shooting line. Most problems come

Writer Kirk Deeter shooting line on a nice cast. Note that his left hand has released the line, and this tight loop will carry the extra line forward with ease.

from releasing the line too early, which directs the shooting line straight up in the air rather than out in front of you. After you release the line, funnel the line through the stripping guide by forming an "O" with your thumb and forefinger. This directs the line to the stripping guide, lessens friction, and prevents tangles. With practice, you should be able to shoot at least 20 feet of line comfortably.

LINE CONTROL

Line control is an essential part of casting. After your cast hits the water, the line will be hanging in that "O" you've made with your fingers. Grab the line again with your thumb and forefinger. Never let go of the fly line; some fish strike as soon as the fly hits the water, and if you don't have control of the line, you'll miss your chance.

You can retrieve line by transferring it from your line hand to between the forefinger and third finger, or third and fourth fingers, of your casting hand. Pull the line through these fingers by grasping it behind your casting hand. This is called the *strip retrieve*. As the line is gathered, it can either be coiled in your line hand or just dropped to the ground or water surface next to you. The speed at which you retrieve line is also the speed that your fly will move through the water. When fishing, try to give action to your fly by using this retrieve rather than moving the rod tip. Moving the rod tip around produces slack line, and it's difficult to set the hook or pick up for another cast with a pile of slack on the water.

A helpful drill is to make a cast, shoot some line, put the line between your rod hand fingers, strip in some line, then cast and shoot the line again. When transferring the line from your right to left hand becomes second nature, you're well on your way to mastering line control.

An alternate way to retrieve line is to use the *hand-twist retrieve*. For this retrieve, you don't need to transfer the line to your casting hand. Begin the hand-twist retrieve with the line in the palm of your non-casting hand, palm up. Pinch the line between your thumb and forefinger, at the same time turning your hand upside down. Reach forward with your other three fingers and catch the line on the edge of your little finger. Turn your hand so that the palm is facing up again. You should now have a single small coil of line in your hand. Palm this coil while reaching forward again with your thumb and forefinger, grasping a new section of line. Repeat the process. You'll

With the line held like this, you are in perfect control at all times—ready to cast, ready when a fish strikes, ready to strip line.

To strip line when retrieving slack or to make a fly move, just pull line with your line hand while holding it between the fingers of your rod hand.

soon have a handful of small coils that will pay out and shoot through the guides without tangling.

The hand-twist retrieve is useful when you want your fly to move through the water at a slow, steady pace. It's not as versatile as the strip retrieve, because you can't re-

To gather more line, make a longer strip.

To gather even more line, hold coils in with the last two fingers of your line hand.

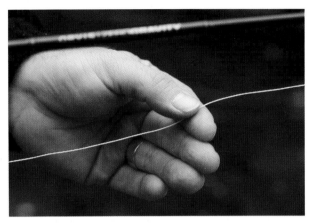

Start the hand-twist retrieve by grabbing the line between your thumb and forefinger, with your palm facing up.

Reach forward with your other three fingers and catch the line on the edge of your pinky.

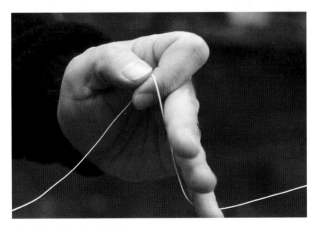

Now turn your palm up again.

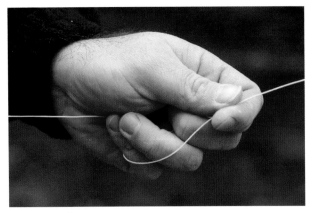

You'll end up with a small coil of line in your hand.

You'll soon have a palm full of coils that will uncoil instantly when you shoot line.

Palm that coil and reach forward again with your pinky.

Turn your palm up again and palm another coil.

trieve line quickly, nor can you impart an erratic action to your fly.

Accuracy in fly casting is achieved merely by pointing your thumb or forefinger (your rudder, remember?), whichever is on top of the grip, at the spot where you want your fly to be delivered. Don't forget to aim a couple of feet high. If you point *down* at a spot, your fly, leader, and line will slam into the water, rather than straightening above the water and settling gently to the surface. A change of direction in fly casting is accomplished by picking up the line with an ordinary straight-up movement of the rod, then pivoting your body and coming forward with the rod at a different angle. A change of direction of more than 45 degrees, however, is best accomplished with a false cast in between.

FALSE CASTING

False casting is merely making a cast or series of casts without letting the line touch the water. Suppose you're standing at the edge of a lake with the line straight out in front of you. You spot a fish cruising along the shoreline to your left, 90 degrees from where your line is sitting. If you pick up the line and try to place it near the fish with a single change-of-direction cast, your presentation will be poor, because the rod can't flex enough when you come forward at an angle that's radically different from your pickup angle. A false cast in between will allow you to alter the direction of your forward cast a little at a time.

To practice the false cast, make your backcast in the standard way and come forward as you would normally—but don't follow through on the forward cast. Stop the rod tip at about 10:30, wait for the line to straighten out in front of you at about shoulder level, and then start another backcast. Repeat the process three or four times; then, on the last false cast, let the rod follow the line to the water as it straightens.

It will take a bit of practice to false-cast without having the line slap the water in front of you. Most problems occur when you stop the rod tip too low or when you don't allow the fly line to straighten both in front and behind you. And don't forget that it's still an up-and-down motion with the rod. Pushing and pulling the rod on your false cast will only cause your line, leader, and fly to slam into the rod. It's okay to use a good bit of wrist on the false cast, so long as your motions are crisp, short, and up-and-down. You'll find that you use more wrist on a false cast, because most of the stroke in both directions is your power stroke. Just make sure that you initiate both forward and back motions on the false cast with your forearm, though—your wrist just does not have enough strength.

A great way to practice the motions for false casting—in fact, a terrific way to work on your power stroke in general—is to cast on the ground at your side. Lay an 80-foot piece of rope or surveyor's tape on the ground beside you. It should be one rod's length off to your side, parallel to the direction of your cast. Now you're going to take the whole fly-casting motion and turn it almost 90 degrees to the side. Do whatever it takes to lay 35 feet of fly line behind you, but make sure all of it lies right alongside the rope. Now, using a power stroke, cast the line forward so that the forward cast lies along the rope in front of you. Stop between back and forward casts so that the line stays on the ground. If the fly line does not lie straight along the rope, you know you've done something wrong. Keep trying until you consistently throw the line on top of the rope.

Now, raise your cast up 45 degrees and try the same thing, this time keeping the line in the air with only enough of a pause between back and forward casts to straighten the line. Once you master that, you can raise the cast vertically until it's comfortable for you. It's perfectly okay to cast on an exact vertical angle, or anywhere from vertical to 90 degrees to your side. In fact, many fishing situations, in tight brush or in windy conditions, call for a sidearm cast. For general fishing conditions with no wind, though, most casters find it most comfortable to cast canted slightly off to the side of the vertical.

False casting performs other useful tasks. It allows you to work out line gradually, shooting a little line on each forward cast without letting the line touch the water. Distance can be obtained this way quicker than putting the line on the surface three or four times, and the water is disturbed less. It also allows accuracy without trial-and-error casts that disturb the water. By watching the line on a false cast, you can estimate where the fly is going to fall and make corrections by changing direction or shooting a little extra line. Finally, dry flies absorb water on the surface, and a few short, quick false casts shake this water off efficiently.

I emphasize *short and quick* because there is a temptation to make half a dozen false casts, or to false-cast 40 or 50 feet of fly line. False casting requires fairly tricky timing, and the longer you try to hold your fly line in the air, the more you compound the problem. There is never any need for more than four false casts. False casting with long lengths of line should also be avoided. Again, the more line you try to hold in the air, the easier it's going to be to lose your timing. And false casts above spooky fish like trout or bonefish will sometimes make them bolt for cover, so if you can get away with one false cast, never use two. If you have to cast 60 feet, false-cast with 40, and shoot the remaining 20 when you follow through on the last one.

At this point, you'll be starting to refine your casting stroke. When false-casting, one way of critiquing your form is to look at the loops your fly line forms on both the back and forward casts. A very efficient cast, one that will let you throw a lot of line with little effort, and one that will slice through the wind better (and one that will look better when people are watching), is a cast that forms a narrow loop, one with a diameter of about 1 to 2 feet. Wider loops cheat the cast of energy. Wider loops come from painting the ceiling of an igloo with the tip of the rod instead of painting a flat ceiling. Watch your tip as it moves through the power stroke, and make your arm and wrist do whatever it takes to keep the tip in a straight line.

A cast that paints a ceiling with a reversed dome (a ceiling with a concave shape), where the tip drops in the middle of the power stroke, will make your loop catch on itself, throwing a tailing loop where the fly and leader catch on the line, or even on the rod. This will also tie wind knots in your leader, often caused by poor casting technique.

Remember that as you're developing your casting style, it will be exactly that—your *own* casting style. There is no right or wrong way to cast a fly, as long as the fly goes where you want it to go, you don't disturb the

This is a bad wide loop, probably caused by "painting the ceiling of an igloo." The fly won't go where the angler wants it, the wind will blow this cast all over the place, and his line will land in a big mess.

Still a more open loop, but a good controlled one. Casting a loop this size is helpful when fishing big weighted nymphs with a strike indicator.

This even tighter loop will be great for precise casts, even in the wind.

water, you don't hook yourself or any innocent by-standers, and you don't exhaust yourself in the process. Just as in tennis or golf or skiing, every person develops a unique style that works for them.

VARIATIONS ON THE OVERHEAD CAST

The overhead cast and false casting can be done in planes other than the straight up and down. You can cast with the rod 90 degrees off to the side, 45 degrees to the side, or at any angle, so long as it's not lower than 90 degrees from the vertical. Below 90 degrees you'll slam the line into the ground or water behind you on the backcast. You can also turn the overhead-cast angle so that you throw the backcast over your opposite shoulder. You'll hear these called such things as *cross-body* casts, *side* casts, and so on, although they aren't different casts—just basic variations on the overhead cast.

These casts can be used to get you out of tight spots. For instance, suppose you're right-handed and there's a tree behind your right shoulder. By angling the backcast over your left shoulder, which is clear of obstructions, you can get the fly on the water without ending up in the tree. Just make sure that your forward and backcasts travel in the same vertical plane. So if you do a cross-body cast across your left shoulder, the line should land off to your right.

Casting off to your right side gives you a horizontal cast. With a cast that is parallel to the water's surface, you can fire your fly in under overhanging trees on the bank of a river or lake. You can also use this sidearm cast to advantage in a brisk wind, as the wind's velocity is always slightly lower just above the surface of the water. Everything else—shooting line and false casting—is exactly the same, except that it's turned on a different plane. When you false-cast with a side cast, your 9:00-to-1:00 power strokes can be nearly parallel to the water instead of perpendicular to it.

Casting to the side or across the front of your body also lets you cast curves into your line—that is, *controlled* curves. For instance, suppose you're right-handed and have a rock directly in front of you. There is a trout feeding on the far side of the rock. Make a side cast off to the right side

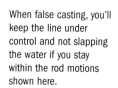

When false casting, you'll keep the line under control and not slapping the water if you stay within the rod motions shown here.

Casting with the rod straight up and down is fine for wide-open spots with no wind, but you can vary the angle of the rod to become more versatile.

of the rock, false-casting a few times. On the last cast, stop your rod at about 10:30 (right after the power stroke), just as if you were going to make another false cast, but let the line fall to the water. Don't follow through with the rod. The line will snap back against the rod, forming a curve that hooks to the right. Hopefully, the fly and leader will fall in front of the rock, with the line off to the right side. You can make the curve even more pronounced by pulling back slightly on the rod after you've come forward.

Casting sidearmed can help you make curve casts around objects.

Casting at an angle that is almost parallel to the water gives you even more extreme curve casts and helps cast under trees. This is about as far as you can go in a sidearmed cast without slamming your line on the water.

Many people are more comfortable angling their cast a little off to their side.

Casting at a horizontal angle can get you into tight spots under trees and other obstructions.

The easiest way to make a curve cast is to begin with a sidearmed cast.

A curve to the left for right-handers can be made in a similar manner by casting across your left shoulder, again stopping the rod high.

Don't become enthralled with curve casts. They're tricky, and even with a lot of practice they can be incon-

As the line begins to straighten above the water, don't follow through with the rod—let the line snap back against it.

The line will hook back into a nice curve.

This right-hander has brush to his right side, so he's casting over his left shoulder to keep his backcast clear.

sistent. You could have reached that trout in front of the rock merely by moving a few feet to the right and presenting a regular overhead cast to him—with much greater chance that your fly would land in the proper spot.

DISTANCE CASTING

There may be times when you need to cast a fairly long line, over 50 feet. Remember: the longer the line you cast, the more difficult it is to be accurate and precise. It's always better to make a short, easy, accurate cast than a difficult, long, sloppy one. Most trout are caught within 35 feet, and even most saltwater fish are caught at less than 50.

The first step toward adding distance to your cast is to raise your arm up a little. Start at the normal starting position, but instead of bringing your elbow up to your shoulder, raise it above shoulder level when you make your backcast. This does two things: it keeps your rod tip higher, allowing you more ground clearance behind you, and it gives you a longer, more powerful arc in which to impart energy to the rod.

Just raising your arm should give you the added power to make most long casts. On very long casts, you can also let your rod tip drift back to almost 2:30 (when

your forearm drifts past your shoulder); just make sure that you give the backcast enough power to prevent it from falling below the tip of the rod. Now, on the forward cast, let the forearm come in front of your body more than on a normal short cast. In a normal cast, your wrist probably ends up about a foot in front of your shoulder, and your upper arm stays even with your body. On a long cast, to increase the length the tip travels, you might end up with your wrist higher and almost 2 feet in front of you. Increasing the distance the rod tip travels is another way of obtaining a longer, more powerful casting stroke.

THE DOUBLE HAUL

A variation of the overhead cast, known as the *double haul*, is the final step in increasing line speed and thus adding length to your casts. The faster a fly line moves, the more momentum it has. Greater momentum allows you to shoot longer lengths of line. The double haul is used for long casts, over 60 feet, and/or when there's a lot of wind, because greater line speed will overcome either obstacle.

The double haul can be done efficiently only with weight-forward or shooting-head lines. Both of these lines utilize about 30 feet of head or thicker line; the remainder of the line is thin-diameter running line. It's easy to see this junction in a shooting-taper line, because the head and fly line are different types of materials, and sometimes different colors. With weight-forward lines, this junction is not immediately apparent, because the head and running line are continuous, the demarcation being where the head tapers down quickly, about 30 feet from the tip of the line. It's important to find this point with either type of line. You'll use the head to load the rod, while the running line will be pulled through the guides by the forward momentum of the head.

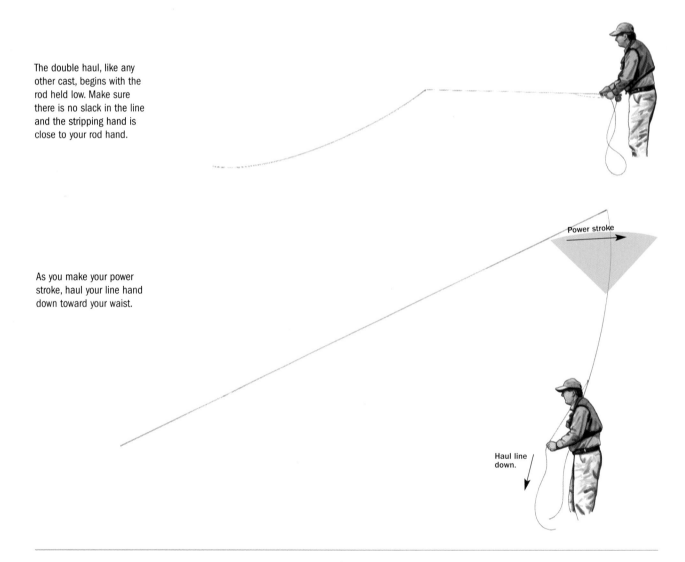

The double haul, like any other cast, begins with the rod held low. Make sure there is no slack in the line and the stripping hand is close to your rod hand.

Power stroke

As you make your power stroke, haul your line hand down toward your waist.

Haul line down.

I'd also recommend that you practice this cast with an 8- or 9-weight line. The extra line mass helps you feel the timing of the hauls—and besides, most times you use this cast, you'll be using a bigger rod anyway.

Start the double haul with about 35 feet of line on the water in front of you. Lower your rod tip to about 2 feet above the water and eliminate any slack by stripping in some line, or else by making a single forward cast. Begin the forward cast as if you were going to pick up a lot of line, bringing your arm up as you cast, letting your elbow come up above shoulder level. Your line hand should be holding the line tightly, quite close to the stripping guide.

Watch the fly line; as soon as all the line leaves the water, haul on the fly line by bringing your line hand down and to the side forcefully. A 1-foot haul is about right to start. As soon as you complete the haul, toward your waist, let your line hand drift back alongside your ear to the stripping guide. The line that you hauled will become part of the backcast. Let the rod tip drift back to 2:30 (almost horizontal) as the line straightens behind you. Use a normal forward cast to complete the entire process.

This is a single haul. It can come in handy all by itself if you have the wind at your back and you're having trouble straightening the backcast.

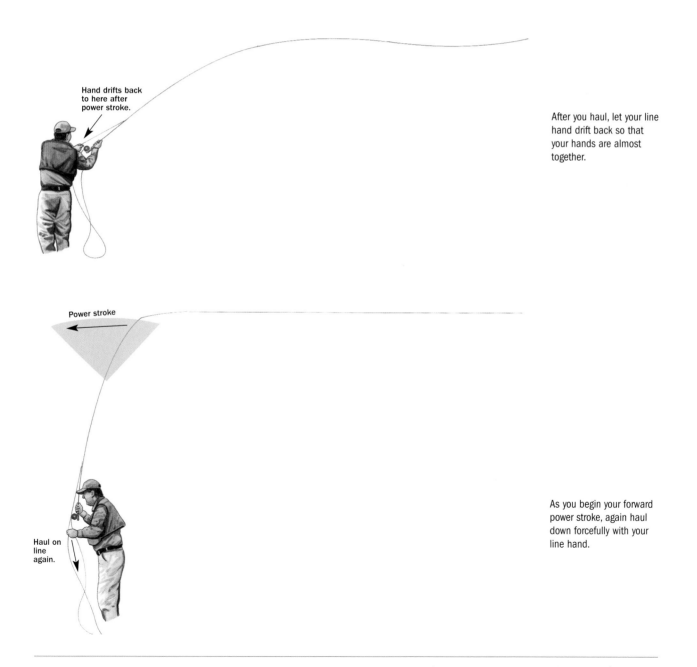

Hand drifts back to here after power stroke.

After you haul, let your line hand drift back so that your hands are almost together.

Power stroke

Haul on line again.

As you begin your forward power stroke, again haul down forcefully with your line hand.

As the casting loop begins to unroll in front of you, release the line.

End of haul just before releasing line.

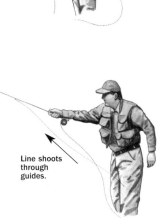

The line will then shoot through the guides with ease, much easier than if you did not use the double haul.

Line shoots through guides.

Once you feel comfortable with the single haul, try a double haul by making a backcast and haul, but make the same hauling motion on the forward cast, at the same time you complete your power stroke. Now you'll haul by bringing your line hand back toward your waist. When the line hand reaches your waist, the rod tip should be at about 10:30. Your casting arm and the rod tip should be one straight line pointing above the horizon. Now, release the line with your line hand. Because you didn't have any slack in reserve, the line will snap against the rod with quite a bit of power and fall to the water.

If you have problems putting this together, and most people do, go back to using a rope on the ground alongside you. Turn the cast over 90 degrees, make a single haul, and let the line fall to the ground. Make sure it lies straight along the line behind you. Now make a forward cast with a haul, again striving to keep the line on top of—or at least parallel to—the rope.

Now practice the double haul with 20 feet of slack line held below your stripping hand, piled neatly on the ground. The powerful line speed you've developed by hauling, combined with the high trajectory of the rod tip, will allow you to shoot great lengths of line.

The high rod tip is essential because, unlike any other type of forward cast, you are actually throwing or propelling line through the air. If the rod tip ends up too low, everything will pile up into the water.

With a shooting-head line, it's possible to shoot 60 to 80 feet of running line on a single cast. Running line has less friction and air resistance than the back end of a weight-forward line, so it travels farther. When using a shooting head, make sure that the last couple of inches of fly line are just inside the guides. Otherwise, you'll form a hinge at the junction of the fly line and the running line and lose a lot of casting power. Fly fishers using shooting-head lines often hold the coils of running line in their teeth or coiled in a

Drift and hauling on the backcast in action: Superb Bahamas guide and expert caster Glister Wallace has just finished the haul on the backcast, and he is beginning to let his line hand drift back.

At the end of the drift, his line hand is all the way back to the rod, very close to his casting hand.

Now he hauls on the forward cast.

And he releases the line so it can shoot through the guides.

stripping basket attached to the chest. In a boat, shooting line can be held in a plastic bucket at your feet.

For optimum performance, you should get the kinks out of shooting-head running line. Point your rod tip at your fishing partner and have him or her pull on the end of the running line as he walks away from you. If no one is around to help, you can hook your front loop over a branch or nail and accomplish the same thing.

The double-haul and shooting-head lines are both designed for one purpose—distance. Neither will straighten a delicate 12-foot leader. They should be used primarily when it's necessary to cast consistently over 60 feet—most often in big steelhead and salmon rivers, lakes, and in saltwater fishing. Sometimes in trout fishing, though, the extra line speed from a single or double haul will help. I've found it useful when throwing a big strike indicator with lots of lead on the leader, or when trying to cast into a very stiff wind.

DEALING WITH WIND

The double haul, with its tremendous line speed, is a great advantage in the wind, but in most cases a simple modification of the forward cast will suffice. It's mostly a matter of common sense. For example, if you have the wind blowing toward you, it's going to be easy to form the backcast and harder to straighten the line in front of you. Put a little less effort into the backcast, be a little more casual about it, but hammer the rod down quickly on the forward cast. When casting into the wind, don't try to *push* the line *into* the wind—slice down *through* the wind. As long as you keep your rod tip from pointing below the horizontal, you can come forward as hard and as fast as the wind dictates without slamming your line into the water. The tighter your loop the better, so work on keeping that rod tip in a straight path.

With the wind coming from behind you, use a forceful backcast and an easy forward cast.

Wind coming from either side presents a different set of problems. If you're a right-handed caster and you have a crosswind blowing from left to right, merely lead your target a foot or two to the left to compensate for the wind. With a wind blowing from right to left, you're asking for a fly in the back of the neck. Here you have three options: either change your position so you don't have to cast across your body; use a cross-body cast; or use a sidearm cast. On a good cast the fly always stays above the tip of the rod, so if the rod tip is pointed 8 or 9 feet off to your right side, you're pretty safe. If you stand there and try to use a standard forward cast, you get the fly in the neck again.

THE TOWER CAST

This isn't really a different cast, but people always ask about it. You should consider using a tower cast when you have brush or a low bank behind you, but you still want to make a standard forward cast. When you make your backcast, lift the line sharply, but at the same time raise the rod as far as you can over your head. This will keep your backcast very high. Complete the forward cast as you normally would. It's not as efficient as the standard overhead cast, and on the forward cast the leader often ends in a pile, but sometimes it's the only option you have.

THE ROLL CAST

The *roll cast* is a useful technique in tight spots and quite easy to learn, but I see it as a last resort in most situations, simply because it's not as accurate or as delicate as a properly executed forward cast. Also, it's harder to shoot a lot of line with it; it can take four or five roll casts to get out 40 feet of line.

The roll cast does offer two advantages: The line never goes behind you, and it can be accomplished with slack line on the water, which would ruin an overhead forward cast. The roll cast can be used when you have an impene-

The tower cast is not the most delicate of casts, but it keeps your backcast very high. Just lift your arm as high as you can on the backcast.

trable wall of trees or brush behind you. If you've made a bad cast and have piles of slack line on the water, a quick roll cast can straighten those coils in preparation for a proper overhead cast. In fact, it's frequently used to get the line in the water quickly when you approach a new spot.

Because the roll cast does not have a backcast, it must be started slowly in order to keep the line from going behind you. To start, very slowly raise the rod tip to the vertical. As you do, bring the rod off to the side just enough to keep the line on the far side of the rod. The line will move toward you, and will form a curve of line between the rod tip and the water. Keep moving the rod tip up and back until part of this curve is behind the rod, forming a semicircle with the rod as the radius. Stop. Wait until everything stops moving. Now, with a forceful motion, using your wrist and forearm as you would on a forward cast, snap the rod tip straight down in front of you. The line should move neatly over the water in front of you in a traveling roll.

The longer your fly rod, the longer the roll cast you'll be able to perform, because the rod tip will travel a longer distance, imparting more force to the line. Still, with any kind of rod, roll-casting over 50 feet in length is a tricky and inconsistent business.

You can change the direction with a roll cast, so long as the line is directed *away* from the side of the rod that the loop is formed on. In other words, a right-handed caster can make a change of direction only to the left of where his rod tip is pointing. If he tries to roll-cast to the right, the line as it rolls will come up under the rod, and the fly will probably catch on the rod.

A roll-cast pickup can be used to lift the line off the water in preparation for a false cast. It is done by making a roll cast but not allowing the line to touch the water in front of you; thus, the rod tip should be directed a little

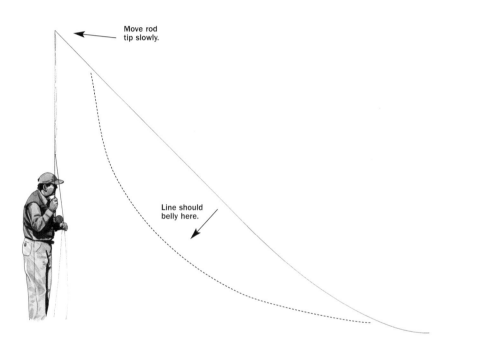

Move rod
tip slowly.

Line should
belly here.

At the beginning of the roll cast, raise your rod slowly and off to the side just a bit.

The proper place to stop your rod before beginning the roll cast, showing both rear and side views.

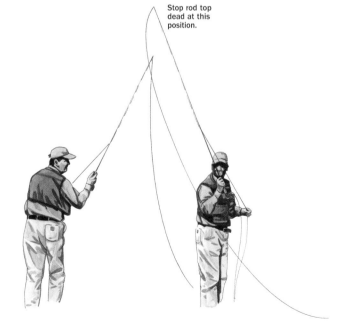

Stop rod top
dead at this
position.

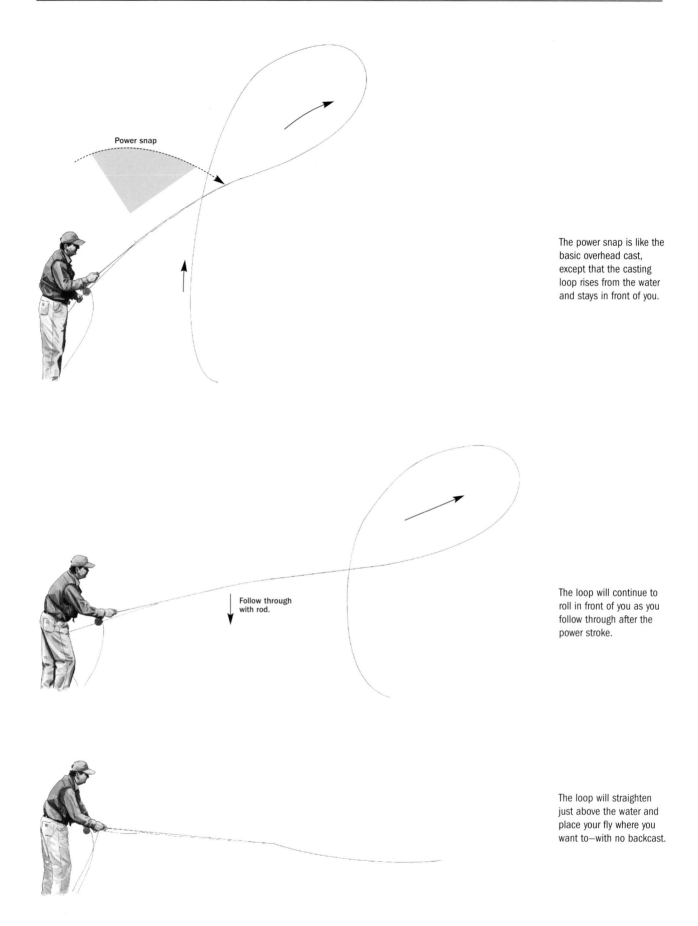

Power snap

The power snap is like the basic overhead cast, except that the casting loop rises from the water and stays in front of you.

Follow through with rod.

The loop will continue to roll in front of you as you follow through after the power stroke.

The loop will straighten just above the water and place your fly where you want to—with no backcast.

In tight spots on small streams like this, the roll cast and the sidearmed cast are essential.

higher than normal. When the line straightens in the air in front of you, make a single false cast and follow through as you would on a normal forward cast. With sinking lines, the roll-cast pickup serves to bring the line to the surface instead of back toward your face, given that it's difficult to lift a sunken line straight off the water. For a deeply sunken line it may take two roll-cast pickups—one to bring the line to the surface, and the other to lift the line into the air.

The roll cast can be performed as a cross-body cast, across your opposite shoulder, but it's an uncomfortable and difficult motion for most people. For right-handers, it is done by slowly bringing the rod tip up and across the front of your body, over the left shoulder. Keep the fly line off to the left of the rod, or the line will roll up into your face when you cast.

SPEY CASTS

The Spey cast is actually a style of casting, comprising many variations on the standard roll cast, and there are many different types of casts that make up Spey casting. Originally developed for use with Spey or two-handed rods (the terms are interchangeable), Spey casts can also be useful in tight spots with a single-handed, ordinary trout rod. Spey casting is beautiful to watch and fun to do, and what was once thought to be an Old-World anachronism used by European salmon fishers has become very popular all around the world, from Russia to Tierra del Fuego.

When trying to cover a large river with a swinging wet fly, there is no better style of casting. Because this cast, when used with a 12- to 15-foot two-handed rod, can pick up 80 feet of line and fire it back to the center of the river in seconds, it's far superior to a short, single-handed rod, where you'd have to strip in 40 feet of line, false-cast with a double haul a few times, and then present the fly. The fly spends far more time in the water and is thus in front of the fish instead of flying through the air.

Entire books and DVDs on Spey casting have been produced. I'll show you two casts, the single Spey and the double Spey, to give you an idea of how they're done. Chances are if you've bought this book, you did not buy it to learn to Spey cast, but these two casts will come in handy in places where you need to make a long roll cast.

Single Spey

Let's imagine you are wading the edge of a river with the current flowing from left to right. You want to cast 50 feet out into the center of the river, but you have no

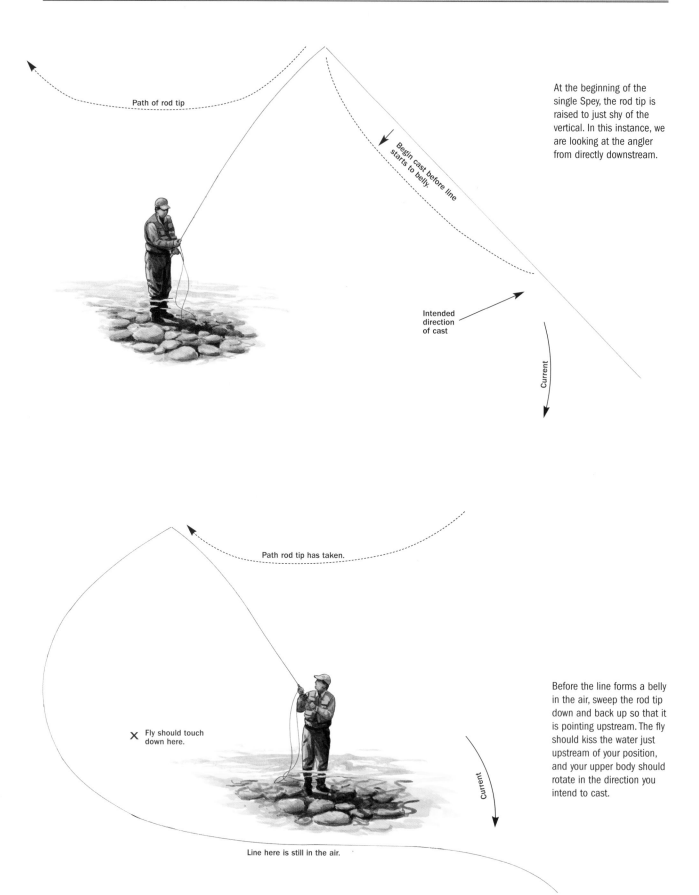

Path of rod tip

Begin cast before line starts to belly.

Intended direction of cast

Current

At the beginning of the single Spey, the rod tip is raised to just shy of the vertical. In this instance, we are looking at the angler from directly downstream.

Path rod tip has taken.

X Fly should touch down here.

Current

Line here is still in the air.

Before the line forms a belly in the air, sweep the rod tip down and back up so that it is pointing upstream. The fly should kiss the water just upstream of your position, and your upper body should rotate in the direction you intend to cast.

If the D-loop has formed properly in the preceding step and the fly has kissed the water just upstream of you, a simple forward stroke should send the line and fly straight across the river.

Current

room to backcast because of thick brush behind you, and the standard roll cast just does not have enough power to get the fly 50 feet away and change direction at the same time.

So you try a single Spey cast. Feed line downstream in the current until you have 50 feet hanging below you. The line should be straight and you should be facing downstream, but with your feet pointing in the direction you want to cast. Put your left hand on the upper grip of a two-handed rod if you're using one. Raise the rod tip to just shy of the vertical, enough to get almost all of the fly line out of the water.

Now, before the line starts to sag, and while it's still straight between the rod tip and the water, rotate your body upstream and dip the rod tip down and then back up with a smooth acceleration, so it follows a half-moon shape with the lowest part in front of your body. The rod will end up pointing upstream. When you do it right, the fly should kiss the water just upstream of your position, just outside the tip of the rod. Now, without stopping, right when the fly hits the water in front of you, raise the rod tip as if to make a roll cast off your left shoulder and make a powerful forward stroke, just as you would in a cross-body roll cast. If you dip the tip in the correct manner and if the fly kissed the water upstream of your position, the line should fire across the river.

If you see the fly kiss the water downstream of your position, stop everything and wait for the current to carry the line back downstream. Then try again. If you attempt this with the fly hitting the water downstream of your position, the fly will catch the fly line—or your nose.

Double Spey

Now let's say we have the same situation, but you have a strong wind blowing downstream. Even if you make a single Spey cast properly, the strong wind might blow the fly into your head. Or perhaps you're not comfortable making a roll cast across your body and would prefer to make it off your right shoulder. This is the place for the double Spey. It's actually an easier cast, because where the fly kisses the water in the middle of the cast is not as critical.

In this case you begin with your right hand on the upper grip of the rod (if you're using a two-handed rod). Make sure the line has straightened completely below you. As in the single Spey, your feet should be pointing straight out into the river and you should swivel your waist so your upper body is facing downstream. Raise the rod as you would for a normal roll cast, still facing downstream. Now smoothly move the rod tip across your body and down, until it is pointing straight upstream and about a foot above the water. Pivot your body as you move the rod. The fly should land just downstream of your position; if it lands upstream of you, start again, because you might impale yourself. If it lands too far downstream, you won't get enough power out of this cast.

Now, raise your rod tip, swing it across the front of your body in a dip, and then raise it again as it gets even with your right shoulder. (The whole idea is to get that half-moon shape on the right side of the rod, and to get enough of a loop so you can perform a standard roll cast.) You'll now find yourself in position to complete the cast

The double Spey cast begins as you would for a normal roll cast by raising the rod tip.

Intended direction of cast

Current

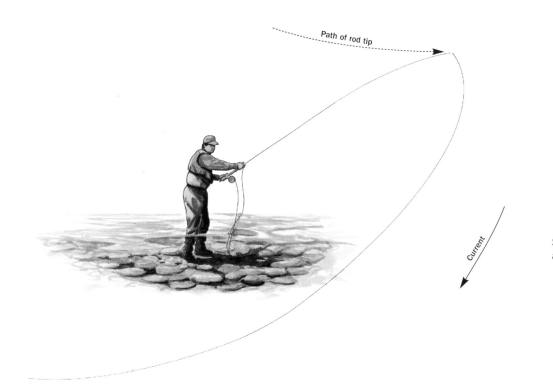

Path of rod tip

Current

Smoothly move the rod tip across your body and down.

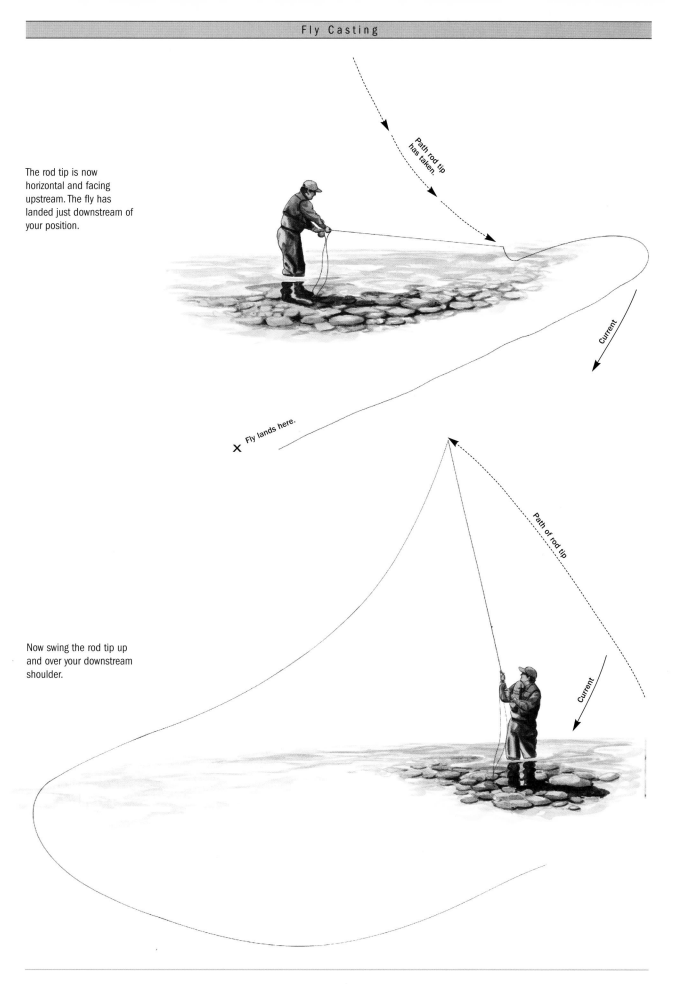

The rod tip is now horizontal and facing upstream. The fly has landed just downstream of your position.

Path rod tip has taken.

Current

× Fly lands here.

Now swing the rod tip up and over your downstream shoulder.

Path of rod tip

Current

From here the final part of a Spey cast is like a standard roll cast with a forceful power snap across the river.

Current

just as you would any plain-vanilla roll cast—and you already know how to do that. The whole motion of the second half of this cast is a smooth lift-dip-and-lift motion.

SLACK-LINE CASTS AND LINE MENDING

When fishing in moving water, there will be times you'll want to manipulate the line with the rod just before or just after the line hits the water. When imitating an insect floating on the surface of the water or drifting in the current, your fly line must move at the same speed as the fly. A river or stream is composed of many different current speeds from bank to bank or from top to bottom; if your fly line is lying in a current that is faster or slower than that in which the fly has been placed, some manipulation is necessary.

The most typical example is when you find yourself in the middle of a fast river with a fish feeding in the slow water next to the bank, directly across from you. If you cast your fly to the fish, the faster water between you and the fish will pull on the fly line, forming a belly in the line and whisking the fly from the slower water near the bank. Not only will the fly be pulled away from the fish before he can see it, but if you're using a dry fly, a little wake will form behind it, making it look like a miniature motorboat. Most in-

Mending a line is merely flipping the line with your rod and turning a line that has bellied in the current into a mirror image.

This angler threw slack line into his cast on purpose, to keep tricky currents from pulling on the fly line, giving the fly an unnatural drift.

The reach cast is merely an aerial mend. Just before the line hits the water, reach out with the rod in whatever direction you want the curve to form.

sects don't skid across the surface of a stream. This unnatural movement, called *drag*, is very apparent, even frightening, to a feeding fish.

In instances like this, drag can be avoided by purposely throwing slack into your line. The faster current has to pull all the slack out of the line before it can begin to pull on the leader and fly. Throw slack either by overshooting your target, overpowering the cast, and stopping the rod higher than normal (about 10:30), or by wiggling the rod from side to side as you follow through on the forward cast.

You have other options in your bag of tricks for avoiding drag. One is to throw a curve cast with the arc of the curve upstream of the fly's position. The faster current will have to invert this curve before it will pull on the fly.

Mending line means throwing a curve into your fly line after the line hits the water. In the circumstance described above, you would cast to the fish directly across from you; then, with the rod held low in front of you with a stiff arm, flip the rod by rolling your wrist in the upstream direction. The result is an upstream curve that the current will have to invert before it will pull on your fly. It's best to release some slack line as you make the mend; otherwise, you'll move the fly when you reposition the line.

The so-called *reach cast* is merely an aerial mend. Just before the line hits the water on a forward cast, you move your rod upstream of where it would have ended up on a standard forward cast. This offers the advantage of not

moving the fly, because you are making the mend just before everything hits the water.

A mend or a series of mends is often used to sink a wet fly deeper and to keep it moving at approximately the same speed as the current. A line that is bellying downstream will pull a fly faster than the current, and also draw it toward the surface. Every time the line bellies downstream, make an upstream mend. On a long cast across the stream you might have to mend line three or four times to get a natural drift. This technique is especially useful with sink-tip lines, because the floating portion of the line is easy to mend. It is almost impossible to mend sinking lines once they are in the water.

Although the most common mend is made in an upstream direction, you may occasionally have to mend the line downstream. A typical situation would be where you are standing in fast water and casting into a slower current. If you don't mend line downstream, the line nearest you will hang upstream of the fly, making the fly drag against the current. In this instance, just reverse the process and flip your wrist in the downstream direction.

Every place you fly-fish will present a different set of challenges. For precise placement of a fly, you should use the standard forward cast whenever possible, but with the many variations of the forward cast, the roll cast, and line mending, you have an impressive set of skills with which to meet many different fishing conditions.

{ KAMCHATKA }

Chapter Six

Flies

FLIES CAN IMITATE ALMOST ANY-thing a fish will eat. Trout flies are tied to resemble the various insects that trout eat, as well as minnows, leeches, and crustaceans. Bass flies imitate frogs, mice, and minnows. Saltwater flies mimic the color and shape of saltwater baitfish, crabs, shrimp, and squid. Prior to the 1970s, most flies were constructed by winding fur, feathers, tinsel, and hair on a hook. Today, lightweight synthetic materials like nylon, Mylar, latex, polypropylene, Antron, and many plastics are used as replacements for, and sometimes improvements upon, natural materials. Some of the best patterns include a mix of materials used for hundreds of years, like chicken hackles, along with flashy modern synthetics.

Flies called *attractors* stimulate nonfeeding fish. Some trout and bass flies look like nothing that occurs in na-

Flies can imitate anything from mice (top) to minnows (middle) to insects (bottom).

ture, and can be considered attractors; no one really knows why fish strike them. Perhaps fish see them in a different light than we do, and actually take them for items of food. Some anglers say that attractor flies arouse curiosity or anger in fish, but this theory is probably more anthropomorphical than biological in origin, and therefore highly dubious. Fish don't have the luxury of striking things from mere whim. They put stuff in their mouths that they are sure is food, and they strike things that present a threat to their territory because they don't have any other appendages for defense.

I believe that fish don't see flies as we do. There can never be a perfect fly, because a perfect fly would not contain a hook. All flies have that great big, obvious point sticking out of them. Every time a fish inhales one of your flies, it has made a mistake.

With our flies we are trying to create the impression of "something alive," not an exact duplicate of live bait. Exact molded-rubber or plastic imitations of fish and insects have been around for years but are soon discarded after a fly fisher tries them, because these stiff, hard facsimiles don't give an impression of life in the water.

HOOKS

Hooks for tying flies come in a variety of styles and sizes suitable for constructing flies that imitate everything from a tiny insect to a large baitfish. Most quality fly-tying hooks are made in Norway, Japan, England, and the United States. All the important manufacturers follow a universal sizing scale, so when an Icelandic salmon-fishing guide says to try a size-8 fly, you can reach for the correct size in your fly box.

Hook Terminology

Eye. The eye of a hook is a closed loop or ring of wire at the front end. It enables you to tie flies to your leader. The most common type is a *turned-down-eye* hook, which means that the eye is bent down from the shank of the hook. *Turned-up-eye* hooks have the eye bent upward from the shank, and the *ring-eye* hooks have a straight eye that is parallel to the shank. Certain types of eyes are supposed to offer better hooking advantages in various situations, but I've never seen any of these theories proven conclusively. Most standard trout flies use turned-down-eye hooks, most salmon flies are tied on turned-up-eye hooks, and most saltwater flies feature ring-eye hooks, but the habit seems to follow tradition more than anything else. As a fly tier, I'm offended by a classic dry fly on a ring-eye hook, but I'm sure if it's properly tied, it will catch as many fish as one tied on a turned-down-eye hook.

Shank. The shank is the long, straight part of the hook that is used for the base, to which fly-tying materials are attached.

Bend. The bend occurs between the shank and barb of the hook. Bends come in several varieties, such as sprout, limerick, and model perfect, but the subtleties in bend shapes are more for aesthetic than utilitarian purposes.

Point. The point penetrates a fish's jaw so that the bend can hold. Hook points should be sharp but not too long, because long, thin points can easily be broken. The hook point on a fly should be sharp enough to scratch your thumbnail if drawn across it lightly. Examine hook points before you begin fishing and periodically while fishing, especially if you've missed a fish or dropped your backcast. If the point has been lightly nicked, touch it up by drawing it against a sharpening stone or special hook hone. If it is badly broken, the fly should be thrown away and replaced.

Barb. The barb helps to keep the bend in place once the point has penetrated. Because a fly has little weight that a fish can throw or work against, many fly fishers use barbless hooks, or carefully mash down the barb with a small pair of pliers or forceps. Barbless hooks make it much easier to release fish unharmed and are also more easily removed from an ear or finger. Some experts feel barbless flies may even offer hooking advantages because there is less resistance to penetration.

Hook Size and Style

Hook size. Hook size, and thus fly size, is measured by an arbitrary scale based on distance between the point and the shank, also called the *gape*. Hook sizes that are used for flies range from less than ⅛ of an inch in length for the smallest to 3 inches for the largest. The actual size of a fly can be much larger; in some saltwater flies the materials used will extend up to 6 inches beyond the bend of the hook. In the smaller trout-sized hooks we use even numbers 2 through 28; the larger the number, the smaller the fly. Hooks larger than size 2 use a numbering system that increases as the size increases, using a slash/zero after the number to distinguish them. Thus, the hook size scale, in increasing order of size, would be 28, 26, 24, 22, 20, 18, 16, 14, 12, 10, 8, 6, 4, 2, 1/0, 2/0, 3/0, 4/0, 5/0. Hook sizes larger than 5/0 are too heavy to be cast with fly-fishing gear, and hooks smaller than size 28 have a gape that is so small, it's nearly impossible to hook a fish—although I do have a few size-32 hooks on my fly-tying bench, and have actually caught small trout with them.

Shank length. For a given hook size, the standard shank length is about twice the gape of the hook. Some hook styles, however, have a shank length longer or shorter than normal. This gives you a longer or shorter fly with the same hook size. An X system is used to designate these hooks—for example, a size-6, 2X long hook has a shank length equivalent to a standard hook that is one size larger than a size-4 hook, because even though odd-size hooks aren't made, they are still counted in the X scale. A size-22, 1X short hook has a shank length equivalent to a size-21 hook.

Hooks that are 1X to 3X long are generally used for nymphs, or imitations of immature aquatic insects. The 3X to 8X styles are used for long, skinny baitfish imitations called streamers. Short-shank hooks are less commonly used, but a short shank can be an advantage in the tiny, size-20 and smaller hooks, when you want to imitate a small insect but want the hooking advantage offered by a larger gape. Spiders—special dry flies designed to be skated across the surface of the water—are sometimes tied on 2X short hooks. Hooks shorter than 3X give poor leverage when playing a fish and are seldom used.

Wire diameter. The size of the wire used to construct hooks is proportional to hook size. Thus, a size-2 hook is made from heavier wire than a size 4. Standard-wire hooks are generally considered wet-fly hooks; dry flies should be tied with hooks of finer wire, or they won't

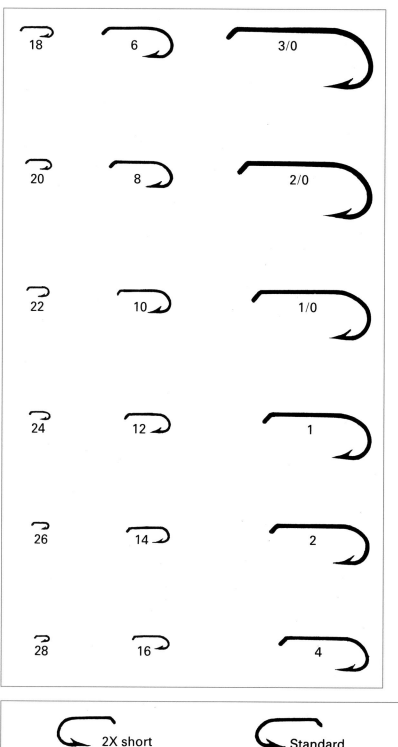

Various hook sizes for flies.

float properly. As with shank length, we use an X system, and a 2X fine hook is made from wire that is two sizes finer than the standard hook in that size. Most dry flies are tied with 1X and 2X fine-wire hooks; 3X fine hooks are available, but they break or bend quite easily. Salmon, saltwater, and steelhead hooks are 1X and 2X stout, or one and two hook sizes heavier, because these species can put a lot of pressure on a diminutive hook.

Hook finish. Most flies are tied on bronzed or japanned (blackened) hooks, which are coated to keep them from rusting. Saltwater flies are always tied on stainless-steel or nickel- or cadmium-plated hooks because of the corrosive properties of salt water.

FLY PATTERNS

Flies are tied according to specific patterns, some of them hundreds of years old, others dreamed up by fly tiers the night before they go fishing. All will catch fish at one time or another, but the ones you see in the fishing catalogs year after year have withstood the test of time, because a trout will eat the same insect tomorrow that trout were eating a hundred years ago. Some patterns are limited in their use; for example, a size-28 black

Differences in fly-hook shank lengths.

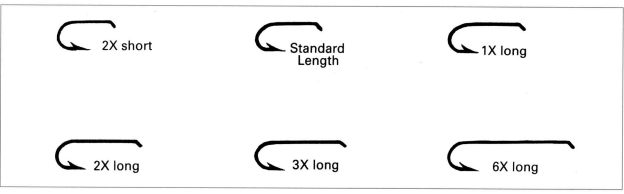

midge will catch trout when they are feeding on tiny midges, but a 20-pound pike or 185-pound tarpon won't even notice this speck on the water. Other flies have broad application. Under the right conditions, a plain black-and-white streamer fly will catch any fish in fresh or salt water that feeds on baitfish—and that includes most of them.

Fly patterns range from sublimely simple to ridiculously complicated. Some steelhead flies are merely clumps of fluorescent yarn that imitate salmon eggs, while the Baron, a classic Atlantic salmon fly, calls for thirty different kinds of tinsel, floss, and feathers.

Parts of a Fly

Head. The head of a fly is right behind the eye of the hook and usually consists of the thread that has been used to tie the fly. Properly made heads are small and neat, and have been finished with a special knot called a *whip fin-*

Wings. Wings imitate the wings of an insect or the back of a minnow. Wings are usually made from feathers, hair, or long synthetic fibers.

Hackle. The hackle imitates the legs of an insect or crustacean and in most dry flies is the part of the fly that provides flotation, by trapping the fly in the surface film. The hackle is almost always made from a neck or body feather of a bird.

Throat. Sparse hackle or hair often replaces the hackle proper on streamer or wet salmon flies.

Tail. The tail extends beyond the bend of the hook, and is usually composed of a small bunch of hackle fibers. On dry flies the tail helps support the fly in the surface film; on some flies it is merely a decoration that adds a bit of color; and on many wet flies and nymphs, it imitates the tails of insect larvae.

Tag, tip, or butt. Some flies have a short piece of tinsel or floss that is actually a part of the body but is a dif-

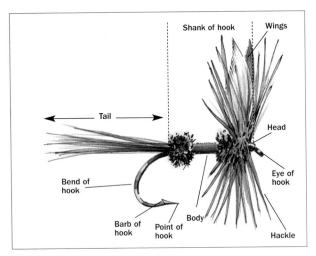

Parts of a typical dry fly and the names of the parts of a hook.

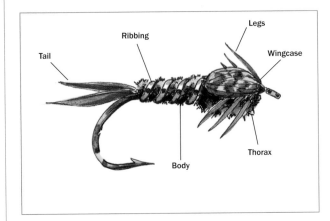

Parts of a nymph.

ish, and then lacquered or epoxied for durability.

Body. The body of a fly is the part that occupies most of the hook shank. Fly bodies can be made from almost any imaginable material, but the most common are fur (or loose synthetic fibers that look like fur), tinsel, wire, nylon or silk floss, wool, plastic, cotton chenille, and spun and clipped deer body hair.

Rib. The rib is a spiral decoration that is sometimes wound around the body. It may imitate the segments of an insect's body or, if made from tinsel, add flash to the body.

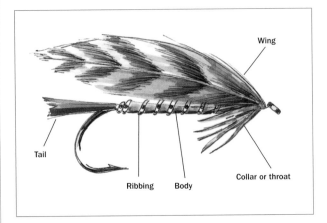

Parts of a feather-winged streamer. Even though the "wing" of the fly is supposed to imitate the back and fins of a baitfish, it's still called a wing.

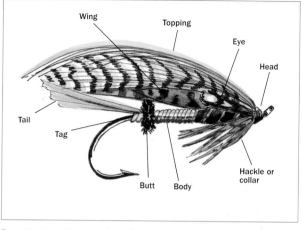

Even though an Atlantic salmon fly is more complicated and has more pieces than a standard fly, the basic parts retain the same names.

An adult mayfly and one imitation used by fishermen to suggest it. Rather than being an exact copy of the insect, the imitation is designed to give a suggestion of the fly as it behaves on the water.

ferent color or material from the rest of the body. The tag is located just in front of or just behind the point where the tail originates. The tag is usually just a decoration, but it may imitate the egg sacs of some insects.

Eyes, cheeks, horns, topping. These are adornments that are commonly found on fancy, complicated streamer or salmon fly patterns. They add nice touches of color to a fly, but their utilitarian value is questionable.

IMITATING INSECTS

Most fly fishing is based on imitating the creatures that fish feed upon. The size, shape, color, and behavior of this food is what we strive to imitate. The plausibility of the first three criteria depends on the fly pattern you use, while the last one depends on the way in which you present your fly.

Most flies used to catch trout and some that are used for bass and panfish are imitations of immature or adult insects. Aquatic insects, the primary source of food for trout, live as larvae underwater. They hatch into winged adults at specific times of year, according to species. When these hatches occur, the insects are extremely vulnerable, so the fish feed with reckless abandon and are quite easy to catch—if you have the right fly pattern.

Mayflies

Mayflies are the genesis of fly fishing. The majority of the flies we use for trout are designed to imitate some stage in

a mayfly's life. Thus, understanding the life cycle of this order of insects is bound to make you a more successful trout angler.

Mayflies are the most common insect in most trout streams and the most important source of food for trout and other stream fish. They are also common in ponds or lakes, but are usually not the main source of food in still waters. Mayflies, like trout, are intolerant of warm or polluted water. The distribution of mayflies throughout the world closely parallels the range of trout, both native and introduced.

Eggs are deposited by adult mayflies by various methods. In streams, the adults usually drop the eggs into the water, and then the eggs sink and fall into crevices on the stream bottom. Many pond insects and some stream dwellers crawl underwater on vegetation and deposit their eggs. The eggs soon hatch into tiny larvae or *nymphs*, which feed on algae and dead plant matter, maturing and growing as the season progresses. Some nymphs burrow into silt on the stream bottom, many varieties cling to the bottoms of rocks, and a few are free-swimming and move like tiny minnows, propelling themselves by expelling water through their abdomens.

Almost exactly one year after they hatched from eggs, the nymphs are ready to hatch. Some species of mayfly may hatch at the same time of day for a few days; others may hatch sporadically throughout the day for almost a month. Just before hatching, the nymphs become restless. Some drift in the current; others clamber around on the

This mayfly nymph, like many species, is a drab olive-brown color. Note the gills along the abdomen, which distinguish it from other aquatic insect larvae.

diately, or it may sit on the surface of the water for a minute or so to expand and dry its wings.

Mayfly nymphs are drab in color, camouflaged against the stream or pond bottom, as are most animals that are preyed on by other animals. Most are olive, brown, tan, or cream in color. The swimming varieties of mayfly are long and skinny, and the species that cling to the bottoms of rocks are flat and wide. Some clamber along bottom debris; in shape this type is halfway between the streamlined swimmers and the flattened clingers. A fourth type burrows in the mud on stream and lake bottoms and has very prominent gills.

All mayfly nymphs have gills along the abdomen. Some have prominent, feathery appendages; in other species the gills are tiny, hair-like filaments that aren't visible without a magnifying glass. Tails are always two or three in number. The legs of mayfly nymphs are often tucked under their bodies when they swim or drift; thus, some artificial nymphs don't even attempt to imitate the legs, or may simulate them with a few fibers of fur that are picked out from the thorax. The wing pads or cases of mayfly nymphs extend across the top of the thorax. Just before hatching, the wing pads become darker and more prominent.

stream bottom and migrate toward the shallows. Then, according to environmental cues that include water temperature and sunlight, the nymphs begin drifting in the current, rising to the surface because of gases that form inside their exoskeletons.

When a mayfly reaches the surface, the exoskeleton splits and a winged form, called a *subimago* or *dun*, crawls out onto the surface film. The adult may fly away imme-

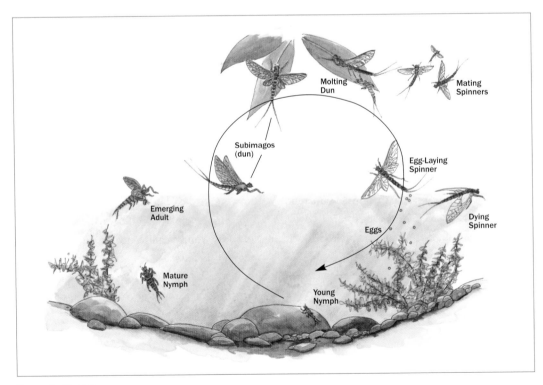

The mayfly life cycle.

Newly hatched mayfly duns have a distinct sailboat-like appearance on the water, and are quite easy to identify. The wings are translucent gray, yellow, or cream, and some species have brown or black mottling. Bodies range in color from almost white to olive, pink, brown, cream, yellow, and black. Mayflies always have two or three slender tails and six delicate legs. Dry-fly imitations usually have more than three hackle fibers for tails and more than six fibers for legs, as nature has the edge in flotation, and

You can tell this mayfly is a spinner by its clear wings and long tails.

we need more materials to keep our hooks on the surface. Harry Darbee, the famous Catskill fly tier, is often quoted as saying, "If the trout could count, we'd all be in trouble."

The adults, if they survive predation by fish and birds, will then fly to streamside brush and molt a final time, changing into the *imago* form, known as the *spinner* stage. The spinners will mate, lay eggs, and die over their parent body of water. Some mayflies mate immediately after hatching, molting in midair, their entire adult stage lasting less than an hour. Most mayflies return to mate within a few days. The life of an adult mayfly is so brief that it doesn't even feed in the adult stage. In fact, their mouth parts are nonfunctional.

After mayfly duns have molted and hatched into spinners, they retain the basic mayfly profile, but colors may change. The wings are transparent, bodies are thinner, and tails are usually longer. Bright yellow or orange egg sacs are often visible in the abdomens of the females. It is by their behavior, though, that spinners are instantly distinguished from duns. While the duns are slow, clumsy

fliers and can be easily captured with a swipe of your hat, spinners are quick fliers and quite agile. Before the mating flights begin, you'll see squadrons of them moving upstream, flying quickly at treetop level with obvious purpose. When mating, they will hover over the water, periodically dipping up and down. These swarms of glistening insects can be so thick that you can barely see the opposite shore.

All of the mayfly stages—nymph, dun, and spinner—are part of a trout's diet when they are available. Because most mayflies do not swim in the current or on the water's surface, but merely drift with it, they are most vulnerable to trout during their hatching stage. Although trout will root nymphs out from under rocks and vegetation, it's a lot of work, and they prefer the easy capture of a nymph drifting in the current or a dun or spinner floating on the surface.

The Sparkle Dun (left), a great imitation for the Hendrickson dun.

Once mayfly nymphs reach maturity, they vary little in size through emergence and mating. Thus, a size-12 nymph will hatch into a size-12 dun, which will molt into a size-12 spinner. Mayflies range in size from a size-6 hook down to a size-28, with most species you'll encounter being sizes 12 through 20.

Colors, however, may vary drastically between life stages. *Ephemerella subvaria*, the species of mayfly anglers call the Hendrickson, has a nymph stage that is brown-olive in overall coloration. The dun has a creamy pink body with medium-gray wings. The spinner has clear wings and a dark reddish-brown body, and the female carries a ball of bright yellow eggs on the end of her abdomen.

Mayfly hatches are predictable not only with regard to the time of year that they'll hatch, but also to the time of day. For example, I know that at 2:00 in the afternoon during the second and third weeks of May on my favorite trout stream, I'll see red-bodied mayflies with gray wings, about size 14, and that they'll hatch for two hours and then stop. I can fish a Hendrickson dry fly, which matches the dun, and catch trout, if I'm lucky, for this two-hour period. I can also catch trout on a Hendrickson nymph an hour prior to the hatch. If it's a warm, clear evening, I'll be able to catch trout on a spinner imitation in the evening, when the flies that hatched yesterday return to lay their eggs.

The Hendricksons will be preceded by, followed by, and overlap with hatches of other aquatic insects. This predictable pattern has been researched and written about in the many entomologies available to the serious trout fisher. The seasonal sequence of hatches will vary with differences in geography and altitude, but in a given section of the country at a given time, you can expect the same hatches year after year.

Many trout streams are so rich in insect life that there is almost always a hatch in progress during the day (few insects hatch after dark), and you may see four or five species hatching at once. Trout can be very selective in their feeding habits, choosing one insect and feeding on it all day long, to the exclusion of all others. That's when the fun begins: By simply watching the trout, or by trial-and-error fly changes, you'll find the fly that is closest to what they're feeding on. Then you're in the ballpark.

Mayfly species vary with each region, but a fly fisher who has a well-stocked fly box can catch trout anywhere in the world. The Blue-Winged Olive dry fly in sizes 14 through 26 will imitate over a dozen species of mayfly in the eastern United States alone, and this fly will also imitate olive-colored mayflies that hatch in Argentina and Chile, New Zealand, England, and the western United States. There are over five hundred species of mayfly in the United States, and to try to achieve a one-to-one correspondence between our imitations and the naturals would be both futile and unnecessary.

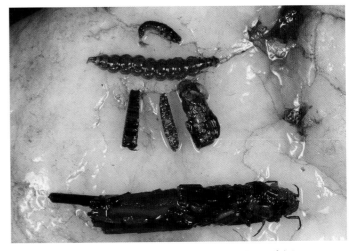

Various caddis larvae from the same riffle show the abundance of these insects in a trout stream. The top two are free-living larvae that don't build cases. The middle three are small species that build cases out of stones. The bottom one is a large species that builds its cases out of sticks and other debris.

Caddisflies

Caddisflies rival mayflies as important food for trout. They also have a larval stage that trout feed on, and some caddis larvae live alongside mayfly nymphs under rocks. Other caddis larvae spin nets that trap food for them. The great majority of caddis larvae, however, build cases from pieces of gravel, sticks, or vegetation. Each species has its own preference as to the type and size of debris it uses for its case, and species of caddis can be identified by the shape of their case or even what size stick or leaf particle they use. The cases serve as protection and as ballast to keep caddis larvae from being swept away in the current. Trout aren't always fooled by caddis camouflage, and if you examine the stomach contents of the fish you've killed, you might find bits of sticks or gravel. You can bet that your trout have been feeding on caddis larvae, or else they've been making a lot of mistakes in their food selection. Trout do make mistakes and pick up a stick or a stone once in a while. If they didn't make mistakes, we'd never catch them.

Unlike mayflies, caddisflies have a stage between the larva and the adult, known as the *pupa* stage. About a week before they hatch, the larvae become inert and change their shape, inside a cocoon that they build around themselves. When the hatch occurs, the pupae cut their way out of the cocoon and rise to the surface. Some species drift great distances; others pop right to the

Trout seem to prefer the caddis pupa to all other stages in a caddisfly's life cycle.

An adult caddis. Note the tent-shaped wings as opposed to the upright wings of a mayfly.

surface. The adult caddisfly emerges from the pupal skin, looking very much like a tiny, drab moth.

Adult caddisflies differ greatly in appearance from mayflies. Their wings are not held upright like tiny sails, but are folded tent-like, parallel to the body of the insect. Caddisflies have long antennae, but lack the slender, delicate tails that characterize mayflies.

Caddisflies range in size from a size-8 hook down to a size-22, with most falling in the 14-through-18 range. Caddisfly hatches exhibit the same seasonal predictability as mayfly hatches and often occur at the same times. Cased caddisfly larvae are almost always white with black heads, while the free-living varieties may be tan, green, or orange. The adults are invariably drab, with tans, browns, and grays predominating, although a few species have bright-green abdomens.

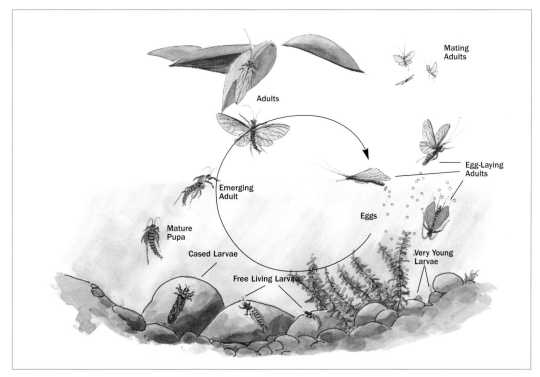

Caddisfly life cycle.

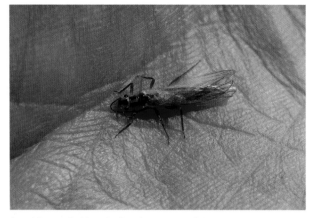

An adult stonefly. Note the flat wings on top of the body.

Two stonefly nymphs. Unlike mayfly nymphs, they do not have feather gills along their abdomen—the gills are on the underside of the thorax.

Caddisfly behavior can be quite different from mayfly behavior. Some species hop, skid, and flutter on the surface of the water. Many leave the water immediately, not even stopping to stretch their wings, as most mayflies do. Some ride the surface of the water sedately for 4 or 5 feet, providing easy meals for the trout and great sport for the dry-fly angler. Caddis adults live for up to a month before they mate and die; thus, they do feed in the adult stage, sipping water and nectar from streamside brush. They often form huge mating swarms at dusk, with battalions of flies moving upstream, bouncing on the water to drop their eggs, and stimulating the trout to feed on the surface.

Stoneflies

Stoneflies are another aquatic insect group that is quite important in a trout's diet. Stonefly nymphs look much like mayfly nymphs, although most species are larger than the average mayfly nymph and have gills under the thorax rather than along the abdomen. Stoneflies have no pupal stage, and the nymphs hatch directly into adults. Most stoneflies do not hatch in the surface film, like caddisflies and mayflies, but crawl onto rocks or logs and then hatch into adults above the water's surface. Thus, although the nymphs are available as trout food, the recently hatched adults don't constitute an important source of trout food unless windy weather blows them back into the stream. Some large stonefly nymphs live for two to three years before they hatch, so they are always available to the fish.

Where mayflies and caddisflies are found in all areas of trout streams and ponds, from fast riffles to weedy bays, stoneflies are invariably found in fast, rocky, highly oxygenated water. The flattened shape of the nymphs reveals their habitat preference, as they are found clinging to the undersides of rocks. Stonefly nymphs are usually dark brown with amber mottling or black, and the adults look exactly like the nymphs, except for the flat wings, which are folded over the body when the insect is at rest.

Stonefly adults, like caddisflies, live for several weeks, subsisting on liquid food, and may fall into the stream on windy days, given that they seldom stray far from the riffle where they hatched. Stonefly mating swarms also make these juicy morsels fair game for hungry trout, as the flies fall spent to the water after mating and egg-laying duties are discharged.

Stoneflies grow larger than mayflies. In fact, the famous salmon fly of western rivers is the largest trout-stream

A swarm of adult midges.

108

During the summer, terrestrial insects become an important part of a trout's diet. Grasshoppers are especially favored by the trout, and by fishermen because their imitations are big and easy to fish.

Crayfish look like tiny lobsters, and trout like them as well as we like their saltwater cousins.

insect and provides a tremendous source of food. Some fly fishers plan their vacations years ahead of time to coincide with the emergence of this fly on the Madison River in late June, because even the largest trout will feed on the surface at this time. Salmon flies may be almost three inches long, imitated by size-2 through 6 hooks, but most stoneflies are in the 8 through12 range. The smallest stoneflies are about a size 18.

Midges

Midges follow a life cycle similar to that of caddisflies: they have a larval, pupal, and adult stage. All three stages are important to trout, the pupal stage being the most important because it drifts in the current. Midge larvae, which look like tiny red, pink, or brown worms, burrow in the silt of lake bottoms or in the slower areas of trout streams. The pupae have a slender abdomen and a bulbous thorax, and the adults have two tiny veined wings and look much like mosquitoes, to which they're closely related.

As might be suggested by their name, most species of midges are quite tiny, sizes 18 to 28, although some are as large as size 14. Despite their tiny size, midges are important trout food because they hatch all year long, and may be the only source of easy food in a trout stream in the middle of winter. In many tailwater rivers (rivers that flow from the cold-water outflow of dams), midges are by far the most important trout food, so despite their diminutive size, you should take them seriously. Trout as large as 10 pounds have been taken on size-22 midge pupa imitations.

Dragonflies and Damselflies

The familiar "darning needles," these brightly colored mosquito predators are much more important in ponds and lakes than they are in streams. The larvae favor slow water, and thus are found only in the still pools of trout streams. The nymphs are quite large (size 4 to 12) and are favorite foods of lake-dwelling trout, bass, and panfish. The adults are usually incidental sources of food for fish, because the nymphs crawl out onto vegetation to hatch.

Terrestrial Insects

When the spring and early-summer hatches of mayflies, caddisflies, and stoneflies dwindle, trout turn to land-bred insects for much of their food. A large trout's explosive rise to a juicy grasshopper is an event to make even the veteran trout fisher tremble. Ants, beetles, leafhoppers, inchworms, crickets, and many other kinds of land-bred insects find their way into the stomach of trout. Terrestrial insects are much more important to trout, bass, and panfish in areas where vegetation overhangs the shore, and on windy days when these insects get blown into the water, the fish will be on the lookout for them.

CRUSTACEANS

In freshwater, scuds, sow bugs, and crayfish are important sources of food for fly-rod quarry. These animals never

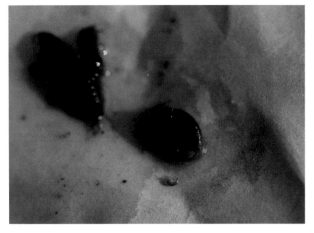

Scuds are small freshwater crustaceans found in rich, weedy trout streams. They provide a high-energy meal for trout and are always in the water because they don't hatch and fly away.

This saltwater baitfish was coughed up by a false albacore after taking the fly above it—pretty close imitation in size and shape.

The blacknose dace is one of the most common baitfish in trout streams.

hatch into winged adults as insects do, so they are available to the fish year-round. Scuds and sow bugs occur in lakes and streams with large expanses of underwater weeds. Scuds look like tiny shrimp, olive or gray in color, while sow bugs look exactly like their gray "pill bug" relatives that live on land. Scuds and sow bugs range from size 10 to 18.

Crayfish, on the other hand, may reach 6 inches in length. They look like miniature lobsters, and apparently gamefish feel the same way about them as humans feel about their larger relatives. Crayfish are found in lakes and streams with clear water and rocky bottoms. They are the number-one food of smallmouth bass where they occur, and are also preferred by large trout.

OTHER INVERTEBRATES

Many other aquatic invertebrates find their way into the stomachs of fish and can be imitated with flies, including leeches, crabs, shrimp, aquatic worms, hellgrammites, aquatic beetles, and even snails.

An understanding of the life cycle of these insects is not essential for success, but it is valuable to know how they behave in the water. In most cases imitations designed for other kinds of animals will work for them. Large black stonefly nymphs, for example, make excellent hellgrammite imitations, and a brown marabou streamer will serve very well when the fish are taking leeches.

FORAGE FISH

Forage fish are small fish that provide food for larger fish. Most freshwater and saltwater gamefish will eat smaller fish; thus, long, skinny imitations of baitfish are essential in anyone's fly box. The most popular forage fish in salt water are menhaden, anchovy, herring, pinfish, pilchards, sand eels, and mullet, all of which are silvery with white bellies and black, blue, or green backs. Freshwater baitfish include the young of most species of gamefish, darters, sculpins, and members of the minnow family like dace and shiners. Saltwater fish also eat eels, up to and including full-grown, 2-foot-long adults. In fact, there is nothing a big striped bass likes better than a big fat eel.

You can usually tell a dry fly (left) from a wet (right) by its full, bushy hackle, although some dry flies are tied without hackle. Wet flies usually also have sparser tails, bigger heads, and are tied on heavier wire hooks.

Sinking and Floating Flies

What's the difference between a dry fly and a wet fly? That is one of the first questions an inquisitive student of fly fishing will ask. Quite simply, a dry fly is designed to float and a wet fly is designed to sink. How?

For a wet fly, the problem is an easy one. All flies are tied on hooks, and hooks are made of metal, which is quite easy to sink. Fly tiers help wet flies sink by tying them on heavy wire hooks and using materials that absorb water quickly. Soft, webby feathers, tinsel, floss, dense synthetics, and most bird feathers absorb water quickly and are essential materials in wet-fly construction. If you want your wet flies to sink very quickly, you can even buy weighted versions. By winding turns of lead or tin wire on the shank of the hook before he ties the fly, a fly tier can make a fly sink quickly. Many nymphs and some saltwater flies are tied using hollow beads or cones that fit over the shank of the hook and are tied in place. The most common materials used are brass and tungsten, and the ones with tungsten sink quicker. "Eyes," made from either metal dumbbell shapes or bead chain, are also added to flies to increase their sink rate.

Most dry flies won't float on their own, or won't float for long without a couple of quick false casts to dry them. Some, made from buoyant cork or plastic or hollow animal body hair, are actually lighter than water, but the delicate insects that most dry flies imitate just cannot be made with these bulky materials. Most dry flies aren't lighter than water, but are pinioned in the surface film, supported by delicate hackle and tails, small amounts of hollow hair like deer or elk hair, and water-repellent furs and synthetics.

Dry flies are tied on hooks made of light wire, and the reduction in weight helps to keep them floating. Many dry flies have stiff, bushy hackle that is wound 360 degrees around the hook. This hackle not only disperses the weight of the fly over a wider area of surface film, but it also increases the air resistance of the fly so it lands lightly. Stiff, shiny rooster hackle floats a fly better than dull, webby hackle, and it is used for both dry-fly hackles and tails. Stiff, hollow deer, elk, or moose hair is also used for tails on dry flies.

Wherever possible we try to use water-repellent materials for dry flies. For bodies, fur or synthetics like polypropylene are better than absorbent wool or floss. Finally, before using dry flies you should spray them with or dip them into some type of dry-fly floatant. These preparations are made from either silicone paste, silicone powder, or silicone with a solvent, and enhance the water-repellent properties of a dry fly.

You can tell most dry flies from wet flies at a glance. Dry flies look light and bushy because of the amount of hackle used; wet-fly hackle is usually sparse and slopes back toward the point of the hook. It's not always so easy, though, because some dry flies are tied without hackle. Their floating properties depend entirely on light wire

Besides traditional trout dry flies, two other types of floating flies are hair bugs (left) and poppers (right).

hooks, stiff tails, bodies tied from water-repellent materials, and a good silicone floatant.

POPPERS AND HAIR BUGS

Unlike true dry flies, poppers and hair bugs are really lighter than water. They fall in that gray area between flies and fly-rod lures, because they come very close in appearance to the plugs that spin and bait casters use, but they're much lighter.

Poppers are hard-bodied cork or plastic bodies that have been cemented to the hook. They are usually painted bright colors, sometimes to imitate frogs and sometimes just in appealing combinations of hues. They may be adorned with hackle, hair, or rubber legs. Poppers may have concave faces, in which case they make loud burps and pops when retrieved, or they can be made with a bullet-shaped head. The bullet-shaped head produces a less-noisy, more subtle disturbance in the water. Both kinds have their place, according to the moods of the fish. Poppers may imitate frogs, mice, or wounded minnows, or they may just be noisy attractors. They are popular with bass, panfish, and pike, and with saltwater fly fishers, who often need to present a large, meaty, noisy fly to interest the fish.

Hair bugs are similar to poppers, being large, noisy, and usually dressed with rubber or hair legs. They are made by spinning hollow deer, caribou, elk, or antelope hair to a hook, often in bands of different colors, and clipping the hair to whatever shape is desired. Hair bugs are porous, so they don't float indefinitely as poppers do, but they are soft and are rejected less quickly once they are grabbed by a fish. Incredibly realistic mice and frog imitations can be made from spun and clipped hair—I once scared a waitress into hysterics with a hair mouse at a Trout Unlimited banquet. Because hair bugs are not as durable as poppers, they are not used for toothy saltwater fish and pike, but are very popular for bass, panfish, and large trout.

DRY FLIES

Dry flies that imitate insects are the most diverse group of flies you'll see offered through a catalog or at a fly shop.

The Adams, a traditional dry fly with hackle and upright wings, has been the most popular dry fly in the world for over thirty years.

There is a good reason for this: Trout are selective feeders, which means that they often pick out one type of insect, find out that it's good to eat, and ignore insects that don't have its shape, size, and color. It is usually the insect that is most abundant on the water, regardless of size. Thus, a trout may feed on size-18 mayflies, ignoring larger juicy mayflies that are on the water at the same time. This selectivity may last for an hour or so, or it may last for weeks, depending on the relative abundance of the insect and how long it hatches. The dry-fly fisher must be prepared to switch flies to accommodate the whims of surface-feeding trout. He's always looking for a dry fly that will work all the time, and thus, each year fly tiers come out with new lines of flies, much like the annual unveiling of Detroit's latest offerings.

This Parachute Pheasant Tail shows the horizontal hackle indicative of these patterns. The fly floats low in the water but is very stable and highly visible.

The Comparadun is one type of dry fly made without hackle. The wing is made from deer hair, which helps keep the fly afloat.

Of course, merely changing the body color of a fly creates a new pattern, and the list of dry-fly types is almost endless. They can, however, be lumped in groups, depending on the construction of the fly or what it's supposed to imitate.

Traditional dry flies. Traditional dry flies are the most versatile of all the types of dry flies. Their construction has changed little in the past seventy-five years. They rely on stiff tails and hackle for flotation. Traditional dry flies were originally tied to imitate adult mayflies, and their wings are tied upright, at a 90-degree angle to the body, to simulate the distinctive upright wing of a mayfly sitting on the water. Some traditional flies leave the wings

A delicate spinner pattern, an imitation of a mayfly spinner that has mated and fallen spent to the surface.

off and rely on hackle to give the impression of both the legs and the sparkle of an adult mayfly's wings.

Parachutes. Parachutes feature a single upright wing with hackle wound around its base, parallel to the hook shank rather than perpendicular to it. Parachutes land lightly and float well. Some fly fishers believe they look more realistic to the fish than flies with standard hackle. They are perhaps the most useful type of dry fly, as they work effectively in fast water or slow, they are easy to see, and they seem to be able to imitate both a mayfly dun

Types of down-wing dry flies. An elk-wing caddis (top), a big Stimulator stonefly imitation (left), and a more delicate feather-wing caddis imitation.

and spinner. The Parachute Adams is the most popular dry fly in the world.

No-hackles, thorax flies, and Comparaduns. The need for an exact adult mayfly imitation under very clear, flat water conditions when trout can look over your fly closely has spawned these innovations in dry-fly construction. The theory is that trout key into the silhouette of a mayfly's wings and body, and hackle obscures this silhouette. These flies utilize little or no hackle, relying on stiff tails, water-repellent fur or synthetic fiber bodies, a good floatant, and light wire hooks for flotation. They are extremely effective for picky surface-feeding trout but do not float well in broken water; however, trout are seldom as selective in fast water, because they can't see your fly as well as on a smooth, unbroken surface.

Spentwings. Spentwings are imitations of mayflies or caddisflies that have fallen spent to the surface of the water after mating. Their wings, rather than being upright as in a freshly hatched fly, lie outstretched in the

Grasshoppers (top), beetles (bottom left), and ants (bottom right) are just some of the terrestrial insects you can imitate with flies.

Four imitations of emerging insects. Clockwise from top left: An emerging mayfly imitation with a buoyant snowshoe rabbit's foot wing, a caddis pupa imitation with a foam body, an emerging mayfly with hackle-tip wings, and a large emerging mayfly with deer hair for the head and wing.

surface film. They are sometimes tied without hackle, or with hackle that is clipped on the top and bottom so they float low in the surface film, just like the naturals.

Down-wings. Unlike mayflies, caddisflies and stoneflies float with their wings parallel to their bodies, instead of upright and perpendicular to them. Down-wings are tied with wings of feather or hair that are tied down along the body of the fly. These flies can be delicate, like those used to imitate tiny caddisflies, or huge, like the big size-6 and -8 "meat flies" used on western rivers as attractors.

Terrestrials. These are imitations of ants, beetles, inchworms, grasshoppers, crickets, and leafhoppers—

land-bred insects that accidentally fall into the water. Terrestrial imitations aren't always easy to identify as dry flies, because they lack the bushy appearance of flies that are designed to imitate aquatic insects. Land-bred insects don't have the delicate buoyancy of aquatic insects. They plop into the water and float low in the surface film, so the imitations need little or no hackle; you want them to land in a clumsy manner and to float low in the water.

Midges. The term "midge" generally refers to any dry fly size 20 or smaller, but this is technically incorrect, because there are many tiny mayfly, caddisfly, and terrestrial species that are imitated by small dry flies. Midges tied to imitate the order of the aquatic insects called midges are extremely simple flies, consisting of a few turns of sparse hackle and a thin fur body. They should float right in the surface film, as most midges are taken as they emerge. Midges tied to imitate tiny mayflies add a few hackle fibers for tails, but they usually don't have wings, either. Tiny ants and beetles, miniature versions of terrestrials, are also tied and are quite effective on midsummer days.

Emergers and floating nymphs. These are a cross between nymphs and dry flies, designed to drift just under the surface or in the surface film. During a hatch, aquatic insects will drift just under the surface, trying to break through the film and shed their nymphal skins at the same time. Trout often hold just under the surface, refusing both high, floating dry flies and sunken nymphs,

A standard size 14 Adams dry fly, top, with a tiny midge adult imitation.

This Adams Wulff has a bulky body, heavy hackle, and big white wings. It's highly visible to both fish and fisherman and is a favorite in rough water.

The Irresistible is a big hair-bodied dry fly that floats like a cork because the body is made from hollow deer hair. It is easy to see on the water and shows a big mouthful to the trout.

accepting only those flies that are barely submerged. Emergers and floating nymphs have the body color and shape of the nymph that is emerging and short, embryonic wings made of feathers, or small balls of fur, hair, foam, or many kinds of synthetic materials. Because emergers imitate the most vulnerable stage of an insect's life (and trout know it), during a hatch they are often far more effective than a dry fly. Emergers can be tied to imitate mayflies, caddisflies, stoneflies, or midges.

Hair-winged flies. Hair-winged flies are robust, bushy dry flies that use durable hair for wings and tails. They float extremely well and are most often used in fast, broken water. These flies are extremely valuable for "fishing the water," which is fishing a dry fly in a likely place when no fish are visibly feeding.

A variant fly has longer hackle and tails than normal and imitates an insect fluttering on the surface.

Hair-bodied flies. Hair-bodied flies are dry flies made from spun and clipped hollow deer or antelope hair. They are tied with lots of bushy hackle and usually with hair wings and tails. Hair-bodied flies, because of the air trapped in the body, are the one type of dry fly that is actually lighter than water, and will float in the roughest of water. Excellent for fishing the water, they are a little too bulky and robust for imitating delicate mayflies during a hatch, but their large, juicy profile will often catch the attention of fish in foamy water that would hide a sparsely tied traditional dry fly.

Variants and spiders. Variants are traditional dry flies but with longer tails and hackle than on traditional dry flies. Whereas traditional dries have tails and hackle that are one and a half to two hook sizes in length, variants

Bivisibles are made entirely from hackle and float very well.

have hackle and tails that are equivalent to a dry fly that is one hook size larger. The long hackle and tail increase both the air resistance and flotation of variants. Spiders are dry flies with very long, stiff, bushy hackle and tiny hooks. They are usually tied on a size-14 or 16 hook, with hackle the diameter of a silver dollar, and most often without bodies or tails. Spiders are fished with manipulation by the angler, "skated" across the water. They are an interesting option when no other fly will work, but often result in short strikes or fish refusing the fly at the last minute. Some fly fishers use spiders to locate large fish, returning later with more conventional flies. Because the variants and spiders land softly and float very well, they are an excellent choice for the beginning fly caster. Because variants float high on the water, some anglers believe that the fish take them for insects that are fluttering above the water. Variants are almost always tied without wings.

At the time of this writing (in 2006), variants and spiders were nearly impossible to find, as they've gone out of vogue. However, I tie my own and use them often, and you might be able to find a sympathetic local fly tier to make some for you (or maybe they'll come back in style).

Bivisibles. Bivisibles are flies that consist entirely of hackle. The hook shank is wound with hackle, usually brown or gray, with a few turns of cream or white hackle at the head. The light-colored hackle at the head makes bivisibles easy to see on the water—thus, the name. Bivisibles are great floaters and, like variants, are probably taken for fluttering insects by fish. Like spiders and variants, they are nowhere near as popular as they were a few decades ago.

SINKING FLIES

Wet flies, nymphs, streamers, most salmon flies, most steelhead flies, and most saltwater flies are designed to sink. They are generally tied with absorbent materials and present a thinner profile than dry flies, as the bulkier or fuzzier a fly is, the more resistance it will offer to the water.

Wet flies. Wet flies are the original flies; all other sinking and floating flies are recent innovations compared to the wet fly. Nymphs were developed in the twentieth century to be more exact imitations of aquatic insects, streamers to be representative of baitfish, and dry flies couldn't be developed until hook technology provided a fine wire hook that could be floated when dressed with the proper materials.

What does the traditional wet fly imitate? Emerging aquatic insects possibly, at times small minnows, and perhaps at times wet flies just trigger something unexplainable in a fish that says "food." Fishing with a wet fly is probably the least scientific way to fly-fish, but at times it's extremely productive, especially when trout are taking insects at the moment they reach the surface and unfold their wings.

The difference between a wet fly and a nymph is merely that a wet fly has wings that lie sloping back over the whole body, like an emerging mayfly, and nymphs have a small wing case that is folded over half of the

A traditional wet fly, left, and a soft-hackle wet fly.

Mayfly nymphs. Clockwise from top left: A Bead-Head Pheasant Tail Nymph, an imitation of a swimming mayfly (burrowing type), a Zug Bug, a copper-bodied imitation of a small mayfly, and a Troutmaster.

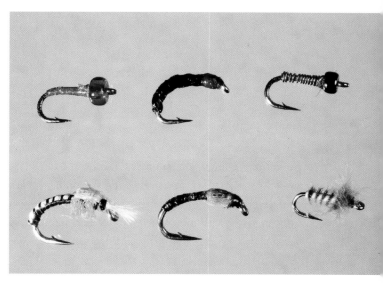

Various caddis nymphs. The three on the top are imitations of caddis pupae, and the three on the bottom are of caddis larvae. The first two larva imitations are of free-swimming caddis larvae that do not build cases, and the third one is an imitation of a type that does build cases from rocks and sticks.

Tiny midge nymphs. The top row are three that imitate the larvae, and the bottom row are pupa imitations.

Three stonefly nymph imitations.

Four different scud imitations. The first three imitate the natural color of the live insect; the pink one imitates a dead scud, as trout often pick up dead ones drifting in the current.

body, like a mayfly that is not yet ready to hatch. Some very simple nymphs and wet flies don't have wings or wing cases, just a fur body and few turns of soft hackle at the head.

Nymphs. Nymphs come in all shapes and sizes, and may imitate animals other than immature insects. Besides mayfly, stonefly, and caddisfly nymphs, artificial nymphs may imitate crustaceans such as scuds, sow bugs, crayfish, or even leeches. A nymph is generally considered to be any sinking fly that is a fairly specific imitation of an aquatic animal other than a minnow.

Thus, for every species of insect or crustacean that fly fishers feel is important as fish food, there is a nymph pattern.

You may have heard of bead head or tunghead nymphs, with brass beads or tungsten beads attached to the head of the nymph. These flies get below the surface even quicker than a nymph weighted with wire, and offer a sparkle in the water that seems to attract trout from long distances. Bead heads and tungheads are merely a style of nymph, and most popular nymph patterns can also be purchased in these versions.

Bead head nymphs. All sink quickly because of the brass or tungsten beads, and add a little flash that seems to attract trout.

Four different kinds of streamers. Clockwise from top left: A featherwing Black Ghost, a Muddler Minnow, a Mickey Finn bucktail, and a Woolly Bugger.

But take heart—you don't need thousands of different fly patterns to catch fish on nymphs. A general representation of the shape, size, and color of whatever the fish are feeding on is all you'll need in most cases. The Bead Head Hare's Ear nymph, for example, the most popular nymph pattern in North America, is probably taken by trout at various times for a mayfly nymph, stonefly nymph, caddis larva, caddis pupa, dragonfly nymph, scud, and even a small crayfish.

Nymphs have the potential to be the most useful flies a trout fisher has in his box, because there are nymphs available in a trout stream or pond twelve months a year. Dry flies are mostly useless to the angler unless there are insects hatching in such numbers to interest the trout in surface food, and even during a hatch when the fish are feeding on the surface, they also take nymphs below the surface.

Streamers, bucktails, buggers, sculpins, and leeches. These are long, skinny flies that are tied to be baitfish, leech, or crayfish imitations, or perhaps just "lures," as the English call them. Sometimes all of them are lumped into a general bucket called "streamers." Streamers proper were developed when anglers found that long, skinny chicken hackles tied on a hook would catch fish that were feeding on smaller fish. It is generally thought that the modern streamer fly was first used around the turn of the twentieth century in Maine to imitate the smelt that landlocked salmon feed on, but research in

fly-fishing literature has proven that English fly fishers were catching saltwater fish on feathered lures fifty years earlier. You can go one step further and use a marabou streamer, which has a wing made from soft, downy feathers from under the wing of a turkey. Marabou breathes and pulsates in the water, and often excites gamefish.

Bucktails are streamers tied with hair instead of feather wings. The Black Ghost bucktail (one of my favorites) is exactly the same as the Black Ghost streamer, except that the wing is made of the white hair from a deer's tail instead of white hackle feathers. Bucktail makes a more durable wing than hackles, but it doesn't have as much action in the water. I like to use bucktails in fast water, reserving the more lively hackled streamers for slow streams and lakes.

Buggers are simply flies with fuzzy hackle and flowing tails. They may imitate leeches, crayfish, baitfish, damselfly larvae, and who knows what else. They just work. The Woolly Bugger is the most popular fly in the world, period, and will catch almost any gamefish that swims in fresh or salt water

The addition of a spun-and-clipped deer-hair head and collar to a streamer or bucktail produces an important variation called a muddler or sculpin. The original Muddler Minnow was tied this way to simulate the flat, blunt head and wide pectoral fins of a bottom-dwelling baitfish called a sculpin, which is a favorite food of large trout and bass. The muddler, usually tied weighted or fished on a sinking line to keep it where sculpins dwell, has accounted for more large trout than any other fly in the past forty years. The deer-hair head appears to produce some kind of vibration in the water, and Muddlers are excellent flies even when the water is dirty and visibility limited. Muddlers or Sculpins can be tied with wings of hackle, hair, or marabou—the effectiveness of the fly doesn't seem to be affected so long as it incorporates that deer-hair head. Sometimes a bunch of yarn is substituted for deer hair, but it does not seem to be quite as effective.

Leeches are simple flies, typically with just a fuzzy body and a long, flowing tail. They of course imitate leeches, a favorite trout food, but may just act as attractors. Leeches are more common in lakes and ponds, so these flies are very popular in still waters.

SALMON FLIES

Atlantic and Pacific salmon are born in freshwater rivers, grow fat in the ocean or large lakes, and return to their natal rivers to spawn. They do not need to feed for nourishment on their spawning runs, but will occasionally take worms, aquatic insects, minnows—and flies.

There are many theories as to why Atlantic salmon take flies. A logical explanation is that salmon have a ves-

Atlantic salmon flies, like these full-dress featherwings, can be gorgeous creations.

tigial, instinctive memory of feeding in rivers when they were young, and our flies trigger a reflex. An old salmon angler in Nova Scotia once told me, "Your fly's getting in the way; they don't like anything getting in the way when they're moving, so they swat it with their mouth." That would certainly explain why salmon take flies more readily when they're moving than when they're resting.

Regardless, Atlantic salmon do take flies. Where most trout won't move more than a few inches to feed, an Atlantic salmon may come from 10 feet away to inhale a large wet fly. It doesn't make sense, but it's a lot of fun.

Most Atlantic salmon fishing is done with large wet flies or streamers that are attractors in the purest sense of the word. The bodies of these flies may be richly embellished with brightly colored floss, hackle, and tinsel for visibility in fast rivers. Two basic kinds of wet flies are used: *feather wings* and *hairwings*. The feather wings are older, traditional European patterns and may incorporate from one to twenty different kinds of feathers. In addition, simpler salmon feather-wing flies called Spey flies, with long, flowing hackles, have become very popular, probably due to a combination of both their beauty and their action in the water. Hairwings are simpler, more durable flies, and many salmon anglers feel they are just as effective. Hair seems to have a more lifelike action in the water, so many fly tiers duplicate the classic feather-wing patterns with hair by substituting dyed hair for the less-durable feathers.

Tube flies, originally used on European salmon rivers and in Iceland, are becoming more popular every year. They are thin plastic tubes (the size that hold ink in ballpoint pens) dressed with bucktail, feathers, or synthetic materials. A tube is threaded onto your leader, then a hook (usually a double hook) is tied to the leader, and the tube is pushed over the eye of the hook. Tube flies are ridiculously simple, but they offer the advantage of a large fly without adding a lot of weight to make casting difficult.

When Atlantic salmon rivers warm to over 60 degrees, dry flies can be effective, at least on North American rivers. For some reason, salmon seldom rise to dry flies on European rivers. Salmon dry flies are large, and because of the necessary heavy hook they are tied with lots of bushy hackle or deer-hair bodies. Most of them are merely oversized versions of fast-water trout dry flies.

Flies for steelhead and Pacific salmon can include colorful wet flies like the Thor (top), egg imitations (bottom left), or big nymphs (bottom right).

Nearly all salmon dry flies, such as the Salmon Muddler, Salmon Hornberg, and Buck Bug, are designed to be fished "damp"—that is, in the surface film or just under the surface. These flies are skimmed across the surface, and are often tried as a last resort when the salmon are sulking.

During low-water conditions salmon seem to be frightened by large flies. Low-water flies are sparsely tied wet flies that occupy half to three-quarters of the hook shank. The advantage is that a relatively small fly can be presented on a hook large enough to hold a big salmon. Sparsely tied nymphs, similar to trout nymphs, are also used during low-water conditions.

You'll see some salmon wet flies tied on double hooks. Double hooks offer no real hooking or holding advantage, but add weight and thus are used when you want to fish a salmon fly in deep or fast water. Weighted flies are illegal in most salmon rivers, because it's easy to illegally snag a salmon with a weighted fly (even double hooks are illegal on some rivers). Some salmon anglers also believe that double hooks keep the fly riding upright in faster water. Salmon seem to prefer a fly that is presented broadside to them, and double hooks ensure this profile in tumbling currents.

Pacific salmon rise to flies less readily than Atlantic salmon, but they take flies well, especially when they are fresh, or have just ascended a river. Most Pacific salmon are taken on large, brightly colored streamer flies or oversized steelhead flies. Once they have been in a river for a few days, they can even be taken on nymphs and egg flies.

STEELHEAD FLIES

Steelhead are large, migratory rainbow trout that feed in the ocean or large freshwater lakes. Like salmon, they migrate into rivers to spawn. Unlike salmon, steelhead feed occasionally. Where Pacific salmon spawn in the same rivers as steelhead, the steelhead may follow the salmon and feed on their eggs, which are bright orange-red. Most steelhead are caught on large wet flies that incorporate some red or orange or purple in their dressings. At times, darker, less-colorful flies will also entice steelhead, and nymphs are often used with great success.

Most of what has been said about salmon flies applies to steelhead. Tube flies, Spey flies, and all of the popular salmon flies can be used effectively for steelhead. In addition, egg flies are deadly for steelhead.

Dry-fly fishing for steelhead can be successful, especially in summer, when the rivers are low, warm, and clear. Most dry-fly fishing for steelhead is done with patterns that ride in the surface film, such as muddler-type flies.

BASS FLIES

Largemouth and smallmouth bass were being caught on flies long before plastic worms, spinner baits, and plugs were developed. Early bass flies were large, gaudy wet flies—oversized versions of flies used for brook trout.

Most modern bass flies are either brightly colored attractors or imitations of such large forage as crayfish, minnows, or frogs. Poppers and hair bugs are used as surface lures, as well as some Muddler-type streamers that float just under the surface. Bass flies are often tied with monofilament weed guards or on keel hooks so that they can be slithered over logs and through weed beds without hanging up. When bass are in deep water, streamers or leech imitations fished near the bottom with sinking or sink-tip lines may save an otherwise fishless day.

Just like trout, smallmouth bass will feed on aquatic insects. I always take along a box of trout dry flies and nymphs when smallmouth fishing, although smallmouths

Flies for bass, panfish, and pike should include both big poppers (lower left) sinking flies with lots of action (upper left), and smaller flies for panfish (right), although large bass have been known to eat small panfish flies.

aren't as selective as trout, and a little popper twitched near their feeding stations may make them forget the insects.

PANFISH FLIES

Sunfish, perch, crappie, and other warm-water panfish can be caught with a wide variety of flies. Small versions of bass bugs and sponge-rubber bugs with rubber legs are very effective for bluegill and other sunfish, and standard trout flies, especially terrestrial dry-fly imitations, are useful at times. Many panfish feed on aquatic insects, crustaceans, and small baitfish, so standard trout nymphs and streamers can come in handy.

A properly presented fly is a most efficient way to catch panfish on artificials, because only a fly rod can deliver the tiny artificial lures that mimic the small foods these popular fish eat.

PIKE, PICKEREL, AND MUSKELLUNGE FLIES

These voracious predators feed on large minnows, frogs, and even ducklings and young muskrats. Flies used for these species should be large and flashy, and the most effective kinds are large bass flies and poppers or saltwater

flies. To my knowledge, there are no standard patterns tied specifically for pike, pickerel, or muskellunge, but so long as your fly is big and moving quickly, a hungry pike or pickerel is an easy mark. Muskellunge are caught infrequently on flies—but muskies are rarely caught on any kind of bait or lure.

SALTWATER FLIES

Although saltwater fish have been taken on flies for over a hundred years, this field of fly fishing is still wide open in terms of possibilities for new fly patterns. Most saltwater fish feed on baitfish, crustaceans like shrimp and crabs, or squid, so the selection of flies is quite simple.

Saltwater flies can be lumped into three categories: large, simple streamers, which may be attractors or baitfish and squid imitations; poppers, for surface-feeding fish; and bonefish and permit flies, which are imitations of crab and shrimp and look much like large versions of trout nymphs. Saltwater flies can be instantly recognized because they are always tied on nickel-plated or stainless-steel hooks.

Saltwater streamers are tied with simple tinsel or epoxied-thread bodies and wings of bucktail, hackle feathers, or artificial (nylon) hair. The most popular colors are blue and white, green and white, or all white, because saltwater baitfish such as menhaden, herring, and mullet have white bellies and green or blue backs. Other saltwater streamers, used as attractors, are tied in combinations of red, yellow, and white. They should be tied

Saltwater baitfish imitations: An Epoxy Minnow (top), a Clouser Minnow (middle), and a Lefty's Deceiver (bottom).

Saltwater poppers are usually bigger than freshwater poppers and are tied on stainless hooks to resist corrosion.

with the most durable materials possible, because most saltwater fish have impressive dental work. The heads and bodies should be given at least two coats of epoxy cement.

Saltwater poppers come in the same color combinations as streamers. They are designed to make a lot of noise when retrieved, imitating either a baitfish skipping across the surface of the water or the sound of other fish feeding on the baitfish. They can be made from heavily painted cork or high-density foam.

Bonefish and permit flies are tied for these bottom feeders, as well as other fish that pick crabs and shrimp off the bottom, like redfish, sea trout, and striped bass. They are designed to sink quickly, so that they can be placed near the bottom in front of a feeding fish. Most patterns are tied upside down, to ride with the hook point facing up, and won't catch on the bottom when retrieved. The

An assortment of crabs and shrimp that washed up on the beach where striped bass were feeding, as well as some flies to imitate them.

bucktail or nylon hairwings imitate the legs and tentacles of crustaceans streaming behind them as they scoot from one spot to the next.

SHAD FLIES

Shad, like salmon, live in salt water and spawn in freshwater rivers. When they're on the move, they will take brightly colored wet flies fished just off the bottom. Shad flies are usually just a floss or tinsel body with a hair tail, tied sparsely so that they sink quickly. After their spawning duties are completed, shad will feed on aquatic insects before they return to the ocean and can even be taken with dry flies during heavy mayfly or caddisfly hatches.

Don't be afraid to cross the boundaries between a fly that is meant for one kind of fish or another—and by all means, try flies for fish not mentioned here. The walleye, a superb food and game fish, will take streamer flies and poppers. Bass will take saltwater flies, as will large trout and salmon. Steelhead will take salmon flies, and salmon will take steelhead flies. And one of the secret flies of many professional trout guides is a Clouser Minnow, perhaps the most popular saltwater fly ever developed. Versatility is an important part of our next topic—fly selection.

{ One Last Look—Rainbow }

Chapter Seven

Fly Selection

THE FIRST RULE OF FLY SELECTION is that there are no rules. There is never a right or a wrong fly—only flies that work better than others under certain conditions.

One evening last spring I was fishing a favorite stretch of flat water on a local trout stream that is known for its selective brown trout. I was unusually successful with a dry fly that I had just developed, and throughout the evening I could see two of my friends above me and one below, all apparently doing as well as I was, judging by the frequent bends in their rods. We gathered on the bank after dark.

"You guys must have discovered my secret pattern," I said as they viewed my new creation by flashlight.

"Wasn't even using a dry," said one. "This nymph did the trick for me."

I wouldn't take this fly box with me on a trout-fishing trip. This one is full of flies for striped bass. And on any given day, just a few of these flies might work, but if the fish are really feeding, every fly in the box might result in a strike.

"I was using a standard Sulphur," said the third.

The fourth angler was using a wet fly that resembled none of the other flies.

So much for my secret pattern.

If you're going on a trip to unfamiliar waters, consult fly-fishing magazines and books, which often have lists of flies that are suggested for particular areas. You can also check out relevant websites; most fishing lodges and outfitters post recommended flies for their areas, or you can go into one of the news groups and ask for suggestions—you'll get plenty. Call ahead or visit the tackle shop nearest your destination—the managers or owners of such places are usually eager give you a list of fly patterns for the region and may have one or two local favorites that

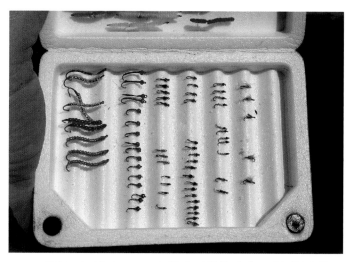

It's important to be prepared with the right flies before a trip. This is the fly box I use in streams with lots of midge larvae and aquatic worms.

can't be obtained anywhere else (buying some flies also might garner some good advice).

Approach fly selection as a challenge rather than a chore. Finding the right fly through experimentation is one of the greatest satisfactions of fly fishing. Remember—the worst thing that can happen is you won't catch any fish.

There are two opposing philosophies on fly selection: the *imitationist*, who believes that with the correct fly you can solve all fishing problems, and the *presentationist*, who believes that any old fly will work so long as it's presented in the proper manner. The most prudent choice is to take the middle of the road.

You can also divide flies into arbitrary groups: attractors and imitators. The latter are those flies that are designed to mimic a specific kind of fish food, like the deer-hair mouse used by bass fishers. Attractors are not designed to imitate specific kinds of food, at least not to our eyes. Though attractors are usually brightly colored and outlandishly large, the fish may take them for something in nature, seeing them in a different light.

Take the Royal Wulff dry fly. With its green peacock herl and red rayon-floss body, plus white wings, it doesn't look like anything in nature. But wait until it gets wet. Peacock herl when wet turns a bronze-olive color, and red rayon floss turns dark brown. What we now have is a brownish fly with a narrow waist and two bulbs at each end. Something like an ant, maybe? The fish might think so.

My point is that fish don't put things in their mouth out of playfulness, anger, curiosity, or boredom. They don't have these emotions. They put things in their mouth so that they can obtain enough energy to spawn and pass their genes along to the next generation.

Fish take attractor flies out of reflex. If a fly is brightly colored, it may stand out more, catching the fish's attention first. Brightly colored attractor flies are used a lot in sterile environments where a fish will attack anything that resembles food. Bright colors catch their attention quicker than muted tones that fade into the background.

Fish take their prey—and thus, our flies—either by sitting and waiting for the current to bring food to them, or by actively pursuing or ambushing their prey. The first feeding strategy occurs only in flowing waters and is characteristic of trout, grayling, landlocked salmon, smallmouth bass, and sometimes saltwater fish in strong tidal currents. Fish may also actively pursue their prey in stream currents, but they *must* ambush prey in still waters. Saltwater fish chasing a school of baitfish, a pike spearing a frog off the surface of a still pond, and a trout cruising for mayflies on the surface of the lake are common examples of ambushers. Of course, bass and trout in streams may also ambush their prey, but the energy expended in chasing the food and fighting the current must be balanced by the calories obtained. Fish, by some marvel of instinct, are quite good at judging this energy balance.

Fish that are actively pursuing prey are far less critical of your fly selection than those who are using the sit-and-wait strategy. The ambusher takes his food when he can get it, never knowing when his next meal might stumble by. The drift-feeding trout has an almost constant supply of food passing overhead, in what a fish-ecologist friend of mine calls "the buffet in the restaurant," his expression for the current bringing food to trout in a stream. Trout don't always

The Royal Wulff, a bulky variation of the Royal Coachman, does not look like anything in nature to us, but it must to the trout.

Fish don't always take their prey in a delicate, passive manner, as you can see with this school of false albacore chasing baitfish.

feed selectively from the buffet, but when they do, you'd better pay attention not only to what insect they're taking, but also to what stage—nymph, dun, spinner, pupa, or emerger.

When trout are actively feeding they give us clues. The most obvious clue is called the *rise*, which occurs when the fish takes an insect off the surface of the water. The rise may be a violent splash, subtle concentric rings in the water with a few bubbles beside them, or merely the head, back, and tail of a fish gently porpoising above the surface. Each of these rises gives us clues as to what fly we should use.

The classic rise occurs when you see an unhurried dimple in the water that leaves a few bubbles behind. This occurs when a trout takes an insect that is resting on top of the water. It may be a mayfly dun, caddis adult, or stonefly, but the unhurried rise indicates that the insect is sitting sedately on the water and the trout knows he has an easy mark. In ponds and lakes the rise will form even, concentric circles;

in a stream, the current distorts the rise into a sharp wedge.

The splashy rise occurs either when the insect is actively fluttering across the surface of the water or when the trout is in fast current. Either way, the fish has to make a quick decision, and the splash gives away his haste. Be careful, though. When a splashy rise occurs without the accompanying bubbles on the surface of the water, your fish may have taken an insect just under the surface. The reason: When a trout takes an insect from the surface of the water, he rises to the top, opens his mouth, and lets the current drop in the insect. When the fish closes his mouth, he expels through his gills the air he took in along with the insect; hence, the telltale bubbles. The splash without bubbles happens when a fish rises quickly to take an insect just below the surface. His momentum may carry his back or tail above the surface, but because he opened his mouth underwater, there won't be any bubbles.

Here's the whole story: A cloud of mayfly spinners in the air and a nice rise in the foreground. If you look closely at the rise, you can see bubbles, indicating that this trout took a fly from the surface.

Splashy rises with bubbles often indicate a trout feeding on adult caddisflies, which skid across the surface of the water, large mayflies that hop and flutter on the water, or a big terrestrial insect like a grasshopper that is trying to oar its way back to land. Splashy rises without bubbles indicate an emerging caddisfly pupa or mayfly nymph.

A third, often misleading type of rise is the smutting or dimpling rise. Usually all you will see is a tiny dimple in the surface of the water, but occasionally you'll also see the back and dorsal fin of the fish behind the rise. This type of rise characterizes fish feeding on either tiny midges, mayflies, or terrestrials, and fish taking spent mayflies or caddisflies that are pinioned in the surface film. Either way, the food is lying flush *in* the film, not on top of the water, like newly hatched mayflies or caddisflies. Emerging insects that are having trouble breaking through the surface tension of the water may also produce this kind of rise. The smutting rise may hide a trout of substantial size, as a big fish can just barely poke his snout above the surface and leave a tiny disturbance.

When fish are feeding below the surface of the water, there are also clues, albeit less obvious ones. Unless the fish are feeding just under the surface, in which case they might leave a swirl with no bubbles, the water must be clear and relatively slow with an unbroken surface for you to see the clues.

Most subsurface feeding happens when a fish is resting his head on the stream bottom or hanging in the current. As a nymph drifts by, he'll merely tip his fins to move for the fly, open his mouth, and let the current wash it in—lazy and efficient, leaving no splashes, no flashes, no clues. If you can't spot the fish camouflaged against the bottom, as in broken or deep water, you'll never even know where he is, much less that he's feeding on something. Subsurface trout fishing involves a lot of guesswork.

You may have heard that flashes below the surface of the water reveal a trout taking nymphs. The flashes occur when a fish turns on his side to dislodge nymphs from the stream bottom, but unfortunately most of the time these flashes indicate suckers or whitefish, which feed this way much more often than trout. Trout prefer to intercept drifting nymphs in the current rather than grub around on the bottom, although they will sometimes root for caddisfly larvae or crayfish.

The other often-written-about-but-seldom-seen phenomenon is the tailing trout. If a trout is rooting in shallow water, standing on his head, his tail may wiggle or wave above the water. The only time I ever saw this was in a shallow, weedy stream where the trout were rooting for sow bugs and scuds in the vegetation.

Trout and other fish feeding on large forage like minnows and crayfish may also leave characteristic water dis-

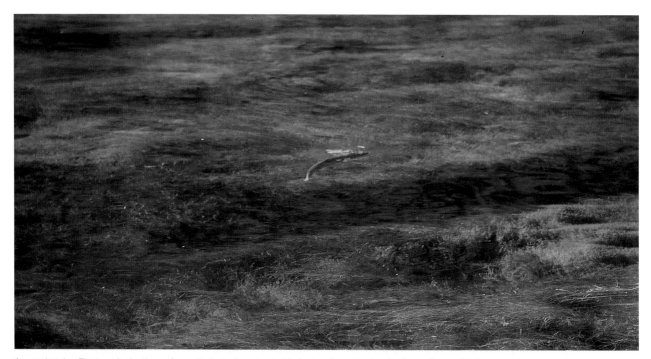

A smutting rise. The trout broke the surface with its back, but probably took an insect just under the surface—a job for an emerger pattern.

turbances. One type is a bulge in the current, accompanied by a quick flash as the fish turns to take a minnow. Another type, usually seen at dawn or dusk, is a torpedo-like wake streaking through the shallows, sometimes with tiny minnows jumping out of the water in front of the wake.

SIZE, SHAPE, AND COLOR

Whenever possible, you should try to determine what the fish are feeding on and pick the fly in your box that most closely resembles the natural food. That's fairly obvious, but which is most important—size, shape, or color?

Size in fly fishing refers to the length of the fly. In most cases it is the most important characteristic for matching natural foods. Experienced saltwater fly rodders say that any color streamer will work when fish like blues or stripers are chasing bait, but if it's an inch or two larger

It's as important to have an assortment of sizes in a fly you trust as it is to have lots of patterns. This is my favorite caddis dry fly, the Eck Caddis, and I carry it (from top) in sizes 12, 14, 16, 18, and 20. As well as imitating many species of caddis, I use the biggest size when moths are on the water and the smallest sizes to imitate adult midges.

or smaller than the baitfish, it will be ignored. There are days on salmon rivers when all the fish will be taken on different patterns but on the same size fly. Trout will often refuse a size-14 fly but eagerly accept an 18. If you can't match anything else to the natural, at least match the size.

Color and shape seem to vie for second place in fly selection. Migratory fish that feed little but take flies seem to have strong preferences for certain colors on certain days, as do trout, bass, and bottom-feeding saltwater fish like bonefish and permit. Bright colors may turn the fish on one day and off the next. Some days they seem to care less about color.

Fish that feed on prey that is below them (like bonefish rooting for shrimp) are very sensitive to colors, as are most fish when the sun is at an acute angle. This is because your flies are illuminated better when the sun is low in the sky. When the sun is high and flies are seen against a backlit sky, colors are difficult for fish to distinguish. Because surface flies are always seen from below, color is less important with dry flies and poppers than it is with sinking flies.

Shape or silhouette is especially important with surface flies. A bass that is accustomed to feeding only on frogs may not be interested in a surface fly with a long, skinny silhouette. When trout are feeding on caddisflies, they *might* take a standard dry fly with an upright wing, but a dry fly with a tent-shaped wing is bound to be more effective. And it certainly makes you feel like you've done your job.

The shape and color of only a part of an animal may be enough to trigger a strike. The Brook Fin, an old wet

A mayfly dun flanked by two imitations—a parachute on the left and a Comparadun on the right.

fly used for brook trout in the north woods, incorporates a wing of red, white, and black—the color of a brook trout's pelvic fin. Why a brook trout will strike the fin of another is a matter for speculation (perhaps territoriality?), but they do seem to have an attraction to it.

Action, or the way a fly wiggles or pulsates in the water, is important at times, especially when fishing for bass. The wiggle of a marabou streamer or the hackle of a Woolly Worm can excite a fish that shows no interest in other flies.

MATCHING THE HATCH

Choosing the correct fly at the height of an insect hatch, when the trout are selective, is the most complicated, exasperating, and, when you find the right fly, satisfying experience in fly fishing. The challenge involves not only what species of insect the fish are feeding on, but also the stage—is it an emerging adult, a drifting nymph, or a spent egg-laying adult?

The ideal situation for dry-fly fishing is when you arrive at a stream or lake to find the trout rising and the water covered with hatching mayflies. You pluck a fly from the air or the surface of the water, lay it on the lid of your fly box, and choose the fly in your box that matches it in size, shape, and color. Then you proceed to catch lots of fish.

It's seldom that easy. Faults in your presentation may tip the fish off to the fact that your fly isn't real (we'll cover those problems in the next two chapters). You can have what is called a *masking hatch*, usually a larger fly that is more obvious to you hatching at the same time as a smaller, less-obvious fly. But the trout may prefer the smaller fly, because it's more abundant or easier to capture.

Every trout-stream insect has a Latin or scientific name, and you may hear other fly fishers using these names. Latin names eliminate confusion about insect hatches between different areas of the country—an *Ephemerella subvaria* is called a Hendrickson in some parts of the country and a Whirling Blue Dun in others. It isn't necessary to know Latin names to catch fish. It isn't even necessary to know the names of the flies in your box until it's time to reorder. As long as you can match the natural to its imitation, you'll be a successful fly fisher.

The secret is observation. Before you start flailing the water with your favorite dry fly, watch the fish that are rising. Find one that's rising steadily and keep your eyes glued to the spot. Did he take the big cream mayfly or the little gray one? Perhaps he keeps rising, but the flies that float over his head remain untouched. Remember the bubbles? If there are none, he's probably taking the emerging nymphs just under the surface.

Here is what usually happens during a hatch: From a couple of days to an hour before the flies hatch, the nymphs or pupae become restless and drift in the current or scamper around on the aquatic vegetation in a lake. Trout pick off these nymphs, but we have no clues unless there has been a hatch for the past few days or your fishing diary or a book on trout-stream insects tells you a hatch is due on this date.

Because the trout are preoccupied with underwater food, they'll probably ignore floating flies, so you'll want to try a wet fly or nymph. Turn over a few rocks on the stream bottom. The flies that are due to emerge will be more abundant on rocks at the stream's edge, and their wing cases will be almost black. Choose a nymph from your fly box that matches them as closely as possible.

At the beginning of the hatch you'll see a few flies in the air and a few on the water. Rises will probably be scattered and erratic. What you're most likely seeing is fish feeding just under the surface; occasionally they'll misjudge and break the surface or cause a swirl. This is the time for a wet fly fished just under the surface, an emerger pattern, or a floating nymph.

Trout feeding just under the surface can be exasperating. You see a fish rise, toss your dry fly to him, he splashes at it, the water bulges under it—and you strike and come away empty. This is called a *refusal*. It may occur because your fly is the wrong size, but often it oc-

Turing over a rock in this river indicates that a caddis imitation would be a wise choice.

curs because the fish doesn't want a fly that is floating that high. He puts on the brakes at the last second, but his momentum causes him to break the surface. You might think that he missed your fly or you didn't strike quickly enough. Don't believe it. An adult trout seldom misses his target, and when he wants a dry fly, it's tough to take it away from him.

Another clue to subsurface feeding is a splashy rise from which erupts an adult fly that flies away. The fish has chased a nymph off the bottom but hasn't been quick enough. This is a very common sight during caddisfly emergence. If you see little moth-like flies popping out of rise forms, put away your dry flies and fish a caddis pupa just below the surface.

During hatches of many mayflies and caddisflies, the trout take the emerging flies throughout the hatch and bother little with the adult flies resting on the water's surface. You may catch a few on dry flies, especially if your fly isn't floating too well, but you would have been more successful using an emerger or wet-fly pattern. In most hatches, however, there will come a time when there will be enough flies on the surface to tempt the trout to take the adult insects—and our high-floating dry flies. Rises will be deliberate, rhythmic, and you'll see bubbles.

Splashy rises indicate fish taking insects that are fluttering on the water; as I've said before, this usually indicates a caddis hatch. A down-wing dry fly of the correct size and color should work. Rises to adult mayflies are usually more sedate, unless the mayflies are very large or the wind is blowing them across the surface like tiny sailboats.

It's usually not good enough to gauge the size and color of a hatching fly by observing it in the air or on the water. Flies look larger in the air, and color in a moving insect can be deceiving. Catch a sample to be sure that your match is correct.

At the height of a hatch you might see fish taking adult flies. Additionally, even though you know you're fishing with the right size and color, and know that your presentation is okay, you still get refusals. This is the time to switch from a standard hackled dry to a thorax fly, no-hackle, parachute, or Comparadun, something with a slightly cleaner silhouette. The change to a different pattern of the same size and color will often fool a difficult surface-feeding trout.

Returning mayfly spinners or egg-laying caddisfly adults can cause intense feeding by the trout, but this situation can be misleading. Because the spent insects are

A traditional Light Cahill dry fly surrounded by some alternate imitations for fussy trout: A CDC Emerger at top right, a smaller CDC Emerger at top left (sometimes just going one fly smaller than the natural will work wonders), a Comparadun (bottom left), and a Sparkle Parachute (bottom right).

You'd better believe that size matters. This big rainbow was feeding on adult midges (note the natural right above the fly) and would probably have ignored anything bigger than the tiny flies it was eating.

lying prostrate on the surface, nothing sticks up above the water and they're difficult to see. The secret is to look up. Aquatic insects can hatch over spread-out periods of time, but they must all mate at the same time. They form mating swarms, which hover and dip above the stream, starting at treetop level and gradually working their way down to the surface of the water. A good way to see them is to look into the sun. When the insects are between you and the sun (or fading twilight), they show up as shimmering dots above the river. If the flies are still pretty high and the fish are rising, it's probably to something else, but when the flies get lower, peer closely at the surface. You should be able to see the dying flies lying with their wings spent, half spent, or fully upright.

Trout may prefer the spinners with either upright or fully spent wings—I've never seen them actually selectively feeding on half-spent flies. If you can't see what they're taking, it's probably a spent spinner; if you see flies disappearing into the rises, they're taking the insects whose wings haven't collapsed yet. The one hallmark of fish taking spent flies is a very steady, deliberate rise. The trout seem to sense that the flies won't get away and they can take their time. The only exception is at the very beginning of a fall of spent insects, when overeager trout (usually smaller ones) slash at the flies just as they touch the water. Small trout may even clear the water in an attempt to catch the flies in midair. While this is a popular theme in calendar art, in real life the big suckers wait until the flies are trapped in the surface film and are an easy meal.

Mayfly spinners with wings that are still upright or caddisflies or stoneflies that have landed or are dipping and laying their eggs are easy to match—just use a standard adult pattern of the correct size and color. After the flies are spent, though, not only are size and color critical, but the fly must lie flush in the surface film. This is the time for a spentwing dry fly such as a hackled spinner or one tied with spinner wings of CDC (duck down feathers), or synthetic yarn and little or no hackle. In a pinch you can also use a parachute, or trim all the hackle from the top and bottom of a standard dry fly with a pair of scissors or your angler's snips.

If this adult caddis were fluttering on the water, you might want to try a high-floating natural like the Elk Hair Caddis.

If the same adult caddis were lying spent in the surface film, a lower-floating imitation like this CDC Caddis would probably work better.

There are thousands of different dry-fly patterns. Most aquatic insects are gray, cream, brown, or olive, and if you have one pattern in each of these colors in sizes 10 through 24, you'll be able to match almost any insect hatch in the world. This approach is much less confusing than trying to fill your fly box with hundreds of different patterns, many of them redundant when it comes to imitating a particular insect.

DRY FLIES WHEN THERE IS NO HATCH

You won't see a hatch every time you go trout fishing, especially early and late in the season. This is the time to "fish blind," or "fish the water." The choice is up to you: dry, wet, nymph, or streamer. No one can tell you what will work; there is never a sure thing in any kind of fishing, and that's what makes it so mysterious and appealing.

Dry flies will work when no fish are rising, especially if the water temperature is between 55 and 65 degrees

Spent spinners, lying flush in the water, are often difficult to see, and you might first spot them fluttering above the water by looking toward the sun.

Fahrenheit. Trout are very active within this temperature range and will respond to almost any kind of properly presented fly. If there is no hatch but you saw a hatch yesterday or the day before, try a dry fly that matches that insect. It will be a familiar morsel to the trout, and they should rise to it without much hesitation.

It's generally futile to fish blind with a dry fly smaller than size 16. A trout that is not actively rising needs a juicy morsel to interest him in surface food, one that will make it worth his while to travel all the way to the surface and expose himself to predators. Hairwing or hairbodied dry flies are best in this situation, because they present juicy silhouettes and are easily visible to the angler. Bivisibles, parachutes, variants, and big stonefly imitations like the Stimulator are productive in this case, for the same reasons. Color doesn't seem to be as important as shape and size when fishing blind, but if one color doesn't work, try others.

From late May through October, terrestrial imitations make excellent "searching" patterns. Land insects are constantly dropping into streams and lakeshores, and after the aquatic hatches dwindle in midsummer, terrestrials become a major part of a trout's diet. Terrestrial insects don't fall into the water on a regular schedule, so the trout may be sitting and waiting for an ant or grasshopper to float overhead, even though they're not rising with a regular rhythm.

Although terrestrials may drift and get blown into all areas of a stream, they are usually most concentrated in areas with overhanging trees or weeds that grow right up to the shore. In rocky mountain rivers with wide gravel banks, terrestrial flies will be less effective than in small woodland brooks or grassland streams with brush right down to the banks.

Shaking the bushes along the edge of a river or pond will tell you not only what kinds of terrestrial insects are available to the fish, but will probably also turn up some mayflies, caddisflies, or stoneflies that hatched the day before. These insects can help you make an educated guess for fly selection, because the trout will recognize them as familiar food.

Imitations of land insects or terrestrials are perfect for days when you don't see a hatch. Grasshoppers (top), beetles (bottom left), and ants (bottom right) are just three of the most popular.

Where deciduous trees overhang the water, ant, beetle, and caterpillar imitations will be most effective. Where grasses and weeds abut the shore, these insects—plus grasshoppers and crickets—will be available to the trout. A walk through a streamside field will tell you if grasshoppers are present and what color and size imitation you should use. In many streams from July through October, grasshoppers are the largest food available to the trout, and imitations are taken with great enthusiasm and confidence.

FLIES FOR TROUT

Nymphs and Wets

Trout biology often says that a great majority of a trout's food is taken underwater. The proportion of trout taken

Three of the best flies for dry-fly fishing when there is no apparent hatch. On top is a Stimulator, bottom left a Royal Wulff, bottom right a Parachute Hare's Ear.

on dry flies, however, is much greater, because the fly fisher can see what the fish are eating—and where they are. Unless the water is clear and you're accomplished at spotting trout before they spot you, most nymph and wet-fly fishing will rely on educated guesses, intuition, and a little luck.

Turn over a few rocks in a stream. Grab a handful of aquatic vegetation in a lake or weedy stream. The insects and crustaceans that you find can serve as models for your subsurface fishing. As with all animals, a trout's diet is based upon familiar shapes, sizes, and colors; the trout develops a "search image" for these items. If most of the nymphs in a stream are brown and olive and size 12 or 14, don't expect the trout to turn cartwheels over a cream-colored size-16 nymph. A black size-6 nymph might even scare them.

Most of the nymphs found in lakes and ponds will be slim and tan or olive, to match the aquatic vegetation or sand that makes up the bottom. Scuds are a very common food in lakes, as are damselfly nymphs. Patterns that imitate these insects are good to start with if you have no other guesses.

In streams with lots of big flat rocks, the nymphs will be mostly large and flat. Something like a March Brown or Hare's Ear nymph in size 10 or 12 will work well in this kind of water. Rivers with small, fine gravel will contain mostly small, skinny nymphs, because the big ones have no place to hide from predators. Slow, clear, weedy streams or spring creeks also contain these slim, tiny nymphs. This water should be fished blind with a slim, lightly dressed nymph like a Pheasant Tail, a Blue Quill Nymph, or a Copper John in sizes 14 through 18.

Turning over a rock reveals a couple of wide, robust mayfly nymphs. A good time to tie on a Hare's Ear or similar buggy-looking nymph.

This mayfly nymph is slim and sparse and better imitated with a Pheasant Tail.

Nymphs and wet flies have their greatest potential early in the season, when no flies are hatching. There are always insect larvae on the stream bottom, because of the seasonal succession of insect hatches; because some insects live two or more years underwater as larvae; and because crustaceans such as sow bugs and scuds live their entire lives underwater. Hendrickson nymphs, for example, are too tiny for catchable-sized trout to bother with after their eggs hatch in May. But by fall the trout will be gobbling them. Is an imitation of the Hendrickson nymph useless in June after the Hendricksons have hatched? Definitely not. There are other nymphs that look like the Hendrickson nymph but don't hatch until late June or July.

Wet flies are less slavish imitations of subsurface food than nymphs, but trout take them just as eagerly. The same suggestions for choosing wet-fly patterns hold for nymphs, plus a few more. Wet flies are excellent imitations

Armed with the Pheasant Tail (top, in a bead-head version) and the Hare's Ear nymph, you'll be ready to match both the wide, robust mayfly nymphs and their skinnier cousins.

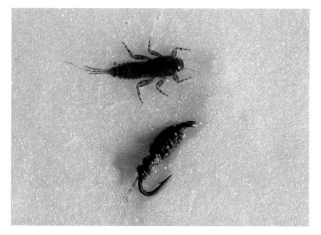

A Hendrickson nymph and a reasonable imitation.

If you see lots of cased caddis on the bottom, there are imitations that simulate their cases.

of drowned or drowning mayfly duns and spinners, and caddis and stonefly adults. Not all the insects that attempt to hatch make it. Some get drowned in fast water; others just fail to crawl out of their nymphal shucks. After a hatch is over, a wet fly fished through the riffles will often add a few bonus fish to your catch. Just match the approximate size and color of the insects that were emerging.

Wet-fly selection often involves just plain chuck-and-chance-it luck. Try a big black one. Try a little olive one. Color in wet flies may sometimes be more important than shape and size, especially in streams where there is little food and the most visible pattern gets the nod from the trout. Bright yellows, reds, and whites may work well in wilderness waters where the relatively gullible brook or cutthroat trout abound, but the more somber, lightly dressed patterns are much more popular in today's heavily fished trout waters.

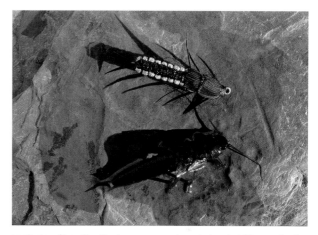

Large stoneflies often live two years as a larva before hatching, so they're always available to trout. Where these large insects are abundant, like the Rocky Mountains and West Coast rivers, a stonefly nymph is a go-to fly when nothing else works.

In the nineteenth century and for the first half of the twentieth century, the accepted way of fishing wet flies was to fish three, four, or as many as seven flies on a single leader, using droppers for each fly. This method lacks the delicacy of presentation needed for most of today's sophisticated trout waters, but fishing two or three different flies (nymphs or wets) at the same time will often tell you which one the fish favor. You can add an additional wet fly to your leader either by leaving the heavier tag end of the barrel knot closest to your tippet a little long, or, simpler yet, by just tying a foot-long piece of tippet material onto the bend of your first fly, and then tying the lower fly onto that piece. Keep the dropper short and no finer than 3X or .008 inch, or else it will tangle with the rest of the leader.

In streams, large nymphs or wet flies, sizes 8 through 12, work best when the water is fast or discolored. In

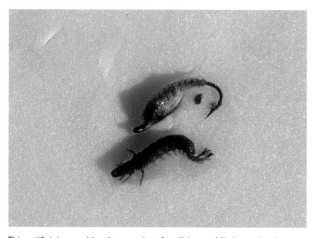

This artificial resembles the prevalent free-living caddis larvae in size, shape, and color.

pools and under clear-water conditions, the smaller 14 through 18 wet flies are more effective. I really don't know why. I can see where the larger flies are more visible in riffled or dirty water, but I'm not sure why it's necessary to switch to a smaller fly when you get to a slow pool. If only the trout could talk . . .

STREAMERS

Trout that live in large lakes may never eat an insect after they reach a foot or so in length; instead, they feed on abundant baitfish like alewives or smelt. Smelt and alewives are gray-green in color with silvery white bellies. Streamers and bucktails that incorporate these colors in sizes 2 through 8 are popular in New England ponds, in the Great Lakes, and in large western reservoirs where big salmonids feed on these forage fish.

On the other hand, Dr. Robert Bachman, the noted brown-trout behaviorist, never once saw a trout eat a minnow in over three thousand hours of observing a wild, undisturbed population of stream trout. Why? Trout in streams often take our streamers and bucktails. The answer lies in the words "never once *saw.*"

Bachman is sure that the trout fed upon minnows after dark and when the water became high and dirty after a rainstorm. Under normal water conditions, in the daylight, a minnow is just too fast for a large trout, and the trout expends too much energy at too great a risk. After dark or during a flood, minnows become disoriented, and a trout has the edge.

Trout-stream minnows fall into three broad categories: long and thin with a horizontal black stripe (dace and shiner); slightly deeper in the body with vertical bands (darter and sucker); and short and stubby fish that are flattened horizontally (bottom dwellers like sculpin). An investigation of shallow areas will tell you what kinds are present and what size they are.

A sparsely dressed bucktail fly with bands of white, black, and brown hair like a Black-Nose Dace from the Thunder Creek series, or a Zonker, will imitate the various dace and shiners. If the minnows show vertical bars, you might select a streamer tied with barred Plymouth Rock chicken hackles like the Gray Matuka, or a bucktail with hair that has a vertical barring—the Squirrel Tail is a good example. Finally, bottom-dwelling fish like

sculpins and darters are best imitated by a Muddler, Woolly Bugger, or one of the new Sculpin variations. Most of the best new streamer patterns you see are some form of sculpin—with good reason. Sculpins live in nearly every trout stream, they are slow and easy for trout to catch, and they provide a lot of calories for one meal.

A blacknose dace from a trout stream. Best to imitate this one with a fly with horizontal stripes.

This shot of a sculpin shows why flies with bulky heads work well in streams with lots of sculpins. Trout love them.

Even though trout in streams seldom take minnows under normal, clear-water conditions, streamers are surprisingly effective. A large trout will seldom pass up a crayfish, and such bulky patterns, especially those with some brown and yellow in them—like the Yellow Matuka, the Dark Edson Tiger, the Orange Blossom Special, or the McGinnis Extra Stout—might be taken for a crayfish fleeing from a potential predator. Tiny streamers in sizes 8 to 12 may also look to the trout like stonefly nymphs, damselfly nymphs, or leeches.

The Blacknose Dace bucktail imitates this common trout-stream minnow and other baitfish with longitudinal stripes.

The Muddler Minnow is just one of many streamers that imitate sculpins, which are a favorite food of large trout.

Streamers reach their full potential when there is absolutely no activity on a trout stream—whether it's early in the season, when the water temperature is too cold for insect hatches; during slack periods in season; or late in the season after the hatches are over. At these times streamers may be just lures—large, nonspecific chunks of something that's alive and good to eat.

If the water is dirty or has some "color" to it, bright streamer patterns usually draw the most strikes. The reds and yellows of a Mickey Finn bucktail, a Yellow Marabou streamer, a Tequeely, or the contrasting black and white

of the Black Ghost bucktail will catch the fish's attention. Larger sizes, 2 to 6, are a good bet when visibility is low. Because Muddler-type flies with their deer-hair heads seem to produce a vibration that fish pick up with their lateral line, you might want to stack the deck and fish a big Yellow Marabou Muddler. Rubber legs added to a streamer also increase the noise value of a fly and add wiggly action that makes them look alive.

Under clear-water conditions, trout may chase big, bright streamers but will usually turn away without striking. Something less flashy, on the order of a size-10 or 12 Black-Nose Dace bucktail, appears to be large enough to be noticed but subtle enough to be inhaled.

Big rivers and fast water will require larger streamer patterns to attract a trout's attention. On the Madison

The Woolly Bugger, which has probably accounted for more large trout (in fact probably more trout, period) than any other fly in the past twenty years might imitate a sculpin or a leech or a crayfish.

The McGinnis Extra Stout also has the bulk, coloration, and wiggly legs of a crayfish.

River in Montana, for instance, fly fishers use big, sizes 2 and 1/0, Marabou Muddlers to fish for fall-spawning brown trout. A streamer this big on a small, infertile mountain stream where growth is slow may actually be larger than the majority of the fish population. A streamer bigger than a size 10 or 12 might frighten trout that aren't used to seeing large minnows or crayfish.

FLIES FOR OTHER FRESHWATER FISH

Bass Flies

When we talk about selecting flies for freshwater bass, it's important to make a distinction between the largemouth bass, which inhabits warm, weedy waters with silty bottoms, and smallmouth bass, which will be found in clear lakes and rivers with rocky bottoms and cooler water temperatures. The redeye and spotted bass, close relatives of the smallmouth that occupy a limited range in the southern United States, can be lumped with the smallmouth as far as fly selection is concerned.

Smallmouth bass often live in trout streams and will feed upon insect hatches side by side with the trout. It generally takes a heavy hatch of insects to interest smallmouths, though, and you'll seldom find them feeding on mayflies or caddisflies that are smaller than size 16. Standard trout wets, nymphs, and dries will work during hatches, although smallmouth, unlike trout, can often be taken with a small popper or hair bug even when they're feeding on insects that are much smaller.

The larger the smallmouth, the less inclined he will be to feed on insects except the largest ones. Big smallmouths prefer to ambush their prey, and minnows and crayfish rate very high on their menu. Hellgrammites (the large, black larvae of the dobsonfly) are also found frequently in smallmouth stomachs.

Streamer flies and nymphs in sizes 4 through 12 should be included in your fly box if you're after smallmouths. The Crayfish bass fly or a brown Woolly Bugger will imitate these crustaceans, and you should also have a large black nymph like the Montana, especially in streams where hellgrammites are present. A good selection of imitator-type streamers for the various minnows will round out your selection. Two you shouldn't be without are the Muddler Minnow and the Black Matuka.

Smallmouths also take brightly colored attractor-type streamers. White, black, yellow, red, and combinations of these colors in sizes 4 through 12 are popular with smallmouth fly fishers. The fish often show a decided preference for one color over another, so finding the right fly is often a matter of trying different patterns until you discover the right color combination.

An excellent collection of flies for smallmouth bass. Clockwise from top left: A big black nymph to imitate hellgrammites, a Sneaky Pete bullet-head popper, a noisier cup-shaped popper, a Clouser Minnow with weighted eyes, and a Woolly Bugger.

Early mornings and evenings in lake shallows and in the tails of pools on rivers are times to try floating bass bugs or poppers. Smaller bugs, sizes 4 through 12, are best for smallmouths, in black, brown, yellow, green, chartreuse, and red-and-white. Where the water is clear, you should lean toward the smaller sizes that make less commotion on the surface, like hair bugs or bullethead minnows. In murky water you'll be able to catch the bass' attention better with the large poppers with concave faces, ones that make enough noise to be noticed.

Largemouth-bass flies are generally larger than smallmouth flies. Although small largemouths will occasionally eat insects, individuals over a foot long prefer larger food like frogs, mice, and minnows. Largemouths can swallow prey that is quite large and have even been reported to take water snakes and small muskrats.

Flies used for largemouth bass should reflect their habitat. Largemouths prefer to ambush their prey from the protection of heavy cover like submerged weed beds, lily pads, and sunken logs, so flies used for largemouths should incorporate some sort of weed guard to keep your flies from catching on weeds and other obstructions. You'll find working your streamer or bug outside a weed bed to be futile, yet if you drop it into the center of the weeds and work it through open spots, you'll catch bass. Common types of weed guards include keel hooks, which ride upside down, and monofilament loops, or the wing of a fly may be tied so that it covers the hook point.

Choosing flies for largemouth bass depends less on matching their food than on the mood of the angler and his quarry. Of course there are hair bugs that look just like frogs and mice, but you're hardly going to see a bass sipping mice selectively, one right after another. Nor are you going to wait for a bass to eat a mouse, then toss your fly to him. You want to appeal to his ambushing instinct—show him something that looks like a juicy morsel.

Surface lures—bugs and poppers—are the most exciting way to catch largemouths. Bass will take surface lures whenever they're in shallow water—usually at dawn and dusk, and all day long during the spring spawning season. If there is a lot of cover or structure, like logs or lily pads, there may be bass lurking in shallow water all day, but they seldom stray far from deep water or structure when the light is bright.

Surface lures for largemouths are more effective in the larger sizes, 4 through 4/0. Don't rule out tiny size-12 bluegill bugs, though, when you're sure the bass are in

shallow water but they refuse everything else. Green, yellow, black, and brown are the most popular colors.

I like to start with a standard cork or plastic popper in size 1/0 or 2 in one of the above colors. If the bass strike short or boil under the popper without taking it, I'll switch to either a smaller popper in the same color or a softer, more subtle hair bug. Often a small hair bug in natural brown deer hair will do the trick when the traditional bright-colored bass bugs fail.

Bass visibly boiling near shore and among aquatic vegetation may mean they're feeding on frogs or minnows; largemouths boiling in open water almost always means they're herding schools of minnows near the surface. This is the time for a Keel Bug, Prismatic Muddler, Zonker, Woolly Bugger, or Marabou Muddler. These flies, with their streamer-like wing and deer-hair head, look like crippled minnows struggling just under the surface.

When the surface water is cold (below 60 degrees) or very warm (over 75 degrees), bass will be found in deep water. At these times you'll want to use one of the large streamers tied for bass. They are usually weighted or tied with bead-chain eyes to get them down quickly. Most use wings of marabou, which gives them a wiggling, pulsating action, much like the plastic worms that bait and spin casters use. In fact, the Gulley Worm is not designed to imitate a specific bass food—it's designed to imitate plastic worms that spin and bait casters use so effectively. For subsurface lures, the darker colors—black, brown, and olive—work best, although white is sometimes effective, especially in murky water.

Panfish Flies

Selecting flies for panfish is quite easy—these species are always eager to take anything that vaguely resembles a small minnow, insect, or crustacean. Bluegills are so easy to catch on flies that a small one will often smash a huge bass popper, although the really big bluegills are a little more cautious, and it may require some observation to see what they're feeding on.

Study the feeding habits of the panfish you're after before selecting flies for them. Even though bluegills get larger than other sunfish, they feed almost exclusively on small insects and crustaceans. Thus, a tiny popper, dry fly, or nymph will catch more bluegills than a streamer. Rock bass, white bass, white perch, yellow perch, and crappie,

Flies for largemouth bass. Top: A sinking Gulley Worm, the fly-rodder's answer to the plastic worm. Middle: A rubber-legged streamer, a crayfish imitation, and a noisy popper. Bottom: Hair Mouse.

Panfish flies. Top row: A small round-headed popper and a sponge bug. Bottom: A small bright streamer, a trout dry fly, and a nymph.

on the other hand, prefer small minnows, less than 2 inches in length, so streamer flies in sizes 8 through 12 are the most productive flies for these fish.

A small selection of trout dries, nymphs, and streamers, plus some tiny cork poppers or sponge-rubber bugs in various colors, should be all you'll need to catch all species of panfish.

Even though they grow quite large, walleyes are often considered to be panfish. Walleyes are almost exclusively minnow feeders and have a decided preference for red-and-yellow flies. The best fly for walleyes I've ever used is a large Mickey Finn bucktail in sizes 2 through 6. If walleyes are herding minnows on the surface, a black or yellow popper will take them as well as any surface lure. Black is especially good after dark, because it's most visible silhouetted against the night sky.

STEELHEAD FLIES

Steelhead flies must be visible for long distances to be effective. When anglers usually target this species, the fish are not actively feeding and must be attracted to the fly. So in a raging torrent the fly should be large (up to size 1/0), and in low, clear water it may be effective to fish flies as small as size 12 or 14. Average steelhead flies for normal water conditions are sizes 4, 6, and 8.

Steelhead and lake-run rainbows have a penchant for bright colors. The traditional West Coast wet flies incor-

porate red and white, and such patterns as the Thor and Skykomish Sunrise are still among the most popular. Fluorescent greens, reds, and oranges, as well as deep purple, are being used more and more for steelhead; the high visibility of these colors in deep, dark steelhead rivers seems to draw strikes when standard flies go unnoticed.

If the standard bright colors fail to entice steelhead, a change-of-pace fly should be tried. The Skunk, a black-and-white pattern, is one of the best.

Most steelhead fishing is done with hairwing wet flies, and unlike salmon, steelhead take flies more readily near the bottom. To get down to the fish, steelhead flies may use bead-chain heads (like the Comet series) or heavy wire bodies (like the Brass Hat and Paintbrush patterns). Such flies might also be streamers with brass or tungsten coneheads. Many fly tiers avoid the use of weighted steelhead patterns, preferring a fast-sinking line and short leader to get down to the fish. (Steelhead anglers often cast long distances at very high line speeds, and a weighted fly under these circumstances can be a dangerous projectile.)

In streams with runs of Pacific salmon, flies that imitate eggs or clumps of eggs are devastatingly effective for steelhead. Such patterns as the Two-Egg Sperm Fly, Babine, and Glo Bugs in fluorescent red, pink, and orange, fished right along the bottom, will simulate loose salmon eggs. The same patterns in bright green or chartreuse work well in streams that have spring runs of steelhead, because the fish will feed on bright green sucker spawn.

Large nymphs that imitate stoneflies or burrowing mayflies are very effective on summer steelhead on the

Traditional steelhead wet flies. Clockwise from top left: A Spey fly, a Green-Butt Skunk, a Fall Favorite, and a Thor.

Egg flies. Clockwise from top left: A large chartreuse egg fly, a small orange Glo-Bug, a small pink Glo-Bug, and an egg clump.

Tube flies for steelhead or Pacific salmon. Top: A bright tube fly with weighted eyes so it sinks faster. Middle: A large black Bunny Fly. Bottom: A marabou Popsicle. These flies are tied on plastic tubes instead of hooks, and the hook on the left can be attached to a fly after the leader is threaded through the hollow tube and tied to the hook.

West Coast and for the steelhead that migrate into streams in the Great Lakes area of the East and Midwest.

Tube flies have become very popular for steelhead, and large flies that interest steelhead in fast, dirty water can be made without resorting to a large hook or a heavy fly. The most effective tube flies for steelhead are made with red, orange, black, or purple marabou, and the very large ones, up to 4 inches long, are often made by winding black rabbit fur around a hook to give the fly a very enticing action.

Steelhead that are holding in pools during low-water conditions in summer can be taken with small wets, flies fished "damp" or just under the surface, and occasionally on dry flies. Damp flies are tied with buoyant deer-hair

heads or wings so they ride just under the surface. Common examples are the Grease Liner, Muddler Minnow, and Dragon Fly. If a river is very low and clear and the steelhead are holding in pools, a dry fly may be effective. Steelhead dry flies are very similar to those used for Atlantic salmon, with hair wings and lots of hackle for good flotation.

ATLANTIC SALMON FLIES

Most of the Atlantic salmon caught on flies are taken on large wet flies, sizes 5/0 through 12. Where sizes 4 and 6 have been considered to be the standard sizes for salmon, there is a growing tendency, especially in Iceland and North America, to use the smaller 10s, 12s, and even 14s. The larger flies are more effective in high, fast, or dirty water; the smaller sizes are used during midsummer or when the water is low and clear.

For example, if you arrive at a salmon river when it's in flood stage, you'll probably see most of the fish caught on large flies, sizes 3/0 through 2. The next day, as the water drops, 4s and 6s may take the most fish, and by the end of the week, if it doesn't rain, you may have to go to 10s and 12s to raise fish. You may also stroll out into a

Steelhead nymphs. Clockwise from top left: An imitation of a large swimming mayfly nymph, a Steelhead Stone, and Rusher's Steelhead.

salmon river during low water with a big size 1/0 and take the biggest fish in the pool—but that's salmon fishing: never predictable.

To be most effective, the salmon should see a wet fly broadside, and the wet fly seems to be most effective when it's a foot or two under the surface. Single-hook wet flies may tumble in broken water or skim across the surface in fast water; hence, the double hook: doubles ride hook down even in the most broken currents, so they show the fly broadside to the fish more often. In addition, the extra weight of a double hook will keep the fly riding a little deeper. There doesn't seem to be any strict rule as to when you should use doubles or when to use singles, but a switch from a single to a double in the same size and pattern may rise the only salmon of the day.

Four kinds of Atlantic salmon wet flies. Clockwise from top left: A DeFeo Salmon Nymph, a Silver Rat Hairwing, a full-dress Green Highlander feather wing, and a Cosseboom hairwing tied on a double hook for weight and stability.

When salmon don't respond to traditional wet flies, experienced fly fishers often try nymphs as a change of pace. The drab colors and different silhouette of a nymph pattern are so far from the traditional bright, flashy salmon patterns that they may work when nothing else does. Nymphs seem to work best under low, clear-water conditions and in smaller sizes, 8 through 12.

Low-water flies are another option when a small fly is needed. Because they occupy only half to three-quarters of the hook shank and are very sparse, you can present a small fly to the salmon with the hooking and holding advantages of a larger hook. A size-8 low-water fly, for example, is equivalent to a size-12 standard wet fly. The salmon seem to ignore the extra hook sticking out beyond the fly.

Color in salmon flies is a matter of great controversy. Most authorities agree that you should have bright flies, something with green or yellow or orange in them; light-colored flies, with silver tinsel bodies and light wings; and dark flies, with black bodies and wings. The general rule is "bright day, bright fly—dark day, dark fly," and it seems to work under most circumstances.

Every salmon river has its preferred colors, and the fish seem to be consistent about their choice of colors. The color of the water and the bottom may affect the visibility of particular colors. For example, flies with yellows and greens are most visible in tea-colored water—and they catch a lot of salmon in this kind of water.

It's a good idea to use a fly of the same size and color that has been catching fish, or one that has been recommended by your guide. If the favorite doesn't work, experiment with flies that haven't been shown to the salmon in a while, something with a totally different shape, like an Ingall's Butterfly or a Salmon Muddler.

Salmon will rise to large dry flies, especially when the water temperature is between 60 and 70 degrees. Below 60 degrees they may take dries, but wets are much more productive; above 68 degrees, salmon are difficult to take on any type of fly. Dry flies used for salmon are bushy, high-floating flies in sizes 1/0 through 12. The Wulff and Irresistible patterns are popular, along with big bivisibles and hairwing flies like the MacIntosh. As with wet flies, high water calls for big patterns that are easily seen by the fish, and low water may require dries as small as size 12. A size-12 Black Gnat is an excellent salmon dry fly during low-water conditions.

Atlantic salmon dry flies. Clockwise from top left: A MacIntosh, Bomber, Buck Bug, and White Wulff.

In some rivers, especially those in northern Maritime Canada and Russia, many salmon are taken on dry flies. In others, notably Icelandic and European rivers, salmon never rise to dry flies—in fact, salmon dry flies are almost unknown in Europe.

Color seems to be of little importance with salmon dries, but shape and especially size are critical. Try various sizes. If a salmon rises to inspect your dry but doesn't take it, try a smaller size.

PACIFIC SALMON FLIES

Like Atlantic salmon and steelhead, Pacific salmon feed little when on their spawning migration and are more easily caught on flies just after they have entered a river and the memory of feeding is still fresh.

Flies for Pacific salmon. Clockwise from top left: Conehead Rabbit, Spring Wiggler, Glo Bug, Egg Cluster, and Hareball Leech.

There is a substantial sport fishery for Pacific salmon in the estuaries of spawning rivers, before the fish have begun their migration. Pacific salmon readily take large streamer flies in estuaries in the Pacific Northwest, and in the Great Lakes where they have been introduced. Patterns should be large, sizes 1 through 3/0, and should imitate the baitfish on which the salmon feed. Much of this fishing is done by trolling, so large tandem streamers are often used. The Herring and Candlefish bucktails are the most popular flies on the West Coast and are named after the baitfish they imitate. These patterns have silver bodies with green-and-white or blue-and-white wings, and any large streamer pattern that has these colors should work. The same streamers will also work for Great Lakes salmon, because the alewife, the predominant baitfish there, has the same coloration.

Once Pacific salmon have been in the river for a week or so, they are difficult to take on flies, although large steelhead wet flies, big nymphs, egg flies, or big white or orange streamer flies can be effective in certain rivers.

Landlocked Salmon Flies

Landlocked salmon are Atlantic salmon that do not have access to the ocean. They live in cold, clear lakes in the northeastern United States and move in and out of streams and rivers that feed these lakes.

During the spring and summer months, landlocked salmon may feed on insect hatches in both lakes and rivers. Flies should be chosen just as you would for trout—and landlocks can be as selective as trout.

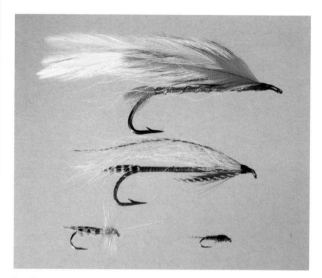

Landlocked salmon flies. Top: A Nine-Three Featherwing streamer, a traditional smelt imitation. Middle: A Magog Smelt bucktail. Bottom: A caddis dry fly and a small Pheasant Tail nymph.

During spring and summer landlocks feed heavily on smelt, and streamer flies with smelt coloration—greens, grays, blue, and whites—are by far the best flies. The Gray Ghost, Nine-Three, and Supervisor are good examples of landlocked-salmon streamers.

Landlocks also have a strong attraction for yellow flies, and the Dark Edson Tiger bucktail and Yellow Marabou account for many landlocks, especially in the fall, when the fish spawn in rivers that feed their lakes. Once fish have moved into a river for a few days, though, you'll often find that small nymphs, even down to a size 20, will catch many more landlocks than the conventional streamer flies. My favorite fall landlock fly is a size-18 Pheasant Tail nymph.

PIKE AND PICKEREL FLIES

The same flies used for largemouth bass will catch pike and pickerel, especially large streamer patterns and large poppers and hair bugs. Saltwater streamers like Lefty's Deceiver and the Blonde series also work well. The best colors are red-and-white, red-and-yellow, or all white, and a tinsel body seems to add some attraction. The Mickey Finn trout bucktail in larger sizes is a favorite of many Canadian pike enthusiasts.

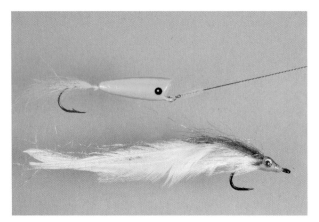

You can use large bass and saltwater flies for pike, but it's a good idea to use a wire bite guard, shown on the popper here.

Bucktails and cork poppers rather than streamers and hair bugs are usually used, because the sharp teeth of these species can cut a less-durable fly to shreds.

Sizes 3/0 through 2 are best for pike, but the smaller pickerel may take size-4, 6, and 8 patterns more readily.

Occasionally a duller pattern will work better for pike and pickerel, especially on very bright days or in very clear water.

SHAD FLIES

Shad ascend freshwater rivers on the East and West Coasts in the spring months. While they are moving, they seldom stray far from the bottom of the river; thus, quick-sinking, simple wet flies tied on heavy hooks or on weighted hooks are used. Shad do not feed before spawning, so highly vis-

ible colors are used, notably reds, whites, and yellows. You can buy or tie special shad flies, but I've found that trout streamers and small saltwater patterns with heavy eyes like the Clouser Minnow and Crazy Charley work well for shad when they are in the mood to hit a fly. The best sizes are 4, 6, and 8, with the larger flies used in fast water and the smaller ones in slow, clear water. Red glass beads are sometimes strung on the tippet before the fly is tied on, for extra color and to get the fly deeper.

In June, after the shad have spawned and they are working their way back to the ocean, they will feed and can be taken on nymphs, wet flies, and even dry flies. Once, during a heavy spinner fall of Brown Drake mayflies on the Delaware River, I took a brown trout, a

Shad flies are usually small and bright, and most have metal eyes to help them get down quickly.

rainbow trout, and two shad from a riffle one evening, all on the same dry fly.

SALTWATER FLIES

Saltwater fly selection is relatively simple. With a few baitfish imitations in a couple of colors and three or four sizes, two sizes of poppers, and a selection of crab and shrimp imitations, you can catch almost any saltwater fish that can be taken on flies.

All saltwater gamefish feed on baitfish at one time or another, from the bottom-feeding bonefish in the shallows right up to sailfish in the open ocean. Length is the most important consideration when saltwater fish are actively feeding on baitfish, so fly size can be critical. Small striped bass are about the most selective fish in salt water, and if they're feeding on 2-inch baitfish, a streamer that is 4 inches long may go untouched. If the fish are herding baitfish near the surface, you'll see the baitfish clearing the water, trying to escape; it's an easy matter to estimate their size and choose your fly size accordingly. If the fish are feeding in deeper water, you may have to determine the correct size by trial-and-error fly changing.

The depth at which you retrieve your fly is also important. How deep your fly is presented is determined to a great degree by the density of floating, intermediate, sinking, or fast-sinking fly line, but different kinds of flies have various sink rates. In general, the larger the fly, the quicker it will sink; thus, bonefish, which are generally caught in very shallow water, may be taking a size 6 while permit in the same vicinity but in deeper water might require a size 2.

Lefty's Deceiver is one of the most popular and versatile saltwater baitfish imitations.

If you can see the color of the baitfish that your quarry is eating, it's always a good idea to match them as closely as possible. Most saltwater baitfish have dark backs—blue, black, or green—with silvery white bellies, sometimes with a black medial stripe. Lefty's Deceiver patterns in blue-and-white, green-and-white, and black-and-white combinations should handle most of the baitfish-imitating situations you'll ever encounter.

Poppers increase the enjoyment of saltwater fly fishing, because all the action is in full view. You can see your fly all the time, and you can see the fish with its open mouth charging your fly. Poppers can be used when species like bluefish or stripers are herding baitfish at the surface, and big 7/0 poppers are used for giant fish of the open ocean like sailfish, amberjack, or cobia. More so than any other kind of fly, poppers call attention to themselves by making noise and throwing spray out in front of them. A bluefish that is charging a school of baitfish will be drawn to a noisy popper more quickly than to a streamer that is competing with all the other baitfish in the school for attention.

Poppers can also be used as attractors, drawing stripers or bluefish out of 10 feet of water to investigate the commotion. Redfish, with their weak eyesight, are often brought to the surface by a small popper. Experienced fly fishers say that the sound a popper makes resembles the noise a frightened shrimp makes when it scoots to the surface.

The Skipping Bug is a classic saltwater popper.

Bonefish Flies

Fly fishing for bonefish is all about strategy and presentation, and although there are hundreds of bonefish patterns, you really don't need to carry many. Bonefish cruise shallow water hoping to root out or scare all kinds of critters from their hideouts in turtle grass, sand, or coral, and a bonefish will typically nail anything that scoots out in front of it, as long as it is a reasonable facsimile of food they've seen before. The most important part of bonefish fly selection is to have a variety of sink rates. Fish in very shallow water will spook when a heavy fly splashes near them, plus a heavy fly quickly sinks and gets hung up on the bottom. Here, you want a bonefish fly without metal eyes and with no weight. Crazy Charlie or Gotcha patterns with plastic eyes are very popular and effective.

The most typical bonefish scenario is a fish in about 2 feet of water. Here, lightly weighted patterns with small eyes of bead-chain sink quickly enough to get near the bottom in front of a cruising fish, yet they're not so heavy that they spook fish. The Whisper Crab, standard Gotcha, and Bonecrusher are good patterns for this situation.

When bonefish move into water so shallow that their backs are out of the water when they swim, or when they're waving their tails in the air (called "tailing fish" in a similar way that the expression is used for trout), you need a fly that you can cast very close to them without making a splash. Here, you want to use flies with no weight added; or, if the flies have eyes, they should be made of lightweight plastic. Additionally, when bonefish are in turtle grass, you don't want your fly to get lost in the weeds, so a lighter fly suspended over the bottom is more easily seen.

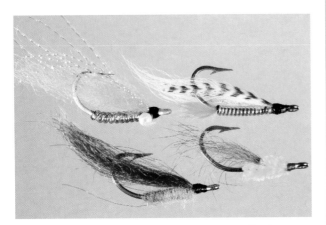

These lightweight bonefish flies all have either no eyes, or like the one on the upper left, plastic eyes. They are designed to be fished in shallow water.

In very warm or cold water, bonefish often stay deep, around 3 feet and deeper. This is also where most very large bonefish are caught. Here, you need a quick-sinking fly with metal eyes, like the Crazy Charley or Gotcha tied with machined metal eyes, small Clouser Minnows, or a quick-sinking crab fly like the Flexo Crab or Del's Merkin, both of which are tied with heavy metal eyes.

Because bonefish eat a variety of foods, including aquatic worms, shrimp, crabs, and small baitfish, they are seldom selective, but you at least want to throw something to them that looks familiar and does not cause alarm. For that reason, it's best to choose lighter tan or pink flies over light-colored sand bottoms, medium-hued flies over a mixed coral bottom, and dark flies over eel grass.

Bonefish have small mouths, and the flies used for them are smaller than most saltwater species. The most common sizes in the Florida Keys, where some of the biggest bonefish in the world swim, are sizes 2 and 4. In the Bahamas, where you see a good variety of bonefish, sizes 4 and 6 seem to produce best. In Central America and Mexico, most fish are smaller, and size 6 (or even 8) will tempt them. I always carry some bonefish flies on the large end, and some tiny size 8s wherever I go. You could run into a school of smaller fish in the Keys, and you could also run into some 10-pound bruisers in the Bahamas or Mexico.

These bonefish flies, for deeper water, all have metal eyes to sink them quickly.

Permit Flies

Although the elusive permit has been caught on tarpon and bonefish flies by anglers fishing for other species, if you're going to pursue this fish, you need to have some specific crab imitations. Because permit feed in deeper water than bonefish, and they run larger, you'll need to carry larger flies, size 2 or 1/0. A crab fleeing from a gamefish dives to the bottom quickly to burrow into the sand, so whatever crab pattern you use, make sure it has heavy metal eyes so it sinks fast. You should match the general shade of the bottom you're fishing over. For light sand bottoms, the translucent tan of the Flexo Crab is perfect. For darker bottoms, the browns and greens of Del's Merkin Fly are better.

Flies for permit. Clockwise from top left: Del's Merkin, Flexo Crab, Dorsey's Kwan.

Tarpon Flies

Tarpon are not terribly selective in their feeding habits. They eat mullet, pinfish, shrimp, crabs, aquatic worms, and probably anything else that resembles a meal. "Baby" tarpon, those inhabiting mangrove swamps and canals, feed more actively, and standard baitfish flies like the Clouser Minnow and Deceiver, as well as popping bugs, will take them. Because undisturbed tarpon (the ones that eat better) swim near the surface, you want patterns that have an almost neutral buoyancy; thus, the tendency in tarpon fly design to use big saddle hackles or rabbit fur, as these bulkier materials retard the sink rate of a fly and give it a wiggly action that seems irresistible to tarpon. Metal or bead eyes are not recommended unless you plan to fish the deep, muddy rivers of Costa Rica with fast-sinking lines. If you use standard tarpon flies like the Black Death or Cockroach, bigger flies, sizes 3/0 and 4/0, work better because these brackish waters are typically tea-stained and you need a highly visible fly to interest the fish.

Tarpon flies. Clockwise from top left: Malzone's Black Death, Ruoff's Lay-Up Fly, Malzone's Medium Blonde, Malzone's Green Weenie.

Tarpon that swim along the coast in clear water are a different story. These are typically fish that are migrating, not feeding actively. They seem to be much spookier than their inland cousins, so in clear water, smaller, duller, more subtle flies are your best first choice. Flies like Ruoff's Lay Up Fly, the Cockroach, and brown-and-tan Tarpon Bunny flies are top recommendations. These clear-water flies should also be in smaller sizes, such as on a 1/0 or 2/0 hook.

Redfish and Sea Trout Flies

Redfish and sea trout are not related and don't even resemble each other, but they swim side by side throughout the southern Atlantic and Gulf Coasts and feed on the same critters—shrimp, crabs, and baitfish. They are often found in dirtier water than bonefish (which feed on the same kinds of food), so the flies used for these guys should be

Redfish flies. Clockwise from top left: Kirk's Rattle Rouser, Flexo Crab, Psycho Circus, Ruoff's Back Country Popper, Clouser Minnow.

bigger and more brightly colored. Redfish in particular have poor eyesight, so colorful flies like a Chartreuse Deceiver, Yellow and Red Sea-Ducer, or the brighter variations of the Clouser Minnow in sizes 2, 1/0, and 2/0, work better than the smaller bonefish flies. Crab and shrimp imitations in sizes 2 and 4 are also very effective, as are small saltwater poppers.

Barracuda Flies

Barracuda are long, skinny, and fast, and prefer their flies that way. It's probably because one of their favorite preys is needlefish. There are specific barracuda flies tied to imitate needlefish, and the most popular colors are green (to match the natural color of their prey) or orange (probably just because it is so visible). Big baitfish patterns like the Lefty's Deceiver will also entice cuda when they're in the mood to strike. There does not seem to be much magic to cuda fly selection: Throw at one and strip like mad; if it doesn't eat, it was probably not due to the fly pattern but to the mood of that particular fish. The next one may jump all over your fly.

Top, a needlefish imitation for barracuda. Bottom, a big bright feathered streamer for sharks.

Snook Flies

Snook lie in wait to ambush baitfish, shrimp, or crabs. Like barracuda they are moody, and when in the mood will strike almost anything. When they're not, no fly in the world will catch them. For fish that are back in mangrove roots or along current edges, large attractor patterns like the Lefty's Deceiver or Clouser Minnow in sizes 1/0 to 3/0 work fine, as will saltwater poppers like the Skipping Bug. When fished at night along lighted docks, they seem to be far more selective. Usually the baitfish in these places are small and almost translucent, and a size-4 or 6 Epoxy Baitfish may work better than the bigger, brighter flies.

Flies for snook. From top: Chris' Razor Back, Lefty's Deceiver, Epoxy Minnow, Skipping Bug.

Shark Flies

Sharks can be moody or very aggressive, but the one constant in choosing shark flies is that they should be big and bulky. Sharks have poor eyesight but are superb at sensing vibrations in the water. Big tarpon flies, Lefty's Deceivers, Skipping Bugs, or any other baitfish patterns in white or other bright colors, from sizes 3/0 to 5/0, are effective. If I'm tossing to sharks, I'll just choose the biggest, bulkiest, most obnoxious fly in my box that I want to get rid of, because there's not much left of a fly once you land a shark.

Flies for Tuna and their Relatives

There are many fish in the tuna/mackerel family that are fun to take on a fly. In this bunch I'll include Atlantic and Pacific bonito, false albacore, Spanish mackerel, Cero mackerel, king mackerel, blackfin tuna, yellowfin tuna, and even bluefin tuna. There are many others around the world, but these are the most popular with fly fishers. All of these fish have relatively small mouths with fine teeth and feed on smaller baitfish. Even 150-pound bluefin tuna sometimes prefer a surprisingly small and subtle fly. The best flies for these species are general baitfish imitations, but tuna can be surprisingly selective.

I'd carry an assortment of skinny baitfish patterns, like the Epoxy Baitfish, Lefty's Deceiver, Clouser Minnow, or Crease Fly. Perhaps even more important is to have a variety of sizes, from ½ inch long (size 4 or 6) to as long as 6 inches (sizes 2/0 to 3/0). Try to match the size of the baitfish you see when these fish herd their prey on the surface, or if you are chumming for them, try to match the size and shape of the fish you're using for chum.

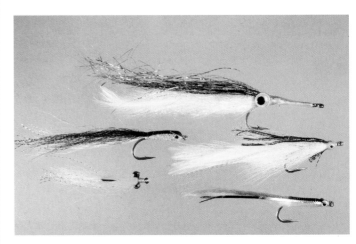

Flies for various members of the tuna family. Clockwise from top center: Ballyhoo, Lefty's Deceiver, Cowan's Albie Anchovy, Clouser Minnow, Epoxy Minnow.

Striped Bass and Bluefish Flies

Both of these species are often found together in mixed schools, so you can use the same flies for both. Let's dispose of the bluefish first. If they're in a feeding mood, they'll eat almost anything that moves. Bluefish are so aggressive that I like to fish for them with big hard-body poppers like the Skipping Bug, as you can often pull bluefish from a long distance away, or from deeper water, with a popper. Bulky baitfish imitations like Lefty's Deceivers in blue-and-white or bulky Clouser Minnows will catch them when they're close to the surface feeding on baitfish (which is almost all the time, night or day).

Traditional baitfish imitations for striped bass. Clockwise from top left: Clouser Minnow, Lefty's Deceiver, Skipping Bug, Cowan's Magnum Baitfish, Crease Fly, Epoxy Minnow.

Striped bass over open water will also take large baitfish imitations, but these guys are far more selective. They might take a 4-inch baitfish fly while feeding on 1-inch sand eels; then again, they might not. In open water, you'll often find striped bass feeding on squid; in that case, a white Deceiver or one of the specific squid imitations will catch their interest.

The closer to shore stripers move, the more selective in their feeding they seem to be, so if you're fishing in sight of the beach, it's wise to pay attention to what they're eating. Big ones could be crashing into schools of menhaden, in which case you'll need the biggest fly you

These crab (left) and shrimp (right) imitations, commonly used for bonefish and permit, can be deadly on striped bass in shallow water.

can throw. The next evening they could be into small glass minnows or sand eels (a long, skinny fish, not an eel), and a sparsely tied Epoxy Minnow in size 8 might be the only fly to draw any strikes.

Stripers in shallow water will also feed on crabs and shrimp, as well as baitfish. Clouser Minnows work here, as well as the same crab and shrimp patterns you'd use for bonefish and permit. Although you'd typically use the larger size 2s and 4s, I've seen days when the only fly stripers would take is a size-8 shrimp imitation like a Crazy Charley bonefish fly.

OTHER SALTWATER SPECIES

There are so many other saltwater species that can be taken on a fly it would (and has) taken up entire books on the subject. Sailfish, marlin, jack crevalle, trevally, grouper, flounder, dorado, roosterfish, yellowtail, and perhaps hundreds of other species have been or could be caught on a fly. I've tried to give you a sampling of the most popular ones, and all of the flies listed in Table 8 below will catch these species, as well as the more common glamour fish.

WHEN TO CHANGE FLIES

How do you know when to change flies, and how long do you stick with a particular pattern? Generally, if the fish are visible and they ignore your fly or chase it without taking, you can do two things: either change flies, or change your presentation slightly.

If you're fishing to a rising trout and he either splashes at your fly or ignores it, you know something is wrong. Catch another natural insect and make sure your imitation is correct. Watch the rise form. Is he really taking insects on the surface?

At the other end of the scale, if you're fishing blind and don't know where the fish are, you might want to keep the same fly on your tippet for hours. Atlantic salmon may ignore your fly for ninety-nine casts and take the fly on the hundredth. You may be fishing a nymph deep on a sinking line in a trout lake, not knowing where the fish are. Here, you might keep moving, covering the water thoroughly. If the nymph you're using is a proven favorite, why switch?

FILLING YOUR FLY BOX

Let's say you're taking a fishing trip and have a recommended list of flies from a guide or fishing lodge. How many of each should you have?

I feel naked without at least four flies in each size of each recommended pattern. This may sound like an inordinate amount, especially if your recommended list is quite large. Look at it this way—even a proficient fly caster expects to lose at least two flies in the trees or on submerged logs or rocks during a day of fishing, plus one fly lost by striking a large fish too hard. If you only have one or two of the pattern that's working and you leave them in the trees, your long-awaited fishing trip is going to be spoiled. Flies are cheap compared to gasoline or travel expenses.

When you first start fly-fishing, you may have trouble identifying hook sizes and patterns merely by eyeballing them. This will come in time, as there is no shortcut. I suggest that you keep patterns and sizes together in a fly box and attach a sticky label to the top of each compartment of your fly box, writing on it the pattern and size in pencil. Not only will you learn fly names more quickly, but it will also make it much easier to reorder your favorite patterns.

RECOMMENDED FLY LISTS

The following are lists of flies that should be useful for the favorite fly-rod fish we've discussed. Like all such lists, they have the inherent drawback of my own biases on fly selection, but they're a good place to start if you have no other source of information.

Table 5: Recommended Flies By Fish Species	
TROUT—EASTERN U.S.	**SIZES**
Dry Flies	
Adams Parachute	12-20
Light Cahill	12-20
Blue-Winged Olive Parachute	14-24
Hendrickson Comparadun	12-16
Quill Gordon	14-18
Ausable Wulff	10-14
Black Ant	14-20
Black Midge	20-24
Tan Elk-Wing Caddis	14-18
Rusty Spinner	12-18
White-Black Trico Spinner	20, 24
Parachute Beetle	14-18
Yellow Humpy	12-18
Rabbit's Foot Emerger, PMD	14-18
Rabbit's Foot Emerger, Olive	16-18
Griffith's Gnat	16-22
X-Caddis	14-18
CDC Emerging Caddis	14-18
LeTort Hopper	8-14
Nymphs and Wets	
Bead Head Hare's Ear	8-16
Zug Bug	10-16
Olive/Gray Scud	12, 14
Pheasant Tail	14-18
Bead Head Pheasant Tail	14-18
La Fontaine Sparkle Pupa	12-18
Prince	10-16
Wets	
Hare's Ear Wet	10-14
Soft Hackle Hare's Ear	10-16
Leadwing Coachman	10-14
Blue Quill	12-16
Streamers and Bucktails	
Black Woolly Bugger	4-12
Conehead Muddler Minnow	6-12
Tunghead Marabou Muddler, Black	6-10
Black-Nose Dace	6-12
Gray Ghost	6-12
Black Ghost	4-10
Moto's Minnow	6-10
Bead Head Light Brite Zonker	6-10
TROUT—WESTERN U.S.	
Dry Flies	
Western Green Drake	10, 12
Pale Morning Dun Parachute	14-20
Adams Parachute	12-20
Blue-Winged Olive Thorax	14-22

Tan Elk–Wing Caddis	12-18
Royal Wulff	12-18
Yellow Humpy	10-18
Rusty Spinner	14-18
Olive Spinner	14-18
White/Black Trico Spinner	18-22
Orange Stimulator	4-8
Bugmeister	8-14
Schroeder's Parachute Hopper	8-12
Parachute Beetle	12-18
Rabbit's Foot Emerger, PMD	14-18
Rabbit's Foot Emerger, Olive	14-18
Griffith's Gnat	16-22
X-Caddis	14-18
CDC Emerging Caddis	14-18
Olive RS2	16-22
Rusty Emerger	14-18

Nymphs

Kauffman's Stone	4-8
Bitch Creek	4-8
Bead Head Hare's Ear	8-16
Bead Head Pheasant Tail	12-18
Speckled Sedge	12-16
Bead Head Prince	10-18
Zug Bug	10-16
Czech Mate Nymph	12-16
La Fontaine Sparkle Pupa	12-18

Wets

Black Woolly Worm	6-12
Leadwing Coachman	12, 14
Hare's Ear	10-14
Dark Cahill	12, 14
Light Cahill	12, 14

Streamers and Bucktails

Brown Matuka Sculpin	2-6
Black Woolly Bugger	4-10
Moto's Minnow	4-8
Black Tunghead Marabou Muddler	4-8
Double Bunny	2-6
Conehead Zuddler	4-8
White Conehead Marabou Muddler	2-12
Muddler Minnow	2-12
Olive Matuka	6, 8
Black Leech	4-8

SMALLMOUTH BASS
Floating Flies

Sneaky Pete Popper	4, 8
Yellow/Black/White Bass Popper	4
Peeper Popper	4
Black Bluegill Bug	12

Streamers and Bucktails

Muddler Minnow	4-12
Black Bead Head Woolly Bugger	4-8
Black Matuka	6-10
Conehead Zuddler	6-10
White Conehead Marabou Muddler	6-12
Crayfish	4-8
Yellow Matuka	6, 8

Nymphs

Montana	4-12
Hare's Ear	8, 10

LARGEMOUTH BASS
Floating Flies

Bass Popper	1/0
Yellow Minnow Popper	1/0
Dry Rind Frog	2, 4
Hair Mouse	2
Sneaky Pete	4
Yellow Keel Bass Bug	4

Sinking Flies

Woolly Bugger	4
Gulley Worm	1/0
Gulley Ultra Craw	1/0
Florida Muddler	4/0
White Marabou Muddler	1
Silver Prismatic Shiner	2

ATLANTIC SALMON FLIES
Wet Flies

Green Butt	2-10
Cosseboom	4-8
Rusty Rat	4-8
Silver Rat	4-8
Undertaker	4-8
Blue Charm Low-Water	4-8
Salmon Muddler Double	4-8
Green Highlander	4-8

Dry Flies

Buck Bug	4-8
Bomber	4-8
Royal Wulff	4-8

STEELHEAD—WEST COAST OCEAN RUNS

Wet Flies

Thor	4-8
Purple Peril	4-8
Black Woolly Bugger	4-8
Comet	4-8
Skunk	4-8
Skykomish Sunrise	4-8
Polar Shrimp	4-8

Dry Flies

Royal Wulff	4-8
Grease Liner	4-8

STEELHEAD—LAKE-RUN FISH IN GREAT LAKES AND ALASKA

Wet Flies

Babine	4-8
Glo Bugs (Orange, Red, and Chartreuse)	6
Cluster Egg	8
Royal Coachman	4-8
Fall Favorite	2-8

Streamers

Black Woolly Bugger	4-8
Egg-Sucking Leech	4-8
White Conehead Zuddler	4-8

Nymphs

Steelhead Stone	6-12
Steelhead Hammer	6-12
Bead Head Pheasant Tail	10-12
Montana	4-8
Hare's Ear	6-12

SALTWATER FLIES—OPEN OCEAN SPECIES

Blue/White Skipping Bug	2/0
Yellow Skipping Bug	2/0
White Deceiver	2/0, 2
Sailfish Streamer	4/0
Blue/White Deceiver	2/0, 2
Yellow Deceiver	2/0, 2

SALTWATER FLIES—INSHORE SPECIES

Pink Shrimp	2-6
Brown Snapping Shrimp	4, 6
Permit Fly	1
Green Mantis	4, 6
Horror	4
White Deceiver	2/0, 2
Blue/White Deceiver	2/0, 2
Chase Tarpon	4/0
Gold Cup	4/0
Yellow Skipping Bug	2/0
Blue/White Skipping Bug	2/0
Honey Blonde	2, 1/0, 3/0

BONEFISH FLIES

Crazy Charley, Plastic Eyes	4, 6
Crazy Charley, Bead Eyes	4, 6
Crazy Charley, Metal Eyes	4, 6
Gotcha	4, 6
Meko Special	4, 6
Cowan's Bonefish Scampi	6, 8
Simram	4
Whisper Crab	6

PERMIT FLIES

Del's Merkin	1/0, 2, 4
Flexo Crab	2

TARPON FLIES

Ruoff's Lay Up Fly	2/0, 1/0
Black Death	3/0, 2/0, 1/0
Malzone's Medium Blonde	3/0, 2/0, 1/0
Brown Tarpon Bunny	2/0, 1/0
Malzone's Greenie Weenie	3/0, 2/0, 1/0

REDFISH AND SEA TROUT FLIES

Flexo Popper	2
Lefty's Deceiver, Green/White	1/0, 2
Clouser Minnow, Red/White	2
Bendback	2
Flexo Crab	2

BARRACUDA FLIES

Double Hook Barracuda Fly	2/0
Lefty's Deceiver, Chartreuse	2/0

SNOOK FLIES

Lefty's Deceiver, Green/White	1/0, 2
Clouser Minnow, Red/White	2, 2/0
Skipping Bug	2, 2/0
Epoxy Minnow	2-6

SHARK FLIES

Skipping Bug	2/0
Shark Fly	4/0
Lefty's Deceiver, Red/White	3/0

FLIES FOR TUNA AND THEIR RELATIVES

Clouser Minnow, Olive/White	2/0, 2, 6
Lefty's Deceiver, White	2/0, 2, 6
Lefty's Deceiver, Olive/White	2/0, 2, 6
Epoxy Baitfish, Chartreuse	2-6
Crease Fly, Blue/Silver	4

STRIPED BASS AND BLUEFISH FLIES

Clouser Minnow, Olive/White	2/0, 2, 6
Clouser Minnow, Chartreuse	2/0, 2, 6
Lefty's Deceiver, White	2/0, 2, 6
Lefty's Deceiver, Olive/White	2/0, 2, 6
Epoxy Baitfish, Chartreuse	2-6
Skipping Bug	2/0, 2
Gurgler	2
Tabory's Snake Fly, Black	2/0, 2
Del's Merkin	2, 4
Crazy Charley, Deep version (metal eyes)	4, 6
Cowan's Baitfish, Olive/White	2/0

{ Venus Setting—Evening Rises }

Chapter Eight

Stream Tactics

CURRENT ADDS MYSTERIES AND challenges to fishing. Resident trout and smallmouth bass don't move around much in streams, preferring to find a spot that offers them easy meals without costing them a lot of energy. A knowledge of the needs of stream fish plus a basic understanding of stream hydraulics will enable you to "read the water," which is an angler's term for being able to predict where trout and bass hold in streams.

THE STREAM ENVIRONMENT

Before we can discuss finding fish in a stream, you should understand the following terms in relation to moving water:

Pool. A pool is a relatively deep area in a stream, generally with fast water at the upstream end (or head), a broad flat expanse of slow water (or middle), and a narrower, gradually faster area of current (known as the tail). Pools can be anywhere from 3 feet long in a mountain brook to half a mile long on big rivers.

Riffle. Riffles usually separate one pool from another. They are areas of more rapidly descending topography than pools; the water is shallower, faster, and the surface of the water is more broken.

Runs. Runs are midway in depth between pools and riffles, and narrower than either pools or riffles. The water, at least on the surface, is faster than in a pool.

Pocket water. Pocket water is a run or deep riffle with big rocks or boulders on the bottom, causing the surface of the water to be frothy and heavily broken.

Undercut bank. An undercut bank is formed in a pool, riffle, or run when the current erodes the bank under the surface of the water, making a trough of water that is overhung by rocks or soil.

This pool on Wyoming's Shoshone River has it all—large rocks at the head to break the current, submerged rocks in the middle to provide further cover from predators and a refuge from fast currents, good cover along the bank in the form of more rocks, and smooth water at the tail of the pool where drifting food will be concentrated both vertically and horizontally. If possible, it's best to observe a pool from above, from quite a distance away, before you begin to fish it.

Although this riffle on Idaho's South Fork of the Snake River looks shallow and featureless, it will hold plenty of trout in its deeper slots. Also, trout may move into shallow riffles to feed when there is an insect hatch, if there is a deep-water refuge nearby.

Deeper than a riffle with fast current, this run on Montana's Madison River holds plenty of trout in places where they have protection from the brunt of the current.

Brawling pocket water like this on California's Merced River is fun but tricky to fish. Like any other fast water, look for places where trout find a slight break in the current.

In this Montana meadow spring creek, the best cover will be found along the undercut banks.

TROUT ENVIRONMENTS

Trout in streams need water temperatures in the proper range, a place to feed where they won't expend more energy than they obtain by feeding, a place to run and hide when predators threaten, and proper spawning habitat. An understanding of all of these except the last will help you find fish in a stream. Trout will move out to spawn sometime between late fall and early spring, depending on the species, but they'll return home when you begin to fish for them next spring.

Fish, unlike mammals, are cold-blooded and cannot regulate their internal temperature. They need a narrow range of temperatures for survival and also have an optimum temperature range in which feeding levels are at their highest and growth is fastest. For trout, the survival range is from 32 to about 75 degrees Fahrenheit; the optimum range for feeding (and for fishing) is from 50 to 68 degrees for brown trout and rainbows, the most common species. Brook trout and cutthroat require slightly colder water temperatures for optimum growth and feeding.

Below 45 degrees, trout feed little and are almost in a state of suspended animation, not expending much energy and requiring little food. Above 68 degrees they will feed somewhat if the water is broken and has sufficient oxygen concentration. It isn't actually the heat above 75 degrees that kills trout. As water gets warmer it can hold less oxygen, yet the metabolism of the fish increases, and if the water gets too warm the trout simply suffocate.

During the winter and early spring, trout will hold in slow, deep areas where they don't have to fight the current to stay alive. As the water warms above 50 degrees in the spring, they will be found almost anywhere—in riffles, pools, and runs. The temperature everywhere is well within the optimum range. Some trout streams never get over 65 degrees, and the fish will stay in the same places until spawning time, but in those that get too warm the trout will seek colder, more oxygenated water. Springs and small feeder streams are almost always colder, so look for trout below incoming streams and spring seeps during the summer. You can use a stream thermometer to find these spots. Other places to find trout in midsummer are shaded areas of fast, broken water. Even though the water temperature in fast water may be above 65 degrees, there will be sufficient oxygen to support trout here. When the temperature of the stream gets above 75 degrees for more than a day, trout will move to cooler areas. If they can't, they'll die.

Much has been written in trout literature about *cover*: the old brown trout under a rock, the brookie next to a log, or the cutthroat holding beneath an undercut bank. Recent studies have shown that trout prefer to live wherever they can obtain food easily, and that they only need the protection of a rock, log, or undercut bank nearby, somewhere they can bolt to when frightened. Of course, their feeding stations may be near these obstructions, but they may also be right out in the middle of a flat, open pool.

Trout must face upstream, because that's the way they're built. If a fish faced broadside to the current or downstream, he'd be pushed away by the current. The streamlined design of trout enables them to rest their heads on the stream bottom almost effortlessly. When they see an interesting morsel drift by, they merely tip their fins upward and the current carries them up to intercept the food; then they tip their fins down to return to the bottom. The current carries them downstream in the process of feeding; the only time they have to work is to return to their spot, swimming back upstream.

Stream trout are territorial and live and feed in a very small area. They will defend their seat against other trout. If you catch a good trout from a spot this year, there will most likely be another good one there next year. If you release him, the same fish will often be there, as trout live to be up to ten years old and will use the same territory from year to year, unless forced out by a more aggressive fish. But even if that big trout dies, another nice fish will eventually find the same spot, unless the river suffers a catastrophic flood and the riverbed changes.

We can't really predict where these favored spots will be, but we can certainly narrow things down a bit.

Wherever moving water encounters an object it will be slowed down, due to the friction between a hard surface and water molecules. The surface of a stream in the middle of a straight stretch of water is always faster than water near the bottom or near the banks. Where the current meets a rock on the bottom of the stream, there will be areas of dead, slower water in front of, behind, and on the sides of the rock. This phenomenon allows such tiny, almost weightless animals like aquatic insects to move freely in the gravel in a streambed without being swept away. It also gives trout places to live.

Looking at a piece of very fast pocket water, we often think, "How can a trout live in there?" Upon closer examination, we see many different currents, fast in some areas and almost motionless in others. There is an old saying about there being "a trout behind every rock," and in some of the best trout streams there will be a trout behind, in front of, and even on the sides of many rocks. The more varied a stream bottom, the more trout it has the potential to hold. In a good trout stream with adequate temperature and food supply, the only limiting factors to trout abundance will be feeding sites and fishing pressure.

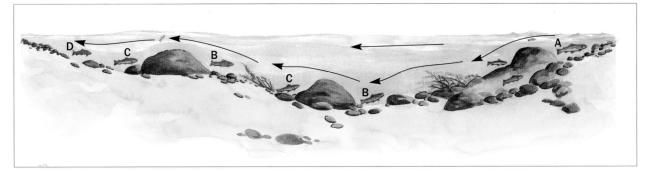

A vertical cross section of a pool showing where trout are most likely to be found: At the head of the pool where the depth first starts to drop off (A), in the depression in front of rocks (B), behind and alongside rocks (C), and in the tail of the pool (D).

Look for trout in places where they have a spot to rest that is in or immediately adjacent to the main current or currents in a stream. You can spot the main current because it will have the fastest water flow, generally the most depth, and it will be the area that carries the most bubbles and debris—and food—downstream. Trout will seldom be found in extremely slow areas of a stream, simply because these places do not provide enough food. Trout may move in and out of these areas occasionally to ambush minnows, but they won't stay there for long.

You will seldom be able to see a trout in a stream, even if he is 10 feet away. Trout are well camouflaged against the bottom of a stream, and they can change their skin shading from light to dark in a matter of days. I've caught brown trout that were feeding alongside a rock or log, and the side that was in the sun was light-colored, while the other side was a couple of shades darker. A trout's camouflage is so good that it's easier to spot fish by their shadows than by trying to see them.

The best time to spot trout is when they are rising. A trout cannot take an insect off the surface without making some kind of disturbance, however subtle.

The following are places that almost always hold trout:

Rocks. The classic situation to find trout is in the slow current behind rocks. There is also a spot of slow current in front of rocks and, to a lesser degree, along the sides of larger rocks. Trout will use rocks anywhere from the size of a grapefruit to half the size of a house.

Where riffles meet pools. Where a riffle runs into a pool there will be a depression formed where the faster water has dug into the bottom. Trout can sit in this depression with little effort, waiting for insects that live in the riffle to drift into the pool. Although adult trout are seldom found in shallow riffles, keep your eye out for slightly deeper depressions in riffles. A good trout can sit in this trench and feed to his heart's content, passed up by most anglers.

Tails of pools. Tails of pools are shallower than the middle, and as the current quickens at the tail there will be a slow area formed along the bottom as the water from the pool hits the shallower tail. Tails of pools are great spots for trout, because they are generally narrower than the middle, so the drifting food is more concentrated here.

Banks. Many streams have a main current flow along the banks, and the banks will break the current enough for trout to have a perfect feeding spot. Trees and bushes that overhang the water also provide trout with a steady supply of terrestrial insects, and trout will take up feeding stations under and near them. Overhanging trees provide protection from predators such as ospreys, eagles, herons, mergansers, and kingfishers. Other than humans, avian predators are a trout's major cause for alarm.

A trout's shadow is often more distinct and easy to spot than the fish itself. Without a shadow to help, this trout lying alongside a log would be very difficult to pick out.

Sometimes a rising trout may make a distinct splash. Other times, it may rise like this, where all you may see is a dimple or wink in the surface. This fish probably took something in the surface film rather than on top of it, and the insect was probably small.

Now an overhead view of where to find trout. The fish at the back eddies (A) are actually facing downstream (but up-current). Points that jut out from the river bank (B) are also prime places. Look for deeper pockets in riffles (C) and pocket water (D). Trout will hold in front of rocks and logs (E), behind them (F), or along their sides (G). Some of the most overlooked places are small side channels in the river (H).

Even though the tails of pools like this one on Wyoming's New Fork River are often flat and shallow, trout feed here because drifting food is concentrated both horizontally and vertically.

A perfect bank for trout in a small Idaho stream: Deeper and slightly slower current that runs up against a bank that offers both rocks and overhanging foliage for protection.

In many large western rivers, most of the large trout will be found a few feet from grassy banks; the centers of the rivers are mainly populated with small trout and whitefish.

Downed trees. Trees that have fallen into a river, whether they are logs lying parallel to the current or "sweepers" (trees still attached to the bank, lying at a 90-degree angle to the current), provide a break in the current and protection for the trout.

Flats. Areas of flat water with moderate currents and a depth of 1 to 3 feet are among the finest trout habitats you'll find, as long as there are rocks or other obstructions on the bottom that provide places for the trout to rest, and shelter should danger threaten.

Flat water will hold more trout than you think, especially if the bottom is rough and uneven like this place on Utah's Green River.

Where fast currents meet slow water. Where there is an interface between fast and slow currents you'll find trout. The fast current carries the food, and the slow current holds the trout where they don't have to move very far for their food.

Where feeder streams enter a larger river. These spots are especially important in large rivers that get warm during the summer, and trout may move from their normal positions to congregate in unbelievable numbers below these sources of cool water during hot spells. Trout do most of their spawning in feeder streams, so look for browns and brookies here in the fall and rainbows and cutthroats in the spring.

Anywhere in spring creeks. Spring creeks, as opposed to rocky (freestone) trout streams, derive their flow mainly from subsurface springs rather than groundwater. They are constant in temperature, stable, and slow flowing, with a profusion of aquatic plants. Because of a rich food supply, slow current, and the profusion of weed beds, trout will hold almost anywhere in spring creeks. Still, the best places to find trout feeding in spring creeks will be close to the banks, or where you see a light spot of gravel or sand between weed beds. These depressions let a trout spot its food better, and like rocks, offer protection from the current.

From the trout's point of view, objects that don't protrude above the surface of the stream are just as good as those that do. Sometimes you'll be able to see them with po-

This midstream rock on Utah's Green River is sure to hold several good trout.

larized sunglasses; other times the surface of the stream will give you clues. Wrinkles or boils on the surface indicate turbulence from submerged objects. In two equally fast pieces of water, you can bet that the one with a broken surface will hold more trout than the one with a smooth surface.

A Trout's Senses

Trout are very nervous fish. The angler who strolls into a trout stream without caution may never see, much less catch, a single trout in an entire day's fishing.

Trout are constantly on the alert for predators. Most of them come from above: herons, mergansers, kingfishers, raccoons, and mink. Otters and such large fish as northern pike are predators that attack from below the surface, but they are much less common, and a trout will tolerate a human swimming with scuba gear much closer than one looming above him.

Trout perceive danger in two ways: visually and through their lateral line system, a network of nerves that senses vibrations in the water. Both senses are extremely acute. To catch trout consistently you must be aware of their scope and their limitations.

Trout can't see objects that are very far away underwater. Because even the purest water has some suspended matter in it, light entering the water from above is diffused, much like car headlights in a fog. You can probably wade to within 10 feet of a trout without his seeing your legs.

The upper part of your body, however, is a different story. Trout can see very well above the surface of the water, judging by the fact that they can leap out of the water to catch a caddisfly in midair. Because of the refractive properties of water, though, a trout can see only a portion of what surrounds the surface, a phenomenon known as his *window*.

The window is a cone that occupies a 97-degree angle above the fish's head. Because light that strikes the surface of the water below 10 degrees above the horizontal plane is reflected and does not enter the water, a fish sees 180 degrees compressed into 97 degrees. Consequently, there is some distortion of objects, especially on the lower edges of the window; objects that are 10 degrees above the horizontal are not seen at all, and much of the outside world that is low on the horizon is distorted, because the remainder of the 160 degrees is compressed into a 97 degree cone.

What does this mean to the angler? Looking at the illustration of the trout's window, you can see that the lower you keep your profile, the less likely it is that a trout will see you. A trout in shallow water is less likely to see

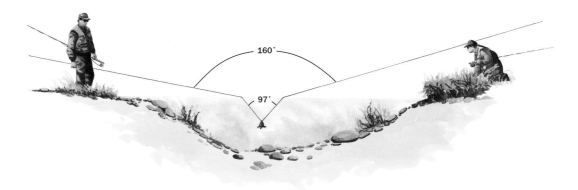

A trout's window. By keeping your profile low, you'll be less noticeable to a wary fish.

you than one that is holding in deep water, because the 10-degree and 97-degree angles remain constant—the fish takes his window with him as he moves up and down in the water.

A fish can see on both sides and straight ahead, and because of the physiology of his eyes, can see in all directions at once, except directly behind him. In a stream, where a trout is facing upstream, you can approach him quite close from downstream. If you are upstream or to one side of the fish, you should stay farther away or cast from a kneeling or crouching position. This is one great advantage of wading—when you are in the water, your profile is lower.

In addition, like all animals (including us), trout will detect movement easier than they will an object that is not moving or moving slowly. Watch a heron stalking a fish and you'll see this phenomenon in action. So when approaching trout, the best thing you can do is to keep your movements slow and subtle. Casting side-armed, so the rod and line are lower and less visible, is another way to cut down on movement.

Why the preoccupation with trout seeing you? Does a trout naturally fear humans?

A trout has an instinctive fear of anything moving above the water. If he sees you or your fly rod moving back and forth, it's likely that he will become frightened and spook. If a trout is rising steadily and stops abruptly, you can assume that your approach has not been careful enough. This is called "putting him down."

Spooking has a number of degrees. A cast that splashes on the water might just make the fish a little nervous. What he'll do is stop feeding, sink slowly to the bottom, and stay motionless for anywhere from a minute to a half hour or more. The best thing to do in this situation is move quietly to the bank, sit down, and wait for him to resume feeding. Approach him more carefully next time.

An overt move on your part, such as entering his window or actually walking near him, will cause the trout to bolt for the cover of a log or rock, and in that case he's probably finished for the day and won't feed for hours.

A trout's vision is not the only thing you have to be concerned with. More trout are spooked because they hear our approach through vibrations in their lateral line than actually see us. I'd be willing to bet that even the most careful fly fisher spooks at least half the trout in every pool he fishes.

A trout can hear anything that sets up vibrations in the water, and can detect your presence from much farther away this way than by seeing you. By careless wading I've spooked trout that were over 60 feet away.

Many things can cause frightening vibrations. Most of them can be avoided by a careful approach. On streams with sod banks, heavy footfalls will warn trout of your approach long before you know that they are rising. The sound of rocks knocking against each other will carry incredible distances underwater; try it sometime when you're swimming. Splashy wading, noisy line pickups, and sloppy casts will also decrease your success.

In very still, slow pools even wading too fast will form ripples that warn the trout of your approach. The solution here is to wade very slowly, moving your feet only inches at a step and taking breaks between steps. On one Catskill stream that I fish it may take me fifteen minutes to wade the 50 feet necessary to get within casting range of the fish.

Water conditions, the weather, and how preoccupied the trout are with feeding will determine how closely you can approach a rising or nymphing trout. In riffled water, not only will the background noise of rushing water cover your approach, but the broken surface also distorts the trout's window. In broken water you can come up behind a trout, approaching him from downstream, sometimes as close as 10 feet. If you're upstream of him, of course, he can still see you, although not as well as in flat water.

The placid surface of a pool will require much more stealth. Not only does the trout have a relatively good window on the outside world, but your wading or careless casting can also send ripples through the water that will tell him something is amiss. In a pool with a smooth surface but relatively swift current, these ripples will be dissipated quickly, but if the current is slow as well, your ripples can carry up to 60 or 70 feet away. Watch the water in front of you. If the ripples threaten to carry themselves all the way to where you think a fish is, or where one is rising, slow down.

Cloudy weather or poor visibility during the early-morning and late-evening hours decreases a fish's ability to perceive individual objects, so they are easier to approach. When the sun is high in the sky, it's much easier for a trout to spot you silhouetted against the skyline or against streamside foliage. Allowing your shadow to fall across a spot where you suspect a fish is sitting is definitely taboo; trout are instantly spooked by shadows from above.

Surprisingly, trout in shallow water, like this rainbow, are easier to approach because their window on the outside world is tightly constricted.

You can also use bright sun to your advantage. A trout is blinded by bright sun, just as we are, because they have no eyelids, and if you can approach the fish so that the sun is behind you but your shadow is not falling on a likely looking spot, all the better.

Some fly fishers go to the extent of wearing dark green or camouflage fishing vests so that they blend in with streamside foliage. I've never been able to quantify the difference between wearing light and dark clothing, but I suspect that if you are careful about the direction from which you approach a fish and move slowly, clothing color is unimportant. This makes sense, as long as you make sure you maintain grass, trees, or a high bank behind you. Otherwise, all that dark clothing just makes a better silhouette.

Rain on the water makes trout lose their caution, probably because of a combination of lower light levels and the distortion on the surface of the water caused by raindrops. Many insects hatch more readily during rain or cloudy weather, and increased feeding activity by the fish also makes them easier to approach.

A trout that is feeding with a steady rhythm is always easier to approach than one that is feeding sporadically or not at all. A combination of factors are at work when he's taking an insect every ten seconds or so, including the fact that he's probably preoccupied with feeding and doesn't have his guard up as he normally would. A trout that is actively feeding will be hanging close to the surface. His window is smaller, so you can approach him closer without his seeing you; plus, he's focusing his eyes on objects that are close to him, so his depth of field is very shallow.

WADING

Wading is as much a skill as fly casting, not only for a careful approach, as we've seen, but also to keep from taking spills or going over the tops of your waders.

Long strides are out when you're wading, unless you're crossing a shallow riffle where you won't be doing any fishing. When wading, you should use your feet to feel your way across the bottom, never lifting your feet more than a foot or so off the bottom—something like a slow shuffle.

The two most important things to remember when wading are that it's always easier to wade downstream than upstream, and it's easier to move your body facing perpendicular to the current (water flows into the side of your legs) than broadside to it (water flows into your knees, front or back).

Suppose you're trying to cross a river of unknown depth. You don't know where the deep spots are. The best thing to do is find the spot that looks most shallow, either a riffled area or one that appears lighter in color. The tail of a pool is usually a good bet. Start at the downstream end of the shallow area and walk carefully upstream at an angle to the current that's comfortable. If the water becomes too deep, you can always retrace your steps. If you try to wade straight across a fast river, the current may push you downstream into a deep hole, forcing you to take a bath. Wading directly downstream presents the same problem; you may find yourself being pushed into a hole, and the power of the current may make it physically impossible to retrace your steps.

When wading fast water or around slippery, round rocks, take care to always have one foot planted firmly on the bottom while the other feels its way forward to find a second firm purchase. Always wade between rocks and boulders, never on top of them. The tops of rocks are weathered smooth by the current, and are unwise places to plant your feet. There is usually an area of sand or gravel just behind and sometimes in front of midstream boulders, giving you both relief from the current and a firm place to plant your feet.

If you're wading in water that's thigh- to waist-deep and start to lose your balance, you can use your fly rod to right yourself. Plunge the rod into the water. It should give you enough support to regain your balance. As long as the water is deep enough and you don't bang the rod on a rock, you won't have to worry about breaking it.

A wading staff is a great boon to those who are not confident wading fast water or who are unsteady on their feet. A staff can help with your balance and to find hidden obstructions and deep spots. Always use the wading staff on your downstream side, pushing forward and slightly upstream as you use it. A convenient emergency staff can be made from a streamside stick. In addition, if you're a poor swimmer or in less-than-perfect shape, a personal flotation device (PFD) might save your life. You can buy fishing vests with the standard kapok or synthetic fiber, but they're terribly bulky and hot. You can also buy small PFDs that you wear around your chest or waist. They are flat and unobtrusive until you pull a ripcord, which fires off a CO_2 cartridge that instantly inflates the PFD.

Wading in shallow water is potentially more dangerous than wading in deep water. There is a temptation to be overconfident and wade quickly in shallow water, increasing the chance that you'll trip on a slippery rock or log. A fall in deep water will give you a bath and a little swim at worst, but a fall in shallow water can cause bruises or broken bones.

If you do lose your footing in deep water and take a plunge, remain calm, try to keep your head above water, and try to keep your feet in front of you so your head doesn't bang against rocks. The current will carry you to shallower water, and it's better to ride out the current than to struggle and swim to shore. If you're a confident swimmer, you may want to swim to shallow water; a fairly decent dog paddle can be done while wearing waders. The old story about a man in waders tipping upside down because of trapped air in his waders is absolutely

When wading tricky currents, remember to keep your body sideways to the current, and look for patches of sand in front of and behind rocks.

untrue. However, an open pair of waders can become a sea anchor, preventing you from moving against the current. Always wear a wader belt and always keep it cinched up. Not only will the belt keep your waders from becoming a drogue, but it will also keep air inside the waders to give you better buoyancy. And in a quick spill where you get right up, it will keep most of the water out of your waders, and you'll be a much happier camper for the rest of the day.

One final word on wading that may save you a spill or two: Turning your body around in deep, fast water is best done by rotating in an upstream direction and leaning into the current slightly. Turning downstream will suddenly place your body broadside to the current, with an irresistible temptation to begin walking downstream. Once your momentum gets going, it's tough to stop moving, and you may find yourself being pushed into a deep hole. Also, consider what you're walking on—piles of sunken leaves can give way, pulling you down; and sunken tree branches can ensnare you and then break, causing you to drop down deeper than you want to go.

DRY-FLY FISHING

Before you begin to approach a rising trout, you should understand the effects of currents on your fly, fly line, and leader, and especially drag. Drag is responsible for as many trout refusing flies as the wrong size, shape, or color of your imitation.

If you cast directly across a current of uniform speed, your line and leader will always move faster than your fly. Imagine yourself directly across from a rising trout. You cast your dry fly 90 degrees to the current, about 2 feet above the riseform. The fly starts to drift directly downstream over the trout, but because the line and leader are moving more quickly than the fly, they begin to pull the fly across and downstream. A tiny V wake appears behind the fly. This is drag, as we spoke of in the section on mending, and it is very apparent from below the surface of the water. Natural insects skip and flutter across the surface of the water, but they don't leave wakes behind them. Drag will ordinarily cause a trout to ignore or refuse your fly.

The effects of drag are heightened when your fly line and/or leader falls in faster currents than your fly, which is a typical situation because trout are usually found in

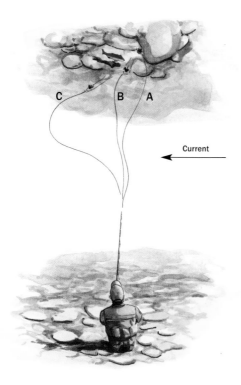

How drag develops: The fly lands in the slower water at A. The faster current in the middle of the river begins to push the fly line downstream, creating a belly in the line at B. Finally at C, the belly gets large enough to skid the fly across the water, giving it a wake that can alert trout that the bug they are about to eat is not acting naturally.

spots that are slightly sheltered from the current. Casting directly downstream on a tight line will cause your fly to drag immediately.

One solution is to approach a rising trout from directly downstream. Not only are you approaching him from his blind spot, but you'll also be placing your line and leader in the same current as the fly, so the danger of drag is greatly diminished.

To present a dry fly to a fish that is rising directly upstream of your position, begin to false-cast, working out a little line on each false cast until it looks as if the fly will land a foot or two above the rise. On the last false cast, follow through and lower your rod tip. Immediately start stripping line just as fast as the current brings it back to you. The line should be coiled neatly in your stripping hand, but if the current is extremely fast, you may not

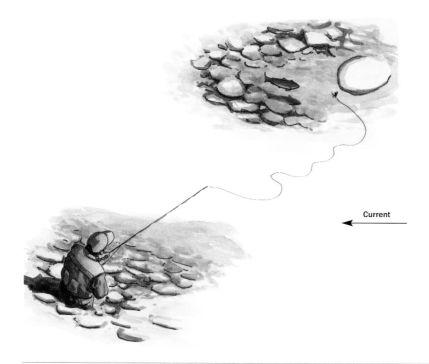

Throwing slack line is one way to minimize or eliminate drag. This can be used with both floating and sinking flies.

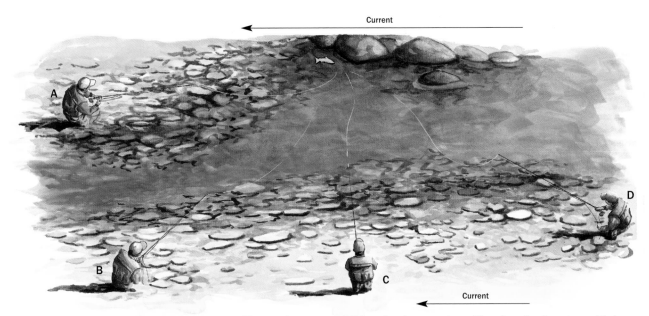

Four ways to approach a trout: From directly downstream (A), quartering upstream (B), from directly across-stream (C), or from directly upstream (D). Any of these angles, plus places in between them, can be used to approach a trout and deliver a fly if you use the proper cast and presentation.

have enough time to coil the line. In that case, just strip in the line and let it fall to the water at your side.

If slack develops below the rod tip, you're stripping too slowly. If the fly moves downstream faster than the current, you're stripping too fast.

Allowing slack line to accumulate below the rod tip causes a couple of problems. A trout will eject a fly almost immediately when he senses its artificiality, and you have to set the hook as soon as you see his rise. Too much slack line prevents you from setting the hook promptly. Second, slack line will be washed downstream, around your legs and behind you, causing tangles when you want to make another cast.

It's best to wait until the fly passes well below the fish before you pick up to make another cast. Ripping the line off the water right below a trout may spook him. Try not to pick up more line than you have to. If you're casting to a fish that is 30 feet above you, let the fly drift until it is 15 feet above you, pick up, and then make several snappy false casts to dry the fly, shooting about 5 feet of line with each false cast by letting it slip through your fingers. If you were right on target on the first cast, there's no need to adjust your line length. If the first cast was too short or too long, put some line back on the reel or strip some off accordingly.

Can you see the problem with casting directly upstream? With this strategy, your leader and possibly your line will land right on top of the trout's head. It's possible

to spook a trout this way, known as "lining" him. A cast that is a little sloppy is especially harmful from this angle, and even the very best casters blow a cast occasionally.

Speaking of blown casts, the worst possible thing to do when you make a bad cast is to rip the line off the water immediately. Let the whole mess drift well below the trout's position, then pick up and try again. Don't get caught off guard, though—bad casts have fooled some magnificent trout.

GET THE RIGHT ANGLE

A straight upstream cast is okay in riffled water, where the added disturbance won't alarm the trout, but on smooth water I prefer an alternative angle that has most of the benefits of an upstream cast and less chance of spooking the trout. It's called a *quartering upstream cast*, and it involves moving your position just a few feet to the right or left of the fish. You'll still be taking advantage of a relatively drag-free float and the trout's blind spot, but only the fly will pass over his head, if your cast has been accurate. Presentation and line pickup are exactly the same as with the straight upstream cast.

The same presentation can be achieved by casting a curve to the left or right, which also keeps your line and most of your leader off to one side of the trout. As I stated in the casting chapter, though, curve casts are inconsistent, and few of us can use them properly on a regular basis.

The quartering upstream cast is the best way to present a dry fly to a trout, but there will be times when this cast is impractical. One instance is when a trout is rising in front of an obstruction like a rock or log. Another is when a trout is rising in the almost dead-calm water behind a rock or next to the bank. If you approach a trout rising behind a rock from below, the fast water to the side of and behind the rock will whisk your line and leader downstream quickly, dragging the fly. In these instances you might try a *quartering downstream cast*, either casting slack into the line or using an upstream curve to prevent the fly from dragging immediately.

False-cast a little over 30 feet of line, aiming for a spot about 2 feet above his position. On the final false cast, check your rod at about 10:00 and pull back on the rod slightly, then drop the rod to waist level. Slack line will be formed, slack that will allow your fly to float drag-free over the trout.

You can also use a sidearm cast, or an upstream reach cast, forming an upstream curve that will have to be inverted before the fly will drag. In contrast to the upstream presentation, you don't retrieve line as the fly is drifting.

After the fly floats over the fish, don't pick it up immediately. Point the rod tip directly downstream, allowing the current to pull the fly and leader off to the side

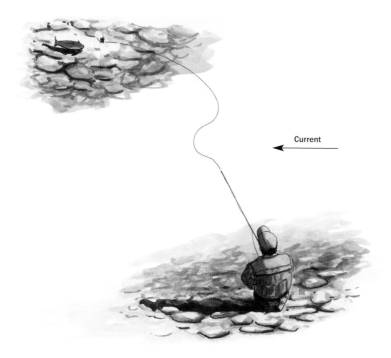

Current

An upstream curve is another way to foil drag. It can be done with a reach cast, a curve cast, or by making a quick mend after the fly hits the water.

Here's a typical example: A trout is rising about 6 inches from the bank, in very slow water. There is an area of fast current just out from the bank. You've tried him with a quartering upstream cast, but the fast current between you and the trout puts a belly into your line that drags the fly almost immediately.

Carefully move sideways, away from the trout, and wade upstream of his position. Remember that the trout can see you now if you approach too closely, because you're out of his blind spot, so you'll have to stay farther away and use a longer cast. Let's say you've moved about 10 feet upstream of his position and 30 feet away from him in a line diagonal to the current.

and below the trout. You can then retrieve and pick up your line for another cast without disturbing him.

In the situation where you have to cast from directly upstream of a trout, where a fish is rising just in front of a low bridge or brush pile, use the same tactics but throw an even looser cast for added slack. To prolong a drift, you can even point your rod tip directly downstream, wiggling it gently from side to side, feeding slack line through the guides.

On many large rivers, especially in the Rocky Mountains, the quartering downstream cast is used extensively for dry-fly fishing. It's said that this presentation is more effective because the fish sees the fly before he sees the leader, but I'm willing to bet it has more to do with the way the fly drifts than whether or not the trout sees your leader.

When float- or drift-fishing a river from a boat, the quartering downstream presentation is the best method to use, because as the boat floats downstream and a dry-fly cast upstream or directly across will drag almost immediately. With a good person at the oars and a cleverly presented downstream cast, it's possible to get a drag-free float of 50 feet or more.

Drag can be very subtle—so subtle that you can't see it from 20 feet away. If you present a dry fly to a steadily rising trout and he refuses it time and again, drag, rather than your fly pattern, may be at fault. Try a slight change in your position, or even try the trout from the other side of the river. Often a change in position will place your cast in different currents—currents that will allow you to obtain a drag-free float.

SOLVING DRY-FLY PROBLEMS

How long should you work over a rising trout before changing flies or giving up and moving on? That depends on your temperament and your confidence. Some fly fishers will work over the same trout for hours, especially if he's a good one, changing flies and positions until the trout is either hooked or spooked. Others may only try a few dozen casts before moving on to find another feeding fish. If there are a lot of fish feeding, changing fish rather than changing flies is not a bad idea, because trout are individuals, and what one refuses the next may inhale eagerly.

A trout's rise rhythm is important when you're fishing dry flies. When there are many natural flies on the water and a trout is holding just below the surface to take advantage of the abundance of food, rises will be deliberate and paced at regular intervals. If you can determine the time between rises, try to pitch your fly to him when you think the next rise is due.

A trout may also rise at infrequent or irregular intervals. Here, the best strategy is to cast to him as soon as he rises, while he's still looking at the surface.

It's always best to cast slightly above a trout's riseform. The force of the current as a trout rises will push him downstream of his observation position, and casting directly to the rise may place your fly in his blind spot. In fast water

where the fish are not easily disturbed, I like to cast 1 to 2 feet upstream of the rise. In slow water, try to lead the rise by at least 2 feet or more so that the disturbance of the fly and leader landing on the water are well above your target.

If you're unsure of your accuracy or exactly where the trout is, always try to err on the short rather than the long side. A cast that's too short will only put the fly behind or off to the side of the trout's vision, so he'll ignore it. A cast that is too long may put the leader, or, even worse, the line, right on top of him.

How much of a drag problem a particular position presents may determine how far above the trout's rise you cast your dry fly. In some spots, especially those with swirly, conflicting currents, or when a trout is rising in slow water adjacent to very fast water, you'll be able to get a drag-free float of only a couple of inches. This may be enough. If it isn't, you'll have to resort to something else.

One solution—the one I like least—can be used when you're directly across from a trout that is rising in slow water and there are fast currents between you and him. Holding your rod tip high helps to keep the fly line out of the fast water so your fly isn't whisked away immediately. The problem here is that it's very difficult to set the hook in this position. In addition, holding the rod high tends to put a belly of line between the rod tip and the water that gravity will pull toward you, dragging the fly anyway.

A midstream obstruction like a rock or log can sometimes be used to advantage. If you can cast so that your line drapes over the obstruction, it may hold your line upstream long enough to permit a drag-free float.

Throwing an extra amount of slack into your cast is probably the best way to conquer very tricky drag situations, and there is a way to exaggerate this effect. Reel in your line, clip off your fly and tippet, and add a new tippet of the same diameter—but longer. Adding a foot or so to your tippet will cause the last part of your leader to land in loose coils, giving you a foot or so of extra drift before drag sets in. In tricky spots, I'll often use a tippet as long as 5 feet. Casting this rig isn't as pretty, but it can be deadly.

Mends can be used to help avoid drag, but I don't like to use them because they are difficult to accomplish without moving the fly as well as the line and leader. Remember to let some line slip from your hand as you mend to help alleviate this problem. I usually use mends only at the end of a drift, when the line starts to belly and drag is imminent anyway.

Holding your rod tip high is another way to keep your fly line off conflicting currents, but this technique is best on short casts.

There are a few times when you'll want your fly to plop into the water with a distinct *splat* that the trout will notice. This technique is especially useful when fishing terrestrial imitations like ants, beetles, and grasshoppers—food that drops into the water. Trout are attracted to the sound of something falling into the water, especially during the summer, when terrestrial insects are abundant. Another time this technique is useful is when large, egg-laying stonefly adults are returning to the water, especially on the salmon-fly hatch.

To make your fly drop onto the water with a tiny splash, just overpower your cast slightly and point the rod tip at the spot where you want your fly to land, rather than aiming high as you usually would.

There are instances where drag is a necessary addition to your presentation, but it must be controlled drag. Caddisfly adults, large stonefly adults, large mayflies, and grasshoppers may move across the surface of the water in a series of hops and flutters. Adult midges may career across the surface like tiny motorboats.

If you notice trout taking the flies that are moving and ignoring those that are drifting motionless, it's time to add some controlled drag to your presentation. This drag must always occur in an upstream or cross-stream direction, and you should position yourself across from or upstream of the trout.

For flies that are skittering across the surface of the water at a steady pace, most often seen with caddisflies and midges, try a skittering presentation. To do this, cast above and slightly beyond the rise, keep your rod tip high, and strip in line at a steady pace while wiggling your rod tip slightly. Your fly must stay above the surface of the water and should not be pulled under, so choose a good floater with lots of hackle. To help keep your fly on top of the water, you might also try greasing your leader with line dressing or silicone dry-fly paste.

Another technique is the slight upstream twitch followed by a drag-free drift, developed and aptly named *the sudden inch* by Leonard Wright. The sudden inch was developed for caddisflies and mayflies that flutter or twitch slightly, then ride the water for some distance. It's an attention-getting device that signals to the trout that your fly is alive and is ready to fly away at any moment.

To perform the sudden inch, you'll need to cast either an upstream curve or a downstream slack-line cast. Your fly should land a few feet above the trout, and you should also be upstream of the trout's position.

As soon as your fly hits the water, raise your rod tip and move it in a quick upstream and upward motion until you see your fly twitch upstream for an inch or so. Then quickly drop your rod tip and let the fly float over the fish in a drag-free manner. The upstream curve or the slack line you've thrown will let the fly drift unhindered until it passes below the trout and out of his vision.

Whether your leader should float or sink when fishing dry flies is a subject that too many people put too much emphasis on. It's true that a floating leader does cast a bigger shadow on the bottom than one that is below the surface, but trout have sticks and blades of grass and other debris floating over them all day long. I do use a commercial leader sink called Mud under delicate conditions, especially in low, clear water, but I use it more because it removes the shine from my leader than because it makes the leader sink. Natural debris doesn't reflect much light, and the flash from a shiny leader may spook trout. In very bright conditions, especially in flat water, it pays to try a PVDF (fluorocarbon) tippet instead of nylon, as this material sinks better and is nearly invisible under the surface.

When trout are taking drifting caddis or midge pupae, or emerging mayflies with that characteristic dimpling rise, you may want to grease all but the last foot of your leader and use an unweighted nymph. Your fly will drift just under the surface of the water, right where the natural flies are. You can get the same effect by using an emerger or floating nymph pattern, or even a standard dry fly that has not been treated with silicone fly dressing.

Even if you're blessed with 20:20 vision, you won't always be able to see your dry fly. It's hard to see a size-18 Blue Dun dry fly in a riffle from 30 feet away. Yet we fish tiny dull-colored flies in fast water, in the rain, and at dusk and after dark. How?

There's no secret. Just cast your fly above the rise, and even if you can't see the fly, strike when a rise occurs in the general area. You can almost always see the rise during the daytime, and at dark you can often hear it, especially in slow water. With practice, you'll be surprised at how well you can track your fly's drift, even when you can't see it.

What do you do if you rise a fish and either you fail to hook him or he refuses it at the last minute, splashing at your fly? The best thing to do is watch him for a while; see if he continues to rise. If you pricked him with the hook, he'll probably stop feeding, but if he just refused the fly or rejected it before you tightened up, he may continue to rise. Rest him for a couple of minutes. Watch his riseform. What kind of insect is he really taking?

The most productive tactic for me in a situation like this is to change to a fly that is one size smaller and perhaps slightly different in shape. For example, if I rise him initially on a size-14 Hendrickson, I might switch to a size-16 Red Quill. There is also a philosophy that says you should show him something radically different, but the fact that he showed any interest in your original offering means that you weren't far off.

A last-minute refusal can also mean that your presentation wasn't quite right. Drag might have been setting in just as he rose to the fly. Try changing your position slightly.

Blind-fishing dry flies, or fishing dry flies when no rises are seen, is a game of imagining that there is a trout rising in a particular spot. Remember those spots trout like best, along the banks, in depressions, and around rocks? Cast to likely spots, taking care that you approach them just as carefully as if a trout were rising there.

A dimpling rise like this might call for a greased leader.

When temperatures are right, trout feed all day long, both below and on the surface. If the water is cloudy, very fast, or very deep, a trout probably won't see your fly, but under clear-water conditions, in water that is 1 to 3 feet in depth, blind-fishing can be very productive.

Blind-fishing is best in riffles or pocket water. Because you don't know exactly where the fish are, and you can approach them much closer in broken water, you'll spook fewer unseen fish here. Choose a visible fly, one with lots of hackle like a variant, or white wings like a Royal Wulff. Work upstream, hitting every fishy-looking spot within your casting range, then walk a few feet upstream and try some new water. A half-dozen casts to each spot is usually sufficient—either there's nobody home, you've spooked him, or he's just not interested.

The only time I've found blind fishing to be truly productive in flat water is during the summer or fall when terrestrial insects are abundant. You have to be especially careful with your wading, moving very slowly so as not to riffle the water. Pitch your terrestrial imitation to places where insects might fall into the water—under overhanging trees and along grassy or shrubby banks.

WET-FLY AND NYMPH FISHING

Dead-Drift Nymphing

You can fish subsurface flies directly upstream, dead drift, just like a dry fly. This presentation produces the most insect-like drift, so it's usually done with nymphs, which are more realistic imitations of natural insects. A nymph drifting without any apparent influence from your line or leader is the most deadly way to fish a sub-surface fly, because it's drifting exactly like a natural insect. However, upstream nymphing is also the most demanding way of fly-fishing, both physically and mentally. You seldom see the fish, you almost never see your fly, and strikes can't be felt because of the slack line. Your only indication of a strike will be a twitch or slight upstream motion of your floating line or strike indicator.

Upstream nymphing requires some special tackle and tactics, and because you must watch the tip of your line, sinking lines are out. It's a way of fishing nymphs deeper than any other method, and to help get them right near the bottom, weighted nymphs, bead heads, or a couple of small split shot on the leader about a foot above the fly are often used. A common strategy is to start with a weighted nymph, adding split shot to the leader until the fly hangs bottom occasionally. A fly that isn't ticking the bottom once in a while is probably not getting deep enough to interest the fish.

A word of caution when using heavily weighted flies or split shot and indicators: Your cast won't behave as it normally would, because the extra weight slows things down and brings the fly dangerously close to your ear. It's best to stick to short casts, lobbing them side-armed rather than trying a standard overhead cast. Keep an open loop by slowing down your power stroke as well—pretty tight loops are for dry-fly fishing.

High-Stick Nymphing

The most common, and usually the best way to fish weighted nymphs, is to fish upstream and across, anywhere from 30 to 70 degrees upstream from an imaginary line that runs directly across the current. For short casts, where you can wade close to where you think the trout are, the best tactic is to make a short cast, and then raise the rod tip to keep as much line as possible off the water. In fact, many anglers lift their rod tips until just the very tip of the fly line touches the water but the rest of the line is in the air, forming a straight line to the rod tip. This is called *high-sticking*. You follow the fly's progress throughout its drift, and the fly will be at its deepest and most effective point when it's directly across from your position. As the fly drifts below you, it begins to rise in the water column and toward your position, and is no longer drifting drag-free. It also seems to be less effective once it hits this point, unless you extend the fly's drift by reaching out with the rod. This technique is most effective in fast, riffled water or in pocket water, as you have to get very close to the fish.

Begin high-stick nymphing by casting the fly quartering upstream.

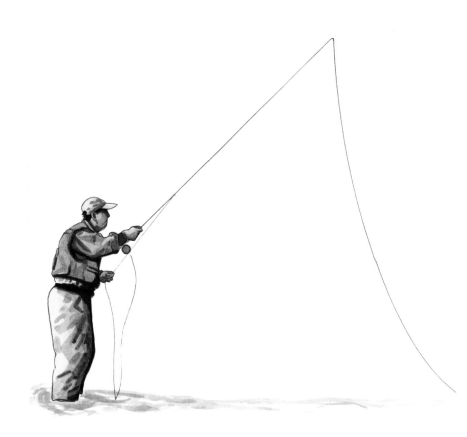

Raise the tip of the rod to keep all or most of the fly line off the water.

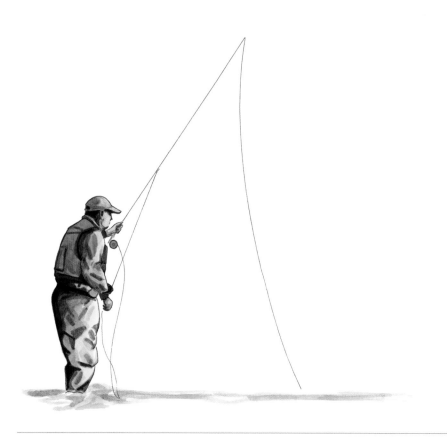

Keep the indicator (or the point where the leader enters the water) under the rod tip as it drifts past you.

Extend your arm downstream to lengthen the drift.

Strike Indicators

You can improve your success with this technique by adding a strike indicator to your leader. Strike indicators are brightly colored pieces of yarn, foam, or plastic, or even floating putty that you place on the upper part of your leader. Some stick on, some attach with special knots, some are threaded over the leader and jammed in place with a stopper. The best ones will stay in place on the leader and not slide down, yet can be moved if the water depth you fish changes. My favorites are those that slip over the leader with a loop-to-loop connection, or the sticky floating putty, because both can be moved quickly.

A general rule of thumb is to place the strike indicator a distance of between 1½ and 2 times the depth of the water from the fly. This is enough to let the fly sink well,

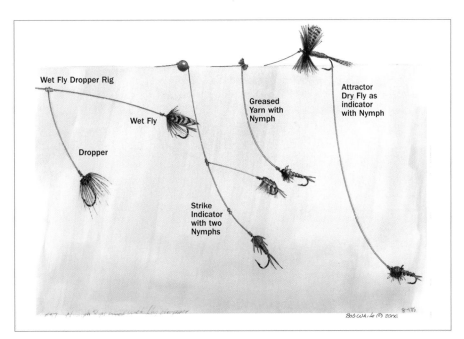

Various multiple-fly setups used with sinking flies. From left to right: A pair of wet flies, one tied on a dropper created by leaving one tag end of a blood knot long. A plastic strike indicator with two nymphs and split shot on the leader (the lower fly could also be tied to the bend of the hook of the first fly). A small piece of greased yarn with a single nymph, best for shallow water and spooky fish. A large dry fly used as both a strike indicator and an attractor for a nymph—a fun setup because a trout might take either fly.

but not so much that you cannot see strikes. You should note that strike indicators are as important for following the drift of your fly as they are at detecting strikes. It's true that a trout can eat your nymph and spit it out without ever making your floating line jump, and strike indicators are better at detecting this subtle motion. But equally important is that you make sure your fly drifts downstream without sliding across the current. Imagine that a stream's currents, instead of one solid sheet of water, are an infinite number of lanes. If you strive to keep your strike indicator (and thus your fly) in the same lane throughout its drift, never crossing over that imaginary yellow line, you catch more trout. The way to do this on short casts is to manipulate your rod tip so that you keep enough line off the water and don't slide the indicator toward you. In addition to this, and when you increase your cast to the point where the line has to fall on the water, you can introduce short mends in the line to keep the indicator in its lane.

You can also fish directly upstream with a nymph, using either a strike indicator or just watching the tip of your floating line. As in dry-fly fishing, this technique is best in riffled water, where the nymph (and perhaps a strike indicator and some weight on your leader) landing on top of the fish won't spook it.

Long-Line Nymphing with Indicators

As you lengthen your casts, you'll have to do more to keep the fly from dragging as you'll have more line on the water. You may have to introduce more frequent and more energetic mends, reach casts, and slack-line casts to keep the indicator in its lane. Mending here is more effective than in dry-fly fishing, as the indicator acts as a buffer or anchor to keep you from moving the fly as you mend.

Nymph fishing with a longer line: Cast quartering upstream to begin.

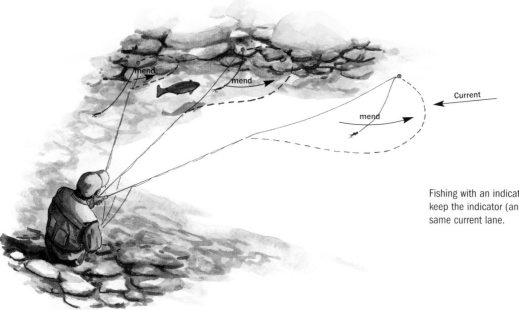

Fishing with an indicator using mends to keep the indicator (and the fly) in the same current lane.

It's okay if your indicator sinks, and it often will. You should still be able to see it just below the surface, and you can still strike and follow the fly's progress. But a fly hanging below an indicator is most effective, and if you can adjust your weight, the size of your indicator, and its placement so your fly drifts about a foot above the bottom, trout in deep water will be able to see your fly, and it will be well within a comfortable range for them to suck it in. Generally, the faster and deeper the water, the bigger the indicator, because it will suspend your fly better and will be easier to see in tumbling currents. At the other end of the scale, in shallow, clear water, a big indicator will spook wary trout. Here, the smallest you can get away with is good advice.

The angler makes another mend. Notice how the indicator stays in the same current lane instead of dragging across the currents.

Make an upstream mend to keep the line from bellying.

Yet another way to follow the progress of your nymph and watch for strikes is to use a high-floating dry fly as an indicator. Plus you double your chances of finding out what the trout are taking. Tie on a dry fly as you normally would, then attach a 12- to 36-inch piece of tippet to the bend of the hook with a clinch knot. Tie your nymph onto this piece and you can fish both a dry and a nymph at the same time. It's a deadly technique, and the trout may take the dry fly as often as the nymph, despite the fact that it has a piece of nylon attached to it.

Really serious nymph fishers usually fish two nymphs at a time. You attach the second nymph the same as in the nymph–dry fly rig just mentioned. It's a terrific

way to test two different patterns, two different sizes, or two different colors at the same time. In this case, the piece of tippet attached to the first fly should be about 18 inches long—any longer and it tangles easily; any shorter and you tend to foul-hook trout that take the upper fly and reject it before you have a chance to strike. By fishing two bead head flies in this manner, you can usually get the flies deep enough with having to add weight to your leader.

The fly gets downstream of his position. If he does not extend his arm downstream at this point, the fly will begin to drag, and it's time to pick up and make another cast.

Sight-Fishing with Nymphs

Upstream nymphing to visible trout in spring creeks and slow, clear pools requires sharp eyesight and stealth. You should be equipped with a long, fine leader, a small weighted mayfly nymph or scud imitation, a floating line, and polarized sunglasses.

You may see the trout move to take a nymph; you might spot his shadow, or see him as an indistinct shape on the bottom. Seldom will you get a good look at the fish, and often you'll fish to a stick or light-colored rock before you realize it's not a trout.

The procedure here is to sneak up quietly to the fish and cast your nymph far enough upstream so it is at his level when it passes his nose. Remember that the farther upstream you cast, the deeper your fly will get. Try to watch both the fish and your fly line at the same time. If the fish opens his mouth or so much as wiggles his fins as the fly passes near him, set the hook. If the tip of the fly line or the leader twitches, do likewise. A small strike indicator might help. Takes will not be vicious, and you won't always see the fish turn or dart for the fly.

A clever strategy to use when nymphing to visible trout is the *induced take*. Just before the fly reaches the fish, strip in a little more line than is necessary to gather the slack or raise your rod tip slightly, drawing the nymph toward the surface. This will often take a sullen trout that refuses a standard dead-drifted nymph.

WET FLIES AND NYMPHS ON THE SWING

Wet flies and nymphs can be fished upstream, downstream, across-stream, and anywhere in between. Although trout sometimes prefer to take wet flies and nymphs drag-free, or dead drift, drag is not as much of a problem, because those little wakes aren't created underwater. Some aquatic insects and crustaceans do swim against or across currents, so sometimes swinging a fly with controlled drag will work better than dead drift.

The traditional and most common way to swing subsurface wet flies is to cast directly across-stream, about 90 degrees to the current flow. The current pulls on the fly line, leader, and fly, causing the fly to swing across and downstream in an arc. In slow currents the arc will be fairly open, and the fly will swing slowly across the current, even breaking the surface and skimming across the water. Your rod tip should point to where the line first touches the water and should follow the line as it drifts downstream.

Strikes can occur almost anywhere in the drift and will show up as either a twitch or unnatural tightening of the line. If there is no slack in the line, you will actually feel the strike as an electrifying jolt. On a tight line, especially if the fly is hanging downstream, the current's force on the line will set the hook for you. If there is slack in the

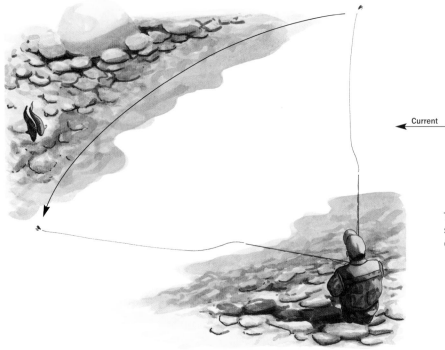

Current

The standard wet-fly drift. If the current is swift, the fly will swing quickly and will stay quite shallow.

line, you must strike immediately. The tightening of the line can mean only one thing—something has grabbed your fly. If you hesitate, he'll eject the fly before you have a chance to set the hook.

Fishing wet flies or nymphs in this manner, without any manipulation by the angler, is an effective way to cover a lot of water, especially if you fish two or three flies on droppers. It's also a relaxing way to fish. You're wading downstream, which requires a lot less effort, and the current is doing all the work for you. All you have to do is take a few steps downstream after each cast and make another cast.

Your line length remains constant, and you don't even have to false-cast. In fact, you should false-cast as little as possible, so that your flies stay wet and sink as soon as they hit the water.

Most strikes will appear toward the end of the drift, just as the fly begins to swing across the current. The fly begins to sink as soon as it lands and keeps sinking until the belly that forms in the line begins to draw the fly across the current and toward the surface. Apparently this looks much like an aquatic insect rising to the surface.

After the fly completes its swing and is hanging directly downstream from you, it's a good idea to strip in line, a few inches at a time, for a couple of feet. Sometimes a trout will follow your fly and hesitate as it stops; the fly swimming back upstream triggers his instinct to strike. On a very long cast you'll want to retrieve some line anyway, so that you can pick up for another cast without working too hard and disturbing the water.

When bringing a subsurface fly directly upstream against the current, keep the rod at a 90-degree angle to the line, to act as a shock absorber against violent strikes. Your line is so tight under these circumstances that it's easy for even a small fish to break your tippet.

Although a wet fly drifting with the current on a tight line is usually effective, you may want to try manipulating the fly slightly as it swings. You can either twitch your rod tip slightly throughout the drift or use short strips or a hand-twist retrieve. Some nymphs swim quite rapidly just before they hatch, and the trout may be on the lookout for this type of behavior.

The problem with the standard across-stream presentation is that, all too often, the fly moves too fast and doesn't get deep enough. A trout is especially reluctant to pursue something that is moving a bit quicker than every-

thing else he's been eating. Why chase something that might get away when a sure meal will drift along soon?

There are a number of ways to slow things down and get your fly deeper. One is to switch from a floating line to a sinking or sink-tip line with a short leader. Lines that are under the surface help keep the fly under, of course, but they also drift slower, because the subsurface currents are always slower than the surface currents.

Another is to hold your rod tip high, about 45 degrees above the surface of the water, following the fly's drift with the rod tip. The more line you keep off the water, the less the line will influence the swing of your fly.

Mending line in an upstream direction is a tactic many wet-fly anglers use to get a better drift. As soon as the line hits the water, mend a loop of line upstream, letting the line that you flip upstream slip from the line you are holding in your stripping hand, rather than from the line that is already on the water. Every time the line begins to belly downstream, mend again, repeating the process throughout the drift.

A slack-line cast is a very useful tactic to use when trout are following emerging insects to the surface. Cast some slack exactly as if you were casting a dry fly directly across-stream. The slack will allow the fly to sink and drift downstream naturally; as the line begins to tighten, the fly will rise quickly to the surface, mimicking the behavior of the natural insects.

You don't always have to cast wet flies or nymphs across-stream, and changing the angle at which you cast can radically change the behavior of your fly as it drifts.

A quartering downstream cast with wet flies and nymphs produces a drift that has less drag because the line doesn't have a chance to belly as much, but it gives a drift that is fairly shallow. You can use mends or a slack-line cast to get the fly a little deeper. This presentation works best when trout are taking emerging caddis pupae and mayfly nymphs.

A quartering upstream cast lets your fly sink deeper before the line bellies and pulls the fly to the surface. It also allows you to use a deadly tactic on a fish that has been spotted splashing at emerging nymphs just under the surface—the *Leisenring lift*. It is performed like this: Cast well above the fish, letting the fly sink on a dead drift as it moves downstream. Follow the fly with your rod tip high as it drifts. When you think the fly is just upstream of the fish, stop following it with the rod tip. The line will belly quickly, drawing the fly to the surface right

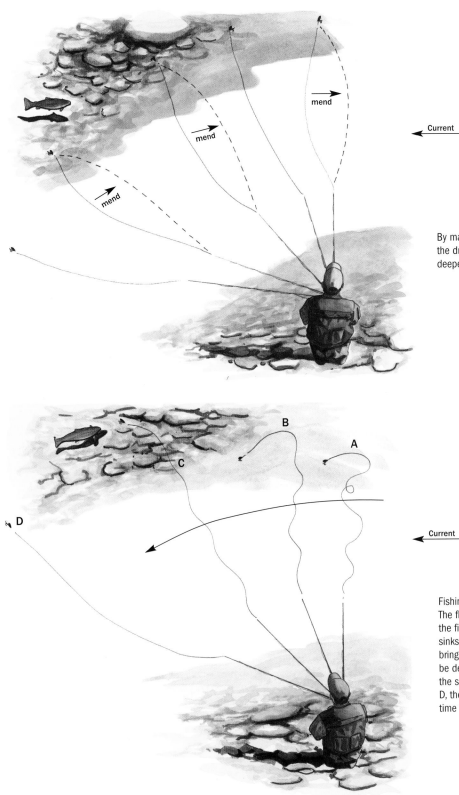

By making frequent upstream mends throughout the drift of a wet fly, the fly will swing slower and deeper.

Fishing a wet fly or nymph on a slack-line cast: The fly is cast well upstream of where you think the fish is lying, with lots of slack (A). The fly sinks on the slack line at B while the current brings it downstream. At C, hopefully the fly will be deep enough and may then begin to rise to the surface, looking like an emerging insect. At D, the fly has swung away from the fish, and it's time to pick up and cast again.

in front of the fish's nose. A similar presentation can be achieved by following the fly with a low rod tip, raising the rod at the same point, just above the fish.

You can also fish subsurface flies directly upstream, dead drift, just like a dry fly. This presentation produces the most insect-like drift, so it's usually done with nymphs, which are more realistic imitations of natural insects.

FISHING STREAMERS

Streamers can be fished just like nymphs and wet flies—across-stream, upstream, and downstream. Streamers will take all of these ways, even dead-drifted directly upstream. They are most effective, however, when you give them some manipulation, either by stripping in line as they drift or by pumping the rod tip to give them life.

Streamers are usually used when nothing else will attract the trout's attention, in high, dirty water, in the cold water of early season, and in very fast, broken water where smaller flies aren't visible.

You can cover a lot of water with streamers, because a trout will usually take your streamer on the first drift, or at least make a pass at it. If he's not interested, no amount of repeated casting will make him strike. If he swirls at your streamer but doesn't take, try one of a different color, or one that's slightly smaller than the one you're using. Some fly fishers also use streamers to locate trout, returning later with a standard dry, wet, or nymph.

A popular way to fish streamers is to cast directly across the current to the far bank, stripping in line in foot-long pulls as the fly swings around in the current. This is one of the most effective ways of float-fishing large western rivers. Strikes to this kind of presentation will be quick and vicious, and the fish will usually hook themselves because of the tight line. Although there is not much finesse involved, introducing some strategy into your presentation will get you more strikes. First, make

sure that you cast your fly right to the bank. Big trout, particularly brown trout, will lie very tight to the bank, where there is protection in the form of boulders and logs. Sometimes, the difference between casting 5 feet from the bank and bouncing your fly right off the shore will make the difference between a great day and a mediocre one.

The other tactic is the direction your fly swims in relation to the current. Regardless of the angle between your cast and the bank, make sure that the fly swims broadside to the current, or if not broadside, at least in an upstream direction. A fly that darts downstream, right into a trout's face, is more likely to frighten your quarry than tempt it. Baitfish don't attack trout, and a baitfish that moves toward—rather than away from—a trout is cause for alarm. Sometimes you can make your fly swim broadside just by the angle at which you cast, but sometimes, particularly when casting to the bank from a moving driftboat, you have to shoot a quick cast upstream of the boat. Just stripping in line will make your fly dart downstream, so the best thing to do is to throw a hard upstream mend just after the fly lands, so that as you begin stripping the fly swims broadside to the current.

In rivers with very fast currents, you should angle your cast downstream to slow the swing of your fly. This works well with a sinking line, but with a floating line it often makes the fly skim just under the surface, too shallow to interest most trout. Just as in nymph and wet-fly fishing, casting slightly upstream or using a sink-

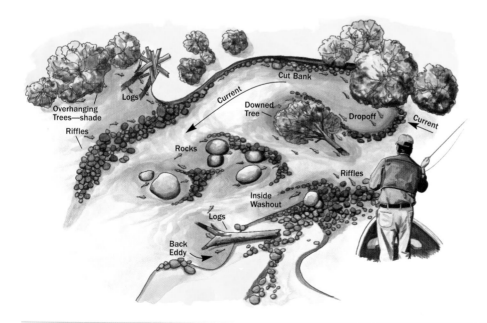

When covering the water from a driftboat or on foot, make sure to hit these spots where trout lie in wait to ambush baitfish.

tip or sinking line will also make your fly ride deeper and slower. In very deep or fast water, try casting upstream-and-across, then mend the fly upstream several times while the fly sinks. You have to cast well ahead of where you think a trout might be lying, but by the time the fly gets below you, it will be much deeper than if you just cast directly across the current or cast at a downstream angle.

A deadly method of fishing streamers, although one that isn't used very often, is fishing them directly upstream. Try to retrieve line just slightly faster than the current, so that your fly darts along the bottom in little fits and pauses, just like a sculpin or crayfish darting from one rock to another. This technique is often deadly if you attach a small nymph behind your streamer, just as you would when fishing a pair of nymphs.

Streamers will also work when cast directly downstream. You can just let your fly hang in the current, using the current to give it life. You can also flip your rod back and forth, making the fly swim from side to side in the same spot. If this presentation doesn't work, try retrieving your streamer back upstream by stripping in line. Try short, quick pulls, long, steady pulls, or even erratic strips. One of these approaches may appeal to the trout.

UPSTREAM OR DOWN?

Older fly-fishing literature tells you that "the dry-fly fisherman always works upstream, and the wet-fly, nymph, and streamer man works downstream." We've seen, however, that you can fish a dry fly downstream or a nymph upstream. Before you start to fish, decide whether you're going to use an upstream or downstream presentation and then move in the same direction as you fish. Otherwise, you'll be fishing in water that you've just walked through, and the trout will probably be spooked.

If you've just covered a pool working upstream with a dry fly, should you turn around and try it with a wet? That depends on the size of the stream. In a small stream, you've just walked near all of the trout in the pool and spooked them. In a large river, however, you probably stayed to the shallow side and didn't get near any of the trout on the far side. They may not even know you're there, so why not give them a whirl with a wet fly?

NIGHT FISHING

On a moonlit night you can often extend the time you fish an evening hatch. Find a flat stretch of water and get into a casting position where the moon reflecting off the surface of the water will illuminate the riseforms. You probably won't be able to see your fly; just strike when you see a rise in the general vicinity of your fly. This isn't true night fishing, however.

Real night fishing means returning to the stream when it is pitch black, when every tree becomes a clutching, invisible obstacle, and even the smallest rock on the bottom is dangerous.

Why night-fish at all?

Most trout are daytime sight feeders and don't eat at night. In every population of brown trout, however, there are a few individuals who, when they grow to over 14 inches, become meat hunters. They seldom feed when the sun is on the water and forgo the traditional aquatic insect diet for minnows, crayfish, and large night-flying moths and beetles that fall into the water. My fish-biologist friend calls them "sharks."

Never night-fish in an unfamiliar stretch of river. The best night fishing occurs on nights with no moon, and a flashlight shone into the water will spook the fish. You need to know every rock on the bottom.

Night fishing doesn't require long, fine leaders. A 7½-foot leader with a 6 or 8-pound tippet is about right. The flies will be large and so will the fish. Fish smaller than 12 inches are rare after dark.

Flies should be large and bushy. Large dries like salmon dry flies or hair bass bugs are good, as are unweighted streamers like the Muddler Minnow or Woolly Bugger. Palmer-hackled wet flies like the Woolly Worm will also produce after dark. The pattern doesn't seem to matter as long as it is bushy enough to produce vibrations in the water. Night-feeding trout use their lateral-line hearing to find their prey.

The best places to night-fish are shallow heads and tails of pools. Unlike daytime drift feeders, night-feeding trout leave their positions and hunt for their food, especially in shallow areas rich in crayfish and minnows.

Your casts should be short, no more than 30 feet, and you should work quietly and slowly downstream. Cast straight across the current and allow your flies to swing. Occasionally a steady hand-twist retrieve

Large brown trout are particularly susceptible to night fishing.

During the heat of the summer, morning and evening are the best times to fish eastern rivers.

throughout the swing will help, especially in slower currents.

Strikes will not be hard; they'll be felt as a sudden, deliberate tightening of the line. Nighttime is no time to baby a big trout—play it as quickly as the heavy leader will allow, as you never know exactly where the snags are after dark.

Best times to night-fish are hot, humid, still nights during the new moon, anytime from midnight until dawn.

TIME OF YEAR AND TIME OF DAY

Streams change with the seasons. Fly fishing is always better when there are insects hatching, and there is a general rule that says the best time of the day for insect hatches is when the temperature is most comfortable for you. In April and May in the East, the best time is the middle of the afternoon, when the sun warms the water and the air. From late May through August, the most pleasant time of day for us is evenings and mornings, and this is when you'll find the fish feeding most actively. In the fall, we return to the midday feeding schedule of early spring.

In the Rocky Mountain region nights are almost always cold, even in the middle of summer. As a result, there are seldom any hatches in this area until the middle of the morning. Best fishing at this high altitude occurs throughout the daytime hours, although you may see some feeding fish in the evening after an unusually hot day.

In late fall, winter, and early spring, trout are most often feeding in the middle of the day.

BIG AND LITTLE TROUT STREAMS

Don't let big rivers intimidate you, and don't be afraid of trying to fly-fish tiny brooks. Big rivers, with their varying currents, are just a bunch of little rivers running together. Divide a big river up into little streams in your mind and fish each one as though it were a separate entity.

In little streams, straight upstream is usually your best approach.

SMALLMOUTH BASS IN STREAMS

Smallmouth bass will be found in streams that warm to over 60 degrees Fahrenheit in the late spring. They occupy places in streams that are similar to places where you'll find trout, but smallmouths aren't as streamlined as trout and prefer the eddies that occur behind rocks and logs, on the edges of fast currents, along rock ledges, and especially in the tails of pools. In large, slow rivers, smallmouths will be found on the edges of weed beds along the banks. Bass will also be found in backwaters and eddies that would be too slow to hold trout.

Smallmouths aren't as selective as trout, nor are they as spooky. You can't splash a lot of water around, nor can you step right on top of them, but you don't have to be as cautious as you would with a wild brown trout.

When smallmouths are feeding on hatching insects, you can use the same tactics you'd use for trout. When they're surface-feeding, though, they'll take almost any floating fly. You might want to drop a small popper in front of a feeding smallmouth, twitching it slightly as it drifts in front of him.

If you can't see any smallmouths feeding on insects or chasing minnows, choose a strategy that allows you to cover as much water as possible. This usually means working downstream, either wading or in a slow-drifting boat. Use either a streamer or a popper, casting to rocks, under overhanging branches, and alongside logs.

Smallmouths usually prefer a fast retrieve, especially with streamers. Steady foot-long pulls will keep your

Divide a big river into little streams and fish each one.

Tiny brooks that look totally impossible for fly fishing can be surprisingly easy. There may be spots that are so brushy you'll have to pass them up, but you'll usually be able to find areas where there is plenty of room behind you for a backcast, even though the banks may be brushy. Fishing straight upstream in tiny brooks is probably the best idea anyway, because casts will be short and you may spook most of the fish trying to work downstream. In a small, bubbly stream you can sometimes approach the fish so closely that you'll barely have to cast more than your leader.

Smallmouth bass in rivers will be found in places with slower current than most trout prefer.

streamer moving fast enough, although you might want to slow down your retrieve if no strikes are forthcoming. With poppers and hair bugs, cast them just upstream of where you think the fish is and make the bug pop by using hard, short strips. You should pull hard enough to make the popper *blurp* and throw a few bubbles each time. About one pop per second is about right, although slower or faster retrieves may produce more results on some days.

When fishing for smallmouths, try to avoid slack line and using your rod tip to give the fly action, which also produces unwanted slack line. Smallmouths have harder mouths than trout and seldom hook themselves, so you must maintain a tight line and strike harder than you would for trout.

A crayfish imitation, fished on a sink-tip line, is a deadly way to catch smallmouths in streams. It is especially deadly in deep, slow pools when smallmouths are reluctant to chase poppers or streamers. Cast across and slightly upstream, letting the sinking tip pull the fly down. Then retrieve with short strips, pausing between.

If smallmouths don't respond to these proven techniques, there are a number of things you can try. One is to fish a hair bug or big salmon dry fly upstream, dead drift, just as you would for trout. This is especially productive in tails of pools.

When the water is shallow and clear, switch from a standard popping bug to a bullethead hair bug or feather minnow, something that doesn't make as much noise. Smallmouths often hide in slow, shallow water, places where you'd never expect to find bass of any size. They wait in these areas to ambush schools of minnows.

You may have days on smallmouth rivers when they chase your streamers or poppers all the way across the river but never actually strike your flies. It's a frustrating experience. The best solution I've found when they're behaving like this is to throw them tiny trout-sized dries or nymphs, sizes 10 through 14. Cast to the spot you last saw the bass chasing your fly, then twitch them slightly to attract attention. Strikes to this kind of presentation will be slow and subtle, more like the way a big brown trout would inhale your fly.

OTHER FISH IN STREAMS

Largemouth bass, walleye, white bass, pike, and pickerel, as well as panfish, may also be found in streams. All of these fish prefer very slow water and will be found mainly in backwaters and eddies. Because these fish will be found in miniature still-water environments within a stream, they can be caught with the tactics discussed in the next chapter.

Migratory fish like salmon and steelhead have different needs than trout because they are migrating and might not be feeding, so they are discussed in chapter 10.

{ BIG WATER }

Chapter Nine

Still-Water Tactics

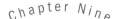

WHEN MOST PEOPLE THINK OF FLY fishing, they think of moving water and trout and salmon, yet lakes, ponds, and reservoirs present fly-fishing opportunities that far surpass those of rivers and streams in number.

Fly fishing—at least, fly fishing that is efficient and fun—is limited to shallow-water fishing. We can fly-fish to about 30 feet under the surface of a lake; after this depth fly fishing would be limited to trolling with lead-core line. Even with an extra-fast sinking fly line, fishing depths of more than 20 feet is a lot of work, and it's tough to cover a lot of area with flies in deep water.

Fortunately, bass, panfish, and pike do most of their feeding in shallow water. Even such deepwater dwellers as lake trout and landlocked salmon, which generally reside in the cool depths of 60 feet or more, can be taken right near the surface on flies during the spring and fall when the water temperature near shore is less than 55 degrees.

Water temperature is as important in still waters as it is in streams. Shallow ponds that warm above 70 degrees and don't have any cool-water depths or spring holes will not support trout. Instead, you'll find warm-water species like bass or panfish, which can tolerate water temperatures

In a big trout lake like this, you're mostly limited to fish that are feeding in shallow water.

above 80 degrees. Alpine lakes that never warm above 60 degrees may have trout in them and nothing else.

Many large lakes and reservoirs, bodies of water that are deep enough to stratify during the summer, are what are called "two-story" lakes. In the early spring, just after ice-out, you'll find trout in the shallows; when the water warms in the early summer, the trout retreat to deeper water, out of reach of the fly fisher. The fly rodder shouldn't forsake these lakes, though, because just as the trout go into deep water, warm-water fish like bass, pike, and panfish become active in the shallows. If the water warms even further during the summer, bass retreat to the depths during the day, but they usually return to the shallows in early morning and evening to feed. And the panfish are always there.

In streams you use the current to help you deliver flies. The current helps you determine where the fish will be. It sometimes even sets the hook for you.

In still waters, unless you're fishing inlet or outlet streams, you don't have the current to help you. Slack-line casts, curve casts, and a high rod tip are not only un-needed, they're undesirable. Whether you fish wet or dry, your line must always be tight, and except in instances where you have trout or bass cruising the surface for insects, your fly must be kept in motion. This is especially important when fishing subsurface flies—a fish may take your sunken fly in still water when it's not moving, but you'd never know it. Fortunately, still-water insects do more swimming than their swift-water counterparts, so a fly that is swimming looks realistic to the fish.

Because fish in still waters seldom stay put for long, you'll probably need a greater variety of fly-line types, unless you fish only shallow ponds, where you can do all of your fishing with a floating line. In streams the deepest you might expect to find trout is 10 feet, and most of the time you'll find them feeding in less than 5 feet of water. In lakes and ponds, trout move throughout the water column on a daily basis, and if you stay up top with a floating line, you'll be missing most of your opportunities. Yes, you can use a weighted nymph or streamer with a floating line, but the problem with that approach is that most baitfish, insects, and crustaceans swim at a steady depth. They don't bob up toward the surface and then sink down (unless insects are hatching), which is exactly what you get when you pull a weighted fly through the water with a floating line.

You'll want at least an sinking-tip line for times when they retreat to the depths, and probably a full-sinking line mounted on extra spools, ready for plumbing the depths. For very deep (up to 30 feet) fishing, if you choose to chase them that far, you'll need an extra-fast-sinking fly line. Although shooting heads sink quickly, they are not as desirable in still waters. Because you'll be doing a lot of line handling, the thin running line becomes a problem, as it tangles more easily than the thicker diameter of a regular fly line.

You can fly-fish from the shore of a lake, but you're fairly limited to the water near shore, and if the banks are lined with trees you'll be restricted to the roll cast or a forward cast that is parallel to the shoreline. You'll be better off getting into the water somehow. Wading will get you around in a lake, but again, you're limited to the shallow water.

Belly boats are becoming very popular for still-water fly fishing. They consist of an inner tube covered with a nylon protective shell that includes a seat, and may also have pockets for fly boxes and other gear. Belly-boat users wear stocking-foot waders and either swim fins or paddle pushers on their feet. Swim fins push you backward and have the advantage of moving you around fairly quickly; paddle pushers move you forward, but they're slower than swim fins.

Belly boats offer advantages over conventional water-craft. Because you're sitting low in the water, you can sneak up quietly to feeding fish that might be spooked by the higher profile of an angler in a boat or canoe. Belly boats are very stable. Fly fishers who chase big rainbows and cutthroats in large western reservoirs prefer them, even during winter storms. They ride with the waves and are almost impossible to tip over. Belly boats can also be toted uninflated into remote lakes, where it would be impossible to carry a boat. Once at your destination, you can inflate your boat with a CO_2 cartridge or hand pump.

Pontoon boats, with two air chambers and a platform in between, are also used in lakes, but they are much harder to control in the wind, even when fitted with a pair of oars. If you venture out in a pontoon boat, make sure you stay in a sheltered cove unless you enjoy rowing a craft with the tracking characteristics of a floating dock.

You can fly-fish in any kind of conventional boat, from a rowboat to a fancy bass boat with swivel seats and a depth finder. The small boats—canoes, punts, kayaks,

Belly boats can take you places no other craft can, especially if you have to carry your boat in to a high mountain lake.

Pontoon boats can be used on lakes, as long as you stay out of strong winds.

Sit-on-top kayaks are great fishing craft—they're stable, quiet, and move faster than a canoe or belly boat. Heritage Kayaks photo.

Canoes are swift, silent, and man-powered and are traditional craft for fly-fishing lakes and ponds.

and rowboats—are preferred, however, because they are more maneuverable and can be brought within range of a rising fish with less disturbance.

As with wading in streams, the less you disturb the water, the better. Getting upwind and drifting into an area where fish are feeding is preferable to rowing or paddling.

There is no special trick to fly-fishing from a canoe or belly boat, except that your movement will be somewhat restricted. If a trout rises directly behind you, it may require a little more care in turning around than when you're standing in a stream. Remember that in all cases, fly-casting should involve only your wrist, forearm, and a little upper arm. It's especially important when fishing from a canoe. Too much body English can send a series of waves out from your canoe, spooking cautious fish.

Because you will be sitting very low to the water, a longer rod helps to keep your backcast high. I would never fish from a canoe or belly boat with a rod shorter than 9 feet.

TROUT IN LAKES

A trout lake or pond is often an intimidating prospect to a stream angler. Here, trout may be around logs or weed beds, but they could just as soon be in open water. They use the security of deep water, rather than rocks or logs, when they are frightened by predators.

Where do you start? The first thing to do is look for rises. The trout have given themselves away at this point; you *know* where at least a few are. Binoculars are essential on very large trout lakes.

Streams entering lakes are always hot spots for trout. Streams bring cooler, more highly oxygenated water to lakes, carry in aquatic and terrestrial insects, and often have concentrations of baitfish around their mouths. Smelt and other baitfish spawn in streams, and trout will cruise the area where a stream enters a lake, waiting for baitfish to ascend or descend.

Trout often use inlet streams for spawning. Browns, rainbows, and landlocked salmon *must* spawn in moving water, so at some time of year they'll be in or near these streams. Look for brook trout, brown trout, salmon, lake trout, and domestic (hatchery-raised) rainbows here in October and November. Most strains of rainbow and cutthroat spawn in the spring, anytime between March and June.

Brook and lake trout have the unique ability to spawn in lakes and ponds, but they must have a gravel-bottomed area with springs near it; otherwise, they spawn in tributary streams, like the other species.

The influence of a stream can extend hundreds of feet out into a lake. There is often a deep channel where the trout can hide while having a plentiful supply of food. A nymph or streamer fished through these channels will often produce trout all day long.

Streams often enter lakes underground, in which case they're called *springs*. They can be found by taking water temperatures at various spots. The area near a spring will be noticeably cooler than the surrounding water in the summer, warmer during the early spring and late fall. Springs may also show up as light-colored patches of sand in clear water.

Be careful when fishing spring-fed lakes or high-altitude lakes, places where shallow water stays comfortable for trout throughout the season. Don't fish out in the middle. The shallows are where you'll find aquatic plants and algae, and thus the insects and baitfish that trout feed upon. The depths may often be barren because sunlight can't penetrate to the bottom.

Outlets of lakes are often good places for trout, because some species will spawn in them, and many baitfish also spawn there. If the outlet has enough current, you'll want to fish it just as you would a stream.

Shoals, drop-offs, islands, points—any interface between shallow and deep water will hold trout, especially in the spring and fall.

This fly fisher was smart enough to fish where an inlet stream feeds a large Adirondack lake.

If you've ever been out on a lake on a windy day, you've probably seen long lines of foam that run perpendicular to the wind direction. These are called *wind streaks*, and are points between waves where turbulence is at a minimum. Foam, debris, and insects become trapped in these areas. If you look carefully at wind streaks, you'll often find trout cruising along the line, picking up drowned and hatching insects.

Trout have the same foods in lakes as they do in streams, plus a few more. Caddisflies and mayflies will be common, but stoneflies will be scarce, except along windswept, rocky shores. Dragonflies, damselflies, scuds, leeches, midges, and baitfish are perhaps the most important trout foods in lakes, so you'll want to imitate these with appropriate fly patterns and fishing techniques. What do trout do in still waters? Do they feed the same way they do in streams?

In shallow, clear, spring-fed ponds, trout—especially brook and brown trout—behave much the same. They sit on the bottom, waiting for food to swim by, rising up to grab a morsel and then returning to their spots. When food is really abundant, as in a midge or mayfly hatch, they'll cruise for their food.

It's fascinating to watch a cruising trout, or "gulper," as they're called in the West. Trout will swim along, gulp two or three or maybe six insects in quick succession, then swim along without feeding, and then gulp again. Or they'll feed with evenly spaced gulps. They may cruise in a straight line. They may even cruise in a circle or a figure eight.

Rainbow trout always cruise, whether they're eating or not, and so do the other species in large lakes. Trout that are exclusively baitfish eaters cruise constantly, on the move for schools of baitfish.

You can see that if you're fishing a shallow pond you might want to stay put, but if you're in a big lake and not catching fish, you might as well move around until you find some.

Dry Flies

Dry flies are less useful for trout in lakes than they are in streams. Still waters have hatches, of course, and you shouldn't leave your dry flies home, but many of the still-water food forms don't hatch; leeches, scuds, and baitfish live their entire lives underwater. Dragonflies and damselflies and many species of mayfly and caddisfly crawl out on vegetation to hatch, so the fish don't have a chance to get to them in the process. These insects have to return to water to mate and lay eggs, though, so spinner falls and mating flights can be important.

Fish in still waters get a long look at your dry fly; unless the surface of a lake is riffled, they get a *very* good look at it. Your leader should be as long and as fine as you dare—a 12-footer is standard. You might even want to extend your leader to 15 feet by making the butt section and tippet longer. Too long a leader will defeat your purpose, however, because if the tippet lands in a big pile around your dry fly, a trout may shy away. You might be able to get away with this in the broken water of a stream, but not in a pond.

Fishing a dry fly blind in a lake is a futile gesture, so you should look for rises. As in streams, dimpling rises mean small flies or spent spinners; splashy rises mean big flies, caddisflies, or emerging nymphs; and bulges mean emerging nymphs or insects that swim just under the surface, like water boatmen or backswimmers.

Rises that are sporadic or erratic should be hit immediately with your fly, while the fish is still looking at the surface. This can be a frustrating experience—you don't know if it's one fish, cruising and rising once in a while, or a bunch of them feeding occasionally. My best results have come from casting a dry in the center of the activity and letting it sit there, even for three or four minutes.

Do you just sit there and stare at your dry fly? Usually. Take all the slack out of your line, without moving the fly, and wait for the strike. Keep your rod tip low, not only to get the line tight so you can strike, but also to keep the wind from blowing around that portion of your fly line between the rod tip and the water.

Sometimes a subtle twitch will make the trout notice your fly, especially if they're only rising occasionally, or there are so many natural flies on the water that the trout ignore yours. Try one twitch, about an inch or so, then let the fly sit motionless again. Try another if you don't get any response. Your fly should be well dressed with fly floatant if you're going to twitch it, and your leader should be greased as well, so that when you twitch the fly it moves lightly across the surface, like the naturals.

When the trout are taking caddisflies or adult midges, you can sometimes use a steady retrieve with great success, making the fly skitter steadily across the surface of the water. Six-inch strips of line with very little pause in between will give you a good steady pace.

When trout are gulping, or feeding steadily and predictably, sit somewhere out of range and observe them. You can usually pick up a pattern. Paddle or drift quietly to a spot where a trout will intercept you. Cast your fly well ahead of him and wait for him to come to the fly. The worst thing you can do in this situation is try to chase a gulper, because you'll usually succeed only in putting him down. You'll sometimes have to wait quite a while for a gulper or group of gulpers to return, but the wait is well worth it.

Wet Flies and Nymphs

Wet flies, other than the soft-hackled wingless variety, are seldom used these days in still waters. The trout get a very good look at your fly when there's no current, and the more representative nymphs are far more successful in still waters. There are many patterns of nymphs that were developed especially for still-water fishing. Because there is no current to make your nymph look alive, soft, pulsating feathers like marabou, ostrich herl, and soft, webby bird hackles are commonly used to give still-water nymphs "action."

Nymph fishing in still waters involves casting the fly and retrieving it back to you by stripping in line. It's as simple as that. A trout may take your nymph as it's sinking, before you begin your retrieve, but these strikes usually go undetected. You need to have a tight line and a moving fly to detect strikes. You'll see your line or leader twitch, or if you're stripping fast or the trout hits hard, you'll feel the strike.

It is very important to keep your rod tip low when working a nymph in still waters. With a high rod tip you'll miss strikes because of the slack line between your rod tip and the water. That low rod tip is also important because of line control.

When your rod tip is hanging in the air, the line doesn't drop straight to the water, it hangs in an arc. If you strip 6 inches of line, the arc straightens and the fly moves 6 inches toward you. Then, however, gravity takes over to put that arc back into the line and the fly moves again toward you, this time out of your control. With your rod tip close to the water, the fly moves exactly as fast as you strip in line. You have complete control over what your fly is doing, even though it may be 40 or 50 feet away.

Besides fly pattern, two other things are important in still-water nymphing: depth, and the speed at which you retrieve. Depth can, of course, be controlled by the type of fly line you use, and the fly can be weighted to get it deeper more quickly. The amount of time you wait before you begin the retrieve will also control the fly's depth.

A good way to find the correct depth is called the *countdown method*. Count to ten before you begin your retrieve on the first cast, fifteen on the second, and so on until you catch a fish or hang up on the bottom.

The type of fly line you use will determine how "flat" your nymph rides in the water. A weighted nymph fished on a floating line will gradually rise toward the surface as it is retrieved, good when aquatic insects are hatching. The same nymph fished on a sinking line will swim in a straight line or actually get deeper as you retrieve it—good for leech and crustacean imitations.

The speed at which your fly swims is controlled by your stripping hand. Unless you know what worked yesterday or exactly what the fish are feeding on—or what speed the guy in the boat next to you (who is catching lots of fish) is using—it's going to be a matter of trial and error.

I like to start with steady 6-inch pulls of line. This is a pretty standard retrieve and will often produce fish. If not, try fast, foot-long pulls, long, slow, steady pulls, or even use a hand-twist retrieve for an extra-slow, steady retrieve.

Leeches and dragonflies are fairly quick swimmers, so if any of these critters are in evidence, try a fast retrieve. Dragonflies move in quick spurts, as they are jet-propelled—they expel water through their abdomens when they want to go somewhere in a hurry.

There is one type of nymph that is either not retrieved at all or is drawn along slowly, just under the surface. This is the emerger or pupal imitation, and it should be fished just as you would a dry fly, with a long, greased leader and floating line. Strikes will be visible as a boil in the vicinity of your fly. You can also add a tiny strike indicator to the leader, or hang a small nymph under a dry fly.

Streamers

The same techniques used to fish nymphs are used to fish streamers, except that in most cases a fast retrieve, or an erratic one, is all you'll need. You're either trying to imitate a wounded or scared baitfish, or just trying to catch a trout's attention. In either case, a fast retrieve will get the nod more often than a slow one. Depth is very important here. Experiment with different sinking lines and how long the fly sinks before you retrieve.

Streamers are more effective than nymphs in very large lakes, especially if you're some distance from shore. There are few aquatic insects in deep water, so if the trout are there, they will be eating baitfish.

On big water, streamers are often trolled. Although it's not fly casting, you are still fishing with a fly and a fly rod, and it's a good way to cover a lot of water. Once the trout are found, you can stop the boat and cast to them.

Trolling is usually done with big, long streamers, sizes 2, 4, or 6; or even tandem streamers, which may be 3 or 4 inches long. Using a long, level leader, usually a piece of 6- or 8-pound monofilament, about 60 feet of fly line is trolled behind the boat, and the boat is driven or paddled in a zigzag pattern off rocky points, islands, and stream mouths. It is a deadly way to catch trout and land-locked salmon just after ice-out, when the fish are near the surface, and is especially popular in New England.

BASS

Catching bass, both largemouth and smallmouth, on a fly rod is a matter of finding them when they're in relatively shallow water. Bass will be found in the shallows, spawning, when spring water temperatures reach the high 50s, and they'll be there all day long. Providing the water temperatures in the shallows remain below 75 degrees, you'll continue to find them in shallow water all season long, but when the water gets too warm, they'll retreat to deeper water, at least during the day. Because the supply of minnows, frogs, insects, and crayfish is pretty slim in deep water, the bass won't stay there all the time. In the early morning and late evening, they'll cruise into the shallows to feed.

Look for largemouths around lily pads, brush piles, cattails, or any other structure that provides shade and protection for both the largemouth and his prey. Large-mouths seldom feed out in the open, so your casting should be as accurate as possible, striving to place your fly as close as you can to these areas. I've seen bass ignore a popper that was cast a few feet from their log, yet pounce on the same fly when it was dropped right next to the log.

While the largemouth likes mud or silt bottoms, you'll almost always find smallmouths over rocky bot-

toms. The two species may sometimes feed side by side over sandy shoals in the evening, but other than that, their habitats are segregated. Smallmouth bass prefer crayfish over any other kind of food, and crayfish are most abundant along rocky shorelines. Rocks anywhere from the size of bowling balls to big boulders are preferred.

A look at the shoreline will give you clues as to where the smallmouths are located. Smallmouths like drop-offs, so if the banks are steep, chances are there will be a drop-off close to shore. A light-colored bottom shading into an area of darker water anywhere in a lake also indicates possible smallmouth habitat. Cast your flies into the area where the shallow water ends and the deep water begins.

Both species of bass will eat insects such as mayflies and dragonflies, especially smallmouths. When they're feeding on insects, use the same nymph and dry-fly strategies you'd use for trout. Poppers and streamers, however, are the most consistent producers of fly-rod bass.

Unlike trout, you don't have to see rising bass to catch them on surface lures. They'll be waiting to ambush prey, and if the water is shallow and clear enough, they'll find your popper or hair bug—and attack it with a vengeance.

The usual strategy with a popper is to cast it into a bassy-looking spot and let it sit for a few minutes without moving it. I don't mean a few seconds, either—wait at least a full minute, or until all the ripples made by the popper landing on the water dissipate. While you're waiting, carefully remove all the slack from your line by stripping until the line is tight. Don't forget to keep the rod tip low to the water.

Look for largemouths around heavy brush piles and other cover.

Perfect smallmouth water from the air: a steep drop-off and lots of boulders in the water.

Strikes will often come at this point, so you should be ready to set the hook at any time. Bass may eyeball a popper for a long time, inches from the fly, suddenly lunging for it with a tremendous swirl.

If nothing hits your motionless popper, give it a little twitch. With a tight line and a low rod tip, strip in enough line to barely move the popper. Let it sit again. Try another twitch. Then strip hard enough to make the popper gurgle. Let it sit again. Try three or four pops in a row. By fishing this way you can see which strategy produces strikes, and you can then use that method exclusively.

Sometimes a steady retrieve, with foot-long pulls starting as soon as the fly hits the water, will work better than the sit-and-wait method. Try all kinds of retrieves until you draw strikes, but avoid using the rod tip to give your popper action. Using the rod tip throws slack into the line and makes it very difficult to set the hook.

Retrieve a popper for as long as you can—don't pick up the line for another cast until the end of the fly line is at most 15 or 20 feet from the boat. Bass may often follow a popper for a long time before they decide to take it. Besides, the shape of a popper makes it difficult to pick up for another cast, especially with a lot of line out. When the popper is close to the boat, you can lift it straight out of the water.

In general, smallmouths prefer a faster-paced retrieve than largemouths. With both species, deep or murky water usually calls for loud, hard pops, while clear or shallow water requires gentle twitches and longer pauses in between.

Hair bugs and bullethead minnows are fished in the same manner. Although they don't pop as loud as hard-bodied poppers, you should still experiment with fast and slow retrieves and hard and gentle pulls.

When fishing for smallmouths, cast right next to protruding rocks and on top of submerged boulders. If the water near shore is deep, don't be afraid to cast your bug right onto shore and then work it back to you. Check your hook point often when doing this to make sure that it hasn't glanced off a rock.

In largemouth country you should toss your bugs as close as possible to logs, brushy banks, and beds of cattails. When fishing large expanses of weed beds, use a weedless popper or hair bug and cast right onto lily pads or mats of floating weeds. Twitch the popper into openings between the weeds and let it sit motionless. Twitch it across the opening, back onto the weeds, and repeat for the next opening.

Streamers can be used for bass in the same place as poppers. Fished with a floating line, they can be crawled over weed beds, next to logs, and over submerged brush piles. Use a fast retrieve for smallmouths and a slower speed for largemouths.

Streamers are more useful than bugs over the whole season. They can be used in the shallows, and they can also be fished on sinking and sink-tip lines when bass are

Fish poppers very slowly for largemouths.

Smallmouths typically prefer a faster retrieve than largemouths.

in deeper water. Bass will be in 20 to 30 feet of water in the spring and fall, when the water temperature is in the 50s, and also during the summer, when surface water temperatures are above 80 degrees. When bass are in deep water, they're fairly sluggish, and a slow retrieve should be used for both largemouths and smallmouths. Use the countdown method and fish your streamers just off the bottom.

The Muddler-type bass streamer is an interesting fly that can be fished either deep or right on the surface. The hollow deer-hair head will keep the fly just under the surface. Fished on a floating line, it imitates a struggling minnow. Try both steady retrieves and a stop-and-go presentation.

The same fly can be used on a sinking line. The buoyancy of the fly makes it ride above the bottom, but the sinking line keeps it swimming deep. You can fish over logs and rocky bottoms without hanging up, as your fly line will slide along the bottom without snagging on obstructions.

Streamers have another big advantage over poppers and hair bugs: The long, slim shape of a streamer is much easier to cast than an air-resistant popper or bug. If you have to cast into the wind, you'll find a streamer to be more manageable than a bug or popper.

PIKE AND PICKEREL

Pike and pickerel feed actively throughout the winter, so they are some of the first fish available to the fly rodder in the spring. They can be found in shallow water most of the spring, near submerged weed beds, drop-offs, and near sluggish tributary streams. When the water warms to over 60 degrees, pike will retreat to 20 or 30 feet, returning to the shallows in the fall. Pickerel will stay in very shallow water all season long.

Just after ice-out, fish a very brightly colored streamer on a sink-tip line in 2 to 6 feet of water. You should retrieve it slowly in early spring, because a pike's metabolism is in low gear then and he won't chase a quick-moving fly.

Pike like the fastest retrieve of all the warmwater species.

The most exciting time to catch pike and pickerel is when the shallows begin to warm and they are actively feeding. Use a floating line and fish streamers and poppers with a very fast stripping motion, just as fast as you can retrieve them. Strikes will be vicious, and because of their sharp teeth, you'll want to use a foot of 30-pound monofilament as a shock tippet.

Pike can be taken on streamers when they're in deep water during the summer. Use a full-sinking line, cast out about 50 feet, and let the line sink almost to the bottom. Then strip like mad.

Unlike bass, pike and pickerel feed actively throughout the day, so they can fill in some otherwise unproductive hours on weedy lakes and ponds.

PANFISH

Bluegills. Bluegills, pumpkinseeds, rock bass, flier, green sunfish, and other small members of the sunfish family can be taken on almost any small fly. They will be found in warm, shallow water, around weed beds, overhanging trees, docks, and pilings.

The best time to catch sunfish is while they're spawning, when the water temperature approaches 65 degrees. You'll see saucer-shaped beds around silty or sandy shallows, usually right out in the open. Anything that lands near these nests will be attacked, and no method is more fun than using a small rubber-legged popper or sponge-rubber bug.

Cast your bug right over a nest. It will often be pounced on immediately; if not, give it a twitch or two. Don't move your fly too fast, as the larger sunfish prefer a slowly retrieved bug to one that is skimming across the surface.

Later in the year they will move to shaded areas near the shore. Sunfish may move into deeper water. Try a wet fly or nymph retrieved slowly and steadily on a sink-tip line. You can also try a weighted nymph tied onto the bend of the hook of a small popper. Make the popper crawl across the surface, or move it erratically with gentle pops. Then let it sit in between for as much as thirty seconds. Not only will the popper attract panfish, but it also acts as a strike indicator for fish that take the nymph as it is sinking.

Sunfish will sometimes get a little selective about their food, especially later in the year. If they refuse your

Panfish like this pumpkinseed sunfish are always willing to take a fly, whether it is a small popper or nymph.

standard bluegill bugs, try a small dry fly on a 4X or 5X tippet. The pattern doesn't seem to matter as much as the more delicate presentation and profile.

White bass, white perch, yellow bass. These closely related species feed on small baitfish and crustaceans and are favorite targets for a small streamer. Look for them in estuaries, shallow bays of large lakes, channels between lakes, and around warm-water discharges of power plants.

Traveling in schools, these spirited fighters herd baitfish near the surface mornings and evenings. When you find a school, toss a streamer or small popper into the area and retrieve it with foot-long strips. During the day they can be taken near drop-off areas and shoals with a streamer fished on a sink-tip line.

Yellow perch. Yellow perch are another panfish that travel in large schools, usually over weed beds in 2 to 20 feet of water. When you catch a perch, stay put—there are bound to be more in the area. They may come to the surface to inspect a popper, but will seldom strike one. Small wets, nymphs, and streamers fished very slowly near the bottom produce the best results.

Crappie. These are voracious minnow feeders that feed in and around weed beds and brush piles, usually over a silty bottom. They seldom pass up a small streamer fished on a sink-tip line in 4 to 8 feet of water.

Walleye. Walleyes are deep-dwelling fish that avoid bright light. They congregate to spawn around large inlet streams in the early spring. At this time they're easy to take on large, brightly colored streamers.

After spawning, walleyes will be found near large gravel or sandbars. During the day you'll need to fish your streamers slowly on a full-sinking line, but on gloomy days or at night, walleyes can be caught near the surface on streamers and poppers.

Because lakes and ponds have more diverse fish species than streams, fly fishing with a universal fish-taker like a streamer can be an interesting proposition. In the spring it's possible to catch a trout, a bass, a pike, and half a dozen species of panfish on consecutive casts. The mystery of not knowing what kind of fish will take your fly next adds a lot to the pleasure of fly fishing in still waters.

{ A WARMING FIRE }

Chapter Ten

Salmon and Steelhead

ATLANTIC SALMON, STEELHEAD, and the various saltwater species are the big game of fly fishing. They all require a lot of persistence, usually heavy tackle, and large flies. The same rod, something around 9 feet long for a 9-weight line, can be used to fish for all of them, except large tarpon, billfish, or tuna, which require a 12-weight outfit.

This chapter requires a familiarity with many of the techniques discussed in chapters 8 and 9, so I would recommend you read those chapters first even if you don't intend to fish for trout and bass. Although Atlantic salmon, steelhead, and Pacific salmon are only distantly related, these fish share a common life history because they all spend most of their time in the ocean (or in the case of Great Lakes steelhead, in huge lakes) and return to moving water to spawn. Atlantic salmon and steelhead may spawn multiple times during their lives; all Pacific salmon die shortly after spawning. Most of the flies you'll use to catch these species are considered attractor flies, as Atlantic and Pacific salmon do not feed during their spawning runs, and although steelhead do feed at some stages of their spawning runs, they are just as likely to take a brightly colored attractor fly.

ATLANTIC SALMON

The Atlantic salmon is tailor-made for fly fishing. It takes a fly well, perhaps better than any other kind of lure or bait. Salmon are superb fighters, their leaping ability equaled only by steelhead and tarpon. There are few rivers in North America where you can legally catch sea-run Atlantic salmon on anything but an unweighted fly.

In our anthropomorphic way of assigning intelligence levels to fish, the Atlantic salmon is one of the dumbest fish that swims. When they are in a taking mood, you can wade clumsily, run a boat over them, and turn around and catch one on the most unlikely fly, with a cast that barely straightens. Yet you can also fish over a dozen salmon "laying in" a clear pool for hours without drawing a rise.

Salmon do not need to feed on their spawning runs, so they never *have* to take a fly. They feed voraciously in freshwater rivers as young parr for one to eight years before they run to the ocean, then grow quickly on a diet of shrimp and capelin. When they return to freshwater

A magnificent Atlantic salmon taken in Quebec by Bebe Bullock. Bill Bullock photo.

Even small Atlantic salmon (called grilse) are exciting leapers, as the splash of this fish on a small Nova Scotia river shows.

rivers to spawn, anywhere from one to three years later, they have plenty of energy stored up, enough to run a 100-mile river, fight an angler's hook, spawn, overwinter, and return to the sea the following spring. Yet we can still elicit a feeding reflex from the salmon with our flies.

Adult Atlantic salmon are divided into two groups: grilse and salmon. A *grilse* is a fish that has been to sea for only one year and weighs from 3 to 6 pounds; a salmon has spent at least two years at sea and weighs from 7 to over 40 pounds upon returning to the river. Unlike Pacific salmon, Atlantic salmon can survive the rigors of spawning and may spawn two, three, or even four times.

In North America, adult salmon return to freshwater rivers anytime from May through October in rivers from the Connecticut north to Labrador. Russian rivers on the Kola Peninsula and Icelandic rivers have a similar season, but Atlantic salmon can be found in the rivers of the British Isles almost twelve months a year. Some rivers are "early run," others are late, and some rivers have a multiple run: grilse at one time and salmon at another. The cue appears to be proper water temperature. Before you plan a salmon-fishing trip, be sure that your vacation time coincides with a likely time for a run of fish.

Salmon will enter a river on a rise of water or high tide, then make tracks for the vicinity of their spawning grounds. Early fish may hold in spring-fed pools for a month or more; late arrivals have been known to travel over 20 miles a day in their haste to mate. Nature times things so that they all arrive in the headwater spawning areas at about the same time, usually in late fall. Laws prohibit fishing over salmon that are actually on the spawning beds, closing the season before the fish begin spawning and sometimes closing upper areas of rivers to fishing.

The best situation for salmon fishing is when a large group of fish moves on a moderate rise of water. Heavy, dirty floodwater makes fishing difficult. When a river is low, clear, or warm, they show less enthusiasm for taking

Classic Atlantic salmon water: The St. Mary's River in Nova Scotia. Good salmon pools may look just like other pools, but experienced salmon fishers know which pools will hold salmon that will take a fly.

flies, although special flies and tactics have been developed for these difficult periods.

Salmon will rest above and below areas that require energy to pass, such as falls and rapids. They will be found anywhere near the main flow of the river, because their purpose is to use that flow to guide them upstream. They'll seldom be found in back eddies or side channels, but may rest in very shallow water if it's near the main flow. Anything that breaks the current—rocks, points, ledges, depressions in the streambed, tails of pools, the intersection of two currents—may hold salmon. During periods of low water, salmon will be concentrated in deep, still pools.

Salmon can often be seen leaping clear of the water, especially in the morning or evening. This does not necessarily mean they will take a fly, but it at least gives you a clue as to where one or more fish can be found. A salmon will sometimes do a slow, porpoising roll, with his head, dorsal fin, and tail breaking the water. This usually indicates potential interest in a fly.

Most salmon fishing is done with wet flies, especially early in the season, when the water is high and cold. In most currents, the fly is merely cast across or quartering downstream and allowed to swing below you. Unless a salmon is spotted, you'll want to cover as much water as possible. The best way to do this is to make a short cast, 30 feet or so, then extend your line a few feet on the next cast. Keep on extending your line until you near the far bank or reach the maximum distance you can cast. Take three or four steps downstream and repeat the process.

Your fly should not swing so fast that it skims across the surface (except in special circumstances), nor should it drift so slowly that it sinks. To keep your fly swinging at the proper pace, cast directly across the current in slow water, angling your casts more in a downstream direction in faster water.

Unlike trout and winter steelhead, salmon will come up for a fly, even if they are lying in 6 feet of water. Your fly should be swinging from 3 inches to 1 foot below the surface. If the water is very high or cold, a sink-tip line may be effective, but most salmon fishing is done with a floating or intermediate-weight line.

With standard wet-fly fishing for salmon, you do not want any slack in your line or leader. Your fly should be under tension at all times, and it is effectively fishing as soon as it hits the water. Slack will not allow the fly to swing properly, and if your leader doesn't straighten immediately, you'll lose some effectiveness on the first part of your drift—until the current puts some tension into it.

Salmon in shallow water are not very spooky, and you won't alarm them unless you block their access to deep water. Make sure that you cover the shallow water near the bank before you lengthen your casts.

Salmon will rest and take flies in traditional holding pools and spots that remain the same from year to year. A good guide is an asset, not only for fly selection but to make sure you fish the right pools. Areas on a particular river that appear great to a stranger may be devoid of fish, even though they look like holding water.

You should try to watch your fly (or where you think your fly is) all the time. A salmon that has risen is one that can usually be taken. If a salmon boils or flashes at your fly but does not connect, rest him for a few minutes by standing quietly, or else casting to another spot. Keep the same length of line and cast to the exact same spot or a bit above it after you have rested the fish. If you rise a salmon, he will usually come back to the same fly; if he doesn't, try a different pattern or size, usually a smaller one.

Salmon take flies best after a rain has raised the water level a few feet and in the early morning and evening when the water is at normal or low levels. They can also be taken during the day, even when the water is low and clear, by using special techniques designed to raise sullen fish.

One such technique is the *greased-line method*, which presents the fly broadside to the current (and to the salmon) throughout most of the drift. The greased-line method also swings a fly with a uniform speed, instead of speeding up at the end of the swing, and may provoke a rise when nothing else will.

The greased-line method is performed by casting across or quartering downstream and mending line every time the line bellies. The rod tip should follow the fly's drift throughout the swing, staying just upstream of the fly. Line is usually mended in an upstream direction, except when you are standing in slow water and the fly is in fast water, in which case you should mend in a downstream direction. In a nutshell, the line between the rod tip and the fly should be kept as straight as possible.

The greased-line method is usually used in conjunction with small, sparse flies such as low-water flies or salmon nymphs.

Another way to raise uncooperative salmon is to use a *riffled fly*. This technique can be used with any wet fly and is performed by first taking a half hitch with the leader around the head of the fly, behind the eye, so that the leader emerges from the side of the fly rather than the front. When the fly is swung in the current, it makes much more commotion than a standard presentation would, and often this added disturbance will interest a salmon enough to draw explosive strikes. It works better on some rivers than others (i.e., certain rivers in Newfoundland, Russia, and Iceland). The hitch should be changed depending upon which direction the current is flowing. If when you are facing directly across the river the current flows from right to left, the leader should stick out from the right side of the fly as you look down the shank of the hook with the eye facing you.

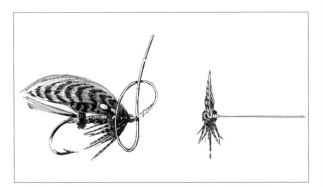

The riffling hitch puts an overhand knot at the head of a fly and creates more disturbance in the water, sometimes very appealing to Atlantic salmon.

If the fly throws spray as it swings, it is moving too fast and you should use an upstream mend to slow it down. If it sinks, you should speed up the swing—increase the line tension by mending downstream.

During periods of low water, salmon will hold in large, slow pools that have such a slight current they resemble ponds. In order to obtain the proper wet-fly speed in a situation like this, you should strip in line as the fly swings, just as you would fish a streamer for trout.

A salmon can also be enticed with the *patent method*, which is merely casting a salmon fly upstream on a slack line. The fly should pass dead drift over the fish. This method cannot be used to cover a lot of water, and the fly loses its effectiveness when it sinks too deep, so it is used for a salmon that has been spotted on the bottom or one that has risen to a fly.

Dry flies can be used for salmon anytime, but are most successful when the water is low and over 60 degrees. A salmon that has been located should be tried first by presenting the fly upstream, dead drift, exactly as you would for trout. This method can also be used to fish blind, but it's tiring because you're wading upstream and will need to false-cast more than with a wet fly.

If an upstream presentation doesn't work, try casting a dry across-stream as you would a wet, and allow the fly to drag violently across the current. This method is especially successful with palmer-hackled deer-hair flies such as the Bomber and Buck Bug, and will draw violent, slashing rises from the salmon.

Nova Scotians use an interesting technique that combines both wet- and dry-fly presentation on a single cast. They use a sparsely tied dry fly that has a slanted hackle, so it looks like a wet but floats when cast upstream. They cast the fly quartering upstream and fish it dry until it drifts just below them, then pull on the line so that the fly sinks. The fly is then fished wet until the line straightens below, and then it's picked up for another cast.

Salmon, especially big salmon, move for a fly slowly, and you should resist the impulse to strike immediately. An experienced trout angler, who is used to setting the hook as quickly as possible, may hook fewer salmon than the novice, whose reactions are slower. With a wet fly, make sure you feel the salmon before tightening the line; many times with a wet fly the tension on the line will set the hook for you. With a dry fly, wait until you see the fish turning toward the bottom before striking.

Leaders for Atlantic salmon, when using a floating line with either a dry fly or wet fly, are usually 9 feet long, with a tippet size of between 3X and 0X (about 9- to 16-pound-test). When using sink-tip lines, a 6- to 7½-foot leader keeps the fly deeper.

The best salmon anglers are those who are persistent and like to cast. The more your fly is in the water, the better your chances of hooking a salmon.

STEELHEAD

Steelhead are rainbow trout that live in the ocean or large freshwater lakes and return to freshwater rivers to spawn. Actually, any rainbow that lives in a lake will use a freshwater river to spawn, as their eggs must have moving water to survive. *Steelhead* usually indicates the race of rainbows that are silvery, quite large, and may migrate upriver hundreds of miles to their spawning ground.

In any population of trout that has access to the ocean, certain individuals will become anadromous, dropping down into the ocean and returning to spawn. In the United States we have sea-run brown trout in a few rivers on Long Island and Cape Cod, sea-run brookies in Maritime Canada, and sea-run cutthroats in the Pacific Northwest. These fish, however, have very limited ranges, and the sport fishery for them as compared to steelhead is limited. They may be caught in estuaries (where they spend most of their time) on streamer flies that imitate prevalent baitfish. When they ascend rivers in the fall to spawn, they are usually caught on standard trout streamers, wets, and nymphs.

Steelhead mate in shallow gravel beds on the stream bottom, where the fry hatch. The fry soon mature into tiny replicas of their parents, with dark oval or crescent-shaped parr markings on their sides. Now called *parr*, they will remain in their natal rivers for one to four years, finally changing into silvery *smolts* and dropping down into the ocean. They will be 6 to 9 inches long at this time.

Adult steelhead, after growing fat on ocean baitfish and crustaceans, return to the same river in which they were born, by some method of navigation that is not entirely understood but is thought to involve the chemical signature of their river, which the steelhead can smell. In general, the longer a steelhead has remained in the ocean before spawning, the larger he will be.

Steelhead may enter a river at any time of the year, but the most common times are spring and fall. There are many distinct races of steelhead, and the time that they are available will vary greatly from river to river. One river may also support more than one race of steelhead, and may have more than one run per year.

Timing and knowledge of local conditions are essential in steelhead fishing. The fish take a fly much better when they are silvery, fresh from the ocean or lake. Steelhead feed very little when they migrate, and as they ascend a river they become less and less inclined to take a fly. *Stale* fish—those that are penned up in a pool, waiting for the proper time to spawn or a rise of water to move upstream—are the most difficult to take on a fly.

Because steelhead are moving but not actively feeding, you must cover a lot of water in order to find the fish.

The pool you're fishing might contain ten fish today and none tomorrow. Unless you have weeks or months to fish a particular river, a guide or someone who has fished the river before can be invaluable. Steelhead will rest in the same spots from year to year. These spots, unless changed by flooding that alters the streambed, will contain steelhead, while spots that look exactly the same to us will be devoid of fish.

Steelhead will most often be concentrated above and below obstructions that require some energy expenditure to pass. A low waterfall or a long stretch of fast water will hold fish that are either waiting to scale the obstacle or are resting after passing it. This makes heads and tails of pools logical places to fish.

Steelhead will also be found in the middle of pools and in long expanses of flat water, but they will be more spread out and difficult to find in these spots, requiring a lot of movement on your part and many casts over unproductive areas.

Look for steelhead above and below rocks on the streambed, on the edge of fast currents, close to the bank in tails of pools, and just under the lips of waterfalls or at the head of a pool. They will seldom be found far from the main current in a river, because even if they're not moving at the present time, they have one purpose: to get upstream as easily as possible. Water that has a smooth flow is usually more productive than water with lots of eddies and conflicting currents.

The various races of steelhead can be lumped into two groups for fly-fishing purposes: summer- and winter-run fish. The tactics used for each group are quite different.

Winter-run steelhead run a river from late fall through early spring. The water in steelhead rivers at this time is high, fast, and cold, and the steelhead will be found on or near the bottom. They will seldom rise to a fly that is more than a couple of feet above them. The most eagerly taken flies are those that are drifting at about the same speed as the bottom currents. They will also attack a fly that is drifting just off the bottom and suddenly rises toward the surface, perhaps an instinctive reaction to something that is getting away.

Either bright flies or large dark patterns are necessary, as is a sinking line of some type; this gear is necessary both to provoke a steelhead and also because the water is often dark and cloudy. Rarely will a floating line with a

Typical West Coast steelhead river for winter-run fish, and typical weather.

weighted heavy fly get deep enough, except in small, shallow streams, to get into the strike zone.

A fly line presents a problem when you are trying for a slow, deep drift. Because the current is always faster in a stream near the surface, the thick fly line between you and the fly will pull the fly away from productive water. Fly fishers who use spinning or bait-casting tackle and lead weights can get their lures near the bottom quicker and keep it there longer, because monofilament line slices through the current and is less likely to be pushed toward the surface. With fly-fishing gear, as soon as the fly is put under tension by the line, it will be pulled toward the surface.

The classic steelhead cast is a quartering upstream cast, using either a sink-tip or a full-sinking line. As soon as the fly and line hit the water they begin to sink, because they are not under tension yet. With a sink-tip line, the floating portion should be mended upstream every time it begins to belly downstream, so that the fly sinks as deeply as possible. To get the fly even deeper, a technique called *stack mending* is used. Here, you throw a series of underpowered roll casts into the line, directed at the point where you suspect the fly is drifting. The fly will be at its deepest point when it is quartering downstream from you; hopefully, it will be near the bottom. Strikes will usually come at this point and will be signaled by a tightening of the line. A steelhead guide once told me, "With fly-fishing gear, you probably have only a couple of feet of drift on each cast when the fly is at the proper

spot—when it's quartering downstream." At any other point in its drift, the fly is riding too far above the fish to be noticed.

You should be hanging bottom frequently when fly-fishing for winter steelhead; otherwise, you're not getting the fly deep enough. To get the fly deeper, you can cast farther upstream, change to a heavily weighted fly, or change to a fly-line type that sinks deeper—from a sink-tip to a full-sinking line, for example.

A trick that is often used to extend the productive drift of a fly is to point your rod tip downstream at the end of the drift, just before the line starts to belly, and feed line through the guides.

A fast-sinking shooting head is the best way to cover a lot of water. Because of the thin-diameter running line, heads can be cast quartering downstream, where they will sink the fly to the proper depth very quickly. All of the unproductive time spent casting upstream to sink the fly is eliminated. To cover a pool thoroughly with a shooting head, you should start at the head of a pool, casting just above areas that look as if they'll hold steelhead. After the fly completes its swing, take a few steps downstream and repeat the process. The next cast will cover the area just downstream of the previous drift.

Summer-run steelhead enter rivers from late spring through early fall, when the water is usually low, slow, and clear. They will be found in riffled water and in pools that have some cool springwater coming into them. Unlike winter steelhead, summer-run fish can be teased into taking a fly that is drifting just under the surface and will even take dry flies if the water is very low and clear.

Summer steelhead are sometimes visible as dark shapes on the bottoms of pools, and you can fish for them with dry flies just as you would for trout, although it may take repeated casts to interest them. If they aren't visible, just work upstream with a big (sizes 6 through 12), bushy dry fly, covering as much water as you can.

Summer fish will also rise well to small, lightly dressed wet flies fished across and downstream with the greased-line method, or with a riffled fly, identical to the way you would fish for Atlantic salmon. Summer-runs present a great opportunity for the fly caster, as fly tackle can be used as efficiently as any other kind of gear under these conditions.

Although swinging a fly on a floating or sink-tip line is the most fun and the most elegant way to catch steel-

close-in fishing, a high-stick technique is used; for longer casts, a straight upstream cast is used; or when quartering upstream, frequent mends are introduced to keep the fly fishing without drag.

Fishing a two-handed rod on the Rogue River in Oregon for summer steelhead.

A typical summer steelhead from the Rogue, taken on a swung streamer.

A hard-running steelhead on Michigan's Pere Marquette, one of the best and most famous of the Great Lakes steelhead rivers.

The other technique, which is not even considered fly fishing by some, is *strip-casting with running line*. Here, a leader is attached to level, floating running line that is about .030 inches in diameter. This line will not cast in the normal manner. Instead, a fairly substantial amount of split shot or sink putty is attached to the leader about 12 to 18 inches above the fly. To cast this arrangement, you dip the weight into the water at your side, then fling the weight out into the river, usually quartering upstream. The rod is kept high, with a straight line to the point where the leader enters the water. The drift of the fly and weight are followed with the tip of the rod, and most of the time you can feel the weight gently ticking bottom throughout the drift. If you hang up on every third cast, remove some weight; if you're not feeling the bottom, add weight in small amounts until you feel some contact with the streambed. Strikes can be very subtle, and you should strike at the slightest hesitation of the line, or when you feel resistance different than the steady ticking of the weight along the bottom.

This strip-casting technique is most often used during the winter, when cold water keeps the steelhead relatively inactive and when they won't move very far for the fly. The

head, there are other, more down-and-dirty techniques that can be used. You should know that the following techniques might get you ostracized from the fly-fishing community on West Coast rivers, however. Just like Atlantic salmon fishing in the Northeast, western steelhead fishing has a long tradition of accepted techniques. Great Lakes steelheading is only about thirty years old, and not being bound by tradition, anglers in this fishery have developed some pragmatic, but not traditional or pretty methods of fishing. One is fishing with floating lines, strike indicators, and usually some weight on the leader. It's exactly like fishing for trout with nymphs; in fact, nymphs are often used, as well as egg imitations. For

Great Lakes steelhead may not be ocean-run fish, but they do grow large in these freshwater inland seas.

advantage is that the thin running line cuts through the water and presents less resistance to the current, so the fly gets to the bottom and stays there throughout the drift. Is it truly fly fishing? Try it and decide for yourself.

Leaders for steelhead when using a floating line are typically 9 feet long, and anywhere from 5X to 0X (5-pound to 16-pound-test) in tippet size. The heavier leaders are used for large fish in heavy water, and the lighter ones for either summer-run fish or fish in clear water on bright days. For sinking and sink-tip lines, 6-foot leaders in the same tippet sizes are adequate.

PACIFIC SALMON

The most important aspect of fly-fishing for Pacific salmon is timing. The ideal situation is when a group of fish has just arrived from the ocean (or the Great Lakes) and they are still bright silver in color. These fish will be very aggressive and will still be interested in slamming baitfish imitations. Once they've spent a few days in the river, they'll be far less aggressive and much harder to take.

For fresh fish, all it usually takes is to get a big, bright streamer in front of their faces. Not all will be takers, but because they enter the river in waves, you should be able to find some in an aggressive mood. You can swing a fly

Silver or coho salmon stay brighter and more aggressive after they leave the ocean and are the most popular Pacific salmon with fly rodders.

in front of them in faster current, or in slower pools it may be a better bet to strip the fly just as you would a trout streamer. *Coho salmon* (also known as *silver salmon*) seem to stay bright and aggressive longer than kings, sockeyes, or chum salmon, and they are the favorite species of Pacific salmon for the fly fisher. Cohos will even chase a streamer stripped just under the surface.

Once Pacific salmon have been in a river for more than a few days, they become less aggressive and harder to catch. The same big, bright streamers will work, but sometimes you'll have better luck with smaller egg imitations or nymphs. More important than anything else is *where* you drift your fly. Unlike steelhead, which tend to lie on the bottom in faster current, Pacific salmon are more likely to be found in the slower sections of pools, and they'll be suspended in the middle of the water column. Thus, a slow-sinking or intermediate line might be a better choice than the fast-sinking line you'd use for steelhead.

Leaders for Pacific salmon should be heavier than those used for steelhead, especially when fishing for king salmon, which can reach 60 pounds. Happily, Pacific salmon are not leader-shy, so your tippet can be from 16 to 20 pounds (.011 to .015 inches in diameter), and a 7½-foot length should be sufficient.

{ A Short Cast to Feeding Bonefish }

Chapter Eleven

Salt Water

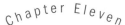

SALTWATER FLY FISHING CAN BE easy if you find fish feeding near the surface. Finding fish is the key; there is so much ocean that merely trying to cover the water with your flies is a fruitless proposition.

A guide can save you weeks of unproductive searching. They know where and when to find the species that you're after. Good saltwater guides are also adept at spotting bonefish on shallow flats, or the subtle ripple or different color made by a school of bluefish when they're near the surface. Many of these signs are overlooked by the untrained eye.

If you're on your own, either on land or in a boat, you can look for clues that indicate good fly-fishing spots. Stripers, bluefish, bonito, king mackerel, and other species that herd baitfish on the surface, can be found almost anywhere. When they're near the surface, you may actually see the water frothing, with baitfish jumping clear of the water. Gulls, terns, and shearwaters are good indicators of this activity. If birds are wheeling above the water without landing, there may be a school of baitfish present; when they begin to drop to the water to pick up dead and crippled baitfish, you can be sure that some potentially good fly fishing is close at hand. Get to that spot

Birds or "nervous water" are a good sign of saltwater gamefish herding baitfish on the surface. This boat in Boston Harbor is in the thick of both.

in a hurry, because the school may sound as quickly as it came to the surface.

If the surface of the water is calm, look for protruding fins, ripples, or wakes that don't look like they're formed by the wind, or dark discolorations on the surface that may indicate a school of cruising fish.

Certain places will concentrate baitfish, so the quarry you're after will be waiting in ambush. Estuaries contain some of the most productive ecosystems in the world. Their nutrient-rich waters support huge quantities of baitfish and crustaceans, and the constant flux of the tide moves food in and out of channels and bays. Look for feeding gamefish on the outside of channels and bays on an outgoing tide, on the inside of these areas on an incoming tide.

Tropical and subtropical flats are among the most consistent sources of fly-rod sport. They host a wide variety of bottom feeders, including bonefish, permit, redfish, barracuda, snapper, sharks, and tarpon. Flats are perfect for fly fishing, because the water is shallow enough to present a fly, regardless of where the fish are, and the fish are usually visible.

Saltwater fly fishing can be as easy as tossing a popper into a chum line or to a sailfish that has chased a teaser. It may also require all the stealth and accurate casting of trout fishing, especially when bonefish or permit are involved. The main problem is getting your fly to the fish as soon as possible. Saltwater fish are constantly on the move when they feed, and you may have only one chance at a fish. Add to this the problem of a big fly (and perhaps a strong wind), and you can see the case for a big rod that will deliver your fly with a single false cast.

Standard procedure is to stand ready with 20 to 30 feet of fly line out beyond the tip of your fly rod, hanging behind you in the water. Another 30 feet of line is pulled off the reel and coiled at your feet. The fly is held in your stripping hand. You'll use the line outside the guides to form a quick roll cast, then make a single false cast, double haul, and shoot the line that was coiled at your feet.

It's important that this shooting line be free of obstructions. Anything that protrudes on the deck of a boat should be covered with towels, rags, or, better yet, a piece of nylon mesh with weights tied to the corners. An improvised shooting basket can be made from a plastic garbage pail. If you're wading in the surf, you should have a stripping basket strapped to your waist.

With poppers, you want to cast just ahead of a surface-feeding fish or right in the middle of a school that is herding baitfish. With a subsurface fly, you want to cast just ahead of a cruising fish, so that when he intercepts your fly it will be at his level. Before fishing with streamers, it's best to make a few trial casts where you can see the fly sink, so that you can estimate its sink rate.

Most saltwater gamefish, with the exception of the bottom feeders, require a fast retrieve. Open-ocean species are fast swimmers, and so are their quarry. Just before they intercept your fly, begin stripping, using 1- to 2-foot pulls of line, with no pause in between. A tight line is essential, and so is a quick, firm hook-setting motion. The rod tip should be as close to the water as possible, in order to maintain a tight rod-to-fly connection.

If a visible fish doesn't respond to your fly as it passes in front of him, the best thing to do is speed up your retrieve, as if the fly is a panicked baitfish. Predator fish will usually make an instinctive lunge toward a fleeing fish. Slowing your retrieve will seldom draw strikes, except with such cautious species as striped bass or bonefish. Stopping your retrieve and letting the fly sit dead in the water will usually cause a saltwater fish to turn away and lose interest, except in a chum line, where the fish are picking up pieces of dead baitfish, or when fishing for species that eat crabs, because a crab's typical defense is to drop to the bottom and burrow into the sand.

Poppers may be fished fast or slow, but they're seldom fished as slow as you would for freshwater bass. A steady retrieve, while making the popper throw up a stream of bubbles and spray, will work best for the species that like a fast-moving fly, such as bluefish, barracuda, marlin, and sailfish. Stripers and redfish may want a popper that barely gurgles, especially when the water is calm.

To get a very fast retrieve with either a streamer or popper, it's sometimes necessary to sweep the rod tip off to the side, using your stripping hand to bring in line and take up slack at the same time. Make sure after each sweep that you return your rod tip in front of you and low to the water, otherwise you'll have trouble setting the hook. A fast, even violent retrieve with a popper is useful when fish are chasing big schools of bait and your fly must compete with Mother Nature's creations. A noisy presentation can also be used to draw the attention of fish that are in deep water.

There are hundreds of species of saltwater gamefish that can be caught on a fly rod. The following are the most popular with fly rodders and should give you representative examples of the opportunities for saltwater fly fishing.

BONEFISH

Bonefish are found in shallow tropical flats throughout the world. The most popular places for fly fishing are the Florida Keys, the Caribbean, and Central America, but untapped bonefish fishing exists throughout the world.

Bonefish feed on mollusks, shrimp, and small baitfish, which they root from aquatic grasses, marl, and crevasses between rocks. They seldom feed more than a foot above the bottom. Bonefish travel in schools that average a half-dozen fish, but some schools may number twenty to thirty fish. On the Yucatán peninsula, schools of over 200 1- to 3-pound bonefish are often seen. The largest individuals, 10 pounds and over, may be solitary or travel in twos or threes.

Bonefish do not jump, but their sizzling runs may peel 100 yards of line from your reel in a matter of seconds. Leaders and line should be as light as possible, because bonefish are very spooky and can be very picky about what they eat.

Look for bonefish in water that is 6 inches to 4 feet deep. In very shallow water their tails will stick out above the water as they feed. This is the most desirable way to find bonefish, as they are easy to approach and to catch when tailing. Bonefish feeding in deeper water may leave trails of mud, which help to spot the bonefish and indicate in which direction they're traveling. Experienced eyes, usually possessed by professional bonefish guides (who are almost essential), can also see their ghostly shapes cruising just above the bottom.

For cruising fish, the fly is presented so that it lands 2 or 3 feet ahead of a moving fish, or far enough so that he'll intercept it as he moves along. If the fish are in shallow water and not moving too quickly, your first cast can land quite close to the lead fish, within a foot or so. If you don't catch a fish on your first presentation, subsequent casts should be placed farther ahead of the fish, as they'll begin to get wise to your presence.

Slow, foot-long strips are then used to interest the fish, although a quick jerk may help to entice a fickle individual. Fly-rod bonefishing can become quite a cat-and-mouse game, because individuals and schools cruise erratically. A cast that lands too near one may cause the entire school to bolt for deeper water, so it's important to see not only the fish you're casting to, but also the others in the school. A fly line that slaps on top of one fish may spook them all. A great advantage of fly-fishing for bonefish is that if you cast to a moving fish and he changes direction, you can pick up immediately and put the fly back in front of him while he's still moving. A spin fisher would have to reel in all his line before making another cast.

If you see bonefish tailing in shallow water, it's best to cast the fly as close as possible without landing your line or leader on top of one. With their heads buried in the bottom, they are not as spooky and may not notice the fly unless it is close to their noses. Let the fly sink close to the bottom, then move it away in short, jerky strips. If you don't see a tail wheel around and follow the fly, pick it up and cast again.

Although it's not considered as challenging, one of the easiest ways to catch bonefish is to cast a heavy fly into a cloud of mud on the flats. These muds are usually made by a school of bonefish rooting in deeper water, and because they are hidden by the mud, they are neither spooky nor terribly picky about what they eat. Cast your fly into the middle of the mud cloud and retrieve it with short, quick strips.

Bonefish are so sneaky that you may not see or feel the strike. They usually take the fly in the pause between strips, even if the pause is very short. Experienced fly-rod bonefishers say that they watch for the fish to stop, tip their heads down and quiver slightly, then set the hook. Striking to a bonefish (and other flats fish) should be done using a *strip strike*, not a lift of the rod tip. By just making a long, quick strip of your fly line, you'll feel resistance if the fish has taken the fly, and if it hasn't taken the fly, your imitation will just look like it's trying to escape, not rocket to the surface. Using the strip strike will

Stalking bonefish on foot is one of the most exciting and challenging things you can do with a fly rod.

give you three or four chances on a single retrieve—lifting the rod tip only gives you one chance.

You won't need a shock tippet for the rubber-mouthed bonefish. A 9- or 12-foot 12-pound leader is standard, although in very shallow water with spooky fish, you might try 8-pound, and with bigger flies in deep water you can get away with 16-pound.

A nice bonefish is released back into Florida Bay by Captain Rick Rouff.

PERMIT

Permit are the holy grail of the flats fisher. Landing just one can be considered the catch of a lifetime, and many successful bonefishers have cast to permit for years without even hooking one. Permit will ignore the most perfectly presented fly that looks exactly like a crab, or else they'll inspect the fly and then flee like they've seen a 5-foot hammerhead. There are few secrets to catching permit other than persistence.

You'll recognize one immediately on the flats. They are much wider and deeper than any other flats fish, and they sport a black, sickle-shaped tail and a long, black dorsal fin. You may see that sickle tail waving in the breeze when they feed in shallow water.

Permit are found in deeper water than bonefish, and because they take crabs off the bottom, you need a heavily weighted fly. You must lead a moving permit by quite a distance in order to get your fly to the bottom. Cast your fly close to you a few times so you can gauge how quickly it sinks. If you see permit cruising, cast well in front of them so your fly is on or near the bottom when they swim by.

A permit on a fly rod is considered the ultimate trophy in saltwater flats fishing.

If permit are tailing, you'll want to cast the fly quite close to the fish—but not right on top of it, or the fish will spook. If a permit seems to pass up your fly, give it a small twitch, just about an inch, to catch the fish's attention. Permit hardly ever chase after a fly like a bonefish, which is why your fly needs to be as realistic as possible—they need to get a good look at it.

Because permit are so spooky, the best days to fish for them are cloudy days with a breeze. If the water's surface is glass-smooth, you'll have a tough time getting a heavy crab imitation close to one before it heads for deep water—that is, if you don't spook it just by your approach.

Standard 9- or even 12-foot leaders in 12- or 16-pound-test are standard for permit. You don't want or need a shock tippet, and I wouldn't scrimp by using a less-expensive nylon leader for them. PVDF leaders sink better, are more abrasion-resistant, and are almost invisible in water. And be sure to check your hook point and your knots; you don't want your one perfect shot at a permit to be ruined by anything other than a permit's coy nature.

TARPON

Tarpon are the most spectacular saltwater fish. These silvery giants reach weights in excess of 200 pounds and will often clear the water for 6 feet vertically and 15 feet horizontally when hooked, throughout a fight that may encompass hundreds of yards and last for hours. Smaller individuals are played for less time, but the battle is just as exciting.

Even "baby" tarpon are a thrill on a fly rod.

Tarpon inhabit shallow, warm water from the southern United States to Central America. They travel in schools, feeding on baitfish and crustaceans. Much of their feeding takes place at night, but they can be enticed to take large streamers during the day. Cold weather will send tarpon into deep water, but when the water temperature rises in the spring, they will migrate into shallow bays. Giant tarpon are found in 6 to 10 feet of water, but "baby" tarpon that range from 2 to 20 pounds can be taken in very shallow water and in the canals that crisscross the Florida coast.

Schools of tarpon can be spotted by their darker shapes or shadows along the bottom, or they can be seen rolling on the surface. A wake of bubbles may indicate a school is nearby. Tarpon have a unique gas bladder that allows them to use atmospheric air to breathe. It's interesting that a 100-pound-plus tarpon with a bucket-sized mouth will often prefer 4-inch flies to large lures. In the Florida Keys, home of giant tarpon of 175 pounds and more, flies are recognized as the most effective way to hook these fish.

An experienced guide may stake out an area and wait for tarpon to cruise by. If you are on your own, try drifting or poling slowly along flats, banks, or mangrove swamps. Baby tarpon in canals can often be stalked from the bank. The best presentation for tarpon is a fly that is stripped with smooth, foot-long pulls with a pause in between, to allow the feathers of the fly to wiggle and pulsate. But the most important part of presenting your fly to a tarpon is not how you retrieve, but the angle between your cast and the fish. A tiny fly swimming toward a 150-pound tarpon will spook the fish. You want to plan your cast so that the fly passes *in front of* a fish and swims away from it, as though it's a baitfish or shrimp that has suddenly realized there's a big predator in the neighborhood.

The easiest angle is to have fish coming directly toward you. Cast so that the fly lands about 10 feet in front of the fish (or in front of the lead fish if they're in a school), and begin to strip the fly when the fish is a few feet from your fly. The problem with fish coming straight at you is that they'll soon see the boat and spook. A better approach is when a school is passing parallel to the boat within casting range. Here, you want to cast *ahead* of the lead fish before it gets even with the boat, so that the fly is moving away from the fish as you begin stripping. If there is a school of fish and the first one does not eat the fly, you may have a shot at one of the fish bringing up the rear.

Tarpon leaders should be long, at least 9 feet, and sometimes 12 feet if the wind is not blowing. Tarpon have very abrasive jaws and sharp gill covers, so a monofilament shock tippet is essential. For smaller baby tarpon of up to 60 pounds, you can get away with a 40- or 60-pound shock tippet, but for the true giants you'll need an 80-pound shock tippet.

REDFISH

Redfish feed on the same foods as bonefish—namely shrimp, crabs, aquatic worms, and baitfish. However, flies used for them should be bigger and brighter, as redfish don't see as well as bonefish and are often found in water with less clarity than ocean flats. These conditions also make them easier to approach, although you shouldn't underrate their caution. I've seen cruising redfish in clear water as spooky as any bonefish, particularly when they're not actively feeding.

Look for redfish in any shallow water that has tidal movement and lots of food. Shallow grass beds, oyster bars, and edges of channels are some of the best places. You may see redfish in the water on a clear day as dark, reddish-brown moving shapes. On cloudy days when you

Redfish are great sport in shallow water and feed on crabs, shrimp, and baitfish. Jimbo Meador holds an average fish from the Louisiana Gulf Coast taken on a crab fly.

can't see into the water, look for their black-spotted tails in the air in shallow water, or look for fins and wakes, or patches of "nervous" water, where something on the surface looks different, like swirls moving opposite to the wind and waves.

Because redfish like to feed in very shallow water, use flies that ride upside down, like the Clouser Minnow or Rattle Rouser, a fly that's doubly effective because the tiny glass rattles used in the fly's construction help redfish find it in muddy water. Poppers are also sometimes effective on redfish and don't hang up in shallow grass—but don't use the same loud pops you use for snook or bluefish. A popper cast to redfish should be worked gently and steadily.

When redfish are tailing or working on mudflats, cast a streamer right next to the fish, let the fly sink just about to the bottom, and retrieve it with short, jerky strips. For cruising fish, lead the fish enough so that your fly sinks almost to the bottom by the time a redfish is right on top of it; then, lead it away with short strips. For blind-fishing deeper channels, a sink-tip line with a short sinking section, from 4 to 10 feet, will get your fly deep enough; but for the flats and oyster bars, you can use a floating line exclusively.

Leaders for redfish are the same as standard bonefish leaders, and a 9-foot leader with a 12-pound tippet is per-fect. Because redfish have a rubbery mouth and no sharp gills or scales, no shock tippet is needed.

SEA TROUT

Speckled sea trout are found in the same waters as redfish, from the mid-Atlantic through the Texas Gulf Coast, and will be mixed right in with redfish, providing the water is clear. However, sea trout seldom venture into dirty or muddy water, which they leave to the redfish. Look for sea trout along drop-offs and channels, at the mouths of inlets, around docks and pilings, and in sandy pockets in grass beds, one of their favorite places to ambush small baitfish.

Because sea trout have much better eyesight than redfish, smaller (1½- to 3-inch) flies fished with a fast retrieve will work better than the slower retrieve used for reds, especially where most of the fish are small, less than 4 pounds. Where you might expect to find bigger "gator" sea trout, try fishing bigger flies with a slower retrieve. Big sea trout also feed well at night, especially around lighted docks. Small poppers will also take sea trout, again fished with a fairly brisk retrieve. Because these fish move quickly, don't "tail" in shallow water, and are not as easy to spot as other flats fish, it's best to cover a lot of water.

Cast as far as you can comfortably control the line, and then retrieve almost up to the boat.

Although sea trout have small, sharp teeth, you don't need to worry about shock tippets with them. A 9-foot PVDF leader with an 8- to 12-pound tippet is all you'll need for these frisky and agreeable fish.

SNOOK

Snook are voracious predators of tropical and subtropical waters, but they can be maddeningly difficult to take. In the tea-stained waters of the Everglades, comfortably hidden beneath mangrove roots and having seen few artificial lures, wilderness snook can seem like the easiest fish in the world to entice with a fly. However, try catching a wise old fish that lives on the current at the edge of a heavily traveled channel or a school of smaller ones feeding under a lighted dock in the middle of the night—and you'll soon think snook are as crafty as permit.

Captain Rick Grasset with a snook taken on a small baitfish imitation under a lighted dock in the middle of the night.

Because snook like to ambush prey from a static position rather than cruise shallow water looking for it, look for them wherever there is structure along a shoreline. Tangles of mangroves, ocean reefs, steep drop-offs along beaches, and crowded harbors with lots of docks will all hold snook. Snook also like to lie in wait for their food (mostly baitfish and shrimp) to be carried to them, so pay close attention to any place with moving water next to a place to hide, particularly little bays and points amid a mangrove shoreline.

The best flies for snook are baitfish imitations and poppers. Poppers are especially useful because they won't hang up on submerged roots. However, where a drop-off is steep or in heavy current, you may have to use a sink-tip or sinking line, because snook are mostly nocturnal and don't like the bright light of shallow water unless they have shade or deep water at hand.

Poppers should be cast as close to cover as possible. Let the fly rest for thirty seconds, then make it pop, let it lie still, then pop it again until you get close to your position. Sometimes snook will follow a popper that moves steadily with frequent pops as well, and may follow the fly for some distance before taking. Streamers should be fished with foot-long strips and then a pause to let the fly flutter and sink. When you find snook feeding on small glass minnows at night—even if they are slamming the baitfish with abandon—it's better to fish a small baitfish pattern in slow, short pulls to make it look like a baitfish that has already been injured, rather than one that has enough energy to get away.

Snook have very sharp gill plates. If you fish a standard saltwater leader without a shock tippet, you'll lose many of them, especially the bigger ones. The best leader is a 9-footer with a 12- to 16-pound-test tippet, plus a 12-inch piece of 50-pound PVDF or abrasion-resistant nylon shock tippet.

BARRACUDA

You can mistake a barracuda on the flats for a large bonefish, but they're actually quite easy to tell apart. First, most of the barracuda you'll see will be laying motionless, waiting to ambush their prey. Bonefish never stop moving. And if you do see a barracuda swimming, its black tail will immediately distinguish it from a bonefish. Look for barracuda at the edges of channels, deep holes, and weed beds, and also tight up against the shoreline.

Barracuda are great fighters on a fly rod, but not as easy to catch as you might think.

Casting to barracuda requires a good cast and a fast strip. Cast well beyond a barracuda, as far as you can, at an angle that drops your line on top of the fish. The best presentation is a fly cast so that the line is 90 degrees to the fish's nose, passing a few feet in front of it. Strip relatively quickly until the fly gets even with the fish, and then strip just as fast as you can, with big sweeps of your line hand or a hand-over-hand retrieve with the rod under your arm. Don't pause the strip until the fly is close to the boat or the fish turns away; if you hesitate for an instant, the fish will turn off.

You'd think a vicious predator like a barracuda would be a sure thing with a fly. I've found just the opposite to

For barracuda, bluefish, tunas, and other fish that like a really fast retrieve, put the rod under your arm and strip hand-over-hand as fast as you can pull the line.

be true; in fact, I find them tougher to catch than bonefish, especially in places with heavy fishing pressure. They seem to be very moody, and if you find one in a taking mood, you should look for others, as something about the water or the weather has made them hungry.

Barracuda are terrific fighters, with slashing runs and breathtaking leaps, especially in shallow water. It's no surprise that you'll need 4 inches of at least 30-pound wire between your tippet and the fly. I've also found that a leader for barracuda should be at least 9 feet long, as these spooky fish with sharp eyesight will turn away if they notice the fly line.

SHARKS

Sharks are taken on flies either in open water around chum slicks or on shallow flats. Some guides don't like them because they can make a mess (I had one bite a flats boat once, actually taking a little chip out of it), but sharks are a ball on a fly rod. In big water over a chum slick, it's a simple matter of getting a big, bulky orange, red, or white fly near one and moving the fly very slowly, or just letting it drift in the chum slick. On the flats, they can be spooky if you drop your line right on top of them, but they often move slower than a bonefish or permit. They usually follow predictable paths, and they're also very easy to spot. Look for their fins slowly wiggling across the surface. They can even be spotted on cloudy, windy days, although sharks, like most flats fish, are more likely to be on a flat and in a feeding mood on calm days.

Wherever you fish for them, don't forget that sharks have poor eyesight. If you're fishing a streamer fly, cast to one side of the fish, within a foot of its head, and draw the fly right out in front of the fish. Sharks hear noises in the water quite well, so you can cast a big popper a little farther away and still draw one's interest. If a shark is coming at you, cast just to one side of its head and strip the fly to match the shark's speed, just in front of it. You'll often get a half-dozen shots at a shark before it either spooks or just moves out of range, so it's a pleasant diversion from the intensity of fishing for bonefish, permit, or tarpon.

Sharks, even little ones, can bite through a heavy shock tippet or wear through it with their abrasive skin. You can use a short 6-foot leader with 16- or 20-pound-test tippet, but you'll need at least 8 inches of 50-pound wire between the fly and the tippet. Also, be aware that

Sharks are plentiful on the flats and are an underrated species on a fly rod. Even the little ones make strong runs in shallow water and are lots of fun.

sharks don't have a true backbone and are flexible enough to turn right around and bite you—so keep them out of the boat. If a shark is hooked near the outside of the jaw, just twist the fly loose with a pair of pliers, and if the fish is hooked deep, the most prudent course is to cut the leader and leave the fly in the fish. If you're using barbless hooks, the fly will shake loose in a day or so.

STRIPED BASS

Stripers are generally fish of shallow water that feed near the surface on baitfish, squid, crabs, shrimp, and eels, so they make an excellent target for the fly rodder. They range from Nova Scotia south to Florida on the Atlantic Coast and have been introduced on the Pacific Coast, where they can be found from Washington State south to Los Angeles. They have also been introduced into the Mississippi delta and into large freshwater reservoirs throughout the country. We still have a lot to learn about their movements, but they spawn in freshwater estuaries in late spring, where they can be found in heavy concentrations. There is also a seasonal migration from south to north in the spring and back south in the fall. Stripers will congregate in the same places during their migrations, year after year. Most fly fishers look for schools feeding on the surface, and then carefully drift along the edge of the school, using poppers or streamers.

Although you can get quite close to a school of stripers when they're feeding, care should be taken not to run a boat through the school. They'll sound and may not come back up in the same area. Stripers are also one of the most selective feeders—you might have to change your fly pattern or retrieve or fly size three or four times before you hit on the right combination. Stripers aren't as selective when they're taking poppers, because the distortion produced by the bubbles hides the size of the fly.

Although stripers may feed all day long, by far the best times are from late evening until daybreak. You'll find them in harbors (as long as the water temperature stays below 70 degrees), in tidal creeks, off swimming beaches, miles offshore, and right in the pounding surf. In other words, when stripers are around, you can find them almost anywhere. The best retrieve speed with both streamers and poppers is a medium pace with foot-long strips, although you might want to try a very slow stop-and-go motion with poppers, especially on very flat water. At night, you can't fish a striper fly too slowly, and fish are often taken on a fly hanging suspended in the water with no movement at all.

Stripers, even fish as big as 40 pounds, will often come up onto sand and mudflats in the middle of the day, looking for baitfish, crabs, and shrimp. You'll need a bright day with little wind to spot them—which of course is when they're spookiest—but with a stealthy approach and presentations like you'd make to bonefish or permit (by leading the fish with a quick-sinking fly), you'll have some of the most exciting (and exasperating) fishing you could have outside of saltwater flats.

Blind-fishing for stripers in deep water is nowhere near as productive, but they can be taken in depths of up to 40 feet using large streamers on a fast-sinking line. Try the edges of channels, reefs, and around large rocks. Because stripers are so much larger than most of the other fish you'll see in northern waters, you can find them on the bottom with a fish-finder and then drift over them repeatedly.

Stripers have a rough mouth but not so abrasive that you need a shock tippet. Most common leaders are 9 feet long, with 12- or 16-pound-test tippets. You often have to make a tough choice when bluefish are mixed in with stripers, as is often the case. Stripers sometimes shy away from flies with a wire shock tippet, but nine out of ten bluefish will bite through an unprotected 16-pound

Magazine editor Sid Evans, left, took this nice Cape Cod striper on a popper under the watchful eyes of captain Tony Biski, right.

tippet. Most anglers prefer to leave off the shock tippet and take their chances, hoping a 40-pound striper is in the mix.

BLUEFISH

Bluefish are among the most voracious predators in the ocean. Traveling in schools of same-size fish, they migrate along the Atlantic Coast from Maine to Florida. The best fly-rod fishing, when schools are feeding near the surface, occurs during June through September in the North and January through March in the South. Bluefish will be found in the same kind of habitat as striped bass, although they prefer slightly deeper water. Unlike stripers, you'll most likely find schools of blues feeding on the surface at midday, although they may feed anytime.

Bluefish prefer a much-faster retrieve than stripers, usually as fast and as hard as you can strip. They will take a popper or streamer equally well, although some fly fishers will use a fast-sinking line and a streamer even when schools are surface-feeding, as larger individuals may feed below the surface, picking off crippled baitfish that are mangled by the school above them. There are times when bluefish will eat anything you throw at them, but they can be selective, especially if they're feeding on small sand eels. They will also sound as quickly as a school of stripers if you run a boat through the school.

Bluefish have razor-sharp teeth, and even if you're catching little "snapper blues" of 2 to 4 pounds, you'll need a wire leader or heavy shock tippet. They are not leader- or line-shy, so leaders can be short and heavy—3 feet of 20-pound-test and a piece of wire is about all you'll need.

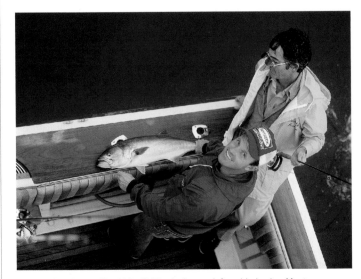

Renowned saltwater fly rodder Spider Andreson, left, guided writer Monty Montgomery into some big bluefish off Nantucket.

Tuna and Mackerel Family

Members of the tuna/mackerel family—including bonito, false albacore, Spanish mackerel, cero mackerel, king mackerel, yellowfin tuna, blackfin tuna, and bluefin tuna—have superb eyesight. It pays to match the baitfish they're eating as closely as possible. Most prefer a fast, smooth retrieve. Make a long, fast strip and bring your line hand quickly back to the stripping guide and begin the next strip immediately. The other option is to tuck the rod under your arm and strip line hand-over-hand into a bucket or stripping basket. If tunas have baitfish corralled into a tight ball and are working back and forth through the ball, cast your fly right into the boils of feeding fish. However, if the fish are moving as they feed, you often have to lead them by as much as 20 feet, because if you cast right to feeding fish, they'll be ahead of the fly before it hits the water.

The false albacore is just one member of the tuna family in the Atlantic that provides great sport for fly rodders. Noted conservationist Andy Goode caught this big one off the coast of North Carolina. All members of the tuna family are very fast and make long runs, often well into your backing.

Most of the time you'll be fishing for these species when you see fish boiling on the surface, as they travel in large schools and herd baitfish on the surface. However, when fishing in a chum slick or behind shrimp boats, it often pays to fish blind with a sinking line and a slower-moving fly. In fact, in general, even though you see fish boiling on the surface, you'll have better luck fishing a sinking line, as many of the fish in a school are slashing at baitfish below the boils you see on the surface.

All tuna and mackerel have such great eyesight that a shock tippet is always a damned-if-you-do, damned-if-you-don't proposition. I never use shock tippets for bonito and false albacore and have never lost a fish to a bite-off, even though their small teeth are quite sharp. However, if Spanish mackerel are in the mix, you'll absolutely have to add a 4-inch piece of fine wire between the tippet and a fly, as these little speedsters are better than sharks or bluefish at cutting off a fly. Many fly fishers use 60-pound monofilament shock tippets for the larger yellowfin, blackfin, and bluefin tuna, but some take their chances with using straight 30-pound PVDF as the tippet, without a heavier shock tippet.

Tuna take a fly in a flash, and immediately take a screaming run, no matter what size they are. And in deep water, they'll often make a long run to the bottom, forcing you into an extended tug-of-war. The key to catching them is to fight them aggressively, as hard as you think your tackle can take, right from the start. Make sure your knots are perfect, the drag on your reel is smooth—and it doesn't hurt to work out with weights a month before you chase them, either. They are some of the most exciting fish you can hook on a fly rod, and once you catch one, even a 12-inch mackerel, you'll be enthralled with their speed and beauty.

The Pacific Coast also offers much good fly-rod fishing for members of the tuna family. Nick Curcione took this one in a harbor in suburban Los Angeles.

{ ONE LAST LOOK—CUTTHROAT }

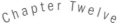

Striking, Playing, and Landing

Most fish lost in fly fishing are lost either at the moment you strike or when you attempt to land them. Playing a fish on a fly rod is a relatively simple matter of making the fish work against the spring of the rod until he gets tired. A fish lost on the strike or at your side is usually caused by operator error, and a fish lost in the middle of a fight is often due to a bad knot or because the fish was just not hooked securely in the first place.

STRIKING

Striking a fish means tightening the line enough to drive the hook into a fish's jaw. Most trout fly hooks are of fine diameter with very sharp points, so the strike requires very little force—in fact, in many instances fish will hook themselves. On the other hand, striking a big tarpon with a 4/0 hook might require several fierce jabs before the hook is set properly.

Striking with a fly rod should be a firm, immediate reaction to a fish that has visibly taken your fly, or an unseen fish that you have felt telegraphed along the rod. The only thing a fish can grab objects with is his mouth, and if that thing doesn't feel just right, he'll eject it quickly. Other than Atlantic salmon, which don't feed anyway, a fish will eject an unwanted object within a second. Atlantic salmon may take flies all the way to the bottom before letting them go.

Some large fish, such as salmon, tarpon, and large trout, move slowly toward a fly, almost as if they were in slow motion. Make sure that you wait until you see the

fish take your fly before striking. There is no need to hesitate in striking unseen fish, because that twitch you feel along your rod or see in your line means that something has grabbed your fly, and any hesitation on your part will give the fish a chance to realize something's wrong and eject the hook.

Tactics for Trout and Other Freshwater Fish

The strike is performed by pinching the fly line tight with your hand and moving the rod tip until you just barely feel the hook hit home. In most cases, you'll be stripping line by pulling it with your stripping hand through the fingers of your casting hand. To strike, merely pinch the line with your casting hand and raise the rod tip at the same time. If you don't pinch the line, it will merely slip through the guides of the rod, and no force will be applied to the hook point.

How hard do you strike? That depends on a number of variables. With a heavy tippet, something over 6-pound-test, you can strike fairly hard without popping the tippet. With a lot of slack line on the water, you may have to strike hard in order to take up all that loose line. On a long cast, it also takes a harder strike, because moving 60 feet of line takes a lot more force than moving 15 feet of line.

The greater the arc you move your rod tip through, the more forceful your strike will be. Slack line on the water may require you to raise the tip from 9:00 to 12:00. If you've been using a high-rod technique to avoid drag, you may have to go back as far as 1:00.

There are times when fish will hook themselves. A fish that takes a wet fly on a quartering downstream cast and a tight line will most often hook himself; all you have to do is gently tighten the line. In fact, if you strike too hard on a downstream cast, you'll often pop your tippet. If you're moving a fly toward you quickly, as with fishing a streamer, the fish has to rush the fly, getting hooked in the process. It's amazing how small a fish can break a tippet when you are stripping in one direction and the fish takes the fly with a fast lunge and quickly turns the other way. Don't forget that force equals mass times acceleration, and if you're pulling against a striking fish, a 2-pound trout can break a 6-pound tippet if you strike at the same time the fish bolts in the opposite direction.

Bass and pike require a fairly hard strike. The hooks you use for these species are large, and large hooks require more force to set them than small hooks. These fish also have bony mouths, which require some force to penetrate. Some of the really big bony ones may require a second and third strike to ensure good penetration.

When striking big fish with bony mouths like tarpon, strike down and sideways with the butt of the rod while also pulling with your line hand.

Striking, playing, and landing a small trout like this does not require any special skills. But as fish get bigger, you'll have to be more careful and plan your strategy.

There are times when you need a gentle strike. Big fish and light tippets require just a hint of a strike, barely enough to tighten the line. With light tippets you'll be using tiny flies anyway, which don't need much muscle to penetrate. I've often heard people say that they never strike with small dry flies, size 20 and under, but unless there is some tension on the line, you'll never set the hook. A tiny fly fished downstream may be set by the tension of the current on the line, but if you're fishing upstream, you *must* set the hook, even if it's a barely perceptible motion.

If you're heavy-handed and sometimes break off fish when striking with light tippets, you can use the *slip strike*, which uses only the friction of the fly line against the guides. As you raise the rod tip, don't pinch the line, but instead, make an "O" with the thumb and forefinger of your line hand, letting the line slip through as you raise the rod tip. The tippet can't break because the tension on the line is so slight.

If the fly is directly downstream from you, try to use a sideways hook-setting motion rather than an upward one. Using a straight upward motion of the rod may pull the fly right out of the fish's mouth. Atlantic salmon fishers avoid "hanging" the fly below them for this reason. If a salmon is going to take, they'd rather have him do it on an across-stream presentation, where he will be securely hooked in the hinge of the jaw.

I've heard fly fishers talk about the relative pros and cons of where in his mouth a fish should be hooked, and how they strike to get the hook in the upper jaw or the hinge or whatever. So far as I can see, we have no control over this, and hooking anyplace in the bone of his mouth is okay with me. If, while you're playing a fish, you see that he is hooked on the skin outside of his mouth, be very gentle when playing and landing him.

Fish are often foul-hooked on the top of their heads or dorsal fins, or even on their tails. This usually results from a fish that moved to your fly and refused it at the last moment. You see him break the surface so you set the hook, just as he begins to roll under the fly. If this happens frequently, you should change your fly pattern or presentation very slightly—something isn't quite right.

Saltwater Species

Nearly all the fish you pursue in salt water have bonier mouths than trout. The hooks are also bigger, so it requires more force to set them. For this kind of fishing, your best bet is to forget about raising the rod tip when you see or feel a strike (not easy for a lifelong fly fisher) and, instead, use the strip strike, as described earlier in the bonefish discussion. For smaller species like bonefish or redfish, you should have a tight line, with the rod tip low and pointing at the fish when retrieving a fly. The best way to set the hook is to make a long, firm strip until you feel the fish, and only then raise the rod tip. Not only does this give you a firm set, but it also gives you another chance, in case you miss the fish or it strikes short.

For example, let's say a bonefish is following your fly and suddenly it tips its body up and hesitates—the sure sign of a bonefish eating a fly. But let's also suppose that at the last minute, the fish decides something is wrong and does not suck in the fly. If you raise your rod tip as you would in trout fishing, the fly leaps away from the fish and may actually fly into the air. This doesn't give you much of a second chance. Yet if you strip-strike, the fly just makes another dart along the bottom, just like a frightened shrimp, and the fish may make another lunge at it.

With big fish that have bony mouths, like large striped bass or sharks, you may have to add a couple of sharp jabs to make sure the hook is secure. Here, you strip-strike as above, but as soon as you feel the pressure of the fish, you add one or two sharp jabs with your stripping hand and the butt of the rod moving in opposite directions.

Tarpon anglers take this example to extremes, because these fish have such bony mouths, and the hooks you use are typically of heavier wire and need more force to penetrate. The strike is a combination of using the butt of the rod and the stripping hand, but when you make the jabs, they should be done by moving the rod low and away from your body, off to one side. You must strike with the butt of the rod, because using the tip of a rod to set the hook is done only with your wrist; you just cannot obtain enough force to set a tarpon hook with your wrist.

PLAYING

It is impossible to break a well-designed fly rod while playing a fish properly, and it is difficult to break a tippet while pulling a fish's dead weight through the water—as long as your knots have been tied properly. Rods are broken if the line-to-leader knot gets caught on one of the last few guides of a rod, putting all the strain on a short section of rod. They are also broken when a fish sounds under a boat and you pull straight up against a fish that is pulling straight down, bending your rod at an angle it was not designed for. Tippets are broken when a fish makes a sudden lunge and you pull back, or if the fish wraps you around a snag.

Small fish can and should be played by merely stripping them in as you would bring in line for another cast. If you can, skip them right across the top of the water, unhook them quickly, and carefully release them. The longer a fish is played, the less chance it has of surviving. Large fish can be brought to shore and laid on the grass briefly for a photograph; they're tough. But to play a small fish for a long time so that the fellow upstream of you sees that you've caught one is a disgusting display.

How do you know when to play a fish from the reel? You won't have any choice. A fish that must be played from the reel will jerk your rod tip down and begin to pull the stripping line from your hand. The object of playing a fish from the reel is to get any stripping line that you might have out from around your legs, out of your stripping hand, or off the deck of a boat. If he makes a quick run and this line catches on something, you're going to lose your fish, your fly, and maybe your tippet. Using the reel also allows you to play a fish against a smooth mechanical drag instead of against the uneven pressure of your fingers on the fly line. A smooth drag is necessary because a fish puts the most pressure on your terminal tackle when he makes a sudden lunge. At that moment his mass times his acceleration puts a lot more strain on your leader than he actually weighs.

Good reel drags are smooth; they require little inertia to get them started, eliminating a "catch" that might allow a fish to snap your leader. If your reel has an adjustable drag, where should you set it? If you're using a light tippet, say 6X or 7X, put the drag on the lightest possible setting. If your tippet is very heavy, over 10-pound-test, set the drag fairly heavy; otherwise, set the drag on its middle setting. If you think the fish is getting away with murder during the fight, tighten it down; if you think he's going to pop your tippet, set it lighter. One thing to remember is that if you're playing a big fish that has taken you into your backing, you should be prepared to lighten up on the drag. The added weight of a lot of line on the water puts pressure on your tippet; plus, as your backing goes out, it's pulling against a diminishing diameter, which requires more force for each turn of the spool.

Reels with exposed rims can be palmed for additional drag when you want to snub a fish. Use the flat of your palm on the bottom of the reel, keeping your fingers away from the spinning handle. Many fly fishers prefer to palm the reel anytime they need drag, so they set the mechanical drag on the reel just tight enough to prevent spool overruns when line is stripped from the reel.

I've seen tests where you can check your drag against a tippet tied to a tree or doorknob or lead weight, but these are static tests and just cannot duplicate the dynamics of a moving fish in the water.

A large fish that makes a sudden run after striking will pull all of the stripping line from your hand and put himself on the reel. Try to guide the line smoothly through the guides; if the line catches on something, lower your rod tip a little, snub him by pinching the line against the rod with your casting hand, and try to free the line.

If a big fish takes your fly but doesn't take right off, keep the line pinched in your casting hand as you should have done for the strike, and reel in any slack between the stripping guide and the reel as quickly as you can. To give yourself a cushion to do this, you can drop your rod tip and give him some slack. Flies weigh so little that a fish has trouble throwing them, as he has no weight to work against.

Now you're ready to go. In any area free of snags, you should fight a fish with the *butt* of the rod at an approximate 90-degree angle to the fish's level. At this position the fish has to work against the spring of the rod, which cushions the tippet. You play a fish with the rod upright or off to your side as long as you maintain pressure on the fish. With large fish, you should use the rod to lead a fish in the direction you want it to go. All you have to do to make a fish go in the direction you want is to turn its head—they can't swim backward.

So if a fish is running directly away from you, the rod should be straight out in front of you, about 45 degrees from the horizontal. As a fish gets closer, if it moves to the

Pulling at this angle when a big fish is close to the boat could result in a broken rod.

left toward a snag and you want it to move to the right, just move your rod tip low and to your right side.

By raising and lowering the rod tip, you can vary the amount of drag and thus the pressure on your tippet. With the rod held upright, the friction caused by the guides increases the force needed to pull line from the reel. By dropping the rod tip, you eliminate this extra drag. If the big fish makes a sudden run, lower your rod tip to decrease the pressure on your tippet. If there aren't any snags, just let him run. When he stops, raise the rod tip back up and try to regain some line.

Because most fly reels are single-action direct drive, you'll have to let go of the reel handle and keep your hand away from it when the fish makes his run. With anti-reverse reels, you can hold on to the handle at all times.

Lowering the rod tip, or *bowing to the fish*, should be done when a large fish like a salmon or a tarpon makes a leap. If the fish lands on a taut tippet, he can easily break it. Besides, a fish that is above water has much more weight to pull against your tippet. If he shakes his head above water while your line is tight, you may part company.

Many areas that you will fish will have objects on the bottom that you'll want to keep both your leader and the fish away from. Coral bottoms and sharp rocks can abrade or sever a leader quickly. A fish can wrap your leader around weeds or brush piles and work the tippet against a stationary object instead of the spring of your rod, snapping the tippet easily. Under these circumstances, play the fish with the rod raised as far over your head as you can. Keeping his head up will force him to swim toward the surface rather than toward the bottom.

FIGHTING FISH IN A CURRENT

Fighting a fish in a current requires some different strategies. Always try to get the fish upstream of you, so that he has to work against the current, rather than you having to pull him back up against the current. If a fish runs downstream, you can either put pressure on him and hope he eventually turns around and comes back upstream, or you can follow him.

To follow a fish and get below him, your best bet is to head for the bank and scramble downstream until you're below him. Don't worry about keeping a tight line until you're downstream of the fish, but keep reeling as you go so that you're always gaining line, or at least keeping things at a stalemate. When you get below the fish, apply pressure on him by moving your rod low and to his downstream side. He'll usually respond by pulling against you and running upstream.

A low rod, using horizontal pressure, is the way to make a fish change directions.

A last-resort trick when you can't follow a fish is to strip some line off your reel and pay slack into the current. When the line bellies in the current below the fish, he may respond by pulling against it and running back upstream.

A fish can be led away from snags. He has no reverse gear or sideways propulsion, so he has to go whichever way his head is pointing. If you can turn his head before he reaches a snag, you'll have won the battle. A typical circumstance is when a fish heads for a streamside tangle of brush.

"Bowing," or lowering the rod on a jumping fish, will keep your tippet from breaking when a fish lands on a tight leader.

Low-rod pressure is also key with fighting big fish like tarpon, where you want to put maximum pressure on them. You can pull much harder low and from the side than you can with the rod directly overhead.

Let's say he's running directly across the current. If you keep your rod tip at 11:00, he'll respond by running right to the snag. Try flopping your rod down to a horizontal position in an upstream or downstream direction. The pressure of the rod tip will force the fish's head away from the snag. He'll have to swim in this direction. You can also use horizontal rod pressure to turn a fish that is running upstream or downstream toward a snag. It's especially useful against an upstream snag, because when he's turned broadside to the current, he'll be pushed back toward you.

What do you do if a fish wraps you around underwater weeds or branches? If you can get to him, the best thing to do is to quickly free the leader from the snag. You can use your hand, an oar or a push pole, or even your foot. Some fish get pinned to a snag, especially with a strong leader, and can be netted right then and there. If you can't get to the snag, try giving the fish slack. Sometimes he'll work himself free and swim away. It's worth a try.

A fish that has buried his head in weeds that are not rooted to the bottom, such as the filamentous algae that grow in spring creeks, can also be freed by pointing the rod at him and slowly walking backward. A slow, steady pull is always better than jerking on the line.

In waters with surface weeds between you and the fish, play the fish with the rod held as high as you can. Try to get his head above the weeds; the instant you slip his head onto the weeds, skitter him on top of them. If there is clear water in front of you, you can continue to play him there, or you can pick him up off the weed bed with your hand.

The worst thing you can do while fighting a big fish is let him rest. Keep the pressure on—make sure your rod is bending and he can't get a second wind. An old rule of saltwater fly rodding is: "If you're more tired than he is when you land him, you haven't been fighting him hard enough."

A high rod will put more drag on a running fish and is a good way to keep them out of snags.

Salmon, steelhead, and large trout may get on the bottom of a river and sulk instead of fight. You've got to get them moving, and one way is to tap on the butt section of your rod, sending vibrations down the line to frighten them. If you're close to the fish, kick and thrash around in the water, or ask your fishing buddy to help. A very effective method, although it sounds silly, is to heave a good-sized rock into the water in the vicinity of the fish (just be ready for a screaming run).

What happens if a fish runs to the end of your backing? The choice is yours. Will the tippet hold? To snub a fish at a point like this, lower your rod tip until it's sticking straight at him and grab on to the line. Your tippet knot will be the weakest link in the system, and most of us would rather lose a fly and a tippet than our fly line and backing.

To get a big fish close to you, it's necessary to pump him. When he finishes his first run, lower the rod tip the instant he stops and reel until the line is tight. Then, holding on to the reel handle, smoothly raise the rod tip or move it off to the side; then move it quickly toward the fish, and reel in the slack. If he starts another run while you're pumping, point the rod tip at the fish, let go of the reel handle, and let him go. With a fish like a big tarpon, this give-and-take battle can last for hours, which is why saltwater and salmon rods have butt extensions. The extension is braced against your lower abdomen to help relieve the tension in your arms.

When a fish is ready to land is a subjective matter. Some fly fishers use the heaviest tippet possible and horse the fish in when they're still thrashing vigorously. If you plan to release your fish, it's a good practice. Others will play a fish until he turns upside down, which is usually considered unsporting and is dangerous to the fish if you plan to release him.

It's safe to say that a fish is ready to land when he stops thrashing violently and begins to swim in tight circles. Most fish will make a final run or two when they see you or the boat. A stream fish will generally head for deep water; just lower the rod tip and try to regain line after he finishes his run. If you're fishing from a boat, he'll often swim for the protection of the underside of the boat. The best thing to do in a case like that is to plunge your rod tip straight down into the water and lead him away from motor, keel, or other obstructions. On a big boat you can walk around to the other side with your rod tip in the water. Another option is to ask the captain to move the boat off to one side so that you are not playing the fish at such an extreme angle.

If you have a strong tippet, the best way to beat a fish quickly is to get its head above water. Once its head is clear, it's all over—as long as you don't let up on the pressure. Skim the fish close toward you and net, lip, or tail the fish before it has a chance to get its head back underwater.

A trick used by stream anglers, especially if they've hooked a big fish on a light tippet, is to kneel down, keep the rod tip horizontal, and sneak the fish into the net or into their hands. If the fish can't see you and you don't make any sudden jerks with the rod, he'll often come in quietly, before he's expended all his energy. This strategy is often used throughout the fight on spring creeks, where big fish, weeds, and light tippets go together. After a gentle strike, they'll nag the fish into the net. It sometimes seems as if the fish doesn't even know he's hooked.

LANDING YOUR FISH

Fly-rod fish can be landed by hand, with a net, gaff, or tailer; or they can be beached.

The grip of the rod should remain in your hand throughout the landing process. You still need the flex of the entire rod to protect your tippet; if you begin to hand-over-hand along the rod toward the rod tip, you'll be taking a chance. If the fish makes a sudden run, all of his weight will be on the section of the rod above your hands. It's an easy way to break a tip section.

When landing a fish, the butt section of your rod should not go past the vertical. Bringing the rod back behind you when a fish is in close quarters is asking for trouble, because a rod is not designed to be bent over double. That not only puts undue stress on the tip of the rod, but it also makes you lose control over the fish, because a tip that is bent over double can rotate 360 degrees around the butt section.

To get a fish close to you, it's better to keep the butt at a horizontal angle while rotating your arm from the shoulder to get the fish close.

If you're using a short leader, try to keep the line-to-leader connection outside the tip-top. With a long leader, like a 12-footer, you may have to reel this connection inside the guides to get the fish close enough. If he decides to bolt and the knot catches on a guide, rotate the rod in your hand quickly so that the knot slips through the guides.

If you choose to release your catch, you can often slide your hand down the leader, grab the fly, and twist the fish free while he's still in the water. Forceps with freshwater fish and long-nose pliers with saltwater fish help you get a firm grip on the fly. Clamp them on the shank of the hook, near the bend, and back the hook out. Both your fly and the fish will suffer less damage. With small fish, if the hook doesn't come free, lift the fish out by the fly and shake him. His own weight is usually enough to work the hook out. The less a fish is handled, the greater his chances for survival.

Forceps or other hook removal tools help fish survive because you can remove the hook quickly.

Most fish can be landed by hand. A trout or bonefish can be landed by gently encircling the middle of his body with your hand. If you plan to release him, keep your hands away from his delicate gills, and don't squeeze too hard, or you'll damage internal organs. A large trout should not be grabbed by the lower jaw, as they have small but very sharp teeth.

You may find it easier to land bass, both freshwater bass and stripers, by gripping their lower jaw with your thumb, which momentarily paralyzes them. But don't hold them horizontally, bending their jaw harshly—keep them hanging vertically in your grip. Obviously, you should not lip species like bluefish and sharks, but you should also be careful of species you're not familiar with. I once stuck my finger into the mouth of a small snapper to remove a bonefish fly he'd eaten, not realizing that these harmless-looking little guys have nasty teeth. I regretted that decision for hours. Be careful of sunfish and others with sharp dorsal spines; grab them ahead of or behind the dorsal fin.

You can land and release many trout just by gently holding them in the middle of the body.

Fish like striped bass can be immobilized by "lipping," or grasping their lower jaw.

A landing net is the surest way to land most fish. Never swipe at a fish with a landing net. Always put the net in the water, lead the fish over the net, and lift the net while dropping your rod tip to slacken the line. Lifting the net into a taut leader could break your tippet. The fish will drop right into your net as you are lifting it. If you're wading in a river, get the fish upstream of you by pointing your rod tip upstream and stepping back a couple of feet. Then slacken your line, let the fish drift downstream over the net, and lift when he passes over it. Fish that are going to be released can be kept right in the net while you remove the hook, so that they have a constant supply of oxygen to their gills.

Gaffing saltwater fish should be done in the same manner: Put the gaff in the water, lead the fish over the gaff, and gaff him from underneath. Although fish can be

When netting a fish, always put the net in the water first, lead the fish over the top of the net, and then lift the net. Swiping at a fish with a landing net is a sure way to lose it.

gaffed in the lower jaw without too much damage, most catch-and-release anglers find other methods to land a fish than this nasty tool.

In rivers with sloping shallows or gravel bars, you can "wet beach" a large fish. If you hook a big one and have no net, plan the whole fight so that you'll end up in a shallow area with little current and a gently sloping bank. When you get the fish in the shallows, walk up onto land and slide the fish into the shallows. Once the fish gets into water so shallow it has to lie on its side, you can reel in your slack line as you walk toward the fish, remove your fly, and take a quick photograph without ever removing the fish from the water.

Fish like permit and Atlantic salmon can be landed by the tail. They have a wide tail and a narrow *caudal peduncle* (the wrist-like part between the tail and the body), which provides an excellent handhold. Grasp a tired fish firmly by the caudal peduncle; the broad tail will keep him from slipping out of your hand. Hand-tailing a fish is a technique that requires some practice, and make sure you have a firm, confident grip on the fish before trying to lift it or move it.

AFTER THE FIGHT

If you're going to keep a couple of fish for dinner, you should be prepared to stop fishing, kill them, and clean them immediately. Get them on ice or in a creel that cools by evaporation, unless the temperature is below freezing. Nothing is more irresponsible than to kill a fish and then ignore it, suddenly finding a couple of hours later that your prize has deteriorated beyond eating.

I hope that you plan to release most of your catch. If you've decided to take up fly fishing, you're obviously looking for more than dead fish in the freezer.

Releasing fish is not the key to preserving our lakes and streams for the future—habitat protection is. Lakes

Releasing trophy fish means they can be enjoyed by other anglers.

and rivers cannot be fished out to the point where natural reproduction can't restock them in a few years. But we're looking for more than a minimum spawning population where we fish. Quality fishing usually means as many adult fish as a body of water can hold, and if we kill off all the trophies, it will take years to grow new ones.

To release a fish, get him back into the water as soon as possible. You should plan to revive him until he can swim away under his own power. Be prepared to revive a fish for as long as you've played it. A fish that has been played will be starved for oxygen. Getting fresh water across his gills will replenish this oxygen, and you can do it by holding him upright while moving his body back and forth, forcing water over the gills.

Revive a fish until it can swim away into gentle current under its own power.

When removing a fly, smaller fish like trout and bonefish will usually remain motionless when held upside down. The less a fish struggles, the less you have to handle it. But most fish can be released without ever taking them from the water, which is the safest way to assure survival.

If you want to snap a quick photo of a fish, I think the best photos are taken with the fish cradled half out of the water or just a few inches above the water. It makes a better composition. Plan a photo with your partner or guide ahead of time. Get the camera ready while the fish is being played, look around for the right background and lighting, and tell your photographer where you plan to land the fish. This way he can check exposures, prefocus the camera, and at the instant you land the fish, he'll be ready to snap a quick photo. Kneel down to get your head and shoulders into the photo, lift the fish for

just a few seconds, and then release it quickly. The clichéd photo of an angler holding a fish high and out in front of him not only makes a lame composition, but it's also hard on the fish.

Revive a stream fish in calm water, but near an area of fast water, so that the water you're reviving him in has plenty of oxygen. Find some clear water not disturbed by all the activity of playing the fish, hold it facing upstream in the current, and gently move it back and forth until the fish leaves your hands under its own power. Never release an exhausted fish in a fast current, as he will never regain his equilibrium and will be battered around by the current.

In salt water, you will follow a similar procedure, except that you may need to move the fish more briskly as there may not be any current to help you. With the first permit I ever caught, I had to jump out of the boat and walk the fish up and down a shallow area for ten minutes before it was able to swim away under its own power. If the water is too deep to wade in, hold the fish alongside the boat and move it back and forth until it revives. If you do release a fish and it turns belly up, get to it again if you can and continue to revive it. If you can't reach the fish, guide it with a stick or boat oar until it is able to right itself and swim away. I've seen tarpon guides dive into 10 feet of water to revive a tarpon that looked like it was okay, but then turned belly up.

A fly-caught fish has the highest chance for survival of any released fish, because the hooks are so small and the fish are usually lip-hooked. Only *single-hook* spinning lures come close. Barbless hooks, made by carefully mashing down the barb of your fly with small pliers or forceps,

With a barbless hook, you can simply reach down and twist the fly free without ever handling the fish.

increase this survival rate even more, because the hook slips out easily and the fish doesn't have to be handled as much. Most fly fishers who use barbless hooks are convinced that they hold fish as well as barbed ones.

A fish caught on a fly occasionally swallows the fly or gets it caught deep in its throat or gills. If the fly can't be removed carefully with your forceps or pliers, cut off the leader as close to the fly as possible. It's better to leave a fly in a fish and release it quickly than to keep a fish out of water for too long, or manhandle it trying to work the fly free. The area around the hook will ulcerate slightly and the fly will fall out within a week.

Even fish hooked deep on snelled bait hooks can be saved this way. I once rose a brook trout to a dry fly that had two large snells protruding from his mouth, and he seemed no worse for wear.

{ First Casts }

Chapter Thirteen

Accessories

CARICATURES OF FLY FISHERS often picture them with vest pockets bulging with exotic paraphernalia. There *are* many gadgets available to fly fishers, and most of them make fishing less troublesome and more fun. Few are absolutely necessary for success. You *can* fly-fish with only a plastic box of flies, a pair of clippers, and a spool of tippet material, plus a rod, reel, line, and leader.

WADING GEAR

Waders or Hip Boots?

Unless you plan to fish only in small brooks, I'd advise you to buy chest-high waders. One of fishing's most chilling experiences is to go over the tops of your hip boots on an April day.

You may not *fish* in water that is over hip-deep, but there will be times when you'll want to cross a stream to get back to the car or to change your casting position. Even small streams can be over hip-deep, especially in early spring.

Hip boots can be very nice in summer, on the other hand, when the water is low and the weather makes a pair of waders uncomfortable. However, almost all quality waders can be rolled down and secured with just a belt, so that you have both chest and waist waders in one. Getting that waterproof fabric off your chest, even if it is breathable fabric, can be a welcome relief in the summer. As of this writing, waterproof and breathable waders have not been developed. If your budget allows, I'd buy both a pair of waders and a pair of hip boots. If

Hip boots are great for small streams, but in a river of any size you'll eventually go over the top of them.

you can afford only one, waders will be more useful over the long run.

Boot Foot or Stocking Foot?

Waders come in two types: boot foot, with the boot molded to the rest of the waders, and stocking foot, with sewn-on feet similar to the pajama bottoms that young children wear. Stocking-foot waders require a separate shoe.

Boot-foot waders range widely in price, but you generally get what you pay for. The inexpensive types are made from stiff, heavy-gauge rubber or nylon. They can be hot and uncomfortable. The more expensive kinds are cut more comfortably, have features like roll-down tops, hand-warmer pockets, and gussets in the leg for a slim but comfortable fit. Most important of all, they're made from waterproof breathable fabric and use laminates of rubber and nylon, which make them lighter, more comfortable, and easier to move in.

There is nothing worse (in a day of fishing, anyway) than walking a mile in hot weather, then entering an icy river with condensation running down the inside of your legs.

Boot-foot waders are easier to get into and out of, but they are less comfortable when you're walking long distances. They are also not as durable as stocking-foot waders. If you get five years of use out of even the best, you're lucky.

These boot-foot neoprene waders are easy to put on and take off, but the plain rubber boot might not offer enough support for some people.

Boot-foot waders are more comfortable and last longer if they fit properly. They should not be so tight that you cannot raise your knee to waist level, nor so loose that they bag in the inseam. Waders that are too short in the inseam will wear in the crotch area, and waders that are too baggy will abrade on the inside of the legs. Boot-foot waders are sized by shoe size. If you are long-legged or short-legged for your shoe size, you have two options: either buy a pair of custom waders (available only in the most expensive brands) or go to stocking-foot waders, which are more flexible and are sized by height. Most of the better styles of stocking-foots come in sizes for short- and long-body lengths, plus different body shapes (small through XXL for men and petite, small, medium, and large for women). Try them on if you can with a heavy pair of wading socks, and make sure you can sit down, get up, and raise your foot up onto a bench without binding.

Boot-foot waders are available with an uninsulated rubber boot or a felt-lined boot for cold-water wading. The boot on boot-foot waders can vary in style and quality. The cheap ones you see for much less than those in a fly shop typically have very light rubber boots without much support. You'll pay for your thrift with sore ankles, and the waders won't last long. Look for boots with extra foxing (the extra rubber stuff around the lower part of the boot), and flex them to make sure the soles are relatively stiff (about as stiff as a street shoe).

You can also buy a hybrid style of boot-foot wader, where true fabric-and-synthetic shoes with a true hard sole and laces are permanently attached to the legs. These are much more secure and comfortable than regular boot-foot waders; you can walk long distances in them, and they're warmer than stocking-foot waders because there is no cold water circulating between the bottom of the waders and your boot.

I'd pick boot-foot waders if you don't like to fuss with putting on a wet (or frozen) shoe over your waders first thing in the morning; if you have strong ankles and don't need a lot of support when wading; or if you fish during the winter. Some people don't like to walk far in boot-foot waders, but I wear them most of the time and have walked miles in just the standard rubber-boot variety without getting blisters or sore feet.

If you don't conform to "average" height and shoe-size proportions, try stocking-foot waders. The waders are sized by your height and the boots by your shoe size, so you're more likely to get a proper fit. Quality stocking-

These hybrid bootfoot waders, called the Tailwaters XTs, are made by actually joining a full wading shoe to a pair of stocking-foot waders, giving the angler the support of a wading shoe with the convenience of boot-foot waders.

foot waders are made from a lightweight laminate, typically three, four, or five layers of fabric. They all have at least an outer layer of durable, abrasion-resistant fabric, a middle layer of a waterproof breathable membrane or coating, and an inner layer of nylon to help transport moisture and make them easier to put on or take off. The lightweight nylon waders weigh only a couple of ounces, so you hardly know you have them on. They're cooler in hot weather, but you'll need to wear long underwear if you use them in the early season. They puncture easily but also patch easily, and they are extremely abrasion-resistant because the nylon is so slippery.

Neoprene waders are thick and have great insulating properties, so they are favored by winter steelheaders and others who fish in cold weather. Made from the same material as a skin diver's wet suit, they are unbearably hot for late-spring and summer fishing. Most serious fly fishers these days use the same breathable waders they use during the summer for cold-weather fishing, adding a layer or two of fleece pants underneath for added warmth. Sur-

prisingly, because you stay drier on the inside of breathable waders during the winter, they end up being warmer than neoprenes. (Neoprene does not breathe, thus creating moisture buildup, which chills you in cold weather.)

Stocking-foot waders offer other advantages over boot-foots. First, you can choose a lightweight pair of wading boots for short jaunts, but then have a serious pair of heavy-duty wading boots for long hikes. You can also buy stocking-foot hip boots and will then need just one pair of wading shoes for both your waders and hip boots. And if your boot tears or you run into nasty barbed wire with your waders, you only have to replace one component of the system.

The only disadvantage of stocking-foot waders is that it takes more time to get dressed for fishing, and after fishing you have a pair of wet shoes and socks to deal with. A special stocking-foot-wader bag or a Ziploc bag will keep your car seat or the inside of your duffel bag dry.

Stocking-foot waders make it easier to get a perfect fit, but they require separate shoes.

Wading Shoes

Stocking-foot wading shoes are more comfortable than the rubber boots attached to boot-foot waders because they are designed like hiking shoes. They come in a canvas sneaker style, which is lightweight, and leather (or synthetic leather) styles, which are heavier but offer more support for long walks. Which kind you buy depends on how long you plan to walk and what kind of river you'll be fishing (as well as what shape you're in). The more rugged the terrain, the more rugged you'll want your wading boots. For short treks down a gentle river with gravel and small rocks, you'll be fine with the lightweight type. Ditto if you plan to do most of your fishing from a driftboat. Serious hikers venturing into remote areas can put a pair of stocking-foot waders and wading shoes into a daypack. They weigh less and take up less room than boot-foot waders. For air travel, they're also easier to pack than boot-foot waders.

You can also buy "wet wading" shoes and dispense with the waders altogether. For warm summer days, a pair of shorts or quick-drying pants and a pair of special wet wading shoes (or just your regular wading shoes) can be a freeing experience.

Most stocking-foot waders are made with an integral wading sock and gravel guard already attached to the wader. If yours wasn't, you'll need to wear a pair of wading socks over the outside of the waders. If you don't, sand and debris will get between the shoes and waders and deteriorate the waders by abrasion. The best kind are special neoprene socks with a cuff that folds over the top of the shoes. These completely eliminate the debris problem. (You can also use an old pair of sweat socks, but they don't work as well and will wear out quickly.)

Whatever the style of waders, I like to wear a pair of wool socks with some elastic in them over my regular socks. They help prevent blisters, and you can tuck your pant legs into them so your pants don't crawl up your leg during a day's fishing. Most trout streams are cool even in the heat of summer, so you'll appreciate the insulating qualities of the wool socks as well.

You'll need a pair of suspenders to hold up your waders. Almost all quality waders today come with them already attached. Make sure that they are the "H" style, which help distribute the weight of the waders across your shoulders. Some waders have two buttons on each side, some have one. Check that the tabs on your suspenders correspond to the button arrangement on your waders.

All quality waders now come with a belt, and you should always wear one. If you take a spill, the wader belt, if tightly cinched, will keep air trapped in your legs, making you more buoyant. You will not turn upside down and float down the river. And even during a brief spill where you get right up and laugh about it, wearing a belt will keep most of the water above your waist—a very comforting thought. Last but not least, a belt helps your waders fit better and distributes the weight of the fabric, so even walking through the woods is easier.

Boot Soles

The type of sole you have on your waders is very important. Most inexpensive varieties come only in a rubber-cleated sole, which is okay for duck hunting or wading in sand and mud, but worthless for stream fishing. Felt soles and heels are needed for a secure grip on slippery rocks. The felt cuts into the algae layer on rocks and gives you a lot more confidence in your footing.

If you already have rubber-soled waders, you can buy an inexpensive kit to glue felts onto your waders. However, be prepared for a major project, and to not be ecstatic with the results. Another option is to buy felt-bottomed or metal-cleated sandals, often called *corkers*, which can be slipped, laced, or buckled over your wading boots. In fact, for very slippery rivers, many anglers wear these over their existing felt soles for added traction. These sandals are not designed for cross-country treks, though, and should be carried until you get to the river.

For extremely fast, slippery rivers, some waders come with bottoms that combine felt with hexagonal metal studs. You can almost walk up the side of an underwater boulder with them, and they are the best choice for older anglers or those who are not as steady on their feet. Just be aware that wearing waders with studs into a wood or fiberglass drift-

These felt-bottomed wading shoes have the extra insurance of carbide studs, for a secure grip on the slipperiest rocks.

boat is a huge faux pas, and if you walk into a guide's boat with studs on your feet, you can bet the next time you call to book a trip, he'll be "busy" (if he doesn't throw you out of the boat on the spot). So if you want studs but plan to fish rivers on your own—and from driftboats—either buy two pairs of wading shoes, or buy a pair of removable cleats.

Another type of sole is a sticky rubber compound that (according to some) has the grip of felt, yet lasts longer, and is easier to use in frozen conditions when ice builds up on felts and makes you feel like you're wearing platform shoes. Some of my fishing buddies swear by it; I am not convinced, and far prefer felt.

These special wet-wading shoes are designed to be worn without waders and are terrific for warm-weather fishing.

Closeup of a sticky rubber wading-shoe sole that has carbide studs for added security. The large white holes are to attach this sole to a wading shoe that has interchangeable soles.

During the summer you can wade "wet," with just a pair of shorts and sneakers. If you fish rivers with slippery rocks, glue some felt or indoor-outdoor carpeting to the bottom of your sneakers. But bear in mind that summer fishing is usually best in the evening, and by the time the sun goes down, you may be wishing you had worn your waders.

If your wading boots have rubber soles, or if you have felt soles and need extra security, these strap-on cleated sandals give extra traction on slippery bottoms.

FISHING VESTS AND PACKS

Fishing Vests

You should always buy a fishing vest with more pockets than you think you'll need. If you don't accumulate more fly boxes and gadgets as you go along, you're a rare individual.

Most fishing vests are made from cotton, a poly/cotton blend, or straight synthetics. The synthetic ones are lighter, last longer, hold their color better, and are less likely to tear on a branch or barbed wire. They are also more expensive than cotton or cotton blends and take longer to get that worn, "I'm an old pro" look. The tighter the weave, the longer the vest will last, and the more water- and wind-repellent it will be. Look for bar tacking

Wading boots come in many different styles and weights, depending on your packing requirements and how much support you need.

A good fishing vest can carry all your fly boxes and gadgets, plus water bottles, net, and a rain jacket.

top of their waders. It rides high so your fly boxes stay dry. A rusty fly is generally ruined, as the wire at the eye and hook point will be weakened.

Vest sizing is not that critical, but you should be able to move freely in all directions. Fill the pockets of a vest before you try it on. If you're going to fish in cold weather, the vest you choose should fit over a sweater and a down vest. It's always better to have one that's too large than one that is constricting when you're all loaded up.

Most vests come with a drying patch, made of either fleece or foam, which can be pinned where it's most convenient for you on the outside of the vest. Wet flies, nymphs, and streamers are placed on this patch after using them, so you don't put them away wet. A fly that is put away wet will rust and may even rust the flies adjacent to it in your box. Dry flies should not be dried on a fleece patch, as this will crush the hackles in a misshapen mess.

Don't economize on a fishing vest. A good one will last for many years. Make sure that the pocket arrangement is convenient for you, and that all the gear you want to take will fit in it, and then some. You can always leave a few pockets empty.

Chest and Waist Packs

For minimalist fishing—those times when you don't need to carry more than a couple of fly boxes, a few tippet spools, and a couple of tools—there are chest packs, waist packs, and backpacks available just for fly fishers. Some of them are complex enough to carry as much stuff as a vest, just in a different arrangement. Times and places these are handy include:

at all pocket corners and stress points, with the thread stitched back and forth many times to secure the fabric.

Fly-box pockets and pockets that will hold heavy objects that fall out when you bend over, like thermometers or mini-cameras, should have large, smooth, nylon zippers. The zippers should open with one hand, because you'll usually have your rod tucked under one arm when you change flies in midstream. Some vests also feature an elastic metal opener that allows you to reach into a pocket for a fly box with one hand, yet will stay securely closed when you are walking or fishing.

Smaller pockets should have Velcro fasteners on them. Velcro is secure and durable and makes one-handed opening easy. Don't buy a vest with snap pockets—snaps don't last long and are tough to open with one hand.

Some vests come in two versions, regular or short. The short vest is designed for those who wade right to the

- small stream fishing, when you only need a few flies and spend most of your day hopping from rock to rock;
- fishing from a driftboat, when a vest gets too bulky or hot;
- when wading for saltwater species, where a vest is too hot, too heavy, and will get wet when you wade too deep or get hit by a cresting wave;
- hiking into remote ponds or small streams;
- fly-fishing for bass, where the weather is usually hot and you don't need to carry more than a box of flies, snips, and a spool of tippet material; and
- fishing from a float tube, canoe, or kayak, where a vest is confining.

This chest pack has a comfortable strap system, and keeps gear up high on the chest without having to wear a full vest.

Saltwater flats, where it's often hot and deep wading isn't necessary, are great places to wear a waist pack.

Chest packs are best for those times when you are float-tubing or wading in bigger rivers, where your bottom half might get wet. For shallow wading or fishing from a boat, waist packs are much less constricting. They

This waist pack can carry lots of gear plus two water bottles.

come as large and complex or as small and simple as you can imagine. Pick the one that best fits your fishing habits.

Lanyard

Sometimes you don't want to wear either a vest or chest pack. Maybe you're fishing from a boat, where all your flies and leaders are in boxes or a kit bag. Maybe you just

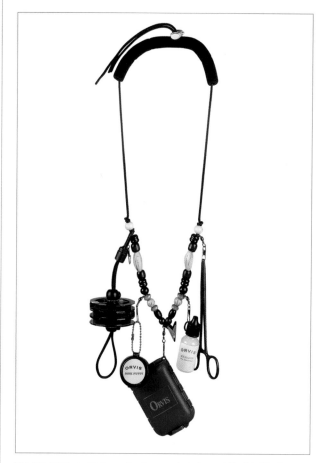

You can get to your tools easily when wearing a lanyard like this. They're very popular with guides and other people who don't like to wear fishing vests.

want a single fly box in your shirt pocket. In this case, a lanyard serves to hold your snips, fly floatant, spools of tippet material, knot-tying gadget, or any other small item you might need, keeping them all around your neck where they are instantly available. Of course, you can also combine a lanyard for your tools with a vest or chest pack. Lanyards can be as simple as a piece of old fly line, or as fancy as a model with handmade beads. Make your own fashion statement. Just make sure that your lanyard has some kind of quick-release breakaway device, in case it gets caught in the brush, or—heaven forbid—in the prop of an outboard motor.

Kit Bag

For fishing from any kind of boat, kit bags are very handy. One can serve as your entire tackle box, with extra reels, camera, lots of fly boxes, dozens of tippet spools, sunscreen, bird guide, binoculars, and even your lunch. They're not very handy for wading fly fishers unless you just keep one in your car to store stuff, but when fishing from a boat, a kit bag may be all you need besides your rod and reel. Some kit bags are water-resistant, which gives you added peace of mind in heavy seas or when rain threatens.

This kit bag will carry reels, fly boxes, leaders, camera, rain jacket, and whatever else you want to throw in a boat or car. This one even has a waterproof compartment and see-through pockets.

Rod and Reel Cases

These are fabric cases with PVC liners that let you carry a rod and reel already strung up and ready to fish without the danger of breaking your rod. And when three or four anglers get together and all use the same car, they typically break down their rods but leave the fly and leader attached. Invariably, after a short ride all four rods have

entwined themselves in a spiderweb of leader material, and it wastes precious minutes of fishing time getting them sorted out—not to mention the impatience that might break a rod tip. Rod and reel cases will prevent this aggravation.

Rod/reel cases will protect a rod and reel in a boat or car, and you'll be strung up and ready to fish.

You can buy these for two- and four-piece rods, for one rod or two. It's a small price to pay to keep your valuable rod and reel collection safe while still ready to fish.

CONTAINERS FOR FLIES

Tackle Boxes

A fly fisher with a tackle box? You bet. I wouldn't go bass or saltwater fishing without one.

It's tough to fit many of the extra-large bass and saltwater flies in fly boxes, and you don't need all those gadgets that trout anglers carry. The long, skinny trays in tackle boxes are great for big streamers and poppers, and you can put your extra spools, insect repellent, clippers, and other paraphernalia in the bottom of the box. Set it in front of you in the boat so everything will be handy.

When trout-fishing from a canoe, I still wear my vest, though, because I haven't yet seen a tackle box that will properly hold tiny dries and nymphs.

Fly Boxes

Your flies should be protected from clothing, gusts of wind, and rain, and they should be kept in some kind of order.

Wet flies, nymphs, streamers, and bass bugs can be kept in any kind of fly box, but delicate dry flies, whose hackle can be easily crushed and matted out of shape, should always be kept loose in individual-compartment boxes. There hasn't been a clip or magnetic arrangement designed that will protect dry flies perfectly.

Compartment Boxes

Compartment boxes come in two types: plastic boxes with a lid that opens to expose all the compartments at once, and aluminum boxes with clear, spring-loaded lids that snap open individually on each compartment.

Traditional aluminum boxes might not be the most practical, but they sure add a lot of elegance to your fly collection.

Plastic boxes are lightweight and indestructible. This one is treated with a special substance to keep hooks from rusting.

The plastic boxes are inexpensive, rugged, and lightweight. They come in all sizes, for midges right up to saltwater poppers. The best designs have lids that fit so tight that tiny midges can't move from one compartment to the next. These boxes are suitable for all kinds of flies, the only disadvantage being that when you open the lid in windy weather, all flies are exposed to errant gusts that

may whisk away some of your prize patterns. Make sure that the compartments are deep enough to hold your dry flies "loose." If a dry doesn't fall out when you turn the box upside down, the compartments are too small. Don't overfill the compartments, either.

The individual-lid aluminum boxes are expensive and heavy, and sometimes the lids get bent out of shape. They are, however, exquisite in appearance and a joy to own. They are not deep or wide enough for a big Wulff or variant dries, and if you try to stuff big dries in these compartments, you'll ruin them. The compartments are not designed for nymphs or wets, but the lids usually contain metal clips, magnets, or a foam pad for other types of flies.

Foam Fly Boxes

Foam boxes have become the most popular boxes on the water. From giant 10-inch boxes for big streamer flies and saltwater flies to tiny midge boxes, they are light, almost indestructible (you can drive a car over one without hurting it), and inexpensive. And they float—a very important consideration if you drop one in a fast river or off the side of a boat.

Foam boxes are the lightest fly boxes you can carry, and they float if dropped into the water.

Some are just flat foam, and you merely stick the flies into the box in any arrangement you like. Others have foam strips, which typically have enough clearance so that dry flies can be held securely without matting or crushing their hackles. Some have a combination of the two arrangements—flat on one side, strips on the other.

Metal-Clip Boxes

Metal clips are used for salmon flies, wets and nymphs, and streamers. They are great for flies larger than size 14, but are not suitable for tiny nymphs.

The metal clips on the box in the background are traditional, especially for salmon flies, but they are not as practical as foam strips.

Magnetic Boxes

These are usually combined with metal clips in the lid. They hold flies securely, but sometimes the flies slip around and get out of order.

Coil-Spring Clip Boxes

You don't see many of these around anymore, but they are one of the finest designs for holding nymphs and wet flies. They are made with a series of stainless steel springs inserted in rows in the box, and hooks are simply placed between the coils, held in place by spring tension.

Foam and Foam-Strip Boxes

These are the only kind of fly box that will hold tiny nymphs and wets, size 16 and smaller, without losing them or dulling their hook points. They are also great for any kind of fly (except dry flies).

Fleece-Lined Fly Books

Fleece-lined fly books are an old traditional design, and they look classy loaded with colorful streamers or salmon flies. Use them with care. If a fly is even remotely damp when you put it in a fleece book, it will rust overnight. Fleece books crush streamer wings out of shape, wings that some poor fly tier took great pains to set properly. And they don't hold many flies for the space they take up in your vest.

Fleece-lined fly books look great, but they often lead to mangled and rusty flies.

Choose fly boxes that appeal to you, making sure that they will hold the kind of flies you're going to carry. Then put your fly boxes in some kind of order. Put all the cream ones in one corner. Put all the size 20s in one compartment. Keep all your spinners in one box. Whatever system you use, it will eliminate a lot of fumbling around when you need that size-14 Quill Gordon. Less fumbling means fewer flies dropped accidentally in the river. You should be able to pick the fly you want even when the last glimmer of twilight is fading.

HELPFUL GADGETS

These are the tools that some of us can't live without, and that others never use. Most can be kept in small pockets or pinned to your vest on a pin-on retriever reel called a *zinger*. If things hanging from the front of your vest bother you, do what a friend of mine does: He pins them on the inside of his vest, so they don't hang out in front every time he bends over.

Clippers or Nippers

These are essential if you plan to stay on good terms with your dentist. Biting the tag ends of your knots removes the enamel from your teeth. Most designs have little pen blades or scissors that come in handy for all kinds of jobs, like cleaning fish when you forget your pocketknife, or trimming a fly to make it smaller or sparser. Make sure you get the kind with straight, flush-fitting jaws. Ordinary nail clippers, with their curved jaws, are just as likely to cut your leader when you are trying to trim the tag end of a knot. For heavier monofilament, heavy-duty styles are made, or you can use the carbide cutters of saltwater pliers.

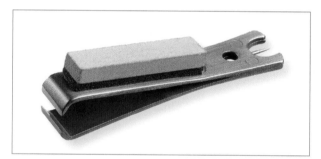

Good fly-fisher's snips should have a sharp, straight cutting edge.

Forceps and Pliers

Forceps are essential if you plan to release your fish. They are much more efficient than fingers for backing hooks out of fish. For pike, bluefish, barracuda, and other toothy species, substitute a good pair of long-nose pliers. You can buy fancy fly-fishing pliers, which are true works of art, or you can use hardware-store pliers. Just remember that the hardware-store variety won't have cutters for wire or heavy monofilament, and if used in salt water, they'll rust or corrode very quickly.

Forceps and pliers can also be used to make barbless hooks, by carefully mashing down the barbs with gentle pressure.

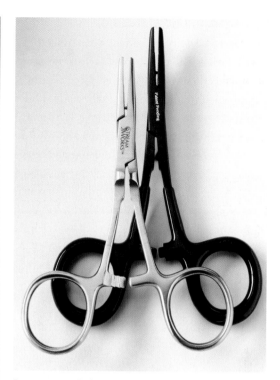

Forceps are useful for holding flies, and especially for removing them from fish.

Scissor Pliers

These combine tiny pliers with serrated scissors and can be used for the same purposes as forceps, plus reel maintenance and crimping split shot to your leader. Dentists look upon using your teeth to crimp split shot to the leader much as they do biting monofilament.

These scissor pliers can remove hooks, but they can also trim flies or cut yarn for strike indicators.

Leader Straightener

Good leader material will straighten when pulled between your hands, but will sometimes cut into your skin. A leader straightener is a leather-covered piece of rubber that you can pull your leader through. Pulling your leader through the rubber side while pinching the leather pad around it generates enough heat to take the kinks out of the nylon. Some people believe that leader straighteners weaken leader material because the heat generated changes the structure of the monofilament. Whether that is true or not, you can almost always get the kinks out of a leader with your hands.

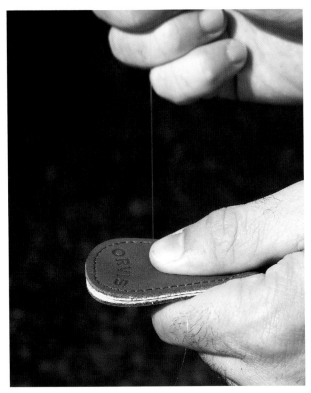

This simple leader straightener attaches to a fishing vest, and you merely pull a leader through it while applying some pressure to take the kinks out of a leader.

Stream Thermometer

A good stream thermometer should have a metal or rugged plastic housing to protect it from bumps. Keep it on a length of old fly line or leader material so you can lower it into a lake or stream without getting your sleeves wet. A stream thermometer will tell you when hatches are due and when fish are spawning. It's also indispensable in the summer, when fish are concentrated near cold-water springs.

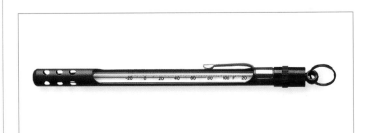

Because water temperature determines how actively fish will feed, a stream thermometer can help you predict their activity and find cool or warm spots in a stream or pond.

Fly Threader

If your near vision is going, this gadget can be a lifesaver. It funnels the leader through the eye of a hook, even in the dark.

Fly threaders can be helpful gadgets—especially after the age of 40.

Knot-Tying Aid

There are various tools designed to make fly-fishing knots simpler. Practice without them first. If you still have trouble, try one of these. About the only knot tool you might need after you get comfortable with the basic knots is a nail-knot tool. Few mortals can tie a nail knot without some kind of mechanical help, and these tools work extremely well.

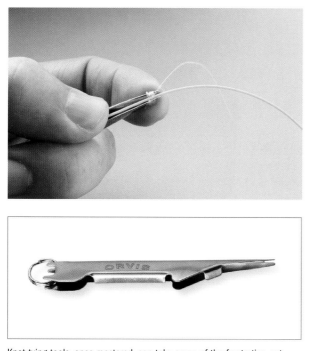

Knot-tying tools, once mastered, can take some of the frustration out of knot tying. Even expert knot tiers use this one, as it makes the tricky nail knot as easy as tying your shoes.

Hook Hone or File

Hooks lose their sharpness if you catch your backcast on a rock, get your nymph snagged on the bottom, or sometimes, when you release a fish by the fly-twisting method. The best hook hones are made from industrial diamond particles, are smaller than a ballpoint pen, and will touch up a point in seconds. For big, stainless saltwater hooks, you might need a coarse diamond file.

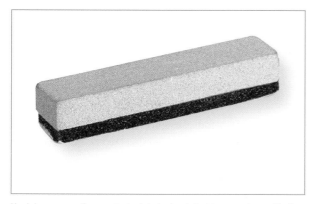

Hook hones are often overlooked, but a hook that is razor sharp will often make fish hook themselves. This one has an adhesive back so you can attach it to your snips or a fly box.

Trout flies can usually be sharpened just by taking a few licks to the point. Bigger hooks, especially saltwater hooks, should be triangulated, which means you sharpen the bottom of the hook and both sides. You can tell if a hook is sharp enough by dragging the point across your thumbnail, with the point perpendicular to the nail. If it sticks and catches, it's sharp enough. If the point slides across your thumbnail, give the hook a few more passes.

Magnifying Aids

Another handy gadget for those whose near vision isn't as sharp as it used to be. There is nothing more frustrating than being unable to thread a new fly onto your tippet. Magnifiers come in all shapes and sizes. Some clip to your hat, and others clip onto your prescription glasses or sunglasses. Some are integrated with lights or snips. Standard reading glasses also work just fine, but are not as convenient; if you buy a pair for fishing, make sure they are least 2.5 diopters in magnification. Threading a size-22 Parachute Adams onto 7X is not the same as trying to read the Sunday paper.

Fly fishers, especially those of us who are a bit older, need some type of vision aid to tie knots and thread flies. This flip-up model that attaches to a hat brim is useful and popular.

Small Flashlight

A small, lightweight flashlight is essential if you fish in the evening or at night. It should be designed so that it leaves both hands free to tie knots, whether you hold it in your teeth, clip it to your vest or hat, or hang it around your neck. Headlamps work great, and are usually powerful enough to help you find your way back to the car. The better ones are sealed with O-rings and are waterproof.

If you fish in the evening or early morning (or the dead of night), you'll need a flashlight to tie knots, untangle a knot in your line, or find your way back to the car. Look for one that clips onto a pocket or hat brim, as this one does, so you can keep both hands free.

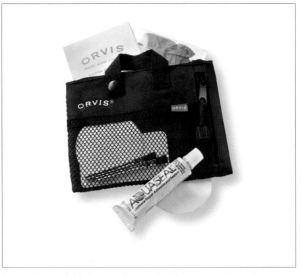

Your wader repair kit does not have to be this extensive, but at least carry a tube of Aquaseal on all your fishing trips.

Insect Repellent

Peak time for mayflies on trout streams is also peak black-fly and mosquito time. I don't need to say any more, except get a bottle of repellent that fits in your vest so you can reapply it while fishing. Keep it away from all plastics, including leaders, lines, and fly boxes, because insect repellent can eat through a fine tippet in short order, resulting in a lost trophy, I apply it using the back of my wrists. Bugs hardly ever bite you on the palm anyway.

Another alternative is insect-repellent clothing. The newer types of clothing are completely safe, you never have to worry about reapplying, and they won't hurt leader material or fly lines. Of course, such clothing costs more than regular fishing wear.

Emergency Wader-Repair Kit

In your vest, you should have a quick-drying method of patching waders. For quick repairs that will last for weeks, duct tape (especially the better brands) is waterproof and very sticky. Use a jigsaw to cut a section from a roll to keep with you at all times. Another option is a plastic stick that you melt with a lighter and dab onto small wader leaks. It dries in minutes and will adhere to most wader materials.

If you're going away from home for a day or more, carry a standard wader-patching kit for larger tears. Such a kit should include some alcohol wipes to clean the area to be patched, some adhesive, material to cover patches (extra wader material usually comes with a new pair of waders, and most of us immediately lose it or throw it away), a plastic knife to apply adhesive, and maybe a pair of disposable rubber gloves. The very best wader-patching adhesive is a brand called Aquaseal. I've repaired many waders over the years with it. I've never found anything better, and I've never had it fail me.

FLOATING AND SINKING AIDS

Dry-Fly Floatant

Dry flies should be dressed with some kind of silicone compound before use. Floatants are available in bottle, powder, aerosol, and paste forms. With the bottle version, you dip your fly in after you've tied it to the leader, then blow on the fly to dry the solvent, and false-cast a half-dozen times. With the aerosol type, you spray the fly and then dry it the same way. If you get the fly into the water before the solvent dries, the silicone will not waterproof the fly properly. With the paste type, you smear a tiny amount on the fly. Use it sparingly—don't gum up the fly. There is no solvent in the paste type, so it doesn't have to be dried. There is also a waterproofing preparation that is applied to flies well before fishing (at least twelve hours) and precludes the need for any

Paste fly flotants come in small bottles and fit in a fishing vest easily.

Strike Indicators

Strike indicators come in a myriad of shapes and sizes. They range from huge plastic bobbers to little tufts of yarn. The yarn ones are light and air-resistant so they don't make a big splash in the water, but the biggest ones are hard to cast. They can, however, usually be removed without removing the fly from the leader and can be adjusted along the length of the leader to regulate for depth.

The plastic or foam ones with holes in the middle are easy to move, but you have to thread them on the leader—unless you buy the type with a slot where you can twist a rubber band around the leader to hold it in place. These float forever and are very easy to see on the water.

The most immediately convenient are foam indicators with sticky backs that you fold over the leader. I don't

streamside preparation. It lasts longer than the stuff you apply on the spot, but I am seldom organized enough to treat my flies the night before a fishing trip.

Silicone Powder

This is sold under such trade names as Shake-N-Float. Once a dry fly has caught a fish, the fish slime that coats it makes flotation difficult. A fly that has been in water will not absorb regular fly floatants, so to redress the fly, you shake some of this desiccant powder into your hand, rub it into the fly, and blow on the fly—moisture and fish slime are instantly removed. This stuff saves lots of time spent changing waterlogged dry flies, and I won't fish dry flies without it. As a matter of fact, silicone powder can also be used as a fly floatant all by itself, on flies that have not even been wet.

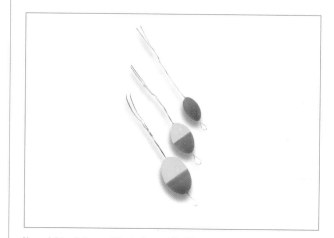

You might call these strike indicators "bobbers"—which in fact they are, just tiny versions you can cast with a fly rod.

Silicone desiccant powder can be a lifesaver when fishing dry flies. The best way to use it is to take a small amount out of the bottle and rub the fly into it.

Yarn strike indicators are slightly more sensitive than the plastic type and cast easier. Besides, they don't look as much like bobbers.

like these because you can't slide them up and down the leader, and they're not reusable. Besides, they often come off the leader, and you find them littering the streamside wherever they are used.

For smaller flies and less weight on the leader, a really slick strike indicator is formed from a buoyant putty that you mold around the leader. You can change the amount or change the position on your leader instantly, or remove it in a snap if you decide to fish a dry fly. It does not stay on a leader as well as the other types, so you have to be careful with your casting, but it is reusable.

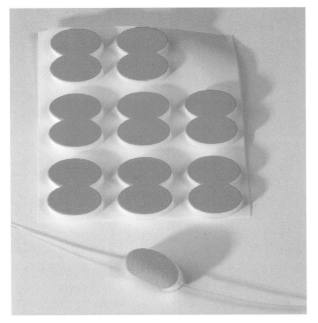

Foam-backed indicators simply fold over the leader and stay put because they are self-adhesive. Unfortunately, this kind of indicator can't be re-used or moved up and down the leader so its convenience also comes with a lack of versatility.

Strike putty is a moldable strike indicator that can be moved easily, and you can change the size you need in a second. It's also reusable.

Fly-Line Cleaner

Modern floating fly lines don't need dressing to float, but they do need to be cleaned periodically. Keep a tin in your vest in case your line gets dirty during the day. You can clean an entire line in a few minutes. Some brands of fly lines need a special cleaner, but Orvis Wonderlines are designed with a special finish that should be cleaned only with soap and water.

Leader Sink

Whether your leader should float or sink with dry flies is a matter for speculation, but it should sink quickly when you're using wets and nymphs. Nylon will float if you get sweat or fly dressing on it, and leader sink removes these. Also, it masks the shine of nylon, which may spook nervous fish. With the advent of PVDF tippet, the need for leader sink has declined, but in a pinch, you can use soap and water or run your leader through some mud. Orvis used to sell a special kind of magical mud for sinking leaders and removing the shine, but at the time of this writing, it was no longer available.

Split Shot

Lead split shot is a necessary addition to your leader when you have to get a nymph right on the bottom. It makes casting difficult, so use as little lead as possible. Start with one or two and add more if you're not getting deep enough. Most fly fishers crimp split shot to their tippet, anywhere from 6 to 20 inches above the fly. You can also leave one tag end of the last blood knot in your leader a

This split shot has a traditional shape, but it's made of non-toxic metal instead of lead.

Another non-toxic alternative is sink putty, a tungsten putty that can be molded to the leader in any size you need. It can be moved or the size can be changed very quickly, and unlike regular split shot it won't weaken your leader.

Landing nets come in various sizes, depending on how optimistic you feel.

little long, tie an overhand knot in the end of it, and add your shot here; the overhand knot keeps the shot from slipping off the end. With this method, if the shot hangs up on the bottom, you may not lose your fly and tippet.

Most shot today is made from tin or other alloys. Although not as heavy as lead, these alloys are not toxic to waterfowl, which ingest lead split shot when getting gravel for their crops. Waterfowl hunting with lead shot is now illegal, and fishing with lead shot may (and should) go the same way, especially because loons have been proven to be especially susceptible to lead poisoning.

Another alternative is sink putty. Made from a tungsten-putty matrix, it is very dense, and you don't need much to get a fly down. Like strike putty, it has the advantage of being instantly modified, whereas split shot has to be cut off the leader to be moved or replaced. Sink putty does not stay on a leader as well as shot, but I feel its advantages far outweigh its drawbacks. It does work better in water below 60 degrees, though, as it softens when the water gets too warm.

ESSENTIAL ACCESSORIES

Nets, Gaffs, and Tailers

A net will save you lost fish and lost flies, and will also enable you to handle fish you plan to release gently. Wading anglers should use as small a net as possible, because a net that is too big only gets in the way. You can always beach a very large fish.

Wooden-handled nets look nice and feel good in the hand, but any small net will work fine. Make sure the mesh isn't too fine; otherwise, your leader and fly will get hopelessly entangled. The best net bags for catch-and-release fishing are made of rubber mesh. It is easier on a fish's skin than nylon or cotton net bags, and flies don't get stuck in it.

You can attach a net to your vest with a spring-loaded retriever chain that attaches to the back of the vest; a French-clip quick release, which hooks onto the net ring under the back of the collar; or a magnetic net retriever, which is the best method of all. Strong magnets hold the net to the back of your vest, yet release when you pull on it. After netting a fish, you just wave the net in the vicinity of the magnet attached to the D-ring on the back of your vest, and it instantly snaps back into place. A squeeze will detach the net from the ring.

There is also a spring-loaded net that folds into a tiny holster and jumps into shape when you pull it out. You should always carry your net attached to the back of your vest. A net that hangs in front or on your side will only get in the way of your stripping line.

Nets used in boats should have longer handles—long enough so you don't have to lean over the side of the boat when netting a fish.

Gaffs are occasionally used for saltwater fish. They are hard on a fish if you plan to release him, except for species with wide bony lips, like tarpon, that can be lip-gaffed without injury.

A *tailer* is a special landing tool used for Atlantic salmon. It is a noose-like device that will grip a salmon without injury, between the narrow rear body and wide

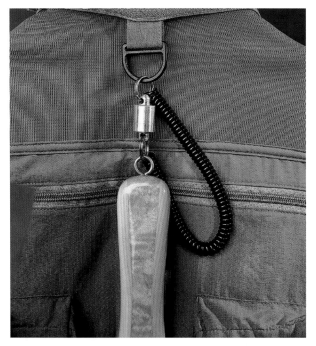

This net retriever is held in place with a strong magnet until you need it. When you are finished landing a fish, you just wave it near the back of your neck and it snaps back into position.

tail of the salmon. It requires some practice to use properly, and most experts now believe they are quite harmful to fish that might be released.

Stripping Basket

On boats or when wading, a stripping basket is used to hold long lengths of shooting line, especially when you're casting

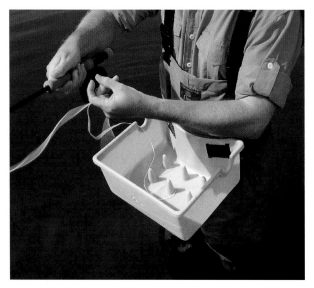

Stripping baskets keep your shooting line in order, especially when fishing in strong surf or when there is a lot of weed in the water.

with shooting heads. It clips to your wader belt around your waist and keeps shooting line from getting tangled around your legs or around objects on the deck of a boat.

Creel

If you can't get your fish on ice immediately, a creel is essential (unless the weather is below freezing). The basket type is traditional, but it's very bulky and does not cool as efficiently as the canvas varieties, which cool by evaporation.

Wading Staff

For those who are unsteady on their feet in fast water, a wading staff can save the day. They give you something to lean on and can be used to test the water depth in front of you. The traditional wooden type can be clipped to your belt when not in use. The emergency wading staff consists of plastic sections held together by elastic shock cord. It stows into a 10-inch-long holster and quickly extends into a 50-inch staff when you pull it out.

If you're unstable on your feet or wade in treacherous currents, a wading staff can literally become a lifesaver. Some types are collapsible and most attach to your belt with a lanyard.

In this kind of current, almost anyone could use the help of a wading staff.

Tweezers

If you fish with small flies, a pair of tweezers makes it easy to pick through fly-box compartments and select the pattern you want.

Hat

A fly fisher's hat is a personal decision, and I wouldn't think of suggesting a particular type. Hats shield your

A long-brimmed hat with neck protection might not be a fashion statement, but it will protect your skin from sunburn and your eyes from eyestrain.

head from wild casts, protect you from insects, and keep the rain off your face. One style, with a brim in back and one in front, keeps sun off your neck and face, and is very popular with saltwater fly fishers.

Polarized Sunglasses

Polarized sunglasses are essential for any kind of fishing where you are casting to visible fish. They cut most of the glare from the surface of the water and give you a much better view of what is going on below. Gray polarized lenses absorb more light and are used on very bright days; they work best in the blue water of open ocean and big lakes. Yellow-brown or amber lenses heighten contrast and are better on cloudy days; these work best on trout streams, saltwater flats, and smaller lakes.

If you are serious about your fishing, invest in glass lenses. Glass still offers better optics than polycarbonate or acrylic lenses; glass lenses also resist scratches better and are easier to clean. Glass is heavier, though, and if the weight of glass lenses is uncomfortable, the higher-quality plastic lenses are almost as good. The worst thing you can do is buy inexpensive polarized glasses. They won't have superior optics, they won't last as long, and they won't have the expensive antireflective coatings you get with the best sunglasses. In addition, if you fish in salt water, make sure you get glasses with a hydrophobic coating on them. When sunglasses get coated with salt spray, they are difficult to clean, and the hydrophobic coating makes the salt spray roll right off the glasses.

If you wear prescription glasses, you can obtain prescription polarized sunglasses or inexpensive clip-ons. Most of the clip-ons are made from plastic and scratch very easily. You may go through a couple of pairs a year.

Polarized sunglasses cut glare from the water's surface and are invaluable in almost all kinds of fly fishing. The best ones are made from optically ground glass, and this amber color is the best shade for stream fishing and shallow-water saltwater fishing.

Sunglasses, of course, will also protect your eyes from eyestrain, from dangerous UV rays (all the good ones block nearly 100 percent of UVA and UVB), and from (heaven forbid) a backcast that gets blown into your face.

Leader Wallet

Leader wallets are used to keep an assortment of different leader lengths and leaders with different tippet sizes in your vest. They are usually made from vinyl, and each leaf can be written on with pencil so that you can keep track of them. Leaders can be coiled around your hand before they are put away; start with the tippet end, wind around your palm, and then wrap the butt end around the loop a few times to keep the coil from unwinding.

Storing your leaders in a wallet will keep them from tangling and all in one place so you can find one easily.

Leader Gauge

Various simple devices to measure the diameter of your leader are available. Most use slots of various sizes that you try to slide your tippet into. A snug but not tight fit indicates the diameter of that particular slot. They are useful when you're using knotless tapered leaders, so you know when the leader has been cut back to the point where you have to add a tippet.

Fishing Mitts

These are wool, neoprene, or polypropylene fleece gloves with the fingertips exposed, so you can tie on a fly or

change tippets while keeping most of your hands warm. They are also excellent protection against mosquitoes and blackflies.

In cold-weather fly fishing, fingerless mitts help keep your hands warm (to some degree anyway) and still let you tie on a fly or fix a leader.

Rain Jacket

Last but not least. Some of the best fly fishing occurs during rainstorms, so you might as well be comfortable while

A good fishing rain jacket will have big pockets to hold fly boxes, a well-designed hood, and cuffs that keep water out of your sleeves.

you're fishing. In a boat, any kind of high-quality rainwear will make things more fun, and the new breathable types are totally reliable and superbly comfortable. And don't think raincoats are only for fishing in Maine or Montana. I would never go to the tropics without a raincoat, as even in 70-degree temperatures, a fast ride to the flats across open water can chill you quickly—and don't let anybody tell you they don't have thunderstorms on the bonefish flats.

If you wear waders and have a full fishing vest, your ordinary rain jacket will be too long and too narrow in the chest. Specially designed wading jackets are cut short so they don't hang in the water and full in the chest so they will fit over a fishing vest. The best ones also sport D-rings in back for carrying a landing net, hand-warmer pockets, and generous front pockets for holding fly boxes. It's no fun having to reach inside your rain jacket for a net or a box of flies when the fish are rising like crazy.

{ POP'S SPORTING LEGACY }

Chapter Fourteen

Care of Fly-Fishing Tackle

MODERN FLY-FISHING TACKLE requires little care. Most of it requires no care at all. Your major investments—rods, reels, lines, and flies—can be kept in perfect working order with a few minutes' time after each day of fishing.

RODS

A fly rod that is broken while playing a fish is rare, and it is nearly impossible to break a well-made rod by casting too hard. Most casters and most fish just do not have enough strength to break a fly rod. The exceptional fly rod that breaks while you are fishing most likely was damaged previously. A hard whack against a rock can cause a tiny fracture that shows up later when stressed, as can a "hook check," which happens when a fly hits your rod on the or forward or backcast, making a tiny crack that opens up later. Weighted flies, particularly big saltwater patterns with metal eyes, are some of the worst culprits. When fishing any fly with added weight, make sure you cast with wide, open loops that keep the fly as far from the rod as possible.

The most common causes of rod breakage are: catching a rod in a car door (by far the most popular) or power window, tripping and falling on a rod, leaving a rod on top of a car and driving off, transporting a rod in an airline baggage compartment, putting a rod together indoors and trying to sneak out a door with 9 feet of graphite in your hand, and taking a rod apart improperly (not getting a straight pull). Another pitfall is yanking a line-to-leader connection through the guides by pulling the leader down toward the butt section, rather than pulling straight away from the tip-top.

Rods are often broken when you try to yank a fly out of a tree. If you get caught in a tree, first try removing it

Pulling the fly line through the guides in this manner is a sure way to ruin your day with a broken rod, especially if a knot catches in the guides.

This is not the best way to break off a fly if you get stuck in a tree. A broken rod tip can happen if you yank too hard and the line gets wrapped around the tip.

Here's a much better way to try to break loose—point the tip of the rod right at the fly and slowly walk backward (but check for deep water behind you before you do).

with a slow, gentle pull. The fly may be wrapped around a twig and not stuck in anything; a gentle pull may remove it. No luck? Then point the rod tip at the fly and slowly walk away. You can't break your rod tip this way.

If you always keep your rod in its aluminum tube and cloth sack when you're not fishing, you will eliminate 95 percent of rod-breakage problems. A rod that is left set up at the end of the day rather than taken apart and put away may not only be a prime target for carelessness—it may also be very difficult to take apart when you *do* want to put it away.

Never put a fly rod away when it's still wet. Lay the rod, cloth sack, and tube (with the cap left off) somewhere warm and dry where they won't be disturbed. Overnight will usually do it. Moisture won't hurt the rod blank, but putting a rod away wet may mildew the rod sack and grip, or oxidize metal reel seats. Fly rods should be stored in a cool, dry place, standing upright in a corner. Leave the cap on the tube unscrewed in case a change in temperature forms condensation on the inside of the tube.

Guides eventually wear out. The constant abrasion of fly line against them will form grooves that are sharp and can ruin a fly line in short order. Someone who fishes hard and whose fly line is dirty will go through a set of guides in five years. Another who keeps his line clean and doesn't fish hard may go a lifetime without requiring a new set. A winding that starts to unwind should be sent away for repair or cut off with a razor blade and replaced. In a pinch, if a guide gets knocked off a rod, you can put it back on temporarily with a small strip of duct tape or electrician's tape.

To check your guides, run a piece of nylon stocking through each one. If it catches, it's time to replace that guide. You can buy a new guide set, a spool of thread, and a bottle of thirty-minute epoxy and do the job yourself, or send the rod off for repair. Major rod manufacturers do this service regularly for a small fee, and they also have pamphlets that show you how to do it yourself.

Cork grips darken with age. This won't hurt the rod a bit, but if it bothers you, they can be cleaned with nail-polish remover (just don't get it on any varnish windings) or with very fine sandpaper.

Keep sand out of screw-lock reel seats, as a single grain can bind the threads. Loosen a stuck reel seat by rocking the reel from side to side. If this is a frequent problem, wash the reel seat with soap and water, then lubricate it by nicking the threads a few times with a bar of soap or paraffin.

All ferrules, whether they are metal ferrules on bamboo rods or the graphite, self-ferrule type, have varnished or epoxied winds of thread over them for security. The difference in flex between the rod and the stiffer ferrule can cause a tiny crack in the varnish, especially in older designs. This happens with all rods and is purely cosmetic; it won't affect the rod's long-term durability or casting qualities. If it's objectionable to you, take a toothpick, dip it in spar varnish, and run it over the crack a few times.

Dirty ferrules will make a rod stick together. To separate stubborn rod sections, first try putting on a pair of rubber gloves or one of those rubber pads used to remove tight lids from jars (to give you a more secure pull), and pull the sections straight away from each other, without bending the rod. If you have no luck, get a friend to stand opposite you and place a hand on each section of the rod, near the ferrule; then place your hands in the same manner, so that you are both pulling the rod as if you were working alone. Pull the sections apart carefully, ensuring that you are both getting a straight pull.

It's easy to take apart a stuck rod with two people. Each places a hand on an opposite side of the ferrule.

Ferrules on all high-quality rods are hand-fitted to each other before they leave the factory. This is why if you break a tip section on your rod, the manufacturer asks you to send both the butt and the tip back to him. He can't just send a new tip section to you, because he can't be sure of the proper fit.

Ferrules that stick constantly should be cleaned and lubricated. Clean both the male and female sections with soap and water, using a Q-tip to get inside the female ferrule. Polish the surface of the male ferrule with a soft cloth. After both sections are completely dry, check the fit. If it's still tight, they'll need lubrication, but never use grease or oil and never rub a ferrule alongside your nose or ear. Greasy substances cause suction in the ferrule and also attract dirt particles. Fiberglass, boron/graphite, and graphite self-ferrules should be lubricated with paraffin; metal ferrules on bamboo rods should be lubricated with dry soap.

Ordinary candle wax is the best lubricant for ferrules, and also will help for a ferrule that is too loose.

With many years of hard use, ferrules will loosen. A loose ferrule will make the rod sections rock against each other, and can break a rod. Never attempt ferrule repair or replacement unless you are a competent rod maker. Return the rod to the manufacturer or send it to someone who offers custom rod service.

Bamboo rods that are subjected to a lot of strain may develop a "set," which is a slight misalignment of the glue joints. The rod will curve off to one side as you look straight down the rod. A minor set won't hurt a thing, but an experienced bamboo rod maker can realign it by heating the section over a flame and pressing it back into shape. Don't try this yourself.

The blanks of modern impregnated bamboo, fiberglass, graphite, or boron/graphite rods need no care at all. They are impervious to moisture, extremes in temperature, and salt water. If a rod looks dirty or dull, it can be buffed back to a high gloss with furniture polish. Varnished bamboo rods should be checked for cracks in the varnish. If moisture gets inside the varnish, a set may result, or if the rod was made prior to World War II (yes, there are quite a number of old bamboo rods still in use) and was glued with animal glues, the glue joints may separate. Revarnishing is expensive and time-consuming, but it's necessary to protect your investment.

With a minimum of care, a well-made fly rod should last for several generations. I occasionally use an old bamboo rod that was built in the 1920s.

REELS

Fly reels used in fresh water should be cleaned and lubricated once or twice a year, or whenever they get dirty. If you don't stick your reel in the sand, and keep it in its case when not in use, you may have to do this only once a year.

Clean your reel in dishwashing detergent and warm water, never with any kind of solvent. A solvent may ruin the finish on your reel and definitely will ruin your fly line. Don't ever spray water into a reel with a hose turned up to a high-velocity stream, as it will only drive dirt deeper into the reel, into places you might not be able to clean. A toothbrush helps to get into tight spaces. Relubricate your reel by applying a light grease to all moving parts, especially the arbor that holds the spool. Heavy grease will gum up the works and may cause your spool to seize up on a fast-running fish. You may want to brush dirt off drag surfaces, but don't ever lubricate a drag sur-

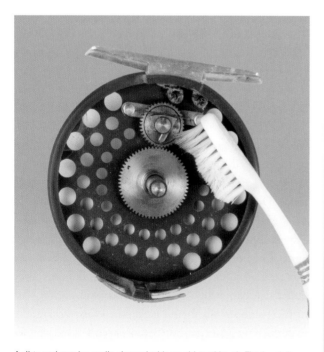

A dirty reel can be easily cleaned with an old toothbrush. The brush is especially useful in getting dirt out of the gear teeth.

face unless the manufacturer's literature specifically tells you to lubricate the drag. Most disc drags are pretty well sealed and almost never get dirty anyway.

Reels that are used in salt water should be washed with soap and warm water and then rinsed several times with fresh water. Take all the line and backing off your reel and rinse them as well. Then apply a light coat of oil to all parts of the reel, including the inside of the spool, except the cork or Teflon pads on disc-drag surfaces. Relubricate all moving metal parts with a light grease. Never use outboard motor lubricant, which is much too heavy.

LINES

Modern plastic fly lines do not need to be dried after use; in fact, you can leave a line on a reel for years without hurting it. Don't store a fly line where it will receive direct sunlight, as UV rays can deteriorate the finish slightly.

The solvents in aerosol fly sprays and the chemicals in insect repellents can break down the plastic finish on fly lines. When you spray a fly using aerosol fly sprays, point the spray *away* from your fly line. After applying insect repellent, rub your fingertips in the sand for a minute so that you don't get any repellent on your fly line, or use the back of your hands to apply repellent. Mosquitoes seldom bite fingertips and palms anyway.

Fly lines get dirty, especially in water that has a lot of algae in it. A floating line that is dirty will not float properly; a dirty line of any type will not shoot as smoothly as it should. In really clean water, you might need to clean your line after a half-dozen trips. In water with lots of algae, or if you strip line onto the ground instead of into the water, it might pay to clean your line after each day of fishing. You'll know when your line needs cleaning—it just won't seem to cast as well as it did the last time, or it may not float well, particularly close to the tip of the line, where it joins the leader. All lines can be washed in a sink with soap and warm water, then run through a towel.

To keep lines clean without ever doing any special maintenance, make a long cast at the end of the day, or let the current pull most of your line downstream. When you reel in your line, pinch it in your shirttail just before the line goes onto the reel, and reel in all your line while doing this. It's much easier to remove algae and other dirt

By washing a fly line in soap and water and then running it through a cloth or paper towel, you'll clean off all the algae and dirt. The line will float better and shoot longer.

while it's still wet, and if you do this every time you go fishing, you might need to clean your line only once or twice a year.

Floating lines, except the hydrophobic kinds, can also be cleaned with special line cleaner, which also lubricates them. You just rub a felt pad on the cleaner and then run your line through the pad while pinching the outside. Fly-line dressing is a greasy or slick coating that can be applied to a line. It works for a few casts, but then starts to pick up dirt and can actually hinder the shooting and floating qualities of a line. Most of the best lines made today have a permanent coating that keeps them slick and hydrophobic without line dressing, as long as they are kept clean.

If you can, always practice casting on water. A few minutes of casting on asphalt can ruin a line. If you can't find any water, wet grass is preferable to asphalt or cement.

Fly lines don't last forever. Eventually you'll notice cracks in the finish of your line, which signals that it's time to get a new one. Most fly lines last two to six years, depending on how hard you use them.

LEADERS

Nylon can be hurt by solvents from fly sprays, by insect repellents, and by constant exposure to the UV rays in sunlight. Store leaders and tippet material in the dark. I don't trust the very fine diameters of nylon, 5X and smaller, after they are two years old. There isn't much margin for error in material that tests a pound and a half,

so if a spool of tippet material is over two years old (few last that long anyway), I throw it out. Reputable tackle dealers constantly rotate their stock of tippet material, so you don't have to worry about buying old stuff. Orvis dates its tippet material with a system similar to that used for food, so you always know you are buying the freshest material.

PVDF or fluorocarbon material is almost completely stable in UV light and never loses its strength. PVDF stored on a spool can be safely used ten years after you bought it, without worrying about loss of strength. This brings up a good point, however; if you do use PVDF, make sure you recover any tippets or leaders you lose in trees or in snags if you can reach them. When you trim knots, put the pieces in a secure place so you can dispose of them later. Because PVDF never breaks down, this trash will stay in the environment for many years if you leave it on the river.

By purchasing leader material that is date-stamped and checking it every season, you'll be sure to get the most strength from your knots.

WADERS

Most of the maintenance time spent on fly-fishing tackle is spent on waders. They won't last forever. The rubber in waders is gradually broken down by UV rays in sunlight, ozone in the air, barbed wire (not so gradually), and abrasion when you walk. Just as you don't expect a pair of pants or shoes to last for a decade, nor should you expect waders to. Waders and wading shoes get a lot of hard use. If you get four years of use from a pair of waders, then you've taken good care of them and have probably not done a lot of hard walking through brush. Many professional guides get only one season out of a pair of waders, and are happy if they do.

Never store waders in direct sunlight, and never near electric motors, which give off small amounts of ozone. The ultraviolet rays from sunlight and ozone given off from electric motors will oxidize the rubber compounds in wader fabric and will shorten the waterproof life of your waders. Waders should be stored in a cool, dry place. Boot-foot waders should be completely dry when you store them; use a hair dryer on the cool setting if they are wet inside. They should be hung, by the boots, on special wader hangers, or folded loosely and put back in the box they came in. Stocking-foot waders can be folded, rolled up, or thrown in a corner—just keep them away from sunlight and electric motors. Be careful to ensure that there are no sharp creases in the fabric, as these can eventually cause weak spots, leading to pinhole leaks along the seam of the crease.

Leather and canvas wading shoes should be dry before you put them away, or they will mildew. The new wading shoes made from artificial leather are mildew-proof and can be stored any old way.

Holes in waders come in three forms: pinhole leaks from abrasion, tears, and seam leaks. Pinhole leaks and tears can be located with a flashlight in a dark closet. Seam leaks can be found by filling the inside of the waders with water and seeing where it leaks out. Alternatively, you can find seam leaks (or any leaks, for that matter) by squeezing the waders tight with air inside, then holding them underwater in a bathtub to see where bubbles escape. Just make sure you look for a steady stream of bubbles, as the DWR (Durable Water Resistant) coating used on the outside of many waders will trap air bubbles as well.

Find the leak, mark the spot with a waterproof marking pen, clean the spot with soap and water or rubbing alcohol, and let the waders dry. For tears and seam leaks, you will have to use a standard patch kit, similar to an inner-tube repair kit. Follow the directions on the package.

Pinhole leaks don't usually require a patch. Repair by coating the area with the cement that comes in your repair kit, or with silicone tile-sealant. Use two or three thin layers, letting each dry before applying the next. Pinhole leaks, small areas of abrasion, and seam leaks should be repaired without a patch. They should be coated with a

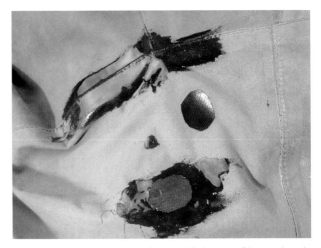

Various wader repairs. Clockwise from top left: An area of Aquaseal used to reinforce a seam that has abraded from poor fit, a simple duct tape repair, a patch placed over a large hole and then covered with Aquaseal, and just a small dab of Aquaseal to fix a pinhole leak.

thin layer of a compound called Aquaseal (available at any fly shop or from any fishing catalog or website). You can apply the cement to either the inside or the outside of the waders. Aquaseal will repair any upper fabric, rubber boots, or neoprene with ease. It is by far the best wader-repair cement yet developed, and a patch made with this compound will outlast the waders.

Bigger rips from sharp sticks or barbed wire may also require a patch. Often, waders come with a piece of fabric that is designed to be ironed on for a repair, and that works reasonably well, but for a serious patch, I'd coat the tear with Aquaseal to an area ¼-inch beyond the tear, wait until it is tacky, and then apply a patch, cut to approximately the same shape as the area you've glued, over the tear. Let this dry overnight and apply a second coat of Aquaseal over the entire patch and its edges. Cut your patches with rounded corners rather than with rectangular or square shapes. The smooth corners are less likely to pull up later.

Aquaseal should dry overnight, unless a special accelerant called Co-Tol Cure Accelerator is also used. In a pinch, there are UV-cure glues available that dry in seconds in the sunlight, or repair sticks that you heat up with a match before dripping on the spot. I have never found either of these to be very reliable or durable. For quick repairs, a piece of duct tape will fix most leaks for at least a day of fishing, or you can buy a special tape used to repair whitewater rafts that is even better and may last a season. For all repair jobs, stuff the inside of your waders with newspaper so you don't glue the legs together.

WADING SHOES

Leather, canvas, or synthetic-fabric wading shoes should be dry before you put them away, or they will mildew. It's also a good idea to rinse any mud or sand from your wading shoes after each use. Sand crystals are sharp, and if they stay embedded in the fabric, they'll cause tiny cuts the next time you use the shoes, and eventually the fabric will give way.

Felt soles on wading shoes and boot-foot waders may eventually wear through, or will sometimes peel away from the sole. For felt that is peeling off, thoroughly clean between the felt and the sole with running water and a wire brush. Make sure the felt is completely dry, and then apply waterproof contact cement liberally in the space between the felt and the sole; wrap duct tape tightly over the boot and the felt, and let dry for twenty-four hours.

Completely replacing felt soles is a nasty and time-consuming job, and luckily, good-quality, high-density felt will last as long as a pair of wading shoes or waders. Nevertheless, you may have a pair of felt soles give out, especially if you fish in places with sharp volcanic gravel. You can buy a felt-sole replacement kit from most tackle shops. The kit will include an oversized piece of felt and contact cement. Carefully peel the old felt away from the soles using a sharp utility knife, similar to skinning a deer. You may have to remove some of the old felt and cement with a coarse grinding wheel as well. Trace the outline of your boot over the new felt, leaving ¼ inch beyond the edges. Coat the felt soles with contact cement and let dry for several hours to get a nonabsorbent base. Then coat both the sole and the felt with contact cement, com-pletely tape the boot and felt with duct tape, and let dry for twenty-four hours. After removing the duct tape, trim the felt sole so it is even with the edge of the sole.

FLIES

I'm a nitpicker about fly care, as are most fly tiers. Flies should never be put away wet. Put nymphs, streamers, and wet flies on your exterior foam or fleece patch and leave there until dry. Blow the moisture from your dry flies before putting them away.

If the inside of a fly box gets wet, be prepared to remove all the flies as soon as possible and lay them out somewhere to air-dry. Do not put them away until they are perfectly dry. Otherwise, you'll end up with misshapen flies and rusty hooks.

This fly was put away wet. The rust on the point will weaken and dull the hook. You'll miss fish with this fly.

The felt on these wading shoes is thin and wearing at the edges. Either the felt or the shoes should be replaced soon.

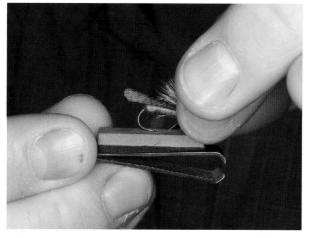

Draw a hook hone against the point, on the bottom and on the sides.

Now the hook is sharp and ready to fish.

Check the point by drawing it against your thumbnail. If it sticks, it's sharp enough.

Dry flies should not be stuffed into compartments that are too small or stuffed too many to a compartment. They should never be put into metal clips. Storing them this way will crush their delicate hackles, tails, and wings out of shape.

Flies that have been mashed out of shape can easily be rejuvenated. With a pair of tweezers, hold them near the spout of a boiling teakettle. The feathers will instantly spring back into shape.

Should you throw away flies that are tattered beyond recognition? I don't know. Flies that have been reduced to a few wisps of thread and fur have taken some pretty nice fish. Maybe you should tuck them away in a corner of your fly box where your buddies won't see them.

Resources

Suggested Reading

Leaders and Knots

Kreh, Lefty, and Mark Sosin. *Practical Fishing Knots.* **Connecticut: The Lyons Press, 1991.** Although not just about fly-fishing knots, all the important ones are here, as well as some lesser-known varieties in case you want to experiment.

Rosenbauer, Tom. *The Orvis Pocket Guide to Leaders and Tippets.* **Connecticut: The Lyons Press, 2000.** The essential knots used by fly fishers and the ones approved by Orvis staff and fishing-school instructors. Also detailed information on the different kinds of leaders and tippet material and when to use them. Fits in a fishing vest or kit bag for quick reference on the water.

Fly Casting

Deck, Tom. *The Orvis Fly-Casting Guide.* **Connecticut: The Lyons Press, 2003.** Beautiful, detailed photographs and artwork, and a complete guide to all kinds of fly-fishing casts, troubleshooting, line handling, including special presentations for trout, bass, and saltwater fly fishing.

Deck, Tom. *The Orvis Pocket Guide to Fly Casting.* **Connecticut: The Lyons Press, 2000.** The basics of fly casting, from overhead casts to roll casts to the double haul. In a compact size, perfect for pulling out when your casting needs a touch-up.

Gawesworth, Simon. *Spey Casting.* **Pennsylvania: Stackpole Books, 2004.** A modern master of this traditional European casting technique shows how to master both traditional and contemporary two-handed techniques, plus ways to use these casts with single-handed rods.

Krieger, Mel. *The Essence of Fly Casting.* **San Francisco: Club Pacific, 1987.** A complete guide to learning to cast, improving your cast, and identifying problems, by one of the most talented and generous mentors in fly casting. Includes detailed diagrams and photographs.

Trout Flies and Hatches

Caucci, Al, and Bob Nastasi. *Hatches II.* **New York: The Lyons Press, 1986.** The best-organized guide to mayfly identification for fly fishers, with detailed keys to the species, suggested imitations, strategies for fishing the hatches, and detailed photographs and line drawings. Covers mayfly hatches throughout North America.

Fauceglia, Ted. *Mayflies.* **Pennsylvania: Stackpole Books, 2005.** A gorgeous look at these most important aquatic insects and their imitations, with superb close-up photography. Contains the best photographs of emerging mayflies ever published. Concentrates on mayfly species east of the Mississippi.

LaFontaine, Gary. *Caddisflies.* **Connecticut: The Lyons Press, 1994.** Truly the definitive study on caddisflies, with a wealth of information on their biology and behavior, plus many innovative techniques for fishing hatches of these important insects.

Meck, Charles. *Patterns, Hatches, and Trout.* **Pennsylvania: Vivid Publishing, 1995.** A helpful overall guide to mayflies, caddisflies, stoneflies, terrestrials, and other trout foods with lots of tactics on how to use them.

Pobst, Dick, and Carl Richards. *The Caddisfly Handbook: An Orvis Streamside Guide.* Connecticut: The Lyons Press, 1998. A field guide on how to identify the most important caddisflies, what fly to use, and how to present the fly during caddisfly hatches. Fits in a fishing vest for quick reference anytime.

Rosenbauer, Tom. *The Orvis Pocket Guide to Trout Foods and Their Imitations.* Connecticut: The Lyons Press, 2000. A basic guide to the major insects, baitfish, and crustaceans that trout eat, and the appropriate flies to imitate them. Fits in a fishing vest for easy reference.

Stream Tactics

Humphreys, Joe. *Joe Humphreys's Trout Tactics.* Pennsylvania: Stackpole Books, 1989. The master of small-stream trout tactics and inventor of the Tuck Cast gives an advanced seminar on how to catch difficult trout.

Lee, Art. *Fishing Dry Flies for Trout on Rivers and Streams.* Illinois: Human Kinetics, 1998. One of the great masters of dry-fly fishing shares his worldwide experience and love of dry-fly fishing. Many innovative techniques and a true graduate class in trout fishing.

Rosenbauer, Tom. *The Orvis Pocket Guide to Dry-Fly Fishing.* Connecticut: The Lyons Press, 2003. Fly selection, technique, reading the water, and fishing to hatches, all in a size that fits in a fishing vest.

Rosenbauer, Tom. *The Orvis Pocket Guide to Nymphing Techniques.* Connecticut: The Lyons Press, 2002. All the basics you need for learning nymph fishing, from fly selection to rigging your leader to finding the best nymphing water. Fits in a fishing vest.

Rosenbauer, Tom. *Prospecting for Trout.* Connecticut: The Lyons Press, 2000. How to catch trout when there is no hatch, with all kinds of flies from dries to nymphs to streamers. Includes sections on trout behavior, what makes a stream rich or poor, and reading the water.

Rosenbauer, Tom. *Reading Trout Streams.* Connecticut: The Lyons Press, 1998. All about what trout need and where they live, with an emphasis on trout behavior and stream hydraulics. All types of water are discussed, including special sections on big and little rivers and seasonal changes.

Straub, Patrick. *The Orvis Pocket Guide to Streamer Fishing.* Connecticut: The Lyons Press, 2006. A complete guide to flies, techniques, and tackle for fishing the flies that catch the biggest quantity of large trout, by a Montana fishing guide.

Streeks, Neale. *Seasons of the Trout.* Colorado: Pruett Publishing, 1998. One of the savviest fishing writers of the Rocky Mountains in a detailed yet concise guide to fishing the hatches of America's best trout rivers.

Still-Water Fly Fishing

Hughes, Dave. *Strategies for Stillwater.* Pennsylvania: Stackpole Books, 1991. A complete guide to fishing for trout in lakes and ponds, with details on the still-water environment, how trout behave in it, the best techniques, and a very detailed section on still-water hatches.

Lepage, Jim. *The Orvis Pocket Guide to Fly Fishing for Stillwater Trout.* Connecticut: The Lyons Press, 2002. The basics and some secrets to catching trout in lakes and ponds, from finding fish to fly selection to presentation, from dry flies to deep nymphs and streamers. Fits in a fishing vest or kit bag.

Tapply, Bill. *The Orvis Pocket Guide to Fly Fishing for Bass.* Connecticut: The Lyons Press, 2003. All you need to know to catch America's most popular gamefish on a fly rod, from poppers and hair bugs to subsurface flies. In a convenient size that fits in a tackle box or kit bag.

Salmon and Steelhead Fishing

Combs, Trey. *Steelhead Fly Fishing.* Connecticut: The Lyons Press, 1991. The bible of western steelhead fly fishers, from the sport's colorful history to tackle, fly selection, and fly presentation.

Shewey, John. *The Orvis Pocket Guide to Fly Fishing for Steelhead.* **Connecticut: The Lyons Press, 2003.** An amazingly extensive guide to fly-fishing for West Coast steelhead, in a size that fits in a chest pack or fishing vest.

Supinski, Matt. *The Orvis Pocket Guide to Great Lakes Salmon and Steelhead Fishing.* **Connecticut: The Lyons Press, 2004.** The basics of techniques, tackle, fly selection, and reading water for both steelhead and Pacific salmon in the Great Lakes. Fits in a fishing vest for easy reference.

Supinski, Matt. *Steelhead Dreams.* **Oregon: Frank Amato Publications, 2001.** Great Lakes steelhead biology and life cycles, fishing all four seasons, fly selection, playing and landing fish, and much more from one of the most experienced Great Lakes steelhead guides.

Saltwater Fly Fishing

Larmouth, Donald, and Rob Fordyce. *Tarpon on Fly.* **Oregon: Frank Amato Publications, 2002.** A well-organized guide to all aspects of tarpon fishing, by a tarpon addict and a full-time tarpon guide.

Samson, Jack. *The Orvis Pocket Guide to Fly Fishing for Bonefish and Permit.* **Connecticut: The Lyons Press, 2001.** All the basics you need to be successful at bonefish and permit fishing, in a pocket-sized guide you can read on an airplane on the way to tropical isles.

Samson, Jack. *Permit on a Fly.* **Pennsylvania: Stackpole Books, 1996.** Longtime permit addict Samson details how to catch the most elusive of fly-rod fish. Includes a generous history of the sport, the best places to find permit, and tactics to catch them.

Tabory, Lou. *The Orvis Pocket Guide to Fly Fishing for Striped Bass and Bluefish.* **Connecticut: The Lyons Press, 2001.** An amazing amount of hard-core knowledge on fly-fishing the Atlantic Coast for these popular gamefish, in a size that fits easily in a kit bag.

Tabory, Lou. *Stripers on the Fly.* **Connecticut: The Lyons Press, 1991.** The dean of striper anglers shares all his secrets, from reading the water to knots to fly selection.

Regional Fly-Fishing Guides

Ross, John. *Trout Unlimited's Guide to America's 100 Best Trout Streams.* **Montana: Falcon Publishing, 1999.** Just what it says—if you want to travel the country in search of the best trout fishing, here is the one place you can find all of them listed, with directions and maps of the best stretches.

Various. *Fly Fisher's Guide to . . .* **Montana: Wilderness Adventure Press.** This book series is a valuable addition to any fly fisher's library. At the time of this writing, the series included Idaho, northern California, Montana, New Mexico, New York, Florida Keys, Yellowstone Park, Wyoming, northern New England, Washington, Oregon, Colorado, Pennsylvania, Michigan, Utah, Alaska, Arkansas, and Texas.

Various. *River Journals* and *Blue-Ribbon Fly-Fishing Guides.* **Oregon: Frank Amato Publications.** Both of these series are terrific, full-color guides to states or regions (the *Blue Ribbon Guides*) or specific rivers (the *River Journals*).

Care of Fly-Fishing Tackle

Leeson, Ted. *The Orvis Guide to Tackle Care and Repair.* **Connecticut: The Lyons Press, 2006.** This book has all you need to know about caring for fly-fishing tackle, from rods and lines to leaders and flies to—especially—waders.

HELPFUL WEBSITES

The following websites specialize in fly fishing, with a mix of current news, fishing conditions, and helpful tips.

www.flyanglersonline.com
www.flyfish.com
www.flyfisherman.com

www.flyfishinginmaine.com
www.globalflyfisher.com
www.midcurrent.com
www.orvis.com
www.troutnut.com
www.sexyloops.com
www.washingtonflyfishing.com

IMPORTANT
CONSERVATION
ORGANIZATIONS

Trout Unlimited

1300 North 17th Street, Suite 500
Arlington, Virginia 22209
(800) 834–2419
www.tu.org

The mission of Trout Unlimited (TU) is to conserve, protect, and restore North America's trout and salmon fisheries and their watersheds. TU accomplishes this mission on local, state, and national levels with an extensive and dedicated volunteer network. TU's national office, based just outside of Washington, D.C., and its regional offices employ professionals who testify before Congress, publish a quarterly magazine, intervene in federal legal proceedings, and work with the organization's 152,000 volunteers in 450 chapters nationwide to keep them active and involved in conservation issues.

The Atlantic Salmon Federation

P.O. Box 807
Calais, Maine 04619-0807
(506) 529–4581
www.asf.ca

The Atlantic Salmon Federation (ASF) is an international nonprofit organization that promotes the conservation and wise management of the wild Atlantic salmon and its environment. It has seven councils, more than 140 affiliate organizations, and represents more than 40,000 conservation volunteers.

Coastal Conservation Association

6919 Portwest, Suite 100
Houston, Texas 77024
(800) 201–FISH
www.joincca.org

The Coastal Conservation Association (CCA) is a nonprofit organization comprised of fifteen coastal state chapters spanning the Gulf of Mexico and the Atlantic seaboard. CCA's strength is drawn from the tens of thousands of recreational saltwater anglers who make up its membership. From South Texas to the upper reaches of Maine, CCA's grassroots influence is felt through state capitals, U.S. Congress, and, most importantly, in the conservation and restoration of our coastal marine resources.

The Henry's Fork Foundation

P.O. Box 550
Ashton, Idaho 83420
(208) 652–3567
www.henrysfork.com

The Henry's Fork Foundation (HFF) is a nonprofit, member-based organization founded in 1984 to preserve and protect the unique qualities of the Henry's Fork watershed located in eastern Idaho. The Henry's Fork Foundation is very active in regional decision-making and policy, and they work with local, state, and federal agencies to ensure better management of the watershed.

Federation of Fly Fishers

215 E. Lewis Street
Livingston, Montana 59047
(406) 222–9369
www.fedflyfishers.org

The Federation of Fly Fishers (FFF) is an international service organization dedicated to the betterment of the sport of fly fishing through conservation and education. Unlike Trout Unlimited, FFF supports all species of fish that are pursued with a fly rod, not just trout and salmon, and it's as active in educational programs as it is in habitat protection. Under its umbrella are more than 300 local fly-fishing clubs.

Index

ABOUT THE AUTHOR

Tom Rosenbauer has worked for the Orvis Company for twenty-eight years, and while there has been a fishing school instructor, copywriter, public relations director, merchandise manager, and was editor of *The Orvis News* for ten years. He is currently the Marketing Director.

Tom has fly fished for over thirty-five years, and was a commercial fly tier by age fourteen. He has fished extensively across North America and has also fished on Christmas Island, the Bahamas, in Kamchatka, and on the English chalk streams. He has ten fly fishing books in print, including *The Orvis Fly-Fishing Guide* (original edition), *Reading Trout Streams, Prospecting for Trout, Casting Illusions, Fly-Fishing in America, Approach and Presentation, Trout Foods and Their Imitations; Nymphing Techniques; Leaders, Knots, and Tippets, The Orvis Guide to Dry-Fly Techniques,* and *The Orvis Fly-Tying Guide,* which won a 2001 National Outdoor Book Award. He has also been published in *Field & Stream, Outdoor Life, Catalog Age, Fly Fisherman, Sporting Classics, Fly Rod & Reel, Audubon,* and other magazines. He lives in southern Vermont with his wife, Robin, and son Brett and daughter Brooke, on the banks of his favorite trout stream.

ABOUT THE ARTIST

Bob White has worked for two decades as a professional artist. Influenced by such masters as Homer, Sargent and Fournier, and by more recent artists such as Pleissner, Francis Lee Jacques, and Eric Sloane, he works in watercolors, oils, pencil, and ink. His paintings hang in the private and corporate collections of sportsmen on six continents. Bob has also worked as a fishing and wing-shooting guide in southwest Alaska for nearly twenty years, and guided sportsmen in Argentina for a decade. He continues to host fly fishing and wing shooting trips to Patagonia, Alaska, Kamchatka and other destinations.

Bob received the Guide of the Year Award in 1988 from *Fly Rod & Reel* magazine. As the 1994 Artist of the Year for the Alaska State Parks Foundation, he produced and donated the artwork for the first Alaska State Parks Foundation print. He has been featured as a guide and artist on ESPN's "Fly Fishing the World" and "Fly Fishing America." He lives in Marine on St. Croix, Minnesota, with his wife, Lisa, his children Jessica, Jakob, Jamie, and Tommy, and their dog, Gus.